VON / FROM WILSON BIS / TO WALDHEIM

Studies in Austrian Literature, Culture, and Thought

Major Figures of Modern Austrian Literature
Edited by Donald G. Daviau

Introducing Austria. A Short History
By Lonnie Johnson

The Verbal and Visual Art of Alfred Kubin
By Phillip H. Rhein

Austrian Foreign Policy Yearbook:
Report of the Austrian Federal Ministry
for Foreign Affairs for the year 1988

From Wilson to Waldheim
Edited by Peter Pabisch

Arthur Schnitzler and Politics
By Adrian Clive Roberts

Translation Series:

February Shadows
By Elisabeth Reichart
Translated by Donna L. Hoffmeister

Library of Congress Cataloging-in-Publication Data

Workshop on Austrian-American Relations, 1917-1987
(1987): University of New Mexico)
From Wilson to Waldheim.

(Studies in Austrian literature, culture, and thought)
English and German.
Held at the University of New Mexico, 1987.
Bibliography:p.
Includes index.
1. United States—Relations—Austria—Congresses.
2. Austria—Relations—United States—Congresses.
I. Pabisch, Peter. II. Title. III. Title: Von Wilson
bis Waldheim. IV. Series.
E138.8.A9W67 1987 303.48'2730436 89-14939

ISBN 0-929497-04-X
ISBN 0-929497-09-9 (pbk.)

270 Goins Court
Riverside, California 92507

Printed in the United States of America

ISBN: 0-929497-04-X (hardback)
ISBN: 0-929497-09-0 (paperback)

VON / FROM WILSON BIS / TO WALDHEIM

Proceedings of a Workshop on Austrian-American Relations 1917-1987

Edited by
Peter Pabisch

Ariadne Press
270 Goins Court
Riverside, California 92507

The Austrian Provinces

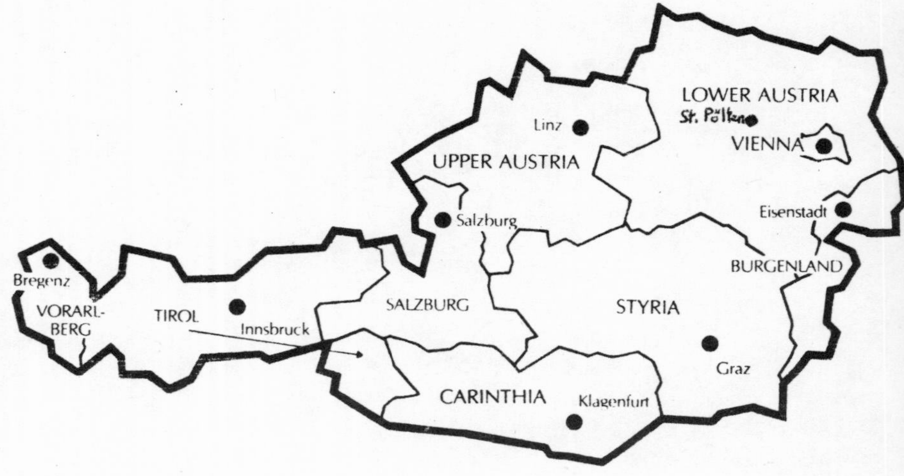

Austria is a federal state with a total area of 32,367 sq. miles (83,855 sq. km) and consists of nine provinces – Burgenland, Carinthia, Lower Austria, Salzburg, Styria, Tirol, Upper Austria, Vienna and Vorarlberg. Austria has common borders with no fewer than seven other countries. These neighbouring states have varying social and economic systems. Their inhabitants belong to the major European ethnic groups: the Germanic, Neo-Latin and Slav peoples (the Magyars of Hungary are an exception, deriving from the Ural-Altaic group).

FROM WILSON TO WALDHEIM

Inhalt / Table of Contents

Introduction

This topic was triggered by the so-called Waldheim controversy which was discussed during a 1987 Austrian Workshop listed by the University of New Mexico as the Third Taos German Studies Workshop. The Workshop was necessary because the "affair" as reported by the press and in the media had many confused by creating one-sided views not only about Waldheim himself, but also about Austria.

It was, therefore, my intent to introduce Austria to an academic forum of college teachers, high school teachers and college students in both the U.S. and Europe from her beginnings as a small country at the end of World War I to the present time.

A book cannot truly recreate the Workshop atmosphere which constantly vibrates and expands during discussions and personal conversations. However, it can highlight the results of a wide spectrum of topics as they were presented following one another so that the participants in the Workshop could hear and discuss as many as they chose. All talks appear in essay form, as scholarly articles, or in some cases as summaries, but they all reveal insights into Austro-American relations during this century. Although the Waldheim controversy was the main theme of the Workshop, it was not the only topic discussed. In fact, only five of the twenty-five talks and discussions dealt solely or with certain aspects of Waldheim and Austria's connection with the Third Reich. The majority of presentations covered the entire time span at hand establishing thereby a thorough, albeit exemplary, historic spectrum. To complete the picture students' examination papers or at least pertinent segments of these have been added. Furthermore, an essay about Taos is contained in the appendix to inform the reader about the location of the Workshop.

May this book also achieve the goal of the Workshop – to enlighten interested readers beyond the boundaries of short-lived sensations.

Peter Pabisch
Albuquerque, August 1988

On 21 May 1987 Austrian Federal Chancellor Vranitzky paid a state visit to U.S.-President Ronald Reagan in the White House. Photo by Terry Arthur

Der Riese und der Zwerg: Amerikanisch-Österreichische Beziehungen 1917 bis 1987

Peter Pabisch

Austria, about the size of Maine, has the status of a sovereign nation, the same as the United States; in this regard these two countries compare to the dwarf and the giant. Before 1918, however, Austria-Hungary was one of Europe's large countries for which America was of no great concern yet. When Austria emerged as a small German country, one-seventh of its former size after 1918, the United States had gained a strong foothold in Europe and began to determine this continent's fate. At first, Austria was friend and foe to the United States, but since the end of World War II the United States has supported Austria decisively so that she could regain her status as a small, yet free nation. A historical overview, in German and English, is appended to this essay and highlights major events in the relations between these two countries—from Wilson's formulation of his 14-Points-Declaration in 1917 to the Reagan Administration's decision in 1987 to enter Kurt Waldheim's name on the so-called watch list.

Im Zusammenhang mit der Kandidatur und späteren Wahl Kurt Waldheims zum österreichischen Bundespräsidenten 1985/ 1986 entfaltete sich eine Krise in den amerikanisch-österreichischen Beziehungen. Sie erreichte die Regierungsebene, als der amerikanische Justizminister Edwin Meese am 27. April 1987 Kurt Waldheim die Einreise in die USA dadurch verbot, daß er dessen Namen auf die "watch list" setzen ließ. Diese Liste bezieht sich auf Personen, die besonders im Dritten Reich im Namen des Naziregimes gegen die Menschenrechte verstoßen haben. Obwohl Kurt Waldheim solche Vergehen nie nachgewiesen werden konnten, wurde er wegen seiner Offizierszeit im Dritten Reich—besonders in der "Heeresgruppe E," die für Partisanenbekämpfung und Menschendeportationen in Konzentrationslager verantwortlich war – einer Mitschuld verdächtigt. Eigenartigerweise gilt dieses Einreiseverbot nur für die Privatperson Waldheims, nicht aber für seine Funktion als Bundespräsident, in der er im Rahmen eines offiziellen Staatsbesuchs amerikanischen Boden betreten dürfte. Inzwischen ist die persönliche Unschuld Kurt Waldheims hinsichtlich seiner angeblichen Mitwirkung an Kriegsverbrechen und Verstößen gegen die Menschenrechte mehrfach bestätigt, obwohl die amerikanische Regierung das Einreiseverbot noch nicht aufgehoben hat. Diese Affäre hat allerdings Fragen an die jüngere Geschichte und Geschichtsschreibung über Österreich aufgeworfen, die noch der Beantwortung und Lösung harren und für die Kurt Waldheims Schicksalsweg repräsentativ und seine Person Symbol geworden sind. Dabei ist die Öffentlichkeit verwirrt und in Lager gespalten, die gewisse Extreme der Ansichten zur Oberfläche gefördert haben. Wegen der unterschiedlichen Größe der beiden Länder – einer Supermacht und eines Kleinstaates – ist die Spannung nicht zum Weltkonflikt geworden, die Kontroverse ist aber geblieben.

Gleichzeitig ist auffallend, daß diese Spannung nicht auf alle Bereiche der zwischenstaatlichen Beziehungen beider Länder ausgeweitet ist. Auf wirtschaftlichem und kulturellem Gebiet hat sich kaum etwas verändert; der Tourismus nach Österreich – auch von Amerikanern – registriert Rekordzahlen; der Waren- und Geldverkehr zeugt vom Vertrauen der Handelspartner zueinander; akademische und künstlerische Programme nehmen in beide Richtungen zu. Nur der sogenannte "Fall Waldheim" trübt das gute Einvernehmen – allerdings nicht in allen Kreisen. Während in Österreich durch diesen Fall eine stärkere Bipolarisierung zwischen extremer politischer Linker und Rechter aufgetreten ist, sind in den USA vor allem akademische Kreise an der Auseinandersetzung interessiert, wo der Fall oft weiterdiskutiert wird.

Der "Fall Waldheim" hat besonders die Frage an die Vergangenheit Österreichs während des Anschlusses 1938 an das Deutsche Reich und danach bis 1945 aufgeworfen, eine Frage, die von offizieller österreichischer Seite lange als "unösterreichisch" verschwiegen oder kurzbündig abgeschoben worden ist. So sind etwa in der englischen Ausgabe des Österreichischen Bundeskanzleramtes über *Austria–Facts and Figures–To the Friends of Austria* (Wien, 1986) dem Dritten Reich achtzehn Halbzeilen gewidmet, wodurch der Eindruck erweckt wird, daß die Deutschen Österreich gegen den Willen des österreichischen Volkes besetzten: "Any resistance to the political and military dictatorship of Nazi Germany seemed doomed to failure" (S. 32). So mutig, nicht selten mit dem Einsatz ihres Lebens, viele Österreicher Widerstand gegen das Hitlerregime leisteten, so eindeutig steht fest, daß sehr viele andere Österreicher den Anschluß willkommen hießen. Diese Tatsache wird in österreichischen Geschichtsbüchern von Format nicht geleugnet. So gab das Bundesministerium für Unterricht unter Bundesminister Drimmel schon 1957 die Dokumentensammlung *Österreich: Freies Land, Freies Volk* als "Arbeitsbehelf im Unterricht" (S. 6) heraus, worin u.a. ein Text der Moskauer Deklaration über Österreich vom 30. Oktober 1943 enthalten ist. Die Regierungen des Vereinigten Königreiches, der Sowjetunion und der Vereinigten Staaten von Amerika anerkennen darin Österreich als das erste freie Land an, "das der typischen Angriffspolitik Hitlers zum Opfer fallen sollte, . . ." Die "Besetzung Österreichs durch Deutschland am 13. März 1938 wird als null und nichtig" erklärt und Österreich sollte wieder frei und unabhängig werden. Wörtlich heißt es jedoch im dritten Absatz: "Österreich wird aber auch daran erinnert, daß es für die Teilnahme am Kriege an der Seite Hitler-Deutschlands eine Verantwortung trägt, der es nicht entrinnen kann, und daß anläßlich der endgültigen Abrechnung Bedachtnahme darauf, wieviel es selbst zu seiner Befreiung beigetragen haben wird, unvermeidlich sein wird" (S. 12). In ihrer Unabhängigkeitserklärung vom 27. April 1945 bekennen sich die Vorstände der politischen Parteien Österreichs zu diesem "Nachsatz" der Moskauer Konferenz (Karl Renner, Adolf Schärf, Leopold Kunschak, Johann Koplenig–S. 16f.).

Die amerikanischen Zeitungsmeldungen der Jahre 1985–1987 über den "Fall Waldheim" gaben meist sehr einseitige Berichte ab, die vor allem hervorhoben, daß Österreich für seine Mitwirkung im Dritten Reich so gut wie nicht zur Verantwortung gezogen worden sei und sich quasi ungeschoren aus dem Staub gemacht habe. Im

Getümmel der Krise stehen sich zwei Fronten gegenüber, die es bislang nicht gegeben hatte. Die Herausforderer in den USA sind eine Gruppe von Exilanten oder deren Kinder, die Österreich 1938 zwangsweise verlassen mußten, nachdem sie oft Erniedrigung durch andere Österreicher, dann Ostmärker, und den Verlust ihrer Besitztümer erlitten hatten. In Österreich ist heute besonders bei den Waldheim vertretenden politischen Kräften mangelndes Verständnis für jene Vorbehalte bei den Amerikanern vorhanden, die schließlich zur Meese-Entscheidung führten. Die Amerikaner, die in der Öffentlichkeit gegen Waldheim aufgetreten sind, entstammen fast ausschließlich jüdischen Kreisen, so daß sich in der Folge in Österreich erneut antisemitische Tendenzen bemerkbar machten, die in der Ära Kreisky (1970–1983) bereits überwunden zu sein schienen. Damit wurde auf historische, nicht immer feindselige Wurzeln österreichisch-jüdischer Beziehungen verwiesen, die im Raum der ehemaligen Monarchie ansetzen und weit vor die Zeiten Schönerers, Luegers und Herzls reichen. Um jedoch die Unruhe der Jahre 1985 bis 1987 in den Beziehungen zwischen Österreich und den USA zu analysieren, muß man Österreich betrachten, wie es 1918 als Deutsch-Österreich gegründet wurde und in der 1917 durch den amerikanischen Präsidenten Woodrow Wilson konzipierten 14-Punkte-Erklärung seinen Ursprung gefunden hatte. Plötzlich deckt sich eine Bandbreite der Beziehungen auf, die die jüngste Mißstimmung relativiert und viele positive Aspekte hervorkehrt. Der "Fall Waldheim" verliert dadurch seine Vordergründigkeit, obwohl er eine Zeit lang die Gemüter bewegte. Sicherlich hat er wie selten ein Ereignis der letzten Jahrzehnte zuvor die amerikanische Bevölkerung auf Österreich aufmerksam werden lassen, aber sein "Fall-Out" hat nicht nur negative Auswirkungen gehabt. Auf Universitätsboden ist das Augenmerk vielfältig auf Österreich gerichtet worden, indem neben der Frage nach der Beteiligung Österreichs im Dritten Reich Epochen wie *Wien um 1900* oder *Mozart und die Musik der Klassik* zur Diskussion stehen, die vom "Fall Waldheim" unberührt sind. Die Bandbreite ist jedoch viel größer, als die öffentliche Diskussion der letzten Jahre vermuten ließe.

Im Nachwind der großen akademisch-künstlerischen Ära

Österreich-Ungarns um die Jahrhundertwende hatte sich im Nachkriegswien der Ersten Republik eine Atmosphäre erhalten, die weltweit ausstrahlte und besonders in den USA Aufnahme fand. Dabei ist an die Zweite Wiener Medizinschule von Sigmund Freud bis Wagner-Jauregg ebenso zu denken, wie an den Wiener Kreis der Philosophie, an die Grundsätze des Otto-Glöckelschen Erziehungswesens – etwa in der Leibeserziehung und ihrer in Österreich etablierten "natürlichen Methode," an die gewaltige Musikszene in Oper und Konzert und an andere Kunstbereiche, besonders der Malerei, der Bildhauerei, des Schauspiel- und des Filmwesens. Die erzwungene Emigration vieler Österreicher in die USA intensivierte diese Auswirkungen derart, daß heute viele amerikanische Einrichtungen – Spitäler, Universitätsinstitute, Konzert- und Opernhäuser, Festspiele und die Filmbranche – auch auf österreichischen Ideenursprung zurückgeführt werden können. Diese Bereiche und Disziplinen sind in den USA inzwischen derart perfektioniert worden, daß seit Ende des Zweiten Weltkriegs ihre Methoden in Österreich Vorbild geworden sind; man denke dabei etwa an die Medizin oder das Computerwesen. In der Tat hat ein ständiges Geben und Nehmen stattgefunden.

Die Politik zueinander entspricht in friedlichen Zeiten den Größenverhältnissen. Da Presse und Politik zusammengehören – wenn auch eher als Widersacher, reflektiert doch jene, was diese bewegt. Österreich war bis zum "Fall Waldheim" selten in den amerikanischen Zeitungen erwähnt. Umgekehrt bringt die österreichische Presse regelmäßig sachliche und unsachliche, haupt- und nebensächliche Neuigkeiten aus dem Land der unbegrenzten Möglichkeiten. Das hängt mit der direkten und indirekten Abhängigkeit Österreichs von politischen Entscheidungen und wirtschaftlichen Hilfen des größeren Landes zusammen, aber auch mit den Mechanismen der internationalen Medienzentren, deren wichtigste sich in den USA befinden.

Woodrow Wilson genießt in den Vereinigten Staaten gemischte Anerkennung. Für die einen war er zu idealistisch und vernachlässigte die Innenpolitik, die anderen verehren den ehemaligen Universitätsprofessor und Präsidenten – zuerst von Princeton University and dann des gesamten Landes – als Wegbereiter der

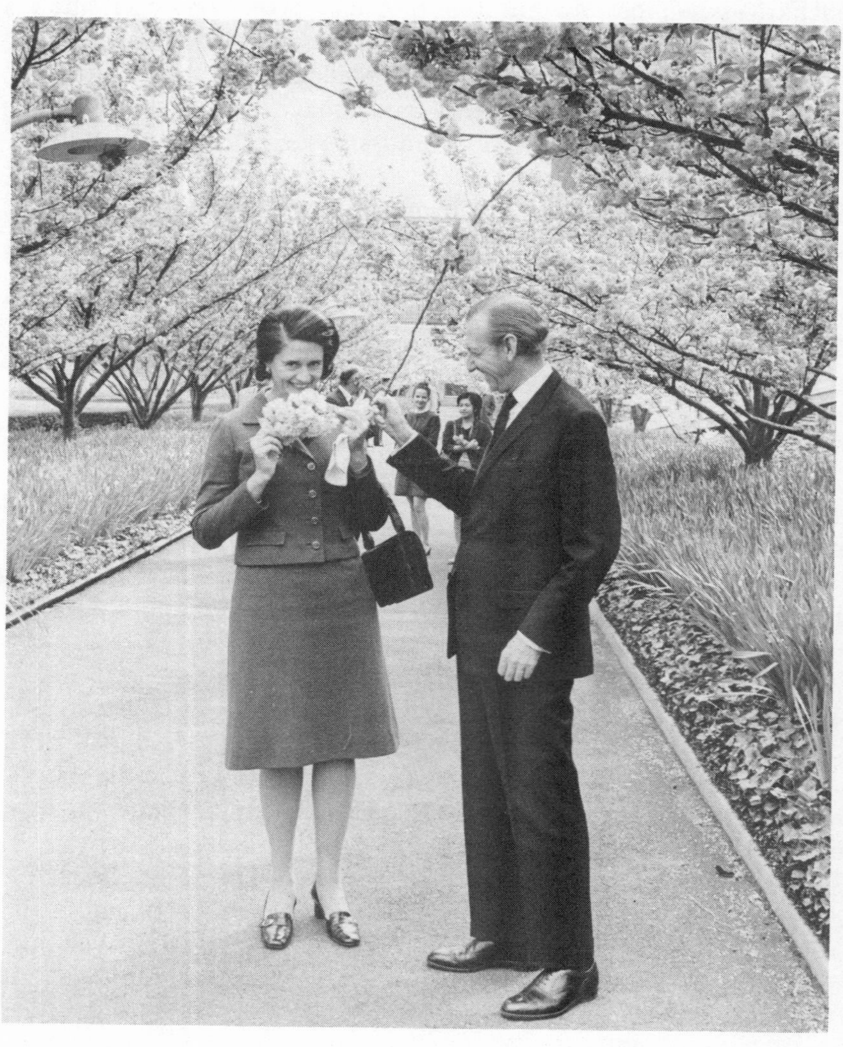

5 May 1972: Secretary-General Kurt Waldheim and Mrs. Waldheim admire the cherrytree blossoms in the United Nations Garden New York.

Photo by UN = T. Chen/JMcG

USA zur Weltmacht. Unbestritten ist zunächst sein Einfluß auf Österreich durch seine Empfehlung zur Aufteilung der Donaumonarchie in nationalistische Nachfolgestaaten. Da er den Völkerbund konzipierte, der Österreich eine Geldanleihe in den wirtschaftlich knappen zwanziger Jahren gewährte, empfiehlt sich Wilson posthum auch dadurch. Daß seine Völkerbundidee in den Vereinten Nationen weiterlebt, denen Kurt Waldheim in den siebziger Jahren als Generalsekretär vorstehen sollte, rückt seine Bedeutung noch enger an das Schicksal Österreichs. Die USA bezeugten weiters ihr freundschaftliches Verhältnis zum friedlichen Österreich, indem sie viele politisch und rassisch Verfolgte – darunter den letzten Staatskanzler der Ersten Republik Kurt Schuschnigg, ebenso wie den Thronanwärter einer von Kreisen der Rechten erträumten, wiedererstandenen Monarchie Otto von Habsburg und viele Flüchtlinge der politischen Linken gastfreundlich aufnahmen.

Daß weiters der in Österreich geborene und aufgewachsene Adolf Hitler zum Erzfeind der USA werden sollte, steht auf einem

April 1985: Former Austrian Chancellor Bruno Kreisky at the Center for Austrian Studies at the University of Minnesota with its former director, history professor William E. Wright.

anderen Blatt der Geschichtsschreibung, gehört aber gerade in dieses Kapitel, da er jene Ostmark schuf, deren Bürger mit ihm gegen die USA in den Krieg gerieten. Diese Jahre der negativen Beziehungen erscheinen durch den "Fall Waldheim" wieder im vollen Licht und belasten das jüngste Verhältnis zum Teil.

Die USA erwiesen sich dennoch schon während des Krieges als Fürsprecher einer Zweiten Republik Österreich und leisteten danach sehr viel, um dem kleinen Land wieder auf die Beine zu helfen, was der Marshallplan klar symbolisiert. Als Besatzungsmacht übte Amerika Einfluß auf das Pressewesen, das Erziehungswesen und den Demokratisierungsprozeß Österreichs. Seit der Unterzeichnung des Staatsvertrags anerkennen die USA Österreichs Neutralitätspolitik. Damit im Zusammenhang akzeptierten sie das Land immer wieder als Treffpunkt internationaler Gipfel und Konferenzen, ja unterstützten Kurt Waldheim und den österreichischen Bundeskanzler Bruno Kreisky in dem Vorhaben, Wien ein Zentrum der Vereinten Nationen werden zu lassen; das erfüllte sich 1979 durch den Bau des "International Centers" der UNO-City.

Österreich hat schon lange viele gelockerte Amerikanismen in den Lebensformen nicht nur seiner Jugend akzeptiert, wie es in Kleidung, Gehaben und Kunstgeschmack – z.B. im Jazz und bei den Liedermachern – in den Vordergrund tritt. Gleichzeitig macht sich schon einige Zeit Widerstand zur Welt- und Militärmacht Amerika geltend, der zuerst gegen den Vietnamkrieg und später die Lateinamerikapolitik der USA gerichtet war. Doch blieb das Verhältnis auf offiziell-politischer Ebene normal und äußerte sich in einer Freundschaftsgeste eher herzlich, als der amerikanische Präsident Ronald Reagan seine Personalchefin im Weißen Haus, die geborene Österreicherin Helene von Damm, als amerikanische Botschafterin nach Österreich entsandte.

Die offiziellen Stellen und die Medien berichten wenig über Österreich, das als kleines Land etwa in der amerikanischen Schule nur im Rahmen des Fremdsprachen- und Geschichtsunterrichts vorgestellt wird, und zwar meist als Teil des Lehrplanes über deutschlandkundliche Fragen. Um diesem Verbund mit Deutschland auszuweichen, stiftete die Regierung Kreisky im Jahre 1976

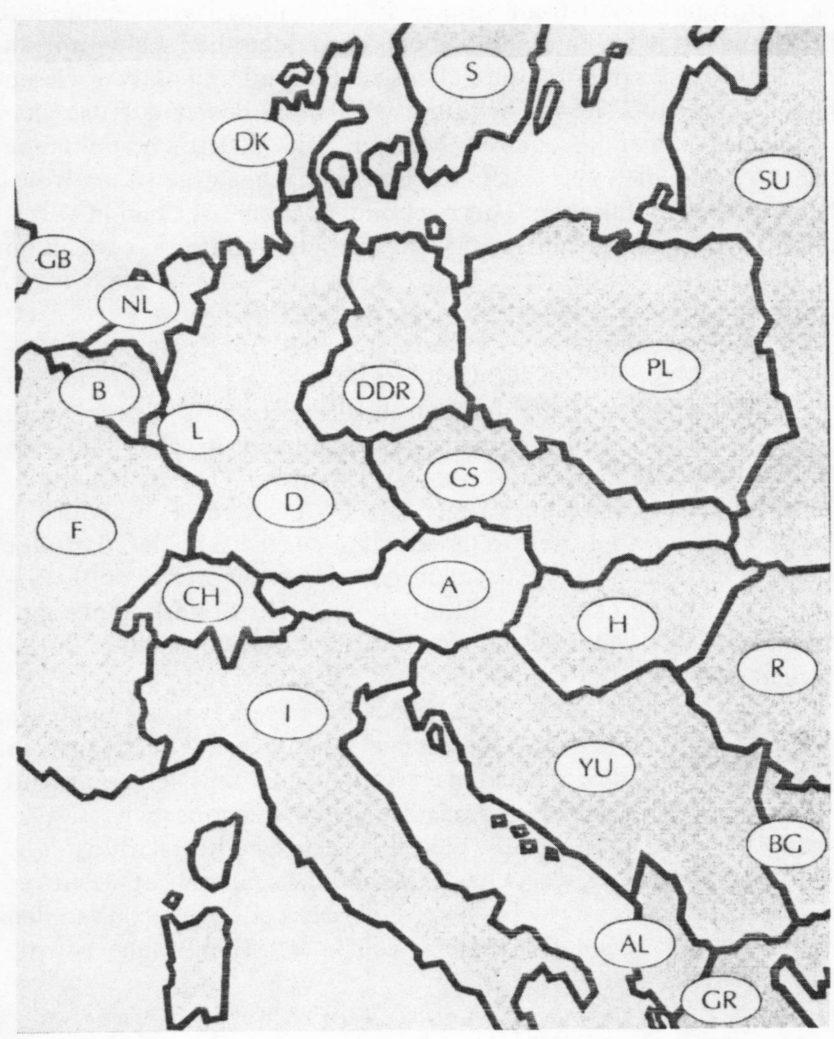

Austria's position in Europe

A Austria, AL Albania, B Belgium, BG Bulgaria, CH Switzerland, CS Czechoslovakia, D. Federal Republic of Germany, DDR German Democratic Republic, DK Denmark, F France, GB Great Britain, GR Greece, H Hungary, I Italy, L Luxemburg, NL Netherlands, PL Poland, R Romania, S Sweden, SU Soviet Union, YU Yugoslavia.

ein Zentrum der Austrian Studies an der University of Minnesota in Minneapolis/St. Paul und einen österreichischen Lehrstuhl an der Stanford University, die sich als zielführend und aktiv erwiesen haben. Ihre aufklärende Wirkung wird noch länger auf das akademische Gebiet beschränkt bleiben. Die öffentliche Meinung bleibt den Medien überlassen, die ihre Kampagne gegen Kurt Waldheim mit einem falschen Österreichbild ergänzte. Als man in Österreich zu Beginn des Jahres 1987 dachte, die Affäre sei endlich im Abflauen, da schockierte Ende April die sogenannte Meese-Entscheidung.

Ein Staatsbesuch des österreichischen Bundeskanzlers Vranitzky im Mai 1987 in die USA brachte zwar keine Widerrufung der amerikanischen Regierungsentscheidung gegen Waldheim, wohl aber die Zusicherung normaler Beziehungen in allen anderen Belangen der Vereinigten Staaten zu Österreich. Die Stimmung in Österreich ist seither eher gegen die USA gerichtet, obwohl die wirtschaftliche und kulturelle Zusammenarbeit beider darunter kaum gelitten hat. Die österreichische Regierung berief auf Initiative Kurt Waldheims eine internationale Historikerkommission, die seine Rolle während der NS-Zeit objektiv und sachlich untersuchen sollte.

Die nüchterne Aufarbeitung des gesamten Fragenkomplexes zur Bekämpfung emotionsbeladener Meldungen über Österreich soll in den Vereinigten Staaten in Symposien von Fachleuten und Studenten geschehen, wie es das Ziel des Workshops in Taos 1987 war. Mit diesem Jahr schließt hier die historische Betrachtung.

Die folgende historische Zusammenfassung einiger wichtiger Daten amerikanischer und österreichischer Ereignisse über den Zeitraum 1917 bis 1987 bezieht sich in der Hauptsache auf die hier vorzustellende Thematik:

(Zusammengestellt in Kooperation mit Magister Monika Chavez)

Einige geschichtliche Ereignisse zum Thema (1917–1987)
Some Historical Events Relevant to Our Topic

Jahr/Year	*Österreich-USA*	*Austria-USA*
1917	USA erklärt den Krieg an das Deutsche Reich.	The USA declares war against the German Reich.
	Wilson entwirft seine 14-Punkte-Erklärung.	Wilson conceptualizes his 14-Point Declaration.
1918	8. Januar: Verkündigung der 14-Punkte-Erklärung.	January 8: 14-Point Declaration is made public.
	12. November: Die Republik Deutsch-Österreich wird ausgerufen; sie soll ein selbständiger Bundesstaat der Deutschen Republik sein.	November 12: The Republic of German-Austria is founded; it is to be an independent federal state of the German Republic.
	Frauenwahlrecht in Österreich.	Women may vote in Austria.
	Starke Auswanderung aus dem ehemaligen Österreich-Ungarn in die USA.	Intensified immigration to the USA from countries of the former Austro-Hungarian Monarchy.
1919	10. September: Unterzeichnung des Friedensvertrags mit dem neuen Österreich: St. Germain-en-Laye.	September 10: Peace Treaty is signed with the new Austria in St. Germain.
	Verbot des Namens Deutsch-Österreich und des Anschlusses an die Deutsche Republik.	Prohibition of the name German-Austria and of the annexation of Austria to the German Republic.
1920	Der Völkerbund konstituiert sich in Genf nach dem Konzept von Woodrow Wilson.	The League of Nations is established in Geneva after a concept by Woodrow Wilson.

Jahr/Year	*Österreich-USA*	*Austria-USA*
1920	Frauenwahlrecht in den USA.	Women may vote in the USA.
	1. Oktober: Österreichs erste Verfassung von Kelsen.	Austria's first constitution by Kelsen.
	Inflation in Österreich.	Inflation in Austria.
	Alkoholverbot in Restaurants in den USA (bis 1933) beginnt.	Beginning of Prohibition in the USA (until 1933).
1922	Der Völkerbund gewährt Österreich eine Geldanleihe.	The League of Nations grants Austria a loan.
1924	Woodrow Wilson stirbt.	Woodrow Wilson dies.
	Unter Präsident Coolidge (bis 1929) ziehen sich die USA in einen Isolationismus zurück.	Under President Coolidge (till 1929) the USA follows political isolationism.
	In den zwanziger Jahren werden amerikanischer Jazz und Mode in Europa populär.	In the twenties American Jazz and fashion become popular in Europe.
1927	15. Juli: Justizpalastbrand; politische Unruhen in Wien.	July 15: The Ministry of Justice in Vienna is set on fire because of political unrest.
1929	Hoover wird Präsident der USA.	Hoover becomes President of the USA.
	Weltwirtschaftskrise.	World economic crisis.
1931	Hoover Moratorium: Stundung aller Kriegsschulden der Europäer durch die USA.	Hoover Moratorium: Europeans are relieved of all debts to the USA.
	"New Deal" – 1. Phase	First phase of the New Deal.

Jahr/Year	*Osterreich-USA*	*Austria-USA*
1933	Hitler kommt an die Macht: Ende der Weimarer Republik im Deutschen Reich.	Hitler gains power – end of the Weimar Republic in Germany.
1934	Engelbert Dollfuss wird von illegalen Nazis in Österreich erschossen.	Engelbert Dollfuss of Austria is shot to death by illegal Nazis.
1935	2. Phase des New Deal unter F. D. Roosevelt beginnt: Sozialversicherung für alle US-Bürger.	Second phase of the New Deal begins under F. D. Roosevelt: Social Security Act.
1938	12. März: Hitler marschiert in Österreich gewaltsam ein. Viele Österreicher heißen den Anschluß willkommen, andere werden als Widerstandskämpfer interniert und sogar exekutiert.	March 12: Hitler marches forcefully into Austria. Many Austrians welcome this *Anschluß* of Austria to the German Reich, others are arrested as resistance fighters and even executed.
	Die USA nehmen viele zwangsexilierte Österreicher, vor allem Juden, auf.	The USA permits many exiled Austrians, especially jews, to immigrate.
	Beginn Österreichischer Exilliteratur.	Beginning of Austrian Exile Literature.
1941	11. Dezember: Hitler erklärt den USA den Krieg.	December 11: Hitler declares war against the USA.
1943	Konferenz der alliierten Außerminister in Moskau: 1. Pläne zur Gründung der UNO. 2. Beschluß, daß Österreich wieder eigene Demokratie werden soll.	Conference of the allied foreign ministers in Moscow: 1. Plans for the establishment of a United Nations Organization. 2. Decision that Austria is to become a democracy again.

Jahr/Year	*Österreich-USA*	*Austria-USA*
1945	4.-11. Februar: Konferenz von Jalta.	February 4-11: Yalta Conference.
	12. April: F. D. Roosevelt stirbt.	April 12: F. D. Roosevelt passes away.
	Mai: Die Alliierten besetzen Österreich.	May: The Allies occupy Austria.
	Karl Renner gründet eine provisorische österreichische Regierung.	Karl Renner establishes a provisionary Austrian government.
	Wien wird wie Berlin in vier Besatzungszonen aufgeteilt – ebenso ganz Österreich.	Like Berlin Vienna is divided into four Allied zones – so is the rest of Austria.
	25. November: Die ersten freien Wahlen nach dem Krieg finden statt.	November 25: First postwar free elections take place in Austria.
1947	26. Juni: Gründung der Vereinten Nationen in New York.	June 26: The United Nations is founded in New York.
1948	Marshall-Plan – ERP-Hilfe beginnt.	Marshall Plan: Beginning of European Reparation Program (ERP).
1949	Die Bundesrepublik Deutschland wird gegründet – ebenso die NATO.	The Federal Republic of Germany is founded as well as NATO.
	Die DDR wird gegründet.	The GDR is founded.
1955	15. Mai: Der Österreichische Stattsvertrag wird unterzeichnet.	May 15: Signing of the Austrian State Treaty.

Jahr/Year	*Österreich-USA*	*Austria-USA*
1955	Eröffnung der Wiener Oper.	Opening of the Vienna State Opera.
	26. Oktober: Alle Besatzungstruppen haben Österreich verlassen.	All Allied troops have left Austria.
1956	16. April: Österreich tritt dem Europarat bei.	April 16: Austria becomes a member of the European Council.
	Ungarnkrise: viele ungarische Flüchtlinge werden in Österreich aufgenommen, etliche reisen weiter in andere Länder – darunter in die USA.	Hungarian crisis: Austria takes many Hungarian refugees of whom quite a few move on into other countries, including the USA.
1957	Die EWG wird in Rom gegründet.	The European Economic Community is founded in Rome.
1959	Die EFTA wird gegründet mit Österreich als Mitgliedsland.	The European Free Trade Association is founded with Austria as a member country.
1960	Österreichisches Wirtschaftswunder setzt ein.	The Austrian economic recovery, also called economic miracle, sets in.
	Kennedy wird zum US-Präsidenten gewählt.	Kennedy is elected president.
1961	Kennedy trifft Chruschtschew zu einem Gipfeltreffen in Wien.	John F. Kennedy meets Nikita Khrushchev for a summit talk in Vienna.
	Plätze und Straßen werden in Österreich nach Kennedy benannt, z.B. Kennedybrücke in Wien-Hietzing.	Places and streets are named after Kennedy, e.g., "Kennedybrücke" in Vienna's district of Hietzing.

Jahr/Year	*Österreich-USA*	*Austria-USA*
1961	13. August: Berliner Mauer wird errichtet.	August 13: Berlin Wall is built.
1965	Österreich lädt die Außenminister der ehemaligen vier Alliierten zur Zehnjahresfeier des Staatsvertrages ein.	Austria invites the foreign ministers of the former four Allies to celebrate ten years of Austria's State Treaty.
	Die Vietnamkrise beginnt. Steigerung in den Vietnamkrieg. Viele Antiamerika-Demonstrationen in Europa and somit in Österreich.	Beginning of the Vietnam crisis. Escalation into the Vietnam war thereafter; many anti-American demonstrations in Europe and, thus, in Austria.
1966–1970	Die ÖVP regiert allein.	Austria's People's Party holds the government.
1968	CSSR-Krise: Russische Panzer fahren in Prag ein. Höhepunkt der europäischen Studentenbewegung.	CSSR Crisis: Russian tanks move into Prague. Climax of the European student movement.
1970–1983	Die Ära Kreisky. Alleinregierung der Sozialistischen Partei Österreichs.	Era of Kreisky. The Socialistic Party of Austria is in charge of the government.
1971	Dezember: Kurt Waldheim wird zum Generalsekretär der UNO ernannt.	December: Kurt Waldheim is appointed Secretary General of the United Nations.
1972	Kurt Waldheims Amt beginnt offiziell und dauert bis 1981.	Waldheim officially begins his term of office, which he holds until 1981.
1973	Watergate.	Watergate.
	Internationale Ölkrise.	International oil crisis.

Jahr/Year	*Österreich-USA*	*Austria-USA*
1976	Zweihundertjahrfeier der amerikanischen Unabhängigkeitserklärung.	Bicentennial of the American Declaration of Independence.
	Zum Anlaß schenkt Österreich den USA ein Zentrum für Austrian Studies an der "University of Minnesota" in Minneapolis und einen Österreichlehrstuhl an der Stanford University in Kalifornien.	As a gift Austria establishes a Center for Austrian Studies at the University of Minnesota in Minneapolis and a visiting professorship at Stanford University.
1979	Die UNO baut ein "International Centre" in Wien.	The UN builds an International Centre in Vienna.
1980	Beginn der Polenkrise: viele Flüchtlinge in Wien.	Beginning of the Polish crisis; many refugees in Vienna.
1982	Helene von Damm wird amerikanische Botschafterin in Wien.	H. v. Damm becomes American Ambassador in Vienna.
1983	Ende der Ära Kreisky. Fred Sinowatz wird Bundeskanzler einer sozialistisch-liberalen Koalitionsregierung.	End of the Kreisky era. Fred Sinowatz becomes Federal Chancellor of a socialist-liberal coalition government.
1986	Wahl Kurt Waldheims zum Bundespräsidenten Österreichs.	Kurt Waldheim is elected Federal President of Austria.
	Proteste während der Wahlkampagne und nach der Wahl Kurt Waldheims seitens des Jüdischen Weltkongresses und anderer US-Bürger, weil Waldheim der Teilnahme an Kriegsverbrechen verdächtigt wurde.	Protests during the campaign and after the election of Kurt Waldheim by the Jewish World Congress and other US citizens, because Waldheim was thought to have committed war crimes.
	In Österreich nimmt der Anti-	In Austria anti-semitic and anti-

Jahr/Year	*Österreich-USA*	*Austria-USA*
	semitismus und Antiamerikanismus wegen der Waldheimaffäre stark zu.	American feelings grow because of the Waldheim affair.
	In den USA wird Österreich verstärkt als Naziland betrachtet, das anders als Deutschland für seine Kriegsvergehen niemals bestraft wurde.	In the US Austria is strongly viewed as a Nazi country that unlike Germany was never punished for her war crimes.
1987	27. April: die amerikanische Regierung setzt Kurt Waldheim auf die Liste unerwünschter Personen für die Einreise in die USA.	April 27: The American government puts Kurt Waldheim's name on the watch list of persons not permitted to enter the USA.
	21. Mai: Bundeskanzler Vranitzky besucht Präsident Reagan im Weißen Haus, um geordnete diplomatische Beziehungen zwischen den beiden Ländern sicherzustellen. Die Entscheidung gegen Waldheim wird nicht aufgehoben.	May 21: Austrian Federal Chancellor Vranitzky pays President Reagan a visit in the White House in order to assure orderly diplomatic relations between the two countries. The decision against Waldheim is not revoked.
	11. bis 16. Juli: In Taos Ski Valley findet der Workshop statt, auf dem dieses Buch basiert. Er ist repräsentativ für die akademische Debatte in der Frage nach der Mitschuld Österreichs an den Geschehnissen des Dritten Reichs.	July 11 to 16: In Taos Ski Valley a workshop relating to this book takes place. It is representative of the academic discussion on the question of Austria's guilt for the events of the Third Reich.
	Kurt Waldheim beruft eine Historikerkommission zur Untersuchung seines Falles ein.	Kurt Waldheim appoints a Historical Commission to investigate his case.
	(Die Ereignisse des Jahres 1988 werden hier nicht mehr berücksichtigt.)	(The events of 1988 are not considered here anymore.)

"Austrian Studies" und "German Studies" Sind die Teile größer als das Ganze?

Valters Nollendorfs

In the United States Austria and Austriaca are taught almost exclusively within the curriculum of German language and culture, because Austria is too small to warrant the introduction of a separate program. Yet Austria is always introduced as independent and free from Germany. By virtue of a contrastive presentation this independence can be understood more obviously by the American student who otherwise has no point of reference to see this difference. Recently established educational guidelines of the US German Studies Association (GSA) recommend such a curricular approach explicitly.

Ich möchte zweierlei vorausschicken—erstens, daß ich kein Österreichexperte bin, und zweitens, daß die rhetorische Frage im Titel meines Vortrags selbstverständlich mit einem "ja" zu beantworten ist. Damit könnte ich auch gleich aufhören. Da ich jedoch einige Aufschlüsse über die wechselseitigen Beziehungen zwischen "German Studies" und "Austrian Studies" geben soll, werde ich mich bemühen, aus der Not eine Tugend zu machen. Erstens werde ich als Nichtexperte meine ganz unvoreingenommene Narrenfreiheit genießen, um einige Hintergründe meiner einfachen Antwort auszuleuchten. Zweitens ist vielleicht auch die einfache Antwort nicht ganz so spannungslos, wie sie zuerst erscheinen möchte. Wir wissen ja im voraus, was am Ende mit Dr. Faust geschehen soll —sowohl in der *Historia* als auch bei Goethe—und doch sind wir immer wieder bereit, den Weg dahin zu betreten.

Wie schon angedeutet, da ich die beiden Begriffe "Austrian Studies" und "German Studies" nicht ins Deutsche übersetzt habe, handelt es sich bei ihnen um englischsprachige, in unserem Fall—amerikanische Begriffe. Die sind dem heutigen Sinn nach

Excerpts from the Guidelines for Curricular Organization at American Educational Institutions developed by the German Studies Association (GSA) as they pertain particularly to Austrian Studies.

GERMAN STUDIES PROGRAMS

**Guidelines for Curricular Organization
at American Educational Institutions
Developed by the**

GERMAN STUDIES ASSOCIATION

1987

This document has been produced by the German Studies Association in response to expressed needs of the profession. It is intended to

— raise awareness about the value of German Studies programs at American schools, colleges, and universities;

— suggest curricular guidelines for institutions which are offering or are planning to offer programs in this interdisciplinary field, and

— furnish a format which the profession may use as a vehicle for further discussion.

The Association is aware that certain differences prevail between education in the United States and in Canada. While these guidelines primarily address education in the United States, they can be adapted with minor modifications to circumstances in Canada.

GERMAN STUDIES PROGRAMS

German Studies has begun to address this growing need. During the last decade, over 100 academic programs with a German Studies focus have been created, with new ones added each year. This growth has been accompanied by scholarly conferences, publications, and by the success of the German Studies Association.

Many of the academic programs are, however, quite small and have been developed without clearly outlined academic or professional goals. Programs vary greatly with respect to purpose, degree of proficiency in the German language required, composition of courses, and administrative structure. The following guidelines are intended to bring about greater uniformity, to establish clearer standards and aims, and to encourage stronger growth of German Studies in America.

II. DEFINITION

German Studies is the interdisciplinary study of the contemporary cultural, social, economic, and political life of the German-speaking peoples in their historical and international context.

III. EDUCATIONAL GOALS

By developing, refining, and strengthening programs in German Studies, American academic institutions will:

A. make a significant contribution to liberal educational and intercultural competence;

B. prepare students for professions and careers, both in the United States and in international settings;

C. prepare future school and college teachers to meet the changing needs of the United States;

D. enrich disciplines participating in German Studies;

E. foster interdisciplinary research;

F. meet information and communication needs of both the private and public sector.

IX. FOREIGN EDUCATION AND EXCHANGE

Educational experience in German-speaking countries and contacts with people from those countries are indispensable for all students, teachers, and scholars in German Studies.

A. Programs in German-speaking countries providing study, work-study, or internship opportunities should be expanded and supported.

B. Opportunities for faculty study and research in German-speaking countries must be available on a regular basis.

C. Students and faculty from German-speaking countries can enrich schools, colleges, and communities. Programs supporting their visits to the U.S.A. need to be strengthened.

D. Faculty exchange programs are indispensable.

E. Additional opportunities for funding the programs outlined above should be pursued at foundations, granting agencies, and appropriate public and private organizations.

X. COOPERATION AND COORDINATION

A. German Studies and Related Interdisciplinary Fields

The relationship of German Studies to other interdisciplinary fields, such as European/West European Studies and Women's Studies, and to such well-defined constituent areas as German-American, Austrian, Swiss, and GDR Studies, should be developed on a cooperative basis at institutional and organizational levels.

B. Institutional level.

Given the interdisciplinary nature of German Studies, cooperation among individuals and among units within each institution undertaking a German Studies program is essential. There should be appropriate interdisciplinary German Studies committees at all institutions with existing or contemplated German Studies programs.

C. Regional level

Regional cooperation among institutions or regional associations is encouraged. Promising initiatives in regional information exchange, organization of special courses and workshops, and provision of access to educational and research opportunities on a cooperative basis should be vigorously pursued.

D. National level

1. The German Studies Association has created a Committee on Academic Programs for the purpose of fostering discussion, disseminating information, assisting institutions in creating and developing programs, establishing networks among scholars and institutions, and conducting other appropriate activities. Contact with this committee should be established.

2. Cooperative efforts in promoting German Studies among professional organizations such as the German Studies Association and the American Association of Teachers of German are encouraged.

3. Communication and cooperation with government agencies, the business and professional communities, and the public at large should be promoted.

E. International level

Communication and cooperation with scholarly organizations, individual scholars and groups of scholars, research, exchange, and information agencies as well as private organizations with aims related to German Studies is encouraged.

etwa in den letzten zwei Jahrzehnten entstanden und größtenteils auf spezifische und allgemeine Entwicklungen an Institutionen höheren Lernens in Amerika zurückzuführen. Ich nenne zwei dieser Entwicklungen:

(1) Die Fremdsprachenkrise, die nach dem durch den National Defense Education Act (NDEA) der späten 50er und frühen 60er Jahre geförderten Aufschwung schon Ende der sechziger Jahre einsetzte und sich bis etwa Anfang der achtziger Jahre fortsetzte: Diese Krise hat im Sprachunterricht an den Universitäten und High Schools in Amerika große Einbußen an Studentenzahl und so einen Rückgang an Professoren und Lehrern bedeutet. Besonders schwer hat die Krise das Studium des Deutschen getroffen. Wenn 1965 der Anteil des Deutschen an amerikanischen Universitäten und Colleges etwa 25% betrug (gegenüber ca. 35% für Französisch und 30% für Spanisch), so beträgt der Anteil des Deutschen heute nunmehr etwa 15% (Spanisch hat inzwischen mit 45% die erste Stelle erreicht; Französisch steht am zweiten Platz mit etwa 30%). Also – von allen Fremdsprachen wurde die deutsche Sprache am schwersten betroffen und erlitt die größten Einbußen.

(2) Die – auch mit der Förderung des NDEA zusammenhängende – Entwicklung des sogenannten "Area Studies"-Konzepts in den sechziger Jahren: "Area Studies"-Programme an Universitäten in den USA galten vorerst der breiten akademischen Erschließung des osteuropäischen Raumes, insbesondere der Sowjetunion. "Soviet Area Studies" und "East European Area Studies" wurden von dem NDEA stark unterstützt und zogen entsprechende "Area Studies"-Spezialisten vor. Das ähnliche Konzept einer breiten, multidisziplinären arealbestimmten akademischen Vorbereitung hat sich auf weitere geographische Gebiete ausgeweitet, so z.B. "West European Area Studies," "Near" und "Far Eastern Studies," "East," "South," und "South East Asian Studies," "Ibero-American," "Latin American Studies" und so weiter. Das Konzept einer multi- oder interdisziplinären Zusammenarbeit blieb aber nicht nur auf geographische Gebiete beschränkt; es

erweiterte sich zu "Women Studies," "Black Studies," "Native American Studies" und als Sammelbegriff "Ethnic Studies," zu denen wohl auch "German-American Studies" gehören mögen, also Studien von verschiedenen Bevölkerungsgruppen, die nicht unbedingt geographisch gebunden sind.

"German Studies" ist unter diesen verschiedenen "Studies"-Gewächsen ein entschieden verspätetes. Die eigentliche "German Studies" Entwicklung begann erst in den 70er Jahren aus den schon genannten zwei Wurzeln – Fremdsprachenkrise und Interdisziplinarität – hervorzusprießen. Unter den nunmehr schon über 100 akademischen German-Studies-Programmen in den USA und Kanada sind nur acht zu verzeichnen, die vor 1972 gegründet worden sind. Das Gros wurden nach 1972 gegründet, wobei die Programmgründung ihren Höhepunkt Ende der 70er Jahre erreichte.

Daß diese Gründung der German-Studies-Programme mit der Fremdsprachenkrise engstens verknüpft ist, scheint schon aus der Tatsache hervorzugehen, daß die bei weitem meisten German-Studies-Programme – noch immer! – administrativ als auch akademisch eine enge, wenn nicht exklusive Beziehung zu den "German Departments" besitzen. Der von mir und Walter Lohnes 1976 herausgegebene Sammelband *German Studies in the United States: Assessment and Outlook* ist fast ausschließlich aus dem Gesichtspunkt der Krise in den "German Departments" geschrieben und gibt Hinweise zur Überwindung dieser Krise. Diese Hinweise können in einem Wort zusammengefaßt werde: Diversifikation, d.h. Erweiterung des inhaltlichen Angebots. Es sollten nicht mehr nur Literatur und Linguistik oder Philologie sondern auch andere Gebiete erschlossen werden, die oft mit dem Wort "Kultur" oder "Culture Studies" bezeichnet wurden.

Eine interdisziplinäre Ausweitung war vorerst eine Seltenheit; es war jedoch von Anfang an klar, daß der Vorstoß ins nicht-traditionelle Curriculum die Kenntnisse der Deutschprofessoren strapazieren würde. Auch der Vorwurf des Dilettantismus wurde gegen "Culture Studies" geltend gemacht.

Zugleich gab es aber Bestrebungen, die Basis der German Studies auszuweiten. Mitte der 70er Jahre wurde im amerikanischen Westen die "Western Association of German Studies" gegründet, wobei anzumerken ist, daß der entscheidende Anstoß von Seiten der Historiker und nicht der Germanisten kam. Diese Organisation ist ungemein schnell gewachsen, hat in einer Art amerikanischem Drang nach Osten den Mississippi überquert, heißt jetzt "German Studies Association" und hat 1987 die zwölfte jährliche Konferenz im Oktober in St. Louis veranstaltet.

Um es noch näherzubringen, 1987 feierte auch die Deutsche Sommerschule zu Taos ihren zwölften Gebürtstag. Gegründet in den Krisenjahren der amerikanischen Germanistik, war diese Gründung zugleich den German Studies gewidmet, denn hier wird den Studenten ganz absichtlich und mit pädagogischem Fingerspitzengefühl ein breites Angebot unterbreitet, nicht nur thematisch sondern auch geographisch. Daß wir heute (1987) mit dem zweiten German-Studies-Workshop beginnen, der den Beziehungen zwischen Österreich und den USA gewidmet ist, ist kein Zufall. Diese Workshops erweitern und spezifizieren zugleich das Angebot der Sommerschule und ermöglichen einen Dialog auf hohem Niveau zwischen fortgeschrittenen Studenten und Fachexperten.

Somit wären wir zum eigentlichen Thema des Vortrags angelangt – den wechselseitigen Beziehungen zwischen "German Studies" einerseits und "Austrian Studies" andererseits. Daß diese Frage an eben diesem Ort erörtert wird und werden kann, ist eigentlich kein Zufall. Vor zwei Jahren fand hier eine "German Studies" Konferenz statt, auf der eine Grundlage zur Ausarbeitung von Richtlinien für German Studies in America geschaffen wurde – die sogenannten "Taos Thesen." Diese Thesen sind auf Grund von weitschweifigen Beratungen, die von einer von mir geleiteten Arbeitsgruppe der GSA ausgetragen wurden, zu "Guidelines for German Studies Programs" angewachsen . Somit ist eine Grundlage geschaffen, die es uns ermöglicht über "German Studies" und "Austrian Studies" konkret nachzudenken.

Fangen wir mit der Definition der "German Studies" an. Die lautet: "German Studies is the interdisciplinary study of the contemporary cultural, social, economic, and political life of the German-speaking peoples in their historical and international context." Diese Formulierung hat der Arbeitsgruppe Mühe gekostet, aber – so glauben wir – ist es uns gelungen, eine weitgehend befriedigende Aussage zu schaffen. Allerdings scheint diese Aussage zutreffender in der englischen Sprache zu sein als eine mögliche Übertragung ins Deutsche. Der Kern dieser Aussage ist in den Worten "German-speaking peoples" zu finden. Wir haben die gemeinsame deutsche Sprache als den Ausgangspunkt gewählt, aber *nur* als einen Ausgangspunkt, denn wir wollen diese Sprache durchaus nicht in ideologisch-mythischem Sinn als die Grundlage eines übergreifenden, alles vereinigenden Deutsch verstehen. Deshalb folgt das Wort "peoples," das auf eine Vielfalt hindeutet, d.h. in der heutigen Welt sowohl Deutsche als auch Österreicher und Schweizerdeutsche einschließt, aber auch kleinere deutschsprechende Gruppen nicht ausschließt. Das Wort "peoples" läßt sich nicht ohne Schwierigkeiten direkt ins Deutsche übertragen. Das kollektive Singular "people" bedeutet im allgemeinen "Menschen" oder "Leute"; als singular konstruiert, bedeutet es "das (*gemeine*) Volk," die Bürger oder die Bevölkerung. Die Pluralform sollte demnach "Völker" bedeuten, aber eben hier werden wir im Deutschen ein wenig stutzig, denn das Wort "Volk" in seiner ideologischen, nationalsozialistischen Bedeutung als das rassistisch determinierte ureinheitliche und anderen Völkern überlegene deutsche Volk entspricht nicht unseren German Studies Zielsetzungen und Absichten. Ich kenne jedoch keine bessere Übersetzung des relativ neutralen und umfassenden Begriffs "peoples," es sei denn mit dem Zusatz "Gemeinschaften." Der politisch-ideologisch geprägte Begriff der "Nation" scheint große, in unserem Vorhaben eingeschlossene Teile der deutschsprechenden Menschen auszuschließen, denn sie bilden nach Wahrig keine "bewußt und gewollt geformte politische Gemeinschaft." Andererseits wollen wir auch das andere Extrem vermeiden, nämlich die atomisierte Bezeichnung "deutschsprechende Menschen." Die Vielfalt der von diesen Menschen durch geschichtliche Entwicklungen bewußt oder unbewußt, gewollt oder zufällig geformten Gruppierungen sollten unter "German Studies" berücksichtigt werden. So lassen wir es dabei, daß "peoples" mit "Völker und Gemeinschaften" im Sinne Wahrigs übersetzt werden kann, und zwar das erste als "durch gemeinsame Sprache und Kultur verbundene größere Gemeinschaft von Menschen" und das zweite eben als eine verhältnismäßit kleinere. Die Banater Deutschen gehören dazu, sowie die Deutsch-Amerikaner und andere deutschsprachige oder doch zuerst deutschsprachige Gemeinschaften, die ihre eigenen von den größeren Gemeinschaften unterschiedlichen sprachlichen und kulturellen Eigenschaften besitzen. So gehört ganz gewiß auch Österreich hinzu, und zwar als ein deutschsprachiges Volk, das zu einer Nation geworden ist. So gehört auch die DDR dazu; vielleicht in umgekehrter und doch nicht weniger zwingender Bedeutung als ein Staat, der sich ein entsprechendes Volk heranbildet. Es ist doch bezeichnend, das es sich "das Volk der DDR" nennt.

Es ist noch richtig hinzuzufügen, daß wir von diesem gegenwärtigen Pluralismus ausgehen. Wir wollen – um Morgensterns "Werwolf" zu paraphrasieren – zu dem Plural keinen Singular hinzufügen, obgleich wir uns auch – wenigstens historisch – damit auseinanderzusetzen haben.

Das ganze German Studies Dokument ist von diesen Pluralismusgedanken geprägt, obgleich – und das werden wir ganz offen zugeben – das Interesse nicht allen deutschsprachigen Völkern oder Gemeinschaften unter allen German Studies Anhängern gleich groß ist. Das akademisch-wissenschaftliche Interesse gilt eben in größerem Ausmaße den großen politischen und kulturellen Fragen der Zeit und der Geschichte. Weiterhin – das muß wieder betont werden – wir richten uns in Amerika nach gewissen amerikanischen Gesichtspunkten, die nicht immer denen der betreffenden deutschsprachigen Völker oder Gemeinschaften entsprechen. Aber eben so können wir auch viel besser gewisse Fragestellungen vermeiden, die in den deutschsprachigen Ländern fast unausweichlich sind. Wir können sie aus einer anderen Perspektive unvoreingenommener beantworten, wie z.B. die Wiedervereinigungsfrage oder die groß- und kleindeutsche Frage.

Im allgemeinen will ich hier auch die Vorteile der Abgelegenheit dieses Bergtals in New Mexiko für unser Vorhaben hervorheben. Wir sind hier in zweifacher Hinsicht auf neutralem Boden, wo unsere Überlegungen möglichst objektiv ausgetragen werden können. Einerseits sind wir von der Bühne des eigentlichen German Studies Geschehens weit entfernt. Zweitens sind wir auch verhältnismäßit von der großen Bühne der amerikanischen Weltpolitik entfernt. Wir sind bei weitem nicht unleidenschaftliche Beobachter des Geschehens – ein jeder, der an German Studies Debatten teilgenommen hat, weiß, wie leicht sich Leidenschaften entzünden – aber wir befinden uns auf relativ neutralem Boden unter relativ objektiven Verhältnissen, eine internationale und interdisziplinäre Gruppe von Vertretern verschiedener Ansichten, mit einem gemeinsamen Ziel – das Wissen zu erkundigen und das Wissen zu vermitteln. Wir werden zwar mit Worten kramen, aber wir werden auch versuchen, die Wirkenskraft und den Samen hinter diesen Worten zu entdecken.

Was ist aber der Stellenwert der *Austrian Studies* innerhalb des umfassenderen Begriffs der German Studies? Sind wir überhaupt berechtigt, diesen Begriff zu gebrauchen? Es wird auch unter amerikanischen Akademikern welche geben, die allzu gern alles unter einen Hut stecken würden. Das wäre meiner Ansicht nach falsch, obgleich auch aus praktischen und wissenschaftsgeschichtlichen Gründen verständlich. Es ist leichter, mit einem einzigen als mehreren Begriffen zu arbeiten. Den gemeinsamen Ausgangspunkt bildet ja für alle "German Studies" die eine deutsche Sprache – deren Beherrschung und Lehre übrigens in den "Guidelines" eine sehr wichtige Rolle zugewiesen wird. Und letzthin sind die meisten Institute in Amerika "German Studies" in Stanford und "Germanic Studies" in Indiana. Historisch-ideologisch wurden auch die vor dem 1. Weltkrieg entstandenen German Departments im Lande weitgehend von Kollegen bevölkert, die entweder aus dem Deutschen Reich stammten oder dort promoviert hatten.

Aber – "the times, they are a-changin'" – und German Studies als ein pluralistisches Konzept muß auch mit Teilkonzepten und Bestandteilen fürliebnehmen. Oder – um es positiver auszudrücken, was ich auch als eigene Überzeugung vertreten kann – die Teilkonzepte und Bestandteile sind eben die, die dem Gesamtkonzept ihre eigentümliche Dynamik verleihen. Diese Dynamik stammt einerseits aus der interdisziplinären Zusammenarbeit und gegenseitigen Einwirkung, andererseits aus der Zusammenarbeit und gegenseitigen Einwirkung verschiedener geopolitischer Überlegungen, nämlich wie die hier zu betrachtenden *Austrian Studies.*

Ich möchte hier die Wichtigkeit dieser Dynamik betonen, dieser wechselseitigen Einwirkung, die im fortdauernden und sich wiederholenden Dialog, wie dieser hier in Taos, ihren eigentlichen Ausdruck findet. Ich glaube nicht nur etwas Eigentümliches in German Studies zu sehen, sondern eine allgemeinere, besonders im akademischen Leben der USA sich einsetzende Richtungsänderung in den Geistes- und Sozialwissenschaften – das Verständnis, daß disziplinäre Grenzen offen bleiben sollten und daß die Überquerung dieser Grenzen erleichtert werden sollte. Wir sind Zeugen davon, wie die traditionellen Disziplinen sich interdisziplinär umgestalten, ebenso wie wir Zeugen davon sind, wie sich das ökonomische und kulturelle Leben etlicher Nationen immer internationaler entwickelt – bei allen charakteristischen und souveränitätsbedingten Unterschieden. Ich glaube, daß diese wechselseitige Dynamik von einer disziplinären oder nationalen oder ethnischen Selbstbesinnung nicht wegführt, eher umgekehrt – daß dadurch die eigene Integrität in besonderem Grade erhöht wird. Also – Interdisziplinärität als Weg auch zu einer disziplinären Erneuerung; Internationalität als Weg zu einer nationalen oder ethnischen Selbstbehauptung.

Die Selbstbehauptung der *Austrian Studies* ist eine Ausdrucksform dieser akademischen Umgestaltung. Und das ist richtig. Aber diese Selbstbehauptung sollte auch ihre Grenzen anerkennen. Es bestehen gute Gründe dafür, *Austrian Studies* von German Studies *nicht* zu trennen, sondern als einen integren und zugleich erweiternden Bestandteil zu betrachten. Sowohl *German Studies* als auch *Austrian Studies* würden davon nur profitieren. Dabei ist darauf zu achten, daß es ebenso wichtig ist, Grenzen zwischen den beiden zu etablieren, als sie auch aufzugeben. Auf die Offenheit, Wechselseitigkeit und Fortsetzung des Dialogs kommt es in erster Linie an.

Dafür, daß *Austrian Studies* ein begrenzender und zugleich erweiternder Begriff ist, gibt es viele Beispiele. So sind die politischen Grenzen zwischen Österreich und Deutschland historisch und auch in der Gegenwart gut etabliert. Es ist klar, daß die Geschichte Österreichs mit mehr ist, als schlechthin die Geschichte

Deutschlands oder eine deutsche Geschichte. Die Verknüpfung der österreichischen mit dieser deutschen Geschichte ist unleugbar, aber ebnen ihre Verknüpfung mit der Geschichte etlicher nichtdeutscher Staaten der Tschechoslowakei, Jugoslawien und Ungarn. Dieser Zwiespalt der österreichischen Geschichte ist an den historischen Karten abzulesen, die die Grenzen des Deutschen Bundes nach 1815 darstellen. Dieser Zwiespalt ist auch an der kleindeutschen Lösung Bismarcks zu erkennen. Damit ist die Geschichte Österreichs sowohl ein Gegenstand von *German Studies* als auch von *Austrian Studies.* Ebenso ein Gegenstand von *German Studies* und von *Austrian Studies* ist, was hier in Taos unvermeidbar zu einem großen Thema wird – die unbewältigte Vergangenheit von Österreich in Hitlers Großdeutschem Reich. Die politische Lösung – Österreich als das erste Opfer Hitlers zu deklarieren – hat sich mit der brisanten Waldheim-Angelegenheit als nicht ganz tragfähig erwiesen, obgleich – und das scheint mir ebenso wichtig – die Angelegenheit meiner Ansicht nach die innere und äußere Stabilität des Staates Österreich im Grunde nicht zu erschüttern vermocht hat. So ist auch nicht zu befürchten, daß etwa Österreichs Vergangenheitsbewältigung der deutschen gleich gesetzt oder aus derselben Perspektive erörtert wird.

Wir können mit gutem Gewissen die Geschichte, auch die noch gegenwärtige, sowohl *German Studies* und *Austrian Studies* zurechnen, ohne damit das Ganze zu reduzieren. Auch in der Zeitgeschichte scheinen sich Ansätze zu einer sich ergänzenden Betrachtungsweise zu ergeben. Österreich ist letzten Endes – in Kontrast zu den zwei deutschen Staaten – erfolgreich als eine Einheit aus dem West-Ost-Konflikt hervorgegangen.

Die politisch-historische Österreich-Frage ist verhältnismäßig einfach. Es gibt rein politisch bestimmte Grenzen. Das ist nicht der Fall, wenn man über die österreichische Literatur spricht, d.h. über die deutschsprachige österreichische Literatur. Die Sprache kennt keine Grenzen; der literarisch-kulturelle deutschsprachige Raum läßt sich nicht beliebig abgrenzen oder einengen. Deshalb wird es, meine ich, immer Streitigheiten über den Begriff "Österreichische Literatur" geben. Diese Streitigkeiten können jedoch in unserem Spannungsfeld *German Studies-Austrian*

Studies ausgetragen werden—hoffentlich mit neuen Anregungen und Einrichtungen.

Daß die Frage nach einer österreichischen Literatur von Ausdauer ist und auch weiterhin bleiben wird, ist schon durch die Regelmäßigkeit belegt, mit der Literaturwissenschaftler sie erörtern. Ich habe persönlich zahlreiche Veranstaltungen miterlebt, an denen akribische und minutiöse Erörterungen zur Frage "Gibt es eine österreichische Literatur?" ausgetragen wurden. Im Jahre 1984 wurde eine Doppelausgabe der Zeitschrift *Modern Austrian Literature* dieser Frage gewidmet (Bd. 17, Nr. 3/4). Eine Bibliographie zu dieser Frage, von Donald G. Daviau und Jorun B. Johns, beläuft sich auf fast vierzig Seiten.

Es gibt also Fragen und Antworten und wiederum Fragen, die weitere Antworten nachsichziehen. Ist "österreichisch" im heutigen Sinne als die Republik Österreich und das ehemalige k.u.k. Österreich-Ungarn zu verstehen? Ist nicht die ganze Literatur, die von heutigen und ehemaligen österreichischen Staatsbürgern geschrieben wurde, dementsprechend österreichisch? In dem engen Sinne wohl ja, aber wir wollen doch mehr—Indizien *einer Art kulturellen "Österreichertums."* Es gibt Schriftsteller, die in diesem Sinne wohl als "österreichischer" gelten dürften als andere. Aber das könnte uns in eine Heimatliteratur-Ecke treiben, die wir wahrscheinlich vermeiden möchten. Ein Peter Rosegger ist wohl "österreichisch," aber ist denn ein Hofmannsthal oder ein Musil weniger so, von solchen problematischen Fällen wie Rilke und Kafka ganz zu schweigen?

Ich glaube, daß die Frage nach einer österreichischen Literatur paradigmatisch sein könnte für die Dynamik einer interdisziplinären und geographisch übergreifenden German-Studies-Konzeption. Auf diese Dynamik und auf die Prozesse, die daraus entstehen, kommt es letzten Endes an. Die Antworten sind wichtig, aber noch wichtiger die Fragen, die diese Antworten herausfordern. Dabei wird sich auch herausstellen, daß meine rhetorische Frage am Anfang dieses Vortrags eben nicht so rhetorisch war und die Spannung nicht ganz gelöst hat. Die Teile sind eben größer als das Ganze, es sei denn, wir fangen mit der Faustischen Frage an: "Du nennst dich einen Teil und stehst doch ganz vor mir?" Eben.

President Woodrow Wilson and the Austro-Hungarian Monarchy

Charles E. McClelland

Woodrow Wilson hatte nie die Absicht, Österreich-Ungarn in alle heutigen Nachfolgestaaten aufzusplittern. Als politischer Philanthrop, der die Idee des Völkerbundes konzipierte, die letztlich in den Vereinten Nationen weiterlebt, hatte er eher die freie Völkerentscheidung im Auge. Jede dieser Nationen sollte selbst bestimmen, ob sie im größeren Staatsverband bleiben wollte oder nicht. Er ahnte den kategorischen Zerfall des Völkerbündnisses nicht, war er doch sogar in seinen gelehrten Schriften ein Fürsprecher der Vielvölkermonarchie. Als ehemaliger Politologe und späterer Präsident der Universität Princeton glaubte Wilson die historische und politische Lage Europas zu verstehen. Seine positiven Absichten wurden als Weltmachtstaktiken mißverstanden; vielleicht wird ihm eines Tages doch ein Denkmal in Wien errichtet.

It has been a little distressing for me to hear in the last few days that Austria is perhaps insufficiently recognized in the fields of Germanistics or German Studies, let alone broader fields of public awareness and discourse in the United States. I think it is doing reasonably well in my field, history, though. Austrian history is taught as a normal part of every Western civilization course in American colleges and these are, if not exactly required, at least very commonly taken by most American undergraduates. Images of Austria, some of them distorted, linger in American minds in part because of such courses. (Perhaps the distortions are there because of the people who teach those courses.) Still, one can agree that the First and Second Austrian republics do not quite gain the attention in America that they might. I am also convinced they do not really gain much attention in Europe either: I don't think most French students know any more about Austrian his-

Österreich vor und nach dem Ersten Weltkrieg

WIR FRANZ JOSEPH DER ERSTE, VON GOTTES GNADEN KAISER VON ÖSTERREICH; KÖNIG VON HUNGARN UND BÖHMEN, KÖNIG DER LOMBARDEI UND VENEDIGs, VON DALMATIEN, KROATIEN, SLAWONIEN, GALIZIEN, LODOMERIEN UND ILLIRIEN, KÖNIG VON JERUSALEM ETC.; ERZHERZOG VON ÖSTERREICH; GROSZHERZOG VON TOSCANA UND KRAKAU; HERZOG VON LOTHRINGEN, VON SALZBURG, STEYER, KÄRNTHEN, KRAIN UND DER BUKOWINA; GROSZFÜRST VON SIEBENBÜRGEN; MARKGRAF VON MÄHREN; HERZOG VON OBER- UND NIEDERSCHLESIEN, VON MODENA, PARMA, PIACENZA UND GUASTALLA, VON AUSCHWITZ UND ZATOR, VON TESCHEN, FRIAUL, RAGUSA UND ZARA; GEFÜRSTETER GRAF VON HABSBURG UND TIROL, VON KYBURG, GÖRZ UND GRADISKA; FÜRST VON TRIENT UND BRIXEN; MARKGRAF VON OBER- UND NIEDER-LAUSITZ UND IN ISTRIEN; GRAF VON HOHENEMBS, FELDKIRCH, BREGENZ, SONNENBERG ETC.; HERR VON TRIEST, VON CATTARO UND AUF DER WINDISCHEN MARK: GROSZWOJWOD DER WOJWODSCHAFT SERBIEN ETC. ETC.

The map shows Austria before and after World War I. Before 1918 the Austrian half of the dual monarchy included all the dark shaded areas; the Hungarian half included the areas in lighter grey. After the way "Österreich" was reduced to the area indicated under its name.

Beneath the map is a complete listing of the official titles of Emperor Franz Joseph I who reigned from 1848 to 1916 or 68 years; he was born in 1830.

Around 1900 the Austro-Hungarian monarchy measured about 91 percent of the size of Texas. The Austrian part was somewhat smaller, the Hungarian part somewhat larger than today's New Mexico. About fifty million people lived in both parts. Modern Austria is more than seven times smaller than the dual monarchy, with a population of almost eight million mostly German speaking people.

tory than their American counterparts, for example. But if we have retained a little fingerhold for Austria in America, I think it has something to do with Austria's immense role in Western civilization and consequently in these history courses. For example, we historians do not especially dwell upon the *Opernball, Spanische Reitschule,* or even the *Musikverein* as specifically associated with the First or Second Austrian Republics; they are European institutions in addition to their Austrian context.

What I am trying to insinuate here, as I am sure you can already see, are the universality and the international dimension of Austrian history prior to 1918 – to speak of "Austria" today as a part of the Habsburg, Danubian or Dual Monarchy, which as an international state made so many memorable contributions. I am not trying to say that "little Austria," *Kleinösterreich,* the First and Second Republics, had nothing to be proud of, quite the contrary. But it seems to me that in order to understand Wilson and the beginning of the First Republic, and indeed a certain amount of the heritage that goes into the Second Austrian Republic, one also has to delve back a little bit into the prior history. (As historians are often tempted to say, if you want to understand the twentieth century, let's begin with Sumer.)

Austria has been throughout most of its history, and I think one can say it still is, inseparable from and unthinkable without the rest of Europe. For centuries before 1871, there was no "Germany" for Austria to join; there was only a welter of German and non-German territories for the Habsburg dynasty, the "House of Austria," to dominate throughout most of modern history. Before 1871, the idea of the German nation-state remained only that, an unrealized dream which, more often than not, conflicted with the dynastic politics of Central Europe. For the thousand years and more before Adolf Hitler, the Holy Roman Empire, the Germanic Confederation, and the German and Austro-Hungarian Empires were multi-ethnic polities. Hitler's own "thousand-year Reich" lasted only twelve years for the Germans, and a mere seven years for the Austrians, although we have already spent considerable time talking about those. It is worth remembering that terms like "the Austrian nation," which I heard mentioned here recently, are as historically questionable as "the German nation" was in the mouth of Hitler. These are intellectual constructs or *Kopfgeburten,* to play with Günter Grass's term. If Hitler did not understand this, it might be because he was a failed Austrian.

I want to make just one other comment relating to some other prior discussions in this Workshop before I get into the substance of my talk. I would like to underline how historically *judenfreundlich* the "official" old Austria traditionally was. Joseph II (1780–1790) was the first major monarch of Europe to emancipate the Jews; the emancipation was not complete, but it certainly was more sweeping, at least in intent, than anything available up to then and precedes the liberation of the Jews by the French Revolution of 1789. In the 1860s once again, the Austrian Empire fully emancipated the Jews, even before Great Britain did. The fact that it did so and was an international, "cosmopolitan" empire was precisely what made Hitler so furious with it and made him welcome the destruction of that monarchy: he saw it as an impediment to the realization of his own dream of a pan-German empire.

An irony in all this is that Woodrow Wilson, who is often credited with the end of the Danube Monarchy, was president of another multi-cultural, multi-ethnic empire, if you want to look at it that way. (Gore Vidal's recent historical novel, *Empire,* stresses the dramatic beginnings, in 1898, of the American Empire.) In any case there are no statues of Wilson, this alleged "father of the First Austrian Republic," to be found in Vienna. Although I do not want to build a statue to him today, I would like to argue that he deserves at least a better memorial than as the unwitting accomplice of Hitler and the pan-Germans.

The "Austria" that collapsed in 1918 was the work of the Habsburg dynasty, and it remained to the end international in nature. The Habsburgs were not even originally from the central provinces that became the Austrian republic. The official title of the last Austrian emperor was King of Hungary and Emperor of the Lands Represented in the Imperial Council – that was the short version. The long version fills two pages of single-space type, with all the individual lands to which he has historic and diverse titles, including the provinces of today's Austria. As the King of Hungary and the titular Emperor over all the other non-Hungarian lands, he presided over a constitutional compromise that had to be renegotiated every decade since 1867. Foreign leaders had difficulty understanding this constitutional system, and historians still tend to refer to "Austria" as a kind of shorthand. But it was a congeries of peoples, religions, languages and customs, in short, a kind of social contract that originally had been imposed by agreement or conquest; but the system was largely accepted by its peoples as at least reformable and, in post-1918 retrospect, as a sort of model of international cooperation. One might dare say that there is a sort of *nostalgie de l'Autriche,* a nostalgia for this "old" Austria in Central Europe today. No doubt today's Austrians are quite happy that they do not have to rule over that area again, but the other "Austro-Hungarian" peoples, particularly after four decades under communism, sometimes see the situation more wistfully.

Austria after 1918 has been a *kleindeutsch,* "little German" state, which was torn to pieces in the 1920s and 1930s by political, class and economic conflicts that I cannot talk about today. It was torn also from its historical moorings of 600 years with the Habsburg dynasty and had to seek a new role between the forces of the Great Powers, to which it no longer belonged, and of whose whims it had become a victim, if even a willing one, as in 1938. Austria's history has been so emphatically a part of Europe's history, and its current world role as a neutral state so significant, whatever world opinion in its swings about Waldheim has to say about it, that its traditions and the "Wilsonian" circumstances of its demise deserve our attention today.

The Austro-Hungarian or "Dual" Monarchy had been set up in 1867 at the conclusion of the Prussian-Austrian war. The Habsburg defeat produced the result that the Hungarians, long interested in their own independence, pressed once again and this time successfully, for some sort of arrangement that would leave them practically governing themselves, except in matters of common defense and foreign policy. The two halves of the monarchy were sundered, had two seprarate parliaments and administered their own internal affairs, so that the Hungarians, the Magyar-speaking majority, tended to lord it over the non-Magyar-speaking groups, such as the Slovaks and the Croats. In the Austrian half, there was a good deal of movement toward reform and ethnic autonomy. By the 1890s, as Mark Twain noted when he was visiting the Austrian Parliament, parliamentary life was so exuberant that it had to be shut down for a while. As Twain reported, not only ideas but curses and objects flew around the lower house: ink stands and words that he said he could not translate in a family magazine (but gave in the original German, Czech, Polish, Italian, etc.). One had not a single unified monarchy, but two monarchies held together with an increasingly tenuous bond, with one showing definite signs of movement, including a democratic franchise before World War I, and for all its roughness, a representative parliamentary body, and the other half, Hungary, attempting to suppress minorities and presenting less promise for change from the point of view addressed by Woodrow Wilson.

Rumania, Hungary, Poland, the Ukraine, Yugoslavia, Italy, Austria and Czechoslovakia, these are the nation-states of which we think today; they were then "Austria." By the way, Arthur May, the source of a lot of what I am going to say, has written the book on this, still unsurpassed after twenty years, *The Passing of the Habsburg Monarchy, 1914–18.*

In order to prevent the disintegration of this multi-national empire, with the various ethnic groups demanding more and more autonomy (or Home Rule, if you want to compare the British/Irish relationship) from the central government in Vienna or Budapest, "Austria" was faced with a big conundrum in 1914. It reacted to this conundrum by going to war to prevent the Serbs, who had an independent kingdom, from continuing to try to detach the Croats and the Slovenes, although these peoples at that time had little interest in Yugoslavia or a Yugoslav state. But the fear in Vienna and Budapest was that if Serbia was going to subvert the Danube Monarchy at its southern flank, it could never have any security. So the assassination of the Archduke Franz Ferdinand in Sarajevo in 1914 by a Serbian-connected terrorist plot gave the Austrian and Hungarian governments the chance they had been looking for to deal with Serbia and, as it were, to

(by sculptor P. Coppini)
Woodrow Wilson Statue on the campus of the University of Texas at Austin. The text on the stone plate beneath the figure reads as follows:

WOODROW WILSON
1856-1924
Professor of Political Economy
President of Princeton University
Governor of New Jersey
President of the United States
Founder of the League of Nations

Photo by News and Information Service
University of Texas at Austin

leap forward out of their difficulties by plunging the country into a war that they felt sure they could win because, for one thing, they thought world opinion was on their side. As we know, this led to a chain reaction of other powers getting into the war: first Russia, then Germany, and then thanks to the Schlieffen Plan, France, finally England, and ultimately, when the price was right, Italy in 1915.

In response to questions by the audience, I refer to the various Treaties made with non-combatant Powers after 1914. In April of 1915, for example, the Allied Powers—Britain, France, and Imperial Russia foremost—assured Italy not only of Italian-speaking regions of Austria—"Italia irredenta"—but also of a great "slice of Turkey"—in Italy's case dominion over the southern coast and islands of what we now call Turkey, as well as free passage of Russian warships through the Turkish straits. The Sykes-Picot agreement also provided for the division of what we now call the "Middle East" among the Allies. The Treaty of Rome and the Sykes-Picot Agreement of 1916 are perhaps the last great examples of imperialistic *hubris* (that we know of) in the twentieth century.

The Treaty of Rome (which was secret) leaked out to the Ottoman Empire and made their soldiers fight harder. Austria-Hungary's ally, Germany, tried to raise colonial rebellions against the British Empire from Ireland to India. Australian and New Zealand troops fought, bled and died on the Turkish beaches, thinking they were "doing it for England." It was a war of messy and stupid campaigns, fought for secret treaties and territorial bribes. In the end the Greek government had to be toppled, "CIA-style," by the British to bring that country into the war in 1917.

In November 1916 Woodrow Wilson was reelected President of the United States, campaigning to keep America out of World War I. I think you might begin to see why such a slogan might have been popular! Of course, only a few months later we were right in it. Wilson, provoked by Germany's unrestricted submarine warfare, thereby set a new standard of forgetting electoral promises that we still have to live with. Emperor Charles I of Austria-Hungary also had ascended his throne in November 1916, hoping to take his country out of this ruinous conflict, which, already quite apparently to many Austrians, was ruining the country. I think one could fairly say that both were men of peace and good will when they came to power, and Charles even tried to use Wilson as a peace-making intermediary, as he had tried to use the Pope, through his brother-in-law, Prince Sixtus of Parma. (Incidentally, Charles' wife, Empress Zita, is still alive in Austria. Her brother, Sixtus of Parma, a French citizen, was willing to negotiate with the Allied powers.) There were several peace initiatives which Charles I launched, all of them secretly, not wanting his German allies to know about them because, who knows, the Germans might come and take over. This was a constant fear in his mind.

Wilson's America had very little quarrel with Austria-Hungary, so little that the two countries remained at peace almost ten months after the American declaration of war on Imperial Germany in April 1917. The one time prior to that declaration of war that Austria and America had a scrape was when Austrian U-boats sank an Italian liner, the *Ascona,* and incidentally killed a few Americans, but the Austrians rushed to pay damages and apologized profusely right away, very unlike the German submarine warfare campaign. Less than a year after America entered the war against Austria-Hungary on 7 December 1917 (that's a December 7 that will not "live in infamy," I think, except perhaps in Vienna), Austria-Hungary had ceased to exist, although America and Austria barely fired a shot at each other.

Wilson's central idea of peace was that of national self-determination, that is, that each national or ethnic group in Europe should have an opportunity to govern its own affairs in some form or another. "Some form or another" is important, because self-determination did not mean independence; it meant asking the people what they wanted to do, and in the Austrian case it could have meant, had the people responded that way, continuing this arrangement under some more liberalized form. But the idea of national self-determination had wound up in fact sweeping away the centuries-old Habsburg dynasty and the multinational empire that it had built. People later began to look back and wonder if Woodrow Wilson hadn't been the person responsible. I am going to argue today that, yes and no, but mostly no.

For one reason, there were many national committees, allegedly representing the ethnic groups within Austria-Hungary, that had been set up toward the end of the war in various foreign capitals: the Yugoslav Committee in London, the Czech Committee in Paris, and other sub-committees around the world as examples. And the Americans gave them a lot of encouragement for reasons I'll explain in a moment. The Slovak Committee invited the Czechs to America and made a deal called the Pittsburgh Agreement, which was supposed to serve as the basis for the future Czechoslovak state, and they even sat down in front of the Liberty Bell in Philadelphia to have a picture made as if to cement their ties symbolically with America and the American Independence movement. (It is also rather ironic that in the photograph the crack is right there next to Masaryk's head. Masaryk was not cracked, but Czechoslovakia, as we'll see later, cracked up, because the beautiful dream in Philadelphia yielded to "great power politics" and ethnic squabbles.)

Thinking of his great fellow-historian Masaryk and the Liberty Bell, Wilson then attended the Paris Peace Conference and had a hand in the various treaties that disposed of Germany and the former Habsburg territories – Versailles, Saint-Germain and Trianon. None of these, of course, was later ratified by the American Senate, so everything Wilson negotiated and many of the points he gave away in order to get his ultimate overriding objective, the League of Nations, were forfeited by the action of the American Congress. Wilson, embittered, defeated, and paralyzed by a stroke, left office in 1921. (He died three years later.) Emperor Charles died in 1922. Wilson's vision of a "Europe of nations" (ironically, Charles de Gaulle would revive this phrase after 1945) lay in ruins, the fuel for another war in 1939, and the Austro-Hungarian Empire was gone forever, according to many historians, because of Woodrow Wilson. As I said earlier, I think the story is a little more complicated.

Austria could be said to have had the least problematical relationship with America prior to World War I. Austria was not an imperial power; it did not have a significant navy, it did not want to carve up China, it was not in competition with the American Empire, much less so than Britain or Russia or Germany, countries that the Americans had much more reasons to fear. Even France seemed to be more of a threat to America than Austria-Hungary. We must also not forget that in 1914 something on the order of perhaps six percent of the American population (or more) consisted of immigrnats from Austria-Hungary. Austria-Hungary provided the *third* largest immigrant group to America in the late nineteenth century after Great Britain/Ireland and Italy, so that there were some two million Poles (of course, not all of them came from Austria), about a million Czechs, about a million Slovaks, and hundreds of thousands of others living in various parts of the United States. This was a constituency both for and against Austria in the United States. Despite the fact that Austria can be squarely blamed for starting World War I because of the circumstance of the assassination of the successor to the throne, there was initially a good deal of sympathy for Austria in the United States. In any case, there was a good deal of sympathy for keeping America out of the war, and once America was in the war, there was very little sympathy for going to war against Austria. Really more for "technical reasons" than any kind of animosity, America and Austria wound up at war. In other words, it was harder for America to be at war with Bulgaria, Turkey, and Germany and not with Austria, than to say, let's put them all in one pot. Also, as an enemy of the Dual Monarchy, America would have more say in her future than as a neutral.

One must also say that Wilson wanted very much to use Austria-Hungary at first to end the European war on a fair basis before the United States came into the hostilities. He was of course very suspicious of Germany and correctly regarded it as the dominant partner in the Central Power grouping. If he could detach Austria from the war, he could weaken Germany and thereby bring the Germans to some sort of terms. Wilson also, we must not forget, mistrusted the Allies (remember: Britain, France, Imperial Russia) and the United States never became an "Ally" in World War I. The technical term was the "Allied and Associated

Powers." We were the associated power; "they" were the Allies.

"They" consisted chiefly of the British Empire, which by any objective standard proved around the pre-1914 world its ruthless self-interest; the Kingdom of Italy, which dispatched a half-million soldiers to die in mountain passes against Austrian boys to buy a Turkish empire; a French Republic riddled with scandal and, indeed, the most massive mutiny of war-weary troops ever seen in a modern army in 1917; and last – not least – the best representative of Allied democracy, progress, and tenderness, the Empire of Nicolas II, or rather at that point the drunken orgiastic priest Rasputin who influenced the royal family of Russia. What American would fight as an "ally" for this degenerate, polluted, plutocratic crowd? Not for the USA, the secret treaties that provided for the carving up of territory after the war, irrespective of any wishes of the peoples there.

When he was reelected in 1916, Wilson launched a peace offensive of his own, encouraged, among other things, by news that Emperor Charles wanted to end the war too. None of the major Allies, Russia, Britain, France, and Italy, nor the Central Powers responded to Wilson's satisfaction, but none of the other powers contemplated at that point the dissolution of the Austro-Hungarian monarchy. "What's wrong with it going on existing?" Wilson thought. It is worth noting that Professor Wilson had analyzed Austria-Hungary, among other countries, in his book *The State* (1889).

How and why Wilson went from being a defender, probably the best defender of Austria-Hungary's right to continued existence in 1916, to one who acquiesced in its breakup and dissolution by the end of 1918 will occupy us for the next few moments. Obviously Wilson had little love for the Habsburg dynasty as such or for dynasties of any type, and he blamed the foolishness of the governments in Vienna and Budapest for plunging Europe into war in the first place. He certainly was not going to try to keep the Habsburg dynasty going, necessarily; it was the idea of this international confederation that the Habsburgs had presided over, that he still considered attractive and perhaps necessary. Wilson, the knowledgeable former professor of government and history, appreciated the way this empire had held together so many quarreling groups. Austria-Hungary represented to him a counterweight – and could be still in the future – against Germany, which he really did fear. He was worried about the future of these rather small Danubian ethnic groups and whether they would be able to make it on their own. Certainly another factor in Wilson's thinking was the influence of Germany on the Austro-Hungarian Empire. In 1917, for example, one of Charles I's peace offensives involving Sixtus of Parma became known to the Germans (it was leaked to French newspapers). The press claimed that he had told the Prime Minister of France that Austria would be happy to make a separate peace and, as far as they were concerned, France could have Alsace-Lorraine, one of its major war objectives, back from Germany. Naturally the Germans were furious and asked, "Wait a minute, are you our Allies or are you the friends of the French?" The Austrians had to shuffle very fast and deny everything. And so once more an opportunity was missed. The Pope, at the instigation of the Austrians, also tried to get the various combatants clearly to state their war aims in the summer of 1917, which none of them would.

What do we have so far: the Austrians had started the war, they deserved some sort of punishment, yet the Allies and Wilson did not want to break up the Empire because of its usefulness in the future as a counterweight to Germany. This situation changed with the Russian Revolution in 1917, and I think this is an important factor in explaining the alteration of American policy. After all, the Germans, you might say, started the game of destabilizing their enemies internally as a way of ending the war. The German General Staff sent Lenin on a sealed train across Europe to make trouble in Russia because the Provisional Government did not want to stop the war. Kerensky said, "Right, we will continue the war, even though we are in the middle of a revolution." Lenin arrived with the statement, "Peace and Bread right now," and that, not communism, was the chief appeal of the Bolsheviks. That is why the Germans were so eager to send Lenin in his train from Switzerland to the Finland Station in Petrograd. The Allies had their own problems with revolutionary rumbles; exhaustion, strikes, and mutinies abounded in the Allied camp. In Germany also there were strikes and riots, and so people were worried what the end of Russian participation in the war would mean. Eventually with some absolutely brutal, punishing bargaining that became a model for the Allies in their turn in Paris in 1919, the Germans, backed feebly by the Austrians, sat down and forced the Russians to sign the treaty of Brest-Litovsk in March of 1918, a move which took Russia out of the war. It also took away most of the territory that the Czars of Russia had conquered in Europe since the time of Peter the Great, irrespective of national self-determination.

Brest-Litovsk meant that the Allies were really now up against the wall without an "eastern front," and consequently the decision to begin to destabilize Austria-Hungary was copied from the German attempt to destabilize revolutionary Russia. If "we" could make Austria-Hungary break up, that would weaken the German cause and thereby perhaps bring an end to the war. Nevertheless, and despite the pressure that was mounting in America (particularly by the Slavic ethnic groups that were now beginning to sympathize with the independence movements within Austria-Hungary), Wilson's Fourteen Points, enunciated in his address of January 1918, in Point Ten called for the freedom for autonomous development of the peoples of Austria-Hungary. *Autonomous development,* not independence. Wilson was not demanding the independence of the component groups. The other points included such things as the creation of a Polish state, but that could be misleading if you don't know the context, because at that time many of the Poles inside and outside of Austria were still in favor of a Polish state that would be affiliated federally with the Austro-Hungarian monarchy in the future. The ideas of a Yugoslav state and of giving over territory to the Italians were also in Wilson's Fourteen Points, but the central issue for us was the autonomous development, the self-determination of the peoples of Austria-Hungary: leave it up to them.

What American policy did between then and the fall of 1918 was essentially drift toward the position that the Allies were already beginning to take, that the breakup of Austria-Hungary was desirable as a means of ending the war. Secretary of State Lansing took that position, starting in May of 1918. The last holdout, the intimate advisor of Wilson who up to the end advocated maintaining the Austro-Hungarian monarchy in some form, was Colonel House. The "éminence grise," the "little man from Texas," had been a main advisor and money backer of Wilson from the beginning of his presidency. Colonel House had traveled extensively in Austria-Hungary before and during the war on missions from Wilson. He understood very well the situation there. One can seek a statue of Wilson, the "negative father of the First Austrian Republic," in vain in Vienna. And perhaps it is right that there is none. But there ought to be a statue of Colonel House.

Let's not forget that there were also centrifugal forces in Austria-Hungary that were tugging away at the monarchy and had been for a long time. Now that the fabric of the monarchy was weakening, these forces asserted themselves even more strongly. Hungary had long since made it clear that it would no longer associate itself with Austria once the war was over. In fact, the Hungarians even refused to deliver food to the Austrian part of the monarchy. The Hungarians, anticipating perhaps the proud 1970s Texas bumper-sticker "Let the Yankees shiver in the dark," had let the Viennese starve rather than deliver grain and other foodstuffs, to give you an idea of how loyal they were. Emperor Charles was trying to placate the non-German peoples of the Austrian half of the monarchy and made a declaration on 17 October 1918 which promised autonomy to all the peoples within the framework of the Empire. This provoked a revolution among the German-speaking population of Austria. They met the next day and declared a National Assembly of German Austria. The internal forces, not just the Slavs, Italians, and so on, were pulling the monarchy to pieces. Not just, or even mostly, Woodrow Wilson.

I think we can terminate this analysis with Wilson's arrival at the point in October of 1918 when he made an armistice with Charles conditional on the independence of the various ethnic groups in Austria. We can see that it took him about two years and that he was not the motor, but rather the brake on the movement toward the disintegration of the Austro-Hungarian Empire.

I would like now to move on to what happened in 1919 at the Paris Peace Conference and how this affected the First Austrian Republic. There was a major conflict between the Fourteen Points of Wilson and the secret agreements of the Allies. This was really about carving up Turkey, and the promises made to Czarist Russia about its rights of access to the Turkish Straits, plus other territorial concessions that had nothing to do with the will or consent of the people involved (the good old European "diplomacy of Imperialism"). Wilson's "new diplomacy" headed right to the first Point of the Fourteen: open covenants openly arrived at, the term "covenant" used in good American Presbyterian terms in preference to the tainted word "treaty." Open diplomacy included the consultation of the peoples involved. Those two systems came into conflict in Paris, and Wilson, I think you can say, was the one that had to yield the most. For example, although promises to Russia were now forfeited by its leaving the war, those made to Italy by France and Britain were still on the table; those awards were inconsistent with the idea of a Yugoslav state and the self-determination of the Slavic-speaking populations. The Italians simply implied, "Well, there is one Italian living there, so it's Italian." This led to interminable conflicts between Yugoslavia and Italy, right through the 20s and 30s, and ended with the invasion of Yugoslavia by the Italians in the early 40s. The desire of the Allies for reparations meant that somebody had to be blamed. Germany of course had to be blamed and made to pay because it could perhaps pay; but somebody had to be blamed in Austria and Hungary too. Since the Allies had become cozy with the Czechs, Yugoslavs and Rumanians, that meant they were blameless as "successor states" of the Empire; only Austria and Hungary proper, much reduced in territory and now, initially, new democratic states, the very kind of institutions Wilson had been demanding, remained to take the blame. Hungary's response was a Bolshevik republic followed by the "regency" of Horthy, which are part of another story. Austria became a democratic republic saddled with the sins of the departed Habsburgs.

Fear of Germany promoted territorial settlements with the other "successor states" to Austria-Hungary, to make them economically and militarily viable at the expense of the principle of national self-determination. That meant that ethnically German and Hungarian areas were given to other countries on the grounds that these territories were economically, militarily, or for some other reason important to the strategic viability of the new states. For example, the Sudeten German area had to be given to Czechoslovakia because the fortifications against Germany, most of the munitions' plants, and a good deal of the industry of Czechoslovakia were located there. The leave it with the rump of German-speaking Austria appeared dangerous, since the Austrian Republic declared it wanted to join the new German (Weimar) Republic; and to give it to Germany was unthinkable, since the point of the Allies was to weaken Germany's future capacity to make trouble. The "self-determination" of the Sudeten Germans would have meant, from the Paris perspective, turning Czechoslovakia, what was left of it, into an indefensible state, as it became in 1938 after the Munich Agreement.

German Austria (and here is the central point for us), as well as the Sudetenland, were prevented from joining the Weimar Republic. This was principally at the instigation of the French, who perhaps understandably argued that they had not fought and bled four years to see Germany winding up with more territory and more people than it had in 1914. Nevertheless, it was a violation of Wilson's promises and of the principle of national self-determination. Hopes of some sort of economic federation in the Danube area, a part of Point Three according to Wilson, were also dashed by conflict among the successor states, which immediately fell upon each other, fighting over scraps of territory and disputed ethnic groups, as well as by the worldwide economic problems of the interwar era.

After Charles I, Wilson was also unthroned. The refusal of the United States Senate to ratify the Paris treaties, Wilson's haughty refusal to seek Advice and Consent as the senators saw it, meant the League of Nations was set up without American participation. Wilson had sacrificed so many things to get that League because he thought it could straighten out all the unfair decisions that had been made in the heat of the Paris negotiation, once tempers had cooled. But the United States had not joined the League, and its non-participation was crucial in explaining why there was later no peaceful redress of all these "wrongs." Ironically, Wilson's words about national self-determination would be used over and over again by the Austrian and German Nazis, including Adolf Hitler, to justify the *Anschluß* of March 1938, as well for the dismemberment of Czechoslovakia later that year. The argument that the Sudeten Germans ought to be given a right to decide their future was the last "Wilsonian" argument of the tinhorn Machiavelli Hitler. Even the attack on Poland in 1939 was connected with the principle of national self-determination, at least in Hitler's mind.

In 1938 the veteran American diplomat at the Paris Peace Conference, William Bullitt, helped the dying Sigmund Freud get out of recently Nazi-occupied Vienna by forcing Freud to agree to write a "Freudian analysis" of Woodrow Wilson which painted the former president as mad. Freud wrote it, but Bullitt was evidently not crazy enough to publish it at the time. It did come out later in the 1960s. It is dismissed today as a serious analysis; it is simply assumed that Freud was doing this as the price to be paid to a rich, embittered American to get him out of Austria. I think it does show how bitter feelings still were about Wilson, though, not only in Austrian but in American circles as well.

I think one cay say that Wilson brought both the best and the worst of American political and intellectual traditions to bear on the problem of Austria-Hungary. He yielded to domestic and allied pressure when he should have stuck to his principles; he was inconsistent. Rather idealistically, perhaps, very "Americanly," he left to the future what he could not get in hard bargaining in the present, hoping that the League of Nations would straighten everything out. He was fêted on arrival in Paris as a maker of peace in 1919, as a bringer of the new diplomacy, but by 1920 he was universally decried by everybody.

I think the Fourteen Points still represent a good basis for international cooperation and friendship in the Danube area (and elsewhere) and stand in stark contrast to the World Policeman role of American Cold War thinking since the 1950s. Many of these principles, I think, have been taken over by Austria and the other successor states since Wilson's time. Ironically, a certain amount of the current prosperity and world role of the city of Vienna derives from its place in the United Nations, the successor to Wilson's League of Nations. It is therefore not too much to say that the world and Austria might have been better off if Wilson's program had been fulfilled after 1918 rather than essentially the program of the Allies and of the leaders of the independence movements within the Austro-Hungarian monarchy. In any case, if there had been no Wilson, the fate of Austria would have been essentially the same, perhaps even worse. Its fate was decided by its own dynasty, which could not come to terms with its peoples, by the narrow nationalism of some of its peoples' leaders (here again the historian Masaryk is a glowing exception), by the cynical greed of the old diplomacy of the Allies, by the international ignorance of the American electorate which turned its back on the League of Nations and Wilson, and of course by the social and economic conflicts that typified Europe in the interwar years.

Wilson also suffered from the hubris of American power and the need to project American values on other societies without knowing them really well. In that sense Wilson, a well-informed and high-minded President, inaugurated a tradition in the American presidency that continues in the hands of increasingly ungifted leaders to this day. Perhaps Kurt Waldheim's election can be seen as a reaction to that tradition of hubris in Austria; certainly in 1986 many Austrians who did not like Waldheim told me they thought he would be elected because the Austrians were tired of being pushed around by the bully America.

If Wilson's ideals mean anything today, "making the world safe for democracy," for example, then I think one had to swallow the election of Waldheim, warts and all, and hope that Wilson's successors in the White House will see it that way too. As Wilson found out, the voice of the people is, if not God, at least sovereign. Even he, like the well-meaning Emperor Charles I of Habsburg-Lorraine, fell before the demiurge of peoples.

In conclusion: although I am not starting a collection, I can hope that someday there *may* be a statue of Wilson, or at least one of Colonel House, in Vienna.

Salzburg – Old Market Place – Café Tomaselli

Photo VOTAVA

Die Salzburger Festspiele und ihre Entwicklung

Ruth E. Lorbe

When Hugo von Hofmannsthal, Max Reinhardt and Richard Strauss initiated this festival in 1920 they envisioned it as a cultural event for the entire population. Salzburg with its rural surroundings was thought to be more congenial to this idea than urban Vienna. They could not predict that their concept would materialize only in part. Although Salzburg has become a center for music, drama and the arts, its tickets and fees can be afforded only by Europe's wealthy. Nonetheless, its excellence in programs and performance has not only kept it alive but made it also an example that many other places in the world have adopted for their festivals, among them that of Santa Fe in New Mexico.

Im Jahr 1928, wenige Monate vor seinem Tod, charakterisierte Hugo von Hofmannsthal in einem Aufsatz über die Salzburger Festspiele, die seit 1920, also damals seit knapp zehn Jahren stattfanden, das Festspielpublikum. Er betont, daß es zwar unmöglich scheinen mag, die Besucher der Festspiele "durch das Dargebotene zur Einheit, zu einem Publikum zusammenzubinden," da ja die Gäste, verschiedenen Gesellschaftsschichten und verschiedenen Interessenbereichen angehörend, aus allen Himmelsrichtungen und Erdteilen für diese kurzen Sommerwochen in Salzburg zusammenströmten. Trotzdem sei "es durch ein Jahrzehnt gelungen: sonst bestünden die Festspiele nicht mehr."[1] Die Festspiele sind – laut Hofmannsthal – in ihrem ersten Jahrzehnt nicht nur "eine in Europa und Amerika berühmte Institution geworden," sondern man konnte damals bereits "von ihrem Publikum sprechen, das sich aus wiederkehrenden und wechselnden Elementen" zusammensetzte, "aber im ganzen doch eine erkennbare Physiognomie gewonnen" hatte, "über die Veränderungen hinweg" (IV, 465).

Wie sah das Publikum des ersten Jahrzehnts aus?

Hofmannsthal unterscheidet eine "großstädtische" und eine "ungroßstädtische" Hälfte (IV, 466). Keine der beiden sei in sich homogen, sondern es seien "in ihren unzähligen Individuen . . . alle Spielarten der Aufnahmebereitschaft, des Theatersinnes, der Schaulust, der Musikalität verteilt, und die Kurven, mit denen man graphisch diese Empfänglichkeiten darzustellen versuchen könnte," hätten "nichts zu tun mit den Linien, welche etwa die sozialen oder nationalen Unterschiede darstellen würden" (IV, 467). Gerade die großstädtischen Vertreter variierten beträchtlich voneinander, entsprechend dem jeweiligen, vom Theaterleben bestimmten geistigen Hintergrund, in dem sie zuhause waren. Hier nun charakterisiert Hofmannsthal, der gut informiert war, die Eigenart der Theateratmosphäre in Berlin, in Paris, in London. Besonders eingehend widmet er sich der Beschreibung des New Yorker Theaterklimas, das in seinen Augen damals gerade eine sehr spürbare Evolution erlebte:

"Noch jung genug, um von allen Seiten zu nehmen, fange" nämlich das New Yorker Theaterwesen "an, über die bloße Rezeptivität hinauszugehen: es [fange] an, zu sondern und in diesem Sondern eine Originalität zu enthüllen und seinen Einfluß auszuüben: den Einfluß seiner weiten Horizonte, seiner Kraft und seines Kraftbewußtseins, seines zu unbekannten Formen und Assoziationen sich umbildenden Puritanertums" (IV, 469). An anderen Stellen bemerkt Hofmannsthal im Hinblick auf das Salzburger Publikum, auf dieses wie er sagt "denkbar bunteste Publikum," daß da nicht nur, "zum erstenmal seit dem Krieg, wieder an einer Stelle von Mitteleuropa eine völlig internationale Zuhörerschaft" versammelt war, sondern daß das Publikum auch sozial bunt gemischt war. So säßen zum Beispiel einfache einheimische bäuerliche und kleinstädtische Menschen aus den Alpenorten neben den Reichen, "Priester und Klosterfrauen zwischen den Amerikanern, den Skandinaviern, den Franzosen und Berlinern" (*Aufzeichnungen*, 299f.). Das sei in gewisser Weise "die erste Wiedererstehung des Europa von früher, mit einer sehr starken, sehr fühlbaren amerikanischen Beimischung" (*Aufzeichnungen*, 304). Fügt man zu diesen Beobachtungen Hofmannsthals die wie beiläufig geäußerte Bemerkung von Annette Kolb über eine Erinnerung an die Salzburger Festspiele im Jahr 1935 hinzu, wo es heißt, daß die New Yorker eingerückt seien und "die Abonnenten der Metropolitan Opera . . . das Feld" beherrschten,[2] dann läßt sich nicht leugnen, daß das amerikanische Kontingent der Salzburger Zuschauerschaft bereits in der ersten, 1938 abrupt beendeten Phase der Festspiele recht beachtlich gewesen sein muß. Und weiter, daß dabei offensichtlich nicht nur die Quantität des über den Ozean anreisenden Publikums auffiel, sondern daß dieses amerikanische Publikum, sozusagen als unbeabsichtigtes Geschenk, ganz bestimmte neue, originelle Qualitäten mitbrachte, Impulse, die die Physiognomie des gesamten Publikums und damit den Geist der Salzburger Festspiele, zumindest in den Anfangsjahren, in auffallender Weise mitprägten.

Somit gehört die Betrachtung der Salzburger Festspiele zurecht in einen Workshop, dessen Aufgabe das Aufzeigen österreichisch-amerikanischer Beziehungen seit dem Ende des Ersten Weltkriegs ist. Schon die wenigen, oben zitierten Augenzeugenberichte bekunden sehr deutlich, daß bei dem geistigen Austausch, der sich in Salzburg von Anfang an sowohl innerhalb des kunstinteressierten und kunstbegeisterten Publikums als auch zwischen dem Publikum und den österreichischen Gastgebern abspielte, die geistigkulturellen Fäden, die hier zwischen Österreich und Amerika angesponnen wurden, einen wesentlichen Faktor bildeten.

In der vorliegenden Darstellung geht es vornehmlich darum, die Entwicklung aufzuzeigen, die zur Gründung der Salzburger Festspiele geführt hat und wie dabei die Pläne und Intentionen der am Zustandekommen der Spiele Hauptbeteiligten das Festspielprogramm vor allem während der Anfangsjahre bestimmt haben. Zugleich soll jedoch immer das Augenmerk auch den amerikanisch-österreichischen Wechselbeziehungen gelten, die sich innerhalb dieses Vorgangs auf verschiedenen Gebieten abgespielt haben.

Die Salzburger Festspiele stellen im Vergleich zu anderen Festspielen nicht nur hinsichtlich des ihnen zugrundeliegenden Gedankens, nicht nur hinsichtlich ihres Programms, ihres Ausmaßes, ihrer Ausstrahlungskraft und der beteiligten Persönlichkeiten etwas Einmaliges dar. Warum?

Obwohl das Jahr 1920 eindeutig als das Jahr der ersten Salzburger Festspiele bezeichnet werden kann, hat die Entwicklung, die gerade Salzburg zum Mittelpunkt besonderer kultureller Ereignisse hat werden lassen, schon lange vorher begonnen. Es handelt sich bei der Gründung dieser Festspiele also keineswegs um die mehr oder weniger spontane Verwirklichung eines grandiosen plötzlichen Einfalls einiger Musik- und Theaterfanatiker, denen es gelungen war, die Behörden von den Vorteilen und der Durchführbarkeit des Unternehmens zu überzeugen und Geldgeber zu mobilisieren. Im Gegenteil: auch wenn es zur endgültigen Verwirklichung umsichtiger, einflußreicher und vor allem genialer Persönlichkeiten bedurfte, die sich, wie in diesem Falle, im rechten Augenblick zusammenfanden, um die Spiele schließlich zu starten, bedeuten die Salzburger Festspiele doch etwas organisch Gewachsenes, etwas, das sich über Jahrzehnte hin entwickelt hat. Trotz vieler Hindernisse waren bei diesem Werdegang glückliche Umstände mit im Spiel. Zu der reichen kulturellen Tradition der Stadt gesellen sich weitere Elemente, die für die Einmaligkeit der Salzburger Festspielatmosphäre verantwortlich sind, die wohl vor allem in den frühen Jahren von den Besuchern empfunden wurde. Annette Kolb betont das wiederholt in ihrem oben erwähnten kleinen Erinnerungsband an die Festspiele. Bei diesen Elementen handelt es sich zum einen um die geographisch günstige Lage Salzburgs, zentral und im Schnittpunkt zwischen den damaligen bedeutenden Kulturzentren des südlichen deutschsprachigen Raums. Wichtig waren weiter sowohl die liebliche Landschaft als auch die einzigartige architektonische Kulisse, die die Stadt bietet. Sieht Stefan Zweig in Salzburg den Rahmen für das Ganze,[3] so charakterisiert Hofmannsthal die Situation noch treffender: "Hier ist nun die Stadt selbst, die Landschaft, von unendlicher Bedeutung. Sie ist weit mehr als Rahmen: der Geist dieser Stadt ist der Regent des Ganzen" (IV, 469). Bestimmt traf das für die erste Phase der Festspiele zu.

War Salzburg seit je als Pflegestätte der Musik, des Gesangs, des Theaterspiels hervorgetreten – man denke etwa an die Bedeutung des Klosters St. Peter für die Musik im Mittelalter, an die

Tradition des Theaterspiels im 17. Jahrhundert, sowohl am erzbischöflichen Hof als auch unter der arbeitenden Bevölkerung der Umgebung, man denke an die vielen volkstümlichen Spiele, die lange schon im Salzburgischen lebendig waren (Kaut, 8) –, so gilt im Hinblick auf de Entstehung der Festspiele die enge Beziehung zwischen Salzburg und Wolfgang Amadeus Mozart als das folgenreichste, ausschlaggebende Faktum. Schon gegen Mitte des 19. Jahrhunderts hatten die ersten Bemühungen eingesetzt, in Salzburg, das politisch damals kaum mehr Bedeutung hatte, Mozart-Musikfeste zu veranstalten, besonders, nachdem im Jahr 1841 in der Stadt ein Institut, genannt "Dom-Musikverein und Mozarteum" gegründet und 1842 das von dem Münchner Bildhauer Ludwig Schwanthaler geschaffene Mozart-Denkmal enthüllt worden war. Bei dem letzteren Ereignis waren übrigens die beiden Söhne Mozarts anwesend. In die zweite Jahrhunderthälfte fallen dann die Gründung des Mozarteum-Orchesters (1880) und, im gleichen Jahr, die Eröffnung des Mozart-Museums "im Geburtshaus Mozarts in der Getreidegasse" (Kaut, 17). Schließlich fanden, inspiriert durch das Vorbild der Richard-Wagner Festspiele in Bayreuth, jedoch wegen finanzieller Schwierigkeiten durch längere Pausen unterbrochen, zwischen 1877 und 1910 achtmal Mozart-Festspiele statt. Das Bayreuther Muster lieferte übrigens auch den Anstoß für den Bau des neuen, dringend erforderlichen Theaters im Jahr 1893. 1914 wurde das neue Gebäude des Mozarteums eingeweiht und Regisseure, Schauspieler und Sänger wurden nach Salzburg gerufen. Bedeutende Namen tauchen auf – unter ihnen der der vor allem durch ihre Mitwirkung in *Don Giovanni* berühmt gewordenen Sängerin Lilli Lehmann, die in finanziellen Notzeiten durch ihre großzügige Unterstützung den Bau des Mozarteums ermöglicht hatte. Neben anderen Koryphäen aus der Musikwelt, die damals in Salzburg weilten, sind Gustav Mahler zu nennen und, für die Entwicklung der Salzburger Festspiele dann von besonderer Bedeutung, Richard Strauss.

Soviel zu den ersten, ganz auf Mozart abgestimmten Festspielen in Salzburg. Sie bilden die natürliche Vorstufe, die hin zu den eigentlichen Festspielen führt. Wie kam es nun zur endgültigen Verwirklichung derselben? Welche Persönlichkeiten, welche Überlegungen und welche Gegebenheiten haben entscheidend dazu beigetragen? Und: welches Konzept für die Festspiele kristallisierte sich heraus?

Bevor wir unsere Aufmerksamkeit dem Spiritus rector der Salzburger Festspiele, dem leuchtenden Dreigestirn Reinhardt, Hofmannsthal und Strauss widmen, bevor wir weitere Helfer nennen, die an der schließlichen Gründung der Spiele mitbeteiligt waren, soll in diesem Zusammenhang kurz der Vorläufer und unermüdliche Wegebahner, nämlich Hermann Bahr, gewürdigt werden. Diesem ungemein vielseitigen, wandlungsfähigen und produktiven Regisseur, Schriftsteller, Dramatiker und Kritiker, der Salzburg kannte und liebte, schwebten schon zu Anfang des Jahrhunderts Festaufführungen in Salzburg vor, die über die ausschließlich Mozart gewidmeten Spiele hinausgehen sollten. Bereits 1903 diskutierte er den Gedanken mit Max Reinhardt und dessen Dramaturg, Arthur Kahane.[4] Bahr, der bekanntlich kommende künstlerisch-literarische Bewegungen analysierte, wenn die jeweils vorhergehenden kaum erst ihren Höhepunkt erreicht hatten, und der auch im Hinblick auf die Fähigkeiten künstlerisch begabter Menschen ein sicheres Urteil besaß, hatte für die Verwirklichung seines Salzburgplanes Reinhardt, Hofmannsthal und Strauss vorgesehen. Außerdem hatte er bereits bestimmte Künstler im Sinn, Tänzerinnen, und auch Architekten und Bühnenbildner, die Bau und Ausstattung eines neuen Festspielhauses übernehmen sollten. Große Opernaufführungen waren geplant. Auch die Geldbeschaffung war eingeleitet. Da Bahr sehr praktisch kalkulierte und die Rentabilität des Unternehmens dessen Gelingen nur nützlich sein konnte, dachte er – ähnlich übrigens wie Max Reinhardt – sogar an ein Fünf-Städte-Theater zwischen Berlin, Hamburg, München, Wien und Salzburg, als dessen Reisedirektor er sich selbst vorsah. Gleiche Bühnendimensionen sollten den Austausch von Kulissen und Dekorationen zwischen den Theatern dieser Städte möglich machen (Kaut, 18). Obwohl sich dieser Plan wie auch ein weiterer aus dem Jahr 1908, demzufolge Reinhardt Theaterstücke in Salzburg inszenieren sollte, zerschlug, gab Bahr, der 1912 nach Salzburg übersiedelte, nicht auf, sondern bastelte weiter an seinem Plan. Bahr ist insofern vor allem wichtig für die Entwicklung der

Salzburg Festival 1970. A scene from Hugo von Hofmannsthal's drama *Jedermann*.
Photo by "Pressebüro Salzburger Festspiele"

Festspiele, als er zur richtigen Zeit und mit untrüglichem Instinkt Salzburg als *den* geeignetsten Ort für zukünftige Festspiele ausersah; und gerade zu dieser Zeit traten auf den Gebieten der Musik, der Literatur und des Theaters geniale Gestalten auf, die bereit und fähig waren, gemeinsam die Idee nach besten Kräften zu fördern und sie schließlich zu verwirklichen. Entscheidende und immer erneute Anregungen und Ermutigungen sind also Hermann Bahr zu verdanken. Obwohl der Erste Weltkrieg viele Pläne auf dem Sektor Kunst unterbrach, beschloß 1916 eine Gruppe interessierter und einflußreicher Persönlichkeiten zunächst einmal die Gründung einer Festspielhaus-Gemeinde, und bereits "im Juni 1917 [–also mitten im Krieg–] genehmigte das Ministerium des Innern die Statuten des Hauptvereins 'Salzburger Festspielhaus-Gemeinde'" in Wien (Kaut, 18). Diese notwendige Basis war allerdings noch keineswegs Garant für das tatsächliche Gelingen des geplanten Unternehmens. Nicht nur war die Salzburger Bühne provinziell und der Verein zwischen Wien und Salzburg gespalten, sondern die inneren Zerwürfnisse und scharfen Rivalitäten gipfelten in einem recht rigorosen Widerstand gegen das vorgesehene Supremat Max Reinhardts bei den geplanten zukünftigen Festspielen. Als schließlich Kaiser Karl I. seine Zustimmung gab, daß Reinhardt Leiter der mit den Hoftheatern verbundenen Festspiele in Salzburg werden sollte, zerbrach die österreichische Monarchie. Auch war in den kargen und bitteren Nachkriegsjahren die Salzburger Bevölkerung verständlicherweise gar nicht für den Festspielgedanken zu erwärmen. Besonders durch die Lebensmittelnot war die Lage derart trostlos, daß im Winter 1919 die in der Franziskanerkirche geplante Aufführung eines von Max Mell umgearbeiteten alten Weihnachtsspiels abgesagt werden mußte, obwohl Max Reinhardt mit den Schauspielern Helene Thimig, Werner Krauß und Alexander Moissi die Proben dafür bereits begonnen hatte. Erst im folgenden Jahr, am 22. August 1920, begannen mit der Aufführung von Hofmannsthals *Jedermann* auf dem Domplatz, in der Inszenierung von Max Reinhardt, die Salzburger Festspiele.

"Wenn die Salzburger Festspiele trotz den Schwierigkeiten der Zeit nach dem Ersten Weltkrieg verwirklicht wurden, so war das dem ungewöhnlichen Glücksfall zu danken, daß sich die

Künstler, die Salzburg als die wunderbare Kulisse theatralischer Feste erkannt hatten, zu einer gemeinsamen Aktion zusammenfanden" (Kaut, 19). Wodurch zeichnet sich nun in dieser Hinsicht der Einsatz der drei hervorragendsten unter ihnen aus? Inwiefern sind zunächst sie für die Eigenart des Phänomens "Salzburger Festspiele" verantwortlich?

Max Reinhardt (1873–1943), von Richard Strauss als "Schöpfer der eigentlichen Festspielidee,"[5] von Hofmannsthal als der "vollkommene Visionär der Bühne" bezeichnet (*Aufzeichnungen*, 349), der, laut Hofmannsthal, "unstreitig dem europäischen Theaterleben den stärksten Impuls" gegeben und eine derart intensive Wirksamkeit ausgeübt habe, daß Vibrationen davon "bis an die Grenzen Europas und bis über den Ozean" gefühlt worden seien (*Aufzeichnungen*, 325), war gebürtiger Österreicher, der seine ersten Schauspielengagements in Salzburg hatte. Als er 1894 als Charakterspieler an das damals von Otto Brahm geleitete Deutsche Theater in Berlin ging, ahnte er nicht, daß er elf Jahre später dessen Leitung übernehmen würde. Abgesehen von einer kurzen Unterbrechung von 1920 bis 1924 wirkte er in dieser Stellung bis 1933, dem Jahr seiner Emigration in die Vereinigten Staaten, wo er 1943 in New York starb. Max Reinhardt, neben Antoine in Paris and Stanislawski in Rußland sicherlich der genialste und einflußreichste Regisseur der Zeit, hatte trotz seiner Karriere in Berlin die Erinnerung an die glückliche Zeit seines Salzburger Theaterdebüts bewahrt. Gerade in den letzten Jahren des Ersten Weltkrieges, als sich seine Ehe mit der Schauspielerin Else Heims löste, seine Bindung an Berlin zeitweilig schwächer wurde und er seinen Tätigkeits- und Wirkungsbereich auszudehnen suchte, trat Salzburg wieder intensiver in sein Bewußtsein. Das bedeutete neues Leben für die Festspielpläne, die Reinhardt, ähnlich wie Bahr, schon sehr früh gehegt hatte. Erfüllt von der Vorstellung, bei zukünftigen Festspielen "dem Theater wieder seine ursprüngliche und seine letzte Form" geben zu können (Kaut, 361), reichte er bereits 1917 bei "der Generalintendanz des k.k. Hoftheaters in Wien" eine "Denkschrift zur Errichtung eines Festspielhauses in Hellbrunn" bei Salzburg ein (Kaut, 19f.). Darin betonte er die Notwendigkeit des Baus eines neuen Festspielhauses als einer Stätte “abseits vom Alltagsgetriebe und an einem Orte, der durch natürliche und künstlerische Schönheit so ausgezeichnet erscheint, daß die Menschen in den sommerlichen Ruhetagen, befreit von ihren Sorgen und Mühen, gerne hinauspilgern” (Kaut, 20). Obgleich man in Wien, wo Kriegssorgen und innenpolitische Krisen weder Zeit noch Interesse für Entscheidungen auf dem kulturpolitischen Sektor erlaubten, auf Reinhardts Denkschrift, die übrigens weitere Theaterpläne und den Vorschlag zur Errichtung einer Hochschule für Bühnenkunst enthielt, vorläufig nicht reagierte, bildet sie ein wichtiges Dokument in der Geschichte der Salzburger Festspiele; denn ein Grundgedanke der Festspiele wird hier eindeutig formuliert: den Menschen an einem durch natürliche und künstlerische Schönheit ausgezeichneten Ort die Möglichkeit zur Erholung und Entspannung zu schaffen und ihnen perfektes Theater zu bieten. In einem Brief aus dem folgenden Jahr erläutert Reinhardt genauer, wie seiner Meinung nach die Festspiele aussehen sollten. Dabei umreißt er das eigentliche Konzept, das ihm vorschwebte: “Unter dem Zeichen Mozarts, des heiteren und frommen Genius Salzburgs, sollten hier Oper und Schauspiel, Lustspiel und Singspiel, das Volksstück ebenso wie die alten Mysterien und Weihnachtsspiele zu einer erlesenen Einheit verwoben werden und jene reine, geistige Schönheit entfalten, zu der sich das Theater unter glücklichen Umständen zu erheben vermag.”[6]

Rückwirkend schränkt er allerdings diesen umfassenden Plan ein. In einem seiner Briefe aus dem Jahr 1927 vertritt er zwar nach wie vor den Standpunkt, daß im Zentrum der Festspiele das Mysterienspiel stehen solle; denn “das volkstümlich religiöse Spiel” sei aus Salzburgischem Boden hervorgewachsen und gehöre in diese Landschaft. Daneben hält er die Einbeziehung der Mozart-Aufführungen in den Spielplan trotz ihrer Kostspieligkeit und der Schwierigkeit, ihr hohes Niveau zu wahren, für durchaus legitim. Alles andere sei höchstens als Verzierung zu betrachten.[7]

Als im August 1919 Leopold Freiherr von Andrian-Werburg, ein Freund Hofmannsthals und Bahrs, in Wien zum Generalintendanten der Hoftheater ernannt wurde (Kaut, 20), gelang es durch Interventionen Reinhardts und Hofmannsthals, Reinhardts Denkschrift wieder ans Tageslicht zu befördern. Die Briefe Reinhardts und Hofmannsthals an Andrian, in denen die Notwendigkeit der Gründung von Festspielen gerade in einer politisch trostlosen Zeit dargelegt werden, liefern weitere Hinweise für die Aufgaben, die Reinhardt für die Festspiele vorsah. So erfährt man z.B. durch Hofmannsthal, daß Reinhardt in einem Brief "die Bedeutung der Sache vom österreichischen culturpolitischen und Prestige-Standpunkt" auseinandersetze, und Reinhardt berichtet, daß es ihm gelungen sei, Andrian davon zu überzeugen, "daß in Salzburg 'eine Triumph-Pforte österreichischer Kunst' errichtet werden müsse. Zu diesem 'Friedenswerk' müßten die Vorbereitungen bald getroffen werden" (Kaut, 20).

Max Reinhardts Konzept der Festspiele ist damit ziemlich deutlich abgesteckt. Im Mittelpunkt, als Kern des Ganzen, sieht er die Mysterienspiele; andere theatralische Aufführungen, vor allem Werke von Mozart, sollten dieses Zentrum umranken, seien aber von sekundärer Bedeutung. Die Spiele sollten Entspannung und geistige Unterhaltung bieten und gerade in den Jahren des politischen Zusammenbruchs eine bedeutende kulturpolitische Aufgabe erfüllen.

Als Reinhardt, dessen Bindung an Berlin sich immer mehr lockerte, 1918, kurz vor Kriegsende, das Barockschloß Leopoldskron bei Salzburg günstig erwerben konnte, es nach seinem Geschmack ausstatten ließ und mit der Schauspielerin Helene Thimig, seiner neuen Lebensgefährtin, darin einzog, stand für ihn Salzburg als *der* Ort für die Festspiele endgültig fest, auch wenn es zu deren Verwirklichung noch zwei Jahre brauchte. Auf Schloß Leopoldskron wurde Theater gespielt, vorgetragen und diskutiert, der Hausherr veranstaltete dort großzügige Feste und lud Künstler und andere Persönlichkeiten aus dem geistigen und öffentlichen Leben ein.[8]

Hugo von Hofmannsthal, Freund und Bewunderer Reinhardts, der diesen "ersten Theaterchef Deutschlands" (*Aufzeichnungen*, 338), wie er Reinhardt nennt, aus engster Zusammenarbeit und dem Besuch vieler von Reinhardt inszenierten Aufführungen her kannte, hat in Aufsätzen und Briefen wiederholt die außergewöhnliche Begabung dieses Theatermenschen par excellence hervorgehoben, der es verstand, seine Visionen zu realisieren, indem er die

Stücke aus dem rein Literarischen löste und auf der Bühne mit neuem Leben versah. Für Reinhardt sei "das Schauspielerische der Schlüssel der Welt" (*Aufzeichnungen,* 330). "Nie," sagt Hofmannsthal, "hat sich jemand weniger gebunden gefühlt durch die nationalen und zeitlichen Grenzen als er: und hierin folgt er ganz der großen Tradition des österreichisch-deutschen Theaters. Er ist, als Individuum, so voll Lebenskraft, daß er alles, auch das sehr Entfernte oder der Zeit nach Entlegene, nur als ein Stück Leben zu sehen vermag. Er sieht nichts historisch, sondern alles unmittelbar – und alles mit der Phantasie des Theatermenschen. Eine fremde künstlerische Persönlichkeit, eine fremde Zivilisation, eine ferne Epoche – diese Schranken existieren für ihn nicht" (*Aufzeichnungen,* 337f.). Von Reinhardts genialer Leistung auf der Bühne ist auch in den Briefen die Rede, die Hofmannsthal zwischen 1922 und 1924, also während der ersten Phase der Salzburger Festspiele, für die New Yorker Zeitschrift *The Dial* geschrieben hat. Sie sollten die amerikanischen Leser mit der künstlerischen Situation in Österreich, vornehmlich in Wien, vertraut machen, da trotz Krieg und Kriegsausgang die Stadt Wien "ihren Rang als die künstlerische und geistige Hauptstadt Südosteuropas" sich bewahrt habe und nach wie vor "viele subtile geistige Fäden" von Wien aus nach Ost und West liefen (*Aufzeichnungen,* 267). Der dritte dieser Briefe ist den dritten Salzburger Festspielen, also denen des Jahres 1922, gewidmet. Hofmannsthal beschreibt darin ausführlich das buntgemischte Publikum, erwähnt die Mozartopern, die unter der Leitung von Richard Strauss und Franz Schalk aufgeführt wurden und konzentriert sich im Rest des Briefes auf die Betrachtung seines eigenen Werkes, des *Salzburger Großen Welttheaters,* das, in der Inszenierung Reinhardts, bei den Spielen im Jahr 1922 in der Salzburger Kollegienkirche uraufgeführt worden war. In Hofmannsthals Darstellung steht die Gestalt Reinhardts dabei im Mittelpunkt; denn das Verdienst, den "außerordentlichen Wirrwarr inkohärenter Individuen und Denkarten zu einem Publikum" zu amalgieren, liege "ganz bei der Inszenierung Reinhardts. Seine mise-en-scène war ganz der Ausdruck der Reife, zu der dieser erste europäische Regisseur sich in den letzten Jahren entwickelt" habe (*Aufzeichnungen,* 300).

Die Phantasie, die Begabung, die unermüdliche Schaffenskraft dieses künstlerischen Weltbürgers bildeten den inneren Motor der Festspiele. Reinhardt hat aber den Geist seines Theaters und damit den der frühen Festspiele nicht nur seinem wie wir gehört haben recht amerikanisch untermischten Publikum in Salzburg mitgeteilt, sondern durch seine vielen Gastspiele in den USA einer *rein* amerikanischen Zuschauerschaft jenseits des Ozeans. Als Beispiel für seinen Erfolg sei hier die Aufführung von Karl Vollmöllers Stück *Mirakel* genannt, das Reinhardt 1925 in Salzburg präsentierte. Er hatte es für Amerika inszeniert, wo es dann "in New York im Century Theatre eine Serie von fast dreihundert Aufführungen erlebte und in den folgenden Jahren, bis 1927, in vielen Städten der USA gezeigt wurde" (Kaut, 57). Bei der Salzburger Aufführung des Stückes wurde übrigens die Rolle der Madonna "von der schönen Lady Diana Manners, der Gattin des englischen Schriftstellers Duff Cooper, und die Nonne von Rosamond, der Tochter des Bürgermeisters von Chicago, dargestellt" (Kaut, 57).

Auch nach der Emigration in die Vereinigten Staaten, von 1933 bis 1937, hat Max Reinhardt alljährlich in Salzburg den *Jedermann* und den *Faust* inszeniert, bis der Einmarsch von Hitlers Truppen in Österreich im Jahr 1938 seine Mitwirkung bei den Festspielen jäh beendete.

Dem Kunstrat, als dem entscheidenden beratenden Organ der Salzburger Festspielhaus-Gemeinde, gehörten außer Max Reinhardt auch der Bühnenbildner Alfred Roller, die Dirigenten Franz Schalk und Richard Strauss und der Dichter Hugo von Hofmannsthal an. Vor allem die beiden letzteren waren neben Reinhardt ausschlaggebend für den ursprünglichen Charakter der Festspiele.

Hugo von Hofmannsthal (1874–1929), damals bereits angesehener Dichter, kritischer Beobachter der zeitgenössischen kulturellen Szene, gebürtiger Wiener, aufgewachsen ganz in der österreichischen Tradition mit offenem Blick über die politischen Grenzen hinaus, aufs innigste vertraut mit dem abendländischen Bildungsgut, setzte sich nachhaltig für die Verwirklichung und das Fortbestehen der Salzburger Festspiele ein, mit Reinhardt als Mittelpunkt. Vielleicht versprach er sich aus der Zusammenarbeit mit diesem Magier der Bühne, in dem er einen ihm innerlich Verwandten erkannt hatte, auch einen Erfolg für seine eigenen Stücke bei den Festspielen; denn "seit 1903 erlebten fast alle seine Dramen ihre Uraufführung bei Reinhardt in Berlin, während das Burgtheater in Wien mit einer einzigen Ausnahme darauf verzichtet hatte, sie in den Spielplan aufzunehmen. In Österreich blieb Hofmannsthal [damals] ein Theaterdichter ohne Theater."[9]

Hofmannsthal hat sich – und darin weit über die oben genannten Formulierungen Reinhardts hinausgehend – besonders intensiv mit der Definition des geistigen Wertes der Salzburger Festspiele befaßt. Persönlich vom Ver- und Zerfall der Habsburgermonarchie und der damit verbundenen Bedrohung der geistigen Vorherrschaft Österreichs in Mitteleuropa betroffen, sorgte er sich besonders um die Überlebenden des Ersten Weltkriegs, "die ihrer geschichtlichen Verankerung beraubt waren. Er suchte eine neue historische Legitimation, die von der Auflösung des Reiches nicht in Frage gestellt wurde" (Walk, 20). Eine Antwort schien ihm Josef Nadlers äußerst fragwürdige und anfechtbare Literaturgeschichte zu bieten, deren dritter Band 1918 erschienen war und die er selbst hoch schätzte. Der Eindruck der Lektüre des Nadlerschen Werkes auf den Dichter zeigt sich – allerdings in Hofmannsthalscher Abwandlung – in den beiden 1919, also noch vor der Gründung der Festspiele verfaßten Aufsätzen "Deutsche Festspiele zu Salzburg" und "Festspiele in Salzburg" (*Prosa III,* 441f.). Auch in späteren Aufsätzen Hofmannsthals zum Thema Salzburg ist die Nähe zu Nadler erkennbar.

Zwei Aspekte, die offensichtlich durch die Lektüre Nadlers angeregt wurden, determinieren Hofmannsthals "ideologische Rechtfertigung der Festspiele": "die Eigenart des bajuwarisch-österreichischen Stammes" und die eigenständige "Barock'-Kultur, die in Salzburg ihren Mittelpunkt habe" (Walk, 20). Er sieht in der kulturellen Ausstrahlungskraft des baierisch-österreichischen geistigen Potentials nach Ost und West, und in der seit dem Mittelalter gepflegten volkstümlichen Theatertradition uralte geistige Werte, die über die politischen Grenzen hinwegreichen und denen der politische Zusammenbruch der Donaumonarchie – und anderer Monarchien – nichts anhaben konnte; denn "gerade die chaotische Nachkriegszeit" läßt in den Augen Hofmannsthals "den schlummernden theatralischen Instinkt im Volk" wieder aufleben (Walk,

21). Die Festspiele sollten also an das stammesmäßige kulturelle Erbe erinnern, das in immer wieder neuer Ausprägung regelmäßig in Salzburg vorgeführt werden konnte. Das Repertoire der Spiele sollte—und hier wird die Abweichung von Reinhardts Konzept erkenntbar—"die gesamte Theaterkunst umfassen, sowohl Musik als auch deutsch- und fremdsprachiges Drama, aufgehoben im geistigen Haus der süddeutschen Bühnentradition." Um die "Tradition bis in die Gegenwart" sichtbar zu machen, sollte man bei der Auswahl der Stücke Vergangenes bevorzugen. "Die Festlichkeit der Mozartschen Opern—der eigentliche Höhepunkt dieser

Mit diesem großzügigen und umfassenden künstlerischen Entwurf, in dem trotz der Betonung des traditionellen Elements die Genreunterschiede unbeachtet bleiben und Oper und Schauspiel, Musik und Wort gleichrangig nebeneinander erscheinen und dem sich auch Reinhardt gebeugt hat, demonstriert Hofmannsthal den Gedanken der organischen Einheit des Theaters. Wie in Bayreuth wird also auch in Salzburg die Verwirklichung des "Gesamtkunstwerks" angesteuert. Allerdings weist das Salzburger Konzept durch seine Vielgestaltigkeit in eine andere Richtung als das allein der Person Wagners gewidmete Bayreuther Muster.

Die von Nadler infizierten Gedanken Hofmannsthals haben sich längst als unhaltbar erwiesen und das von ihm vorgeschlagene Repertoire wirkt heute als zu einseitig traditionell. Das große Verdienst Hofmannsthals liegt jedoch darin, daß er in einer politisch hoffnungslosen Zeit auf geistigem Bereich den Menschen neue, hoffnungsvolle Ziele und Ausblicke eröffnet hat. "An die Stelle des Strebens nach politischer Hegemonie" hat er "die Aussicht auf kulturellen Vorrang" gesetzt (Walk, 21). Noch in anderer Hinsicht ist der Name Hofmannsthal nahezu identisch mit dem Begriff der Salzburger Festspiele geworden. War 1920 mit dem durchschlagenden Erfolg von Hofmannsthals *Jedermann*, den Reinhardt bereits 1911 im Zirkus Schumann in Berlin mit mäßigem Anklang uraufgeführt hatte, der erfolgreiche Auftakt für die Salzburger Festspiele gegeben und ihr Gelingen gesichert, so gehört seitdem, mit nur ganz wenigen Unterbrechungen, inklusive der sieben Jahre unter nationalsozialistischer Herrschaft, das alte Spiel vom Jedermann zum festen Bestand des Salzburger Repertoires. 1922 wurde dann in Salzburg Hofmannsthals eigens für die Festspiele verfaßtes, auf Calderon beruhendes Mysterienspiel *Das Salzburger Große Welttheater* in der Kollegienkirche, dem Barockbau Fischer von Erlachs, uraufgeführt. Es wurde jedoch von der Presse scharf kritisiert, erschien noch einmal 1925 auf dem Salzburger Spielplan und wurde danach abgesetzt. 1931 inszenierte Reinhardt Hofmannsthals Lustspiel *Der Schwierige.* Ein anderes Stück Hofmannsthals, *Der Tor und der Tod,* war das erste Schauspiel bei den ersten Spielen in Salzburg nach dem Zweiten Weltkrieg, im August 1945.

Hofmannsthals Libretti, in enger Zusammenarbeit mit Richard Strauss entstanden, verweisen auf den Wirkungsbereich des dritten der drei Großen, die für das Zustandekommen und den Erfolg der Spiele verantwortlich waren. Denn trotz der vor allem durch Reinhardts Dynamik veranlaßten Betonung des Sprechtheaters hat sich im Salzburger Programm sehr bald die Musik durchgesetzt. Hofmannsthal selbst hatte Mozart als Mittelpunkt vorgesehen, aber auch andere Opern genannt, die seiner Meinung nach nach Salzburg gehörten. Außerdem waren zwei Dirigenten, der eine davon, Richard Strauss, noch dazu bedeutender Komponist, im Kunstrat vertreten. So wurde bereits 1922 bei den Festspielen im Salzburger Stadttheater ein Zyklus von vier Mozartopern aufgeführt, zwei davon, *Don Giovanni* und *Così fan tutte,* unter der Direktion von Strauss. Als dann 1925 im alten Festspielhaus eine bessere Bühne zur Verfügung stand, hielt die Oper ihren eigentlichen Einzug ins Salzburger Programm.

Richard Strauss (1864–1949), gebürtiger Münchner, also auch dem süddeutsch-österreichischen Raum entstammend, weltoffen und lebensbejahend, mit ausgeprägtem Hang zum Theatralischen, war der "musikalische" Mitbegründer der Festspiele. Seit 1898 in Berlin, seit 1908 dort Generalmusikdirektor, von 1919 bis 1924 Direktor der Wiener Staatsoper, Dirigent aller bedeutenden Orchester (Kaut, 29), und ab 1922 Präsident der Salzburger Festgemeinde, gastierte er neben Franz Schalk und anderen Meistern des Taktstocks bis 1943 mit dem Orchester der Wiener Staatsoper regelmäßig in Salzburg. Der von Strauss verfaßte Aufruf zur aktiven Unterstützung des Festspielgedankens beweist, wie sehr seine Vorstellung von der Bedeutung der Spiele gerade in einer vom Krieg heimgesuchten Zeit den Ideen Reinhardts und Hofmannsthals ähnelt. Verständlicherweise liegt bei ihm der Akzent auf dem musikalischen Sektor der Spiele:

> Das Salzburger Festspielhaus . . . soll ein Symbol sein, das erfüllt vom Licht der Wahrheit und dem Abglanz unserer Kultur [ist]. Ganz Europa soll wissen, daß unsere Zukunft in der Kunst liegt, ganz besonders in der Musik . . . In den Zeiten, in denen die geistigen Güter viel seltener sind als die materiellen und in denen der Egoismus, der Neid, der Haß und das Mißtrauen in der Welt zu regieren scheinen, wird der, der unsere Vorschläge unterstützt, ein gutes Werk tun und viel zur Wiederaufrichtung der Brüderlichkeit und Liebe zum Nächsten beitragen. . . .[10]

Von Anfang an setzte sich Strauss intensiv für die Festspiel-Idee ein und machte dafür Propaganda, auch im Ausland, z.B. – wie er in einem Brief berichtet – auf einer Gastspielreise der Wiener Philharmoniker in Brasilien (Panofsky, 235f.). In den ersten Jahren der Spiele wurden in Salzburg, wie oben schon erwähnt, vor allem Mozart-Opern gespielt; denn Richard Strauss, begeistert von der Möglichkeit, Mozart in dessen Geburtsstadt zu spielen, "war es, der zunächst eigensinnig darauf bestand, Salzburg müsse für Mozart das werden, was Bayreuth für Wagner geworden war" (Panofsy, 236). Nur allmählich konnten ihn die Freunde, vor allem Hofmannsthal und Reinhardt, dazu bewegen, auch andere Opern zu spielen. Im Jahr 1926 war zum ersten Mal eine von ihm komponierte Oper, *Ariadne auf Naxos,* in Salzburg zu hören, mit dem Libretto von Hofmannsthal. Bald standen zahlenmäßig Opern von Richard Strauss an zweiter Stelle auf dem Salzburger Programm. Allerdings war von da an Strauss nur selten am Dirigentenpult zu sehen. "Er wollte nicht, daß man ihm Eigennutz nachsagte. Es kam ihm allein auf die Physiognomie der Festspiele an. Und auf seinen Mozart" (Panofsky, 236). Bis 1938 wurden *Der Rosen-*

kavalier, Die Frau ohne Schatten, Die ägyptische Helena und *Elektra–Arabella* erst 1942–in Salzburg aufgeführt, alles Produkte der fruchtbaren Zusammenarbeit von Strauss und Hofmannsthal. Ganz abgesehen von der Wirkung seiner Tätigkeit in Salzburg hat Richard Strauss durch seine Konzertreisen in die Vereinigten Staaten zusätzlich sehr viel zur Ausweitung und Intensivierung der geistig-künstlerischen Beziehungen zwischen Österreich und Amerika beigetragen.

Entscheidend für die Lebensfähigkeit der Spiele–vor allem während der ersten Jahre–war natürlich die pekuniäre Lage. Finanzielle Notzeiten, wie z.B. die Inflation, wirkten sich katastrophal aus. 1923 bestanden die Spiele nur aus *einem* Schauspiel, Molières *Der eingebildete Kranke* und dauerten ganze vier Tage, vom 21.–24. August. Vergleichsweise erstreckt sich *heute* das reichhaltige Programm über eine Periode von über einem Monat. 1924 konnten überhaupt keine Spiele stattfinden. Ausschlaggebend für den Fortbestand der Spiele war auch der Ausbau der Bühne. Bereits 1924/1925 hatte man die Felsenreitschule in das neuerrichtete Festspielhaus miteinbezogen. 1960 wurde die Eröffnung des neuen Festspielhauses gefeiert.

Neben Sprechtheater und Oper eroberten sich bald große konzertante Aufführungen ihren Platz im Festspielprogramm. Erste Konzertveranstaltungen waren im Dom, in der Residenz, in der Stiftskriche St. Peter zu hören. Von 1925 an wurden vor allem die hervorragenden Wiener Symphoniker mit den Symphoniekonzerten der Salzburger Festspiele betraut (Kaut, 221). Zusätzlich sorgten bereits vor 1938, also schon in der ersten Phase der Spiele, Kammerkonzerte, Solistenkonzerte, Konzerte geistlicher Musik, Ballettaufführungen und Tanzabende für ein vielfältiges und abwechslungsreiches Programm.

Nur sporadisch konnte im Rahmen dieser Arbeit auf einzelne Werke im Programm der Spiele hingewiesen werden. Ebenso war eine kritische Betrachtung des Festspielprogramms von den bescheidenen Anfängen bis hin zu der Fülle des heutigen Angebots unmöglich. Das bedürfte einer eigenen Untersuchung, in der auch den mitwirkenden Künstlern besondere Beachtung geschenkt werden müßte. Wichtig im Zusammenhang mit dem größeren

Rahmen der hier vorliegenden Arbeit ist die Tatsache, daß in zunehmendem Maße bei den Salzburger Festspielen neben anderen Ausländern auch amerikanische Künstler mitwirkten, z.B. Nathan Milstein, Grace Bumbry, Leontyne Price und Leonard Bernstein.

Der Einmarsch von Hitlers Truppen im März 1938 beendete mit einem Schlag die erste Phase der Salzburger Festspiele. Daran änderte auch die Tatsache nichts, daß wichtige Inszenierungen, allerdings unter anderen Dirigenten und mit anderer Besetzung, vorerst weiter gespielt wurden (Kaut, 125) und dadurch zunächst der Schein der Kontinuität gewahrt blieb. Das Wesen und der Geist der Spiele waren im Innersten zerstört. Reinhardt kam nicht mehr, Bruno Walter ging – und mit ihm viele andere Künstler. Hofmannsthals Stücke mit Ausnahme des *Rosenkavalier* verschwanden aus dem Programm und neben Mozartopern, als deren Dirigent sich vor allem Karl Böhm auszeichnete, erschienen immer häufiger Opern von Richard Wagner im Spielplan. An Stelle von Strauss trat besonders Wilhelm Furtwängler hervor. Was das Publikum anbetrifft, so war ab Mai 1933 "durch die sogenannte Tausend-Mark-Sperre die Einreise der deutschen Gäste nach Österreich unterbunden" (Kaut, 279); ab 1938 gab es dann *vor allem* deutsche Gäste; Ausländer kamen kaum noch. Schließlich, als der Krieg ausbrach, herrschte das Grau der Uniformen im Publikum vor. Von Hofmannsthals "buntestem Publikum" war nur ein Schatten geblieben.[11]

Eine entscheidende Rolle für die weltweite Verbreitung des Salzburger Programms ist in zunehmendem Maße Film, Funk und Fernsehen zugefallen. Bereits 1925 "übertrug der Rundfunk Mozarts "*Don Giovanni* . . . aus dem Salzburger Stadttheater" (Kaut, 318). 1931, anläßlich einer Aufführung von Rossinis *Der Barbier von Sevilla* durch die Mailänder Scala in Salzburg waren 133 Sender, darunter "83 amerikanische Sender der 'Columbia Broadcasting Company' angeschlossen." Zum erstenmal ging die mehrsprachige Ansage, die für uns heute selbstverständlich ist, "über den Äther in die Welt" (Kaut, 318). "Noch einmal, im Jahr 1945, waren die Übertragungen der Salzburger Festspiele von besonderer Bedeutung. Im August 1945 vereinten sich die Sendegruppen der vier Besatzungsmächte in Österreich zur ersten gemeinsamen Übertragung einer Salzburger Festspielaufführung; es war dies zugleich seit 1937 die erste Übertragung der Salzburger Festspiele nach Amerika. Die Klänge von Mozarts Oper *Die Entführung aus dem Serail* waren als erste musikalische Sendung aus dem befreiten Europa in den Vereinigten Staaten zu hören" (Kaut, 318).

Begonnen als eine österreichische Angelegenheit im Jahr 1920, haben sich die Salzburger Festspiele – vor allem seit dem Bau des neuen Hauses im Jahr 1960 – in den fast 70 Jahren ihres Bestehens zu Europas größten und berühmtesten Festspielen, zu einem künstlerischen Weltereignis entwickelt, zu dem alljährlich viele Tausende von Besuchern, darunter viele Amerikaner, strömen. Natürlich hat sich im Laufe dieser langen Zeit viel geändert, z.B. das Publikum. Nicht nur zahlenmäßig. Nach wie vor findet sich die Schar der Musik- und Theaterexperten und -freunde in Salzburg ein. Daneben aber ermöglichen heute moderne Verkehrsmittel und wirtschaftliche Hochkonjunktur Tausenden den Besuch der Festspiele, bei denen neben echtem Interesse für die kulturellen Darbietungen häufig Sensationshunger und Streben nach gesellschaftlichem Prestige die eigentlichen Triebkräfte für die Reise nach Salzburg sind. Auch ist der ehemalige Rahmen gesprengt, ist Hofmannsthals Programm, dessen Einhaltung noch von ihm selbst als unmöglich erkannt worden war, überholt. Bereits er hatte es, wohl aus der Erkenntnis heraus, daß die Auswahl der Aufführungen mehr oder minder zeitbedingt sein müsse, abgewandelt und erweitert. Trotz der Veränderungen, die die Spiele von ihren Anfängen bis zur Gegenwart erfahren haben, scheint sich *ein* Grundzug des Hofmannsthalschen Konzepts erhalten zu haben: seine Offenheit der internationalen Musik- und Theaterszene gegenüber, die dazu geführt hat, daß seit dem Ende des Krieges bisher jeden Sommer in Salzburg wahres *Welttheater* geboten werden konnte. Es ist zu hoffen, daß trotz der gegenwärtigen politischen österreichischen Krise der weltläufig-liberale Charakter der Spiele erhalten bleibt und nicht durch eine nationalpatriotisch betonte Tendenz in der Programmgestaltung beeinträchtigt wird. Befürchtungen sind nicht unbegründet, nachdem bei den Spielen im Jahr 1987 die Aufführung von George Taboris

From a 1983 performance of *Arabella* by Richard Strauss. Scene in Act II with "Fiakermilli" (Karen Beardsley, soprano) at the Santa Fe Opera.

Photo by Michael Rosenthal

Inszenierung des Oratoriums *Das Buch mit sieben Siegeln* in der Salzburger Kollegienkirche von oben her abgesetzt wurde.[12] Die Chance, durch einsichtiges, großzügiges Verhalten hinsichtlich der Auswahl der aufzuführenden Werke den Anfang einer neuen, zeitgerechten Salzburg-Tradition zu stiften, liegt durchaus in den Händen der zuständigen Autoritäten.

Beziehungen zwischen Österreich und Amerika? Nicht nur haben die Salzburger Festspiele im Laufe der Jahrzehnte zahlreiche Nachahmungen, große und kleine, bekannte und unbekannte, ausgezeichnete und mittelmäßige, an vielen Orten Europas gefunden, sondern ihr Vorbild hat herübergewirkt über den Ozean auf den amerikanischen Kontinent. Viele der sommerlichen Musik- und Theaterfestspiele in Kanada und Nordamerika, darunter auch die Musik- und Opernfestwochen in Santa Fe, in dessen unmittelbarer Nachbarschaft dieser Workshop stattfindet, wären sicherlich ohne die Anregung aus Salzburg nicht zu denken. Das Beispiel der Salzburger Festspiele läßt deutlich das Vorhandensein und die Wirkung bilateraler Beziehungen zwischen Österreich und Amerika auf dem ästhetisch-künstlerischen Sektor erkennen. Wie gezeigt wurde, handelt es sich dabei um einen von verschiedenen Faktoren gespeisten Prozeß, der, ständigen Veränderungen unterworfen, sich auf immer wieder neue Weise diesseits und jenseits des Ozeans bemerkbar macht.

Anmerkungen

1. Hugo von Hofmannsthal, *Gesammelte Werke in Einzelausgaben.* 15 Bände. Herausgegeben von Herbert Steiner. Stockholm und Frankfurt am Main: Fischer, 1945-1959. *Prosa IV* (1966), S. 469. Verwendet wurden außerdem die Bände *Aufzeichnungen* (1959) und *Prosa III* (1964). Die Verweise in Klammern – III, IV, *Aufzeichnungen* – beziehen sich auf Band und Seite.
2. Annette Kolb, *Festspieltage in Salzburg.* Frankfurt am Main: Fischer, 1966, S. 15.
3. Josef Kaut, *Festspiele in Salzburg.* Salzburg: Residenz, 1965, S. 15.
4. Gottfried Reinhardt, *Der Liebhaber. Erinnerungen seines Sohnes Gottfried Reinhardt an Max Reinhardt.* München/Zürich: Droemer Knaur, 1975, S. 363f.

5. Richard Strauss/Hugo von Hofmannsthal, *Briefwechsel,* Gesamtausgabe. Hrsg., Willi Schuh. Zürich: Atlantis, 1970, S. 480.
6. Gottfried Reinhardt, S. 366.
7. Ibid., S. 367.
8. Ibid., S. 398.
9. Cynthia Walk, *Hofmannsthals Großes Welttheater. Drama und Theater.* Heidelberg: Carl Winter Universitätsverlag, 1980, S. 22f.
10. Walter Panofsky. *Richard Strauss. Partitur eines Lebens.* München: Piper, 1965, S. 235.
11. Eine ausführliche Untersuchung der zweiten Phase der Spiele (1938-1945) und der Entwicklung, die nach 1945, also nach dem Ende des Krieges und der Hitlerzeit einsetzte, konnte im Rahmen dieser Arbeit nicht unternommen werden.
12. Siehe dazu Gerhard Roth, Der Würgegriff des Volksempfindens. In: *Die Zeit,* Nr. 34, 21. August 1987 (Overseas edition) und Werner Hofmann, Skandal oder Komödie? In: *Die Zeit,* Nr. 35, 28. August 1987 (Overseas edition).

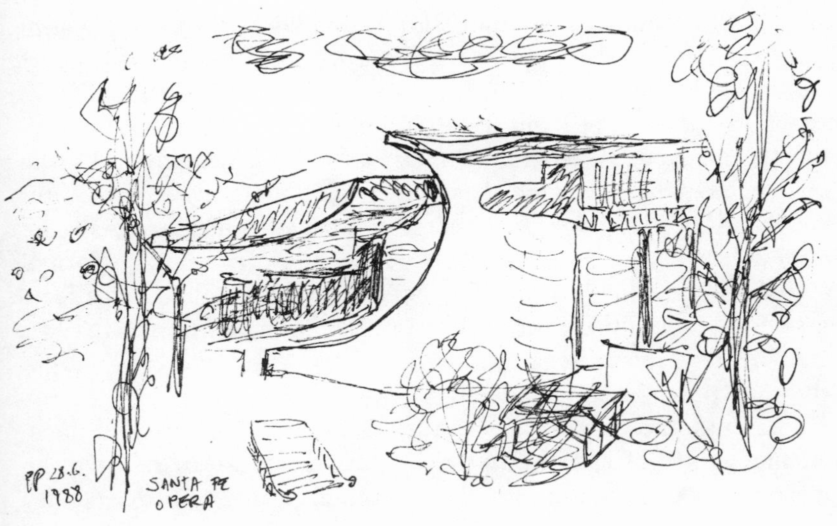

The Santa Fe Opera 1988. Sketch by Peter Pabisch

Congruent Aspects of "Natural" in Austrian and American Physical Education

Nicolaas J. Moolenijzer

Obwohl hier nicht direkte Einflüsse beider Länder auf Konzepte der jeweiligen Leibeserziehung vorgeschlagen werden, weist der Autor auf die Ähnlichkeiten der Auffassungen hin. Die "Natürliche Methode" wurde in Österreich von Gaulhofer und Streicher in den Schulreformbestrebungen der zwanziger Jahre zuerst entfaltet und in ihrem Sinne nach dem Zweiten Weltkrieg fortgesetzt. Turnen und Leibeserziehung ist demnach aus der natürlichen Bewegung zu gestalten und nicht nach militantem Drill. Diese Auffassung herrscht vielfach auch in den Vereinigten Staaten vor.

As with all other facets of education in the United States, physical education has been subject to various foreign influences during its development. In fact, the first school to include physical edcation in its curriculum, the Round Hill School in Northampton, Massachusetts, molded its program directly after that developed by the Swiss pedagogue Heinrich Pestalozzi (Bibliography-10).* Later developments in physical education abroad, in particular the formal German gymnastics ("Turnen") and the equally formal Swedish Gymnastics, made their entree in the United States leaving their lasting imprint on American physical education as may be noted in the ever present practice of "warm-up" exercises, popularly known as "jumping jacks."

Around the turn of the twentieth century, American education had come of age and had developed a nature of its own, an approach to education which, although not uniform, clearly

*Numbers refer to the works cited in the *Bibliography*.

demonstrated a national character. Naturally this does not mean that education had become static and that no new ideas, whether domestic or foreign, were incorporated. On the contrary, profiting from the advances in education-related fields, many new, exciting and progressive practices found their way into the nation's curricula. It is true to say though that, particularly in physical education, adoptions of foreign practices were sparse and, if they occurred, their incorporation came about in a subtle manner.

At first glance it does not seem that Austrian theory or practices of physical education exerted any influence on its American counterpart. However, closer scrutiny of developments in American physical education indicates that, although in an indirect and round-about way, concepts of Austrian physical education indeed have found acceptance and are currently practiced in the United States. Because adoption of these concepts has occurred so gradually and so surreptitiously, most educators are not aware of their origin and consequently never have identified them with Austria.

To be able to demonstrate the relationship between aspects of Austrian and American physical education, it will be necessary to present an overview of the main characteristics of both approaches.

The development of the Austrian School of physical education started at one of the most difficult but also most opportune times in Austrian history. The collapse of the Austro-Hungarian empire after World War I was immediate cause for an almost complete disintegration of the economic and social structure which had perpetuated itself under the centuries-long rule of the Habsburgs.

Even before the war demands for educational reforms had been expressed but the change-over from empire to republic exposed in a dramatic manner the pressing needs for implementation of a new, democratically oriented educational philosophy. In the framework of this educational renewal, which extended to all areas of education, Karl Gaulhofer and Margarete Streicher developed and introduced the concept of *Natürliches Turnen* ("natural" physical education). Although the country was poor and financial support for the new program slim, and although traditional con-

Margarete Streicher (1891–1985), Austrian Professor of Physical Education, co-founder of the "natural method."

cepts and convictions could not be abandoned overnight, Gaulhofer and Streicher benefited greatly from the fact that the time was ripe for a change. Endorsements from physicians, psychologists and educators added validity and support to their method, while theory and practical implementation gradually gained popularity with specialists and classroom teachers. Promotion of their theories was further enhanced by a curious combination of the teaching and supervisory responsibilities of Gaulhofer and Streicher, which gave them rather extensive control over the physical education curricula of the public schools as well as over the preparation of physical education teachers.

At the time the partnership of Gaulhofer and Streicher presented an uncommon phenomenon. Where Gaulhofer had been an outstanding athlete, Streicher lacked any sportive experience. Where Gaulhofer had been subjected to the traditional military gymnastics required for male students, Streicher, who attended a private secondary school for girls, had been exposed to the teaching of Swedish gymnastics and consequently was not tradition-bound. At a time when public opinion in Austria held that a woman's place was in the kitchen, Streicher demonstrated an uncommon independence for its time and place, which resulted in an unprecedented occurrence of becoming an equal partner in developing the future course of physical education. For the development of the Austrian School of physical education, as it later became known, this proved highly significant: from its very beginning both masculine and feminine concepts of education were to determine the goals, direction and methodology of the new method. The cooperation between Gaulhofer and Streicher was so close that it proved impossible to distinguish which part each had contributed to the development of their philosophy. Later on Gaulhofer was to remark: "We have . . . developed together the entire curriculum. Which part each of us has in it perhaps neither of us can tell with certainty, let alone any outsider" (9:5).

Gaulhofer and Streicher, rather than publishing one comprehensive volume presenting their philosophy of physical education, preferred to disseminate their theories by linking them directly to practical experiences, which they presented in the form of workshops and in-service sessions. The materials of the workshop programs were later published as "Grundzüge des österreichischen Schulturnens." The many articles and essays they wrote in support of their theories were later published in book form and appeared in several volumes under the title *Natürliches Turnen.*

Basic to the Austrian School was the conviction that the way "to practice physical education with a child cannot be decided by a system [because] any form of education [should be] determined by the nature of the child and the aim of education" (13:35).

Ergo, physical education must continue to adapt its program to the most recent findings of research in related fields. As a consequence "Natürliches Turnen" should not be regarded as a finished product, which would turn it into a rigid system that would not be able to keep step with the times, but as a method which is suited to grow and expand (8:89).

As their predecessors Rousseau and Guts Muths, Gaulhofer and Streicher did not intend the term "natural" to mean a return to primitive conditions but rather an adaptation of physical activities to the nature of man in all his biological functions, these to include emotional, intellectual, social and physical characteristics. A dichotomy of mind and body was rejected: "Physical education in contrast to moral or intellectual education or besides these two does not exist. There is but one, the "Total Education," which includes the entire young individual whose physique, morals and intellect are so closely knit, that one cannot separate that which really belongs together" (5:11).

Consequently it was urged that "physical education . . . should make itself consciously available to harmonious education" (7:8–9) in order to contribute to the physical, mental, aesthetic, and ethical development of the individual. The concept of "natural" was further defined in terms of "how" and "why" rather than "what," and emphasis was placed on "becoming" rather than on "doing" (7:147). Implications of the concept of "natural" may be identified briefly as follows: (1) an approach to a manner of performance, rather than a system or a group of particular exercises; (2) cognizant of and attentive to biological principles (6:41); (3) as applied to movement, it connotes a process of moving from one state of balance to another exerting minimum expenditure of energy (7:126, 176); and, (4) natural movement is an integrated mental-physical concept and a reflection of the individual's personality, which is characterized by a personal, individual style of performance (8:131).

In sharp contrast to the artificially designed movement exercises of other European systems, the Austrian School, in harmony with its axiom "physical education is education of the individual with the body as point of application" (8:60), advocated the development of the natural functions of man. The development of movements needed for everyday life and for the physical labor which so many people must perform is the most important aim of physical exercises; not the acquisition of skills which nobody needs in daily life (7:76). For this purpose Gaulhofer and Streicher developed in *Natürliches Turnen* a generic classification of exercises, the so-called "Scheme of Pedagogical Physical Exercises" (14:108), which were ranked on the basis of educational concepts. In this organization everyday movements, labor movements, and physical play were employed; all classified generically in terms of their function in the life of the individual. Exercises were related to human purposes rather than to mechanical considerations. Noting that man seldom executes individual functions separately but generally groups them into larger purposeful complexes of coordinated action, the Austrian School stressed the utilization of activities which offered many possibilities for function rather than only for narrow, athletic specialization (8:180; 14:111). Furthermore, the importance of outdoor activities in which nature could be experienced was stressed as an essential aspect of physical education:

> The essence of physical education is practiced during the regular physical education period; but where in the rest of education the requirement "out of the classroom into the world" penetrates more and more, so here too, outdoor games, hiking, swimming, skiing and skating are increasingly recognized as an essential part of physical education without which it cannot attain its goal. We like to take pupils outdoors . . . literally and through this we hope to help them rediscover the road to nature. (7:13)

Afraid of the "great danger [that] physical education would deteriorate from the high level of educational development to drudgery" (7:3) and that their philosophy might crystallize into a rigid system, Gaulhofer and Streicher resisted requests for a detailed curriculum guide. However, to bridge the transition period they regularly published articles which provided new ideas for practical application of their theories. Ever since the principles of the German *Turnen* had been introduced, formal "exercise possibility"-oriented methods had dominated the physical education scene. *Natürliches Turnen* broke with this tradition and focused attention on the individual, on his nature and on his right to be educated according to his nature (14:249). The concepts utilized in the development of the Austrian School proved quite revolutionary to the physical education practices of their time although they correlated closely with views of education prevalent at that time.

This may explain the acceptance of the Austrian School by other European nations, many of which adopted its principles and incorporated its practices into their own programs. In the decade following the introduction of *Natürliches Turnen* many European physical educators attended summer workshops in Austria; and it was during this period that the term "Austrian School" was developed. While translation and substitution of terminology soon helped to make the newly imported concepts indigenous, most modern approaches to European physical education clearly show the marks of the Austrian influence.

Among the affected countries was England, where particularly elementary school physical education was strongly influenced by the practices of Rudolf von Laban (17:101). Laban (1879–1958), mostly known for his contributions to modern dance, had in his early days studied under Streicher in Vienna. During the Hitler regime, which incorporated Austria into the Third Reich, Laban managed to emigrate to England (4:651), where he operated his own Institute for Biomechanics in Addlestone, Surrey (4:651). Because at the time there existed in England little opportunity for women to prepare themselves as physical-education teachers, Laban filled a void by presenting programs which were tailored to their needs. In fact the influence of his "Art of Movement" was so great that he is considered the "reformer" of physical education in England (4:650). That this is not an overstatement may be supported by the fact that the Ministry of Education published several textbooks exhibiting his method (4:709; 11; 12). Close examination of his exercise material and teaching method reveals many Austrian-School practices.

Development of American physical education took a completely different route than the Austrian. Lack of a central agency which could prescribe, dictate or implement national practices of education, including physical education, resulted in a checkered pattern of methods and systems. It is curious that at about the same time that Gaulhofer and Streicher developed their concept of "natural," the American coeducational team of Thomas Denison Wood and Rosalind Cassidy unfolded their program of "natural" movement in a publication entitled *The New Physical Education* (18), which presents many similarities with *Natürliches Turnen.* Unlike the Austrian School, however, the New Physical Education never caught on nationally.

What did occur was the incorporation of athletics, i.e., competitive sports activities into the schools' curricula. Irrespective of its merits or shortcomings, this process of amalgamating sport with learning has become common practice in most of the nation's educational institutions. Contrary to the development of so-called academic programs, which follows the pattern of a pyramid by structuring its curriculum from basic skills to the more complicated, ultimately arriving at highly technical skills, the physical-education curriculum presents the picture of an inverted pyramid. Influenced by the popularity of organized sports predominantly practiced at the college and university level, secondary schools developed their physical-education programs in a similar fashion. Consequently, in those schools where physical education actually forms an integral part of the curriculum, more emphasis is placed on traditional competitive sports activities than on the acquisition of those physical skills that will benefit all students during their formative years and in later life. At the elementary school level conditions for physical education are even worse. Comparatively few school districts can afford physical-education specialists and, although the philosophy of elementary school education adheres to the self-contained classroom teacher, few, if any, elementary school teachers have adequate training in the area of physical education. Although the quality of physical education at the elementary school level, the cradle of all learning, still has a long way to go, there is some indication of improvement, some sign of hope.

During the post-World-War-II years many English teachers emigrated to Canada where they exposed their pupils to the practices of elementary school physical education popular in England (17:109). When considering the closely-knit professional relations between the United States and Canada, it should not surprise anyone that soon similar concepts found their entree into American physical education. Partly due to the groundwork laid by people like Hetherington, Wood, and Cassidy and because of the fact that the nature of the educational program of the elementary school lent itself more easily to change (because there was little, there was not much to change), such new concepts as "movement exploration" and "movement education" had a chance to germinate. Cassidy, still in the forefront, went so far as to suggest that the term "physical education" be replaced by "the Art and Science of Human Movement" (3:14). Much impetus to this change in direction was provided by Betty Meredith Jones from England, whose lectures inspired experimentation and even induced some prominent American physical educators to visit England to gather first-hand impressions (16:539). As a result various Anglo-American workshops were held in England in which the concepts of "natural" movement were promoted vigorously. The Canadian influence mentioned before was reinforced by Margaret Brown, a teacher from Montreal whose efforts were supported by Betty Sommers, a graduate of Vienna, Austria (2:i).

Another far-reaching influence promoting the English version of the Austrian approach to "natural" physical education developed in the 1970s, when the "Project Hope," a federally sponsored program, was able to promote its philosophy of "Every Child a Winner" nationwide (1). This fresh approach, opening vistas of accomplishment for performers of all levels, vigorously promoted by its chief innovator Martha Owens, invigorated many elementary school physical-education programs, as it placed the emphasis on participation by all rather than on that of the few physically accelerated.

Despite the ballyhoo placed on physical fitness and the public concern about physical performance of the nation's youth, legislative bodies continue to be more concerned about economic affairs than about quality programs of physical education, including excellence in teacher preparation. Nationwide elementary school physical education still appears to be regarded more as play and games than as a serious business of fundamental preparation for lifetime skills.

Even without political and education-administrative support, physical education at the elementary school level continues to make steady progress. Austrian concepts of natural movement, including implementation of concepts such as promotion of an individual manner of performance rather than a standard execution, expenditure of minimum energy to achieve maximum results rather than wasting energy to obtain 'beautiful' movements, integration of physical activity into the total educational process rather than an artificial separation of mind and body of academic and non-academic, and, the precept that physical education should provide skills and experiences that relate to the actualities of future life (14:133–135) are reflected in current practices of American physical education.

Although it is not possible to demonstrate a direct influence of the Austrian School of Physical Education on practices in American education, there is ample evidence to support speculation that the modern approach to physical education in North America has its roots in the philosophy of "natural" physical education formulated by Gaulhofer and Streicher.

The Influence of the Vienna Circle on American Philosophy of Science

McAllister H. Hull, Jr.

Der amerikanische Einfluß des Pragmatismus von Charles Pierce und John Dewey auf der einen und F.S.C. Schiller auf der anderen Seite auf den "Wiener Kreis" mag größer gewesen sein, als bisher anerkannt. Dennoch soll die weltweite Wirkung dieses Kreises nicht in Frage gestellt werden. Durch die erzwungene Emigration vieler seiner Mitglieder nach England oder in die Vereinigten Staaten hat sich diese Wirkung unauslöschlich manifestiert. Unbestritten ist demzufolge die Bedeutung Ludwig Wittgensteins, Rudolf Carnaps, Moritz Schlicks, Friedrich Waismanns, Otto Neuraths, Victor Krafts, Hans Hahns, etc. Diese Männer halfen nicht nur mit, die amerikanische Vormacht in der Technik und den Naturwissenschaften auszubauen, sondern sie lenkten die Praxis der modernen Forschung und ihrer Denkvorgänge in zukunftsweisende Bahnen.

One may state the influence of the Vienna Circle on American philosophy of science succintly: for two decades, the approach of the Vienna Circle to the problems of philosophy *was* American philosophy of science. This was the result of the confluence of two – or perhaps three – historical streams: two American and one Austrian.

In the first place, American philosophy toward the end of the nineteenth century had formalized what had been a characterizing mark of American society from the earliest colonial times: pragmatism. Under the impetus of Charles Pierce, the designation was given a formal description as an approach to epistemology in the 1870s, and William James revised and recast it in 1898 as a theory of truth. In some sense Pierce's pioneer work grew out of deliberations of the Metaphysical Club he founded with James and others. John Dewey and F.S.C. Schiller carried the work into the twentieth century. Since James is accused of distorting Pierce's original intent, one may count this as two streams if one wishes. The key question the pragmatists asked was: "What difference does the difference make? "

Their answer, usually couched in observational terms (the fact that this rose is pink and that one orange results in the observation that certain insects are attracted to the one, other insects to the other, and hence that pollination ordinarily is color specific, thus maintaining color as a distinguishing characteristic of types of roses), makes immediate contact with the position of the positivists, as C. W. Morris pointed out.

The second historical stream in American philosophy that prepared it to receive logical positivism warmly was that initiated by Percy Bridgman and called "operationalism." For Bridgman, who received the Nobel Prize in physics for his studies of matter at extremely high pressures, a word or concept in physics was to be defined by the means by which it was measured. This clearly relates to the empiricist flavor of logical positivism as well as to its specific concerns about verifiability.

The third historical stream (I leave the development of logical positivism to another part of my remarks) is recognizable from the time of Moritz Schlick's untimely death at the hands of a deranged student (having once had university police protection for a time when a graduate student had threatened to kill me, I wonder at the University of Vienna in 1936 – the same student was under psychiatric treatment for having threatened Schlick before). The meetings of the *Wiener Kreis* ceased, and could not have been resumed if anyone had wished to do so, for the Austrian Ministry of Education barred scientific or analytical philosophers from any chair at the university – a restriction that was extended throughout Austria and is maintained today, I am told. Whatever the *recent* history, the fact is that the unsympathetic official attitude in 1936 produced a diaspora of the Circle members, from which northwestern Europe, and especially the United States, benefited. The best-known philosophers in America for two decades from 1936 *were* these members of the Vienna Circle.

Thus American philosophy as it had developed through the

first third of this century was receptive to the Vienna approach (and, indeed, had demonstrated this before 1936 by exchange of persons – Americans usually going to Vienna as students, Viennese coming here as visiting professors), while Austrian official attitudes had driven the originators to seek new homes for their ideas.

What was the "Vienna approach," as I've just called it, and how did it originate? I shall not give you a detailed intellectual history of the ideas of the Vienna Circle – it would probably fall before the basic question of pragmatism: what difference would it make? But it is perhaps at least of passing interest to remind ourselves of the origins of positivism – the movement named and systematized by Auguste Compte in the 1820s but with roots in the eighteenth, and even the seventeenth, centuries – and perhaps in Platonic philosophy if one wishes to stretch matters a little. In brief, the view of positivism is that epistemology must be scientifically based, and that the important concepts need to be defined in terms of measurements. Compte was not describing a philosophy of science but – as philosophers are wont to do – a philosophy of everything. In particular, the old Enlightenment program of bringing the social sciences and ethics under the methodology of Newtonian physics was ready-made for Compte, and, of course, one recognizes his debt to the expositor of that methodology in France, René Descartes. More broadly, as the subject developed in other hands, the influence of Hume on British empiricism is notable.

Another intellectual movement, which gave the modifier "logical" to the logical positivism of the Vienna Circle, was the development of systematic studies of the foundations of mathematics and their relation to logic. Non-Euclidean geometry had been discovered by Gauss, Riemann, Lobachevsky, Bolyai, and others. Einstein had turned the force of gravity into geometry. Boole had turned logic into mathematics. Finally, Hilbert, in geometry (following Frege) and Russell and Whitehead (after Peano) in arithmetic, had shown how to base mathematics on logical axioms (in a deeper and more subtle way than all of us learned with Euclid's axioms in school) and to prove theorems about its propositions in logical forms expressed in the equations of propositional calculus. The Viennese wished to adopt this axiomatic, symbolic logical approach for philosophy, and hence called their method "logical positivism." The Berlin Society of Scientific Empiricists—a cumbersome contrast with the simpler title of "Vienna Circle"—was formed at the same time for similar purposes. Hans Reichenbach and Richard von Mises were the leading members of the Berlin group. Reichenbach came to America about the same time as the Viennese.

That the meetings of the Vienna Circle ended after the death of Schlick suggests the importance his efforts had for the life of the group. He had, in fact, started the meetings in 1924 when he came to Vienna as Professor in the University at the instigation of various interested persons, many of whom became members of the Circle.

Schlick had published work on general theory of knowledge (1918) before he came to Vienna—and before the publication of Wittgenstein's first great work. The *Tractatus Logico-Philosophicus* was published in German and English in 1922 with an introduction by Russell, Wittgenstein's teacher at Cambridge, although it was completed while the author was in the army during 1918. I mention his timing because, although Schlick was very modest and hung on Wittgenstein's every word, he had anticipated some of the most important ideas of *Tractatus.* Rudolph Carnap, one of the leading exponents and developers of logical positivism in America after he came to Chicago, was beginning his writing at this time, and it is not profitable for our purposes to try to untangle the influences of these three men: Schlick, Carnap, and Wittgenstein, on the development of the ideas of the Vienna Circle. It may be noted that Wittgenstein never met with the Circle, though he did meet with Schlick and Friedrich Waismann fairly regularly. (Waismann was, at this time, a student of Schlick's, and apparently was liked by the reclusive Wittgenstein.) Carnap and other Circle members were occasionally included, but Wittgenstein's contact with the Circle was principally through Schlick and Waismann.

Wittgenstein's ideas that found fertile ground in the Circle may be summarized as follows:

1. The analysis of the propositions of philosophy requires a

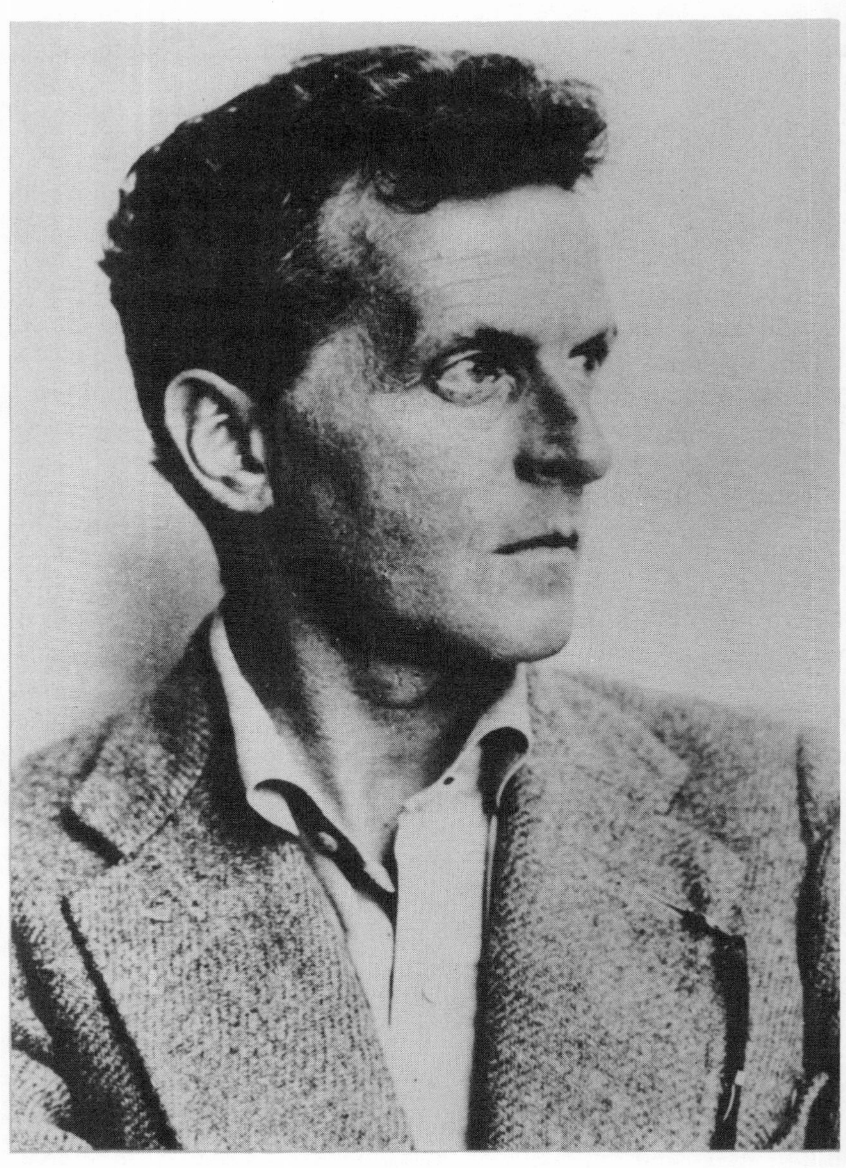

Ludwig Wittgenstein (1889–1951) Photo by "Kanzleramt Pressedienst"

careful analysis of the language in which they are stated.

2. The verifiability of propositions is the only rational basis for entertaining them – hence metaphysics is nonsense, for it contains no verifiable concepts.

3. The job of philosophy is not to develop new knowledge, but rather to sharpen the methods by which the other disciplines do so.

I do not guarantee that if you read *Tractatus* you will immediately see these ideas jumping out at you. Some ninety pages of obscure aphorisms are difficult to glean from. But this is what the Circle members *said* they found in Wittgenstein, and for our purposes, that is enough. We may note that the most cogent attack on *Tractatus* was written by Wittgenstein himself as *Philosophical Investigations* – published posthumously in 1953 (he died in 1951).

I leave to others the questions about why the Circle thrived in Vienna in the decade from the middle 1920s to the middle 1930s of this century, but a listing of some of its members indicates its intellectual vitality: Schlick, Rudolph Carnap, Otto Neurath, Herbert Feigl, Friedrich Waismann, Edgar Zilsel, Victor Kraft (on the philosophical side) and Hans Hahn, Kurt Godel, Philipp Frank, Karl Menger on the scientific and mathematical side. As was the custom then – and now, occasionally – a manifesto was published in 1929: *The Vienna Circle: Its Scientific Outlook.* The problems the Circle wished to study, and its general philosophical position were set forth, and the intellectual forebears were named. The list is very long, but Hume and the Austrian physicist-philosopher Ernst Mach are prominent among precursors, and, of course, Wittgenstein, Russell, Einstein, etc., among contemporaries.

Carnap and Reichenbach edited the journal *Erkenntnis* as an organ for logical positivism, and later, when Carnap went to Chicago, the publication of the *International Encyclopedia of Unified Science* began there.

Today the original program of the Vienna Circle is, with the natural modifications that time and criticism bring, most closely developed in the United States. The program which I am referring to includes the use of symbolic logic to analyze propositions, the insistence on a scientific approach for philosophy, and an overriding concern with the problems of "verifiability" (or, more pragmatically, following Karl Popper – an early critic of the Circle's approach – "falsifiability"). Much American philosophy and most of its philosophy of science is either an application of the methods of logical positivism or a critical analysis of its statements for the purpose of improving the system by studying what scientists actually do – a highly Schlickean idea!

The position of the Circle included a radical rejection of metaphysics – a disease for which it is touted as the cure, it was said – perhaps in a paraphrase of similar comment about another great Viennese movement, psychoanalysis. Hume had already suggested consigning metahysical – and theological – writings to the flames, for they contained "no abstract reasoning concerning quantity or number." Positivism was defined by Compte as a method to replace theological explanations. Hence the Circle was perhaps generous in admitting that metaphysics might have emotive merit, like poetry, but since its propositions could not logically be determined to be true or false, it could not advance knowledge. The attack was mounted because of the *claims* of cognitive content made for metaphysics, not because they were classed as emotive by the positivists. They advanced historical attacks on metaphysics by making its impossibility depend on what could be said (rather than on what could be known).

This follows from the view of language (out of Russell) in the *Tractatus,* which begins with the simplest true (or untrue) statement: simple facts. Legitimate sentences are built exclusively out of these simple ones by the process of conjunction and negation.

Some statements are true by their complete logical consistency with the rules of the language in which they are stated (whether a natural language or an artificial one like the propositional calculus). If this can be determined, such statements are tautologies – such as all the truths of logic. While the proof is lacking due to deficiencies in the work of Russell and Whitehead, most positivists believe that the propositions of mathematics are tautologies. Universally false statements are called contradictions and fall into the same category as tautologies.

If this sounds to you like Kant's analytic statements, we agree. The Circle also concerned itself with the equivalent of Kant's synthetic statement; i.e., with statements whose verifiability lies not in the rules of language but in the data of scientific observation.

Carnap's work on syntax developed the calculus of analytic statements, and his realization that the meaning of some sentences, at least, needed more, led him into semantics—which, however, he developed in the symbolic logical forms he had used for syntax, so his semantics bears little resemblance to the descriptive intuitive approach that frequently goes under that heading.

I have already mentioned that attacks on the principle of verifiability—especially of synthetic sentences—led the positivists to discuss partial verifiability or to take up Karl Popper's alternative, namely, that useful propositions should be *falsifiable*—at least in theory. Of course one problem with the verifiability principle is that it is not itself verifiable. Strictly speaking, neither is the principle of *falsifiability*. This weakens the force of the attack on metaphysics, but I would make two points: the attempt to formalize verifiability or falsifiability of propositions that are advanced as scientific is valuable and the characterization of metaphysics as having no factual content is useful in setting its context. Modern physics has an important metaphysical aspect that at present is indispensable, and it is helpful to have it properly separated from the synthetic statements of the same system that are experientially mysterious. Of course those of us accustomed to enjoying the insights that poetry gives to the way the world works have no difficulty looking to (some) metaphysical propositions for similar enlightenment. But it took twenty years or so for members of the Vienna Circle (Carnap, for example) to come this far.

The position of elementary statements soon was questioned. The perception of sense data, on which these statements depend for their verification, is private, as had been recognized long before by Berkeley. One proposed resolution began with the distinction between the content of experiences and their structure. The former is what is private and logically incommunicable. The latter *can* be verified in the sense that the structure of elementary experiences can be seen by all to be similar. If Dr. Johnson kicks the stone and winces from the impact, I can observe the contact and the wince. If I feel similarly disposed to refute Berkeley, he can observe *my* kick and wince. We share a common language because we describe many such instances in the same way. Our worlds are sufficiently similar that I can accept the information he gives me.

This doesn't satisfy the critics—me or better-informed ones. There really are no statements whose meaning follows entirely from structure. Content at some level becomes important. That is why Carnap had to discuss semantics as well as syntax. Even the assertion that the basic statements of science must refer to public events, to physical statements, is not, in the end, tenable. One must be able to discuss the relation between sentences and what they are used to signify; i.e., one must discuss semantics, from which a correspondence theory of truth may be demonstrated.

The working scientist defines some of the working concepts in terms of sense-data and pays little attention to the difficulties of the philosophers in their attempts to build a logically airtight structure for the epistemology of science. Finally, the logical positivists—members of the Circle and their intellectual successors—have recognized that they will do better to try to understand what a working scientist actually does and to try to put it in good order. The careful discussion of synthetic and analytic statements (including, significantly, that there are no pure cases of either type) helps straighten matters out now and then. One at least can clarify the questions and focus on the difficulty. American pragmatism melded with Viennese positivism makes a powerful tool for philosophical analysis.

The dictate of Carnap—that philosophy is to be replaced by the logic of science—was used reflexively: science was to be logically organized (once it was carefully described) like geometry. A set of axioms was to be set forth, concepts based on sense data defined, and, very importantly, rules of correspondence enunciated that tell one how to go from immediate sense data to what Margenau calls the constructs of physical theories.

Identifying and stating the axioms of science is not a trivial job. But it aids one to identify statements that are really about language rather than about science (not that such linguistic statements are necessarily useless—but they do need to be properly characterized). And the careful identification of the unscientific uses of language continues to be important as pseudoscience moves out of the realm of exploitation books and is advanced as appropriate fare for students in the schools. The complexity of scientific discourse—indeed the difficulty of arriving at uncontested definitions of concepts in science and of its epistemological structure—leads one to sympathize with a Supreme Court that throws a pseudoscience out of the classroom because it would advance a religion, not because it is not science. We shall have to fight the battles again in some arena, and if we can improve our epistemology perhaps we can win on a more satisfying ground.

Improvements over the first efforts of the Circle have, as would be expected, taken place. In particular, the anchoring of the formal deductive structure of Schlick to empirical matters has been developed with Reichenbach's "coordinative definitions" or Carnap's "rules of correspondence," as noted above. Carnap views these as rules of semantic designation for some, at least, of the concepts of the axiomatic systems. Hempel speaks metaphorically of the "upward seepage of empirical juice" providing meaning for the unvisualizable concepts of theoretical physics. The key to what is, very much in the spirit of Schlick's program for philosophy, a logical reconstruction of physical theories, is its power to distinguish between logicomathematical and empirical questions in scientific theories. The former are, in Wittgenstein's sense, tautological (but nevertheless powerful guides to thinking), while the validity of the latter is to be sought in empirical investigation.

In any working theory of the real world, propositions thought to have been already verified—or at least not falsified—are taken over as a sturdy foundation for the new effort. Thus kinetic theory depends on Newtonian Mechanics for the basis of its description of a gas. If one finds that some datum of experience is not represented by kinetic theory, one expects to pin down the culprit postulate by suitable clever experiments, not, as Poincaré's analysis might suggest, to abandon the whole theory. Thus the

Newtonian concepts of Absolute Space and Time lead to contradictions of experience (the Michelson-Morley experiment, for example) and must be replaced by the concepts of Special Relativity. Indeed, the Circle early on put all absolutes into the metaphysics its members eschewed.

The rules of correspondence, become, in the developed view of the Logical Positivists, the central means by which the purely formal concepts are connected with the immediate concepts of observation. A distant goal of this program is to unify the sciences under a single epistemological rubric, even though the analysis so far is most comfortable with the theories of physics.

How comfortable? Critics have pointed out that what Norwood Hanson has called the Vienna bifocal view cannot be pushed all the way to logical purity; i.e., all statements of a real theory cannot be rigorously classified as either logicomathematical or empirical (together with other pairs of labels consistent with these). In particular, observations, especially in the last sixty-five years, are not free from interpretation. That is, one cannot separate a theory from its interpretation. Working physicists build or extend their concepts with a continual interplay between the emerging theory and the experiments they wish to incorporate or interpret (or, explain, if you will – "explanations" is a complex concept in itself that I must pass over for the moment). The hope or expectation of the positivists, that the end result of the physicist's effort will be a theory that can be analyzed on logical positivist principles, is not realized, however. The problem is that there are no finished theories in physics. Maxwell's equations and their interpretation in classical systems is a tidy theory. They even fit without significant modification into special relativity. And the requirements of quantum mechanics lead to a theory of quantum electrodynamics that works brilliantly. But as a logical structure, it is quite unsatisfactory – and has remained that way after thirty years of intense efforts to improve it. It is worth pointing out that while the intense efforts have not produced a formally satisfactory theory, they have remarkably increased our understanding of how to make useful rules of correspondence, and especially what is essential in the theory, as it is applied to new and very abstract ways ("abstract" may be taken to mean that the rules of correspondence needed in such cases are numerous and complex).

While I think some critics of logical positivism pick nits, there is a group, of whom Hanson was one, whose analysis is useful. The tendency to try to discover what physicists really do is an important innovation that stems from the realization that there are no finished theories, only working systems in continual, but rationally controlled, flux. Thus, to the extent that Kuhn's analysis has anything to say, the distinction between normal science and revolutionary science is one of degree, not kind. Newton was not being modest when he said that he "stood on the shoulders of giants"—which does not detract one iota from the judgment that he was the tallest of giants himself.

By offering the criticism of logical positivism that it is, in its purest form, a system designed for sitting ducks whereas real theories are moving targets, I do not mean to suggest that it is wrong-headed or should be abandoned. It is still, in my view, the best means of analyzing theories, and the fact that lively criticism continues to develop its method nearly sixty years after its manifesto attests to its vitality. I have just finished offering a course in the unity of science wherein logical positivism—somewhat liberally interpreted—was the means whereby I knit together the history and modern accomplishments of physics, chemistry, biology and geology (together with an overview of the Enlightenment, its Romantic flip side and the American and French Revolutions). John Howard Northrop has included the disciplines of the humanities, as I have tried to do as a sometime university administrator, and of course the original program of the Circle included the social sciences and ethics, as did Compte's original positivism. My personal position is that the structure of our minds dictates that there is a unity of knowledge, period (not just scientific knowledge), although that is, by its nature, an unprovable proposition and thus excluded from a positivistic analysis.

Let me conclude my formal remarks by discussing the application of logical positivism to some of the—still developing—theories of physics. My former teacher and colleague, Henry Margenau, published a perceptive book in 1950 on *The Nature of*

Physical Reality. This is the account by an able working physicist of the epistemology of physics as it was then. The thirty-seven years since have added marvelous examples he could have used, but have not, in my opinion, changed the value of his observations. That is, the content of physics has changed, but not its epistemology. In 1966, Martin Gardner, who had been a student in Carnap's regular seminar at Chicago, edited, with Carnap's help, a recorded version of Carnap's presentation into the *Philosophical Foundations of Physics*. This, too, I find highly rewarding—a significantly overlapping complement to Margenau's earlier work. Much of what I say here is guided by one or the other of these books.

An important feature of Margenau's analysis is the definition of "construct," i.e., a concept constructed from a chain of rules of correspondence beginning with the immediately perceived and terminating where logical analysis and scientific convenience converge. Such a construct is "electron." I once defined "electron" for someone who asked me as a solution of Dirac's equation—which illustrates the idea of construct very well: what an electron is depends on what the physicist is doing with it. It is the sum of the observations interpreted as attributes of the construct and the theories used for interpretation. It was "discovered" by J. J. Thompson in 1897 and interpreted as a particle having a definite mass and charge, following a well-defined path under the influence of well-understood forces applied in well-confirmed theories. I shall not follow the changes—additions, mostly—in the construct in the last ninety years, but point to my own statement as a part of a complex and reasonable definition one could give today. It is the rules of correspondence that tie Thompson's observations, together with those of Davison and Germer in 1927 that are interpreted by considering the construct as a wave, to Dirac's theory—which is, by the way, incomplete and still developing although it was introduced during the heyday of the Vienna Circle and is very successful as physical theories are judged.

Now the solution of Dirac's equation is a kind of wave function, and one may ask whether the wave function is a construct. One may also ask whether it makes any difference— a good

Piercean question—whether it is a construct or something else, but in the spirit of positivism it needs to have a well-understood place in the theory. Electron is clearly a construct, and we wish to avoid any attempts to idealize it as a concept independently of the rules of correspondence and theories used to formulate the construct. For Margenau, concept and construct are synonymous. Physical reality demands, in good positivistic fashion, that we go no further.

But constructs, as should be apparent from this sketch, are not wholly determined by perception, for logical operations are possible on constructs and not on perceptions. The demands one makes on constructs thus are, strictly speaking, metaphysical: they must be logically fertile, for example, and have multiple connections not only with perceptions but with other constructs. These connections may be formal or epistemic, that is, logical or empirical. Margenau draws a diagram to illustrate this:

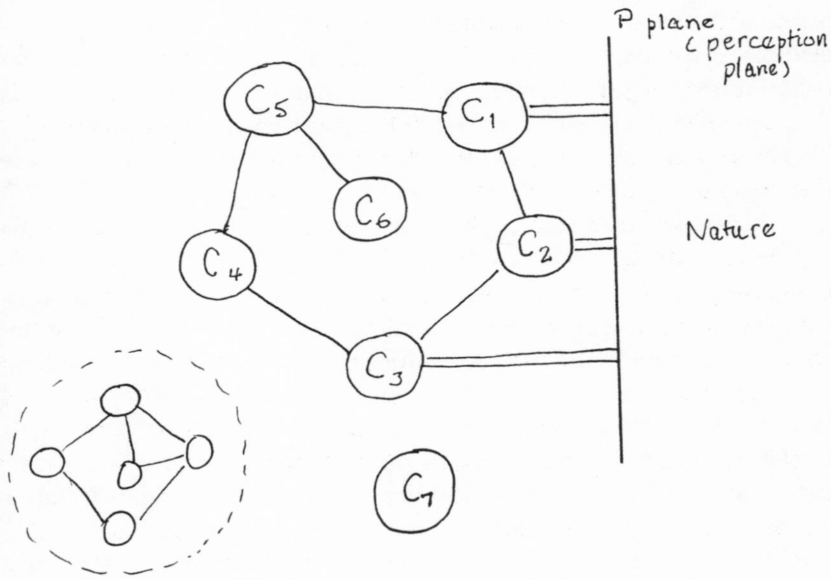

Formal connections are single lines, and epistemic connections double. Most constructs, C_n, are multiply connected, but C_6, for example, hangs on by a single connection. The color of an electron is such a construct. It has no logical fertility, no epistemic connections—in short it has no utility in the theory, although it can be stated and prior to examination, might be thought to be measurable. The construct C_7 has no connections whatever and makes absolutely no difference in the theory. It has no place in science, even speculatively. The constructs grouped together without epistemic connections, and surrounded by a dotted line represent constructs that may be proposed, have multiple connections, but do not lead to any conclusions that may be empirically tested. Margenau refers to them, metaphorically, as "island universes." In the process of developing theories, such groups of constructs are regularly proposed, but eventually are abandoned as unfruitful—unless epistemic connections are found. As opposed to the kind of metaphysics which the Circle rejected, these metaphysical requirements on constructs in fact guide the construction of successful theories—although it must be said that few physicists would consciously undertake the identification and testing of their constructs in the manner suggested. Margenau adds other metaphysical requirements that, while essential, need not detain us in this brief survey. They include a requirement of simplicity and elegance—a guiding principle in developing theories at least since Copernicus.

By this discussion, the wave function, introduced into physics by the great Austrian theoretical physicist Erwin Schrödinger, is not a construct, but is a part of the axiomatic structure of the theory. The absolute square of the wave function is a probability. In particular, if the wave function is an eigenfunction of the position of the construct particle, its square is the probability of finding the particle at the designated value of the position. This interpretation epitomizes the reason that simple ideas of reality no longer suffice in physics and justifies the elaborate epistemology I am touching on. Indeterminancy follows immediately, for if I wish to localize the probability distribution for position with a wave function, I cannot, with the same wave function, arbitrarily localize a probability distribution for momentum. The particular magnitude of the uncertainty is controlled by the equation Schrödinger postulated for the wave function, but that there *is* uncertainty follows from the mathematical representation of waves. Needless to say, many epistemic connections have been found for the probabilities calculated from Schrödinger's equation and its wave function solutions, and for the concomitant indeterminacies. The quantization of, for example, the energy of an atomic system described by an appropriate solution of Schrödinger's equation, follows from the structure of the solution when it is subjected to the boundary conditions of the physical system and the axioms of the theory. These quantized energies are observed – indeed, their observation led to the quantum theory in the first place.

Thus the wave function is a part of physical reality although it is not connected with any epistemic lines to the P-plane. While Carnap does not specifically endorse this extension of the concept of reality, his discussion of the foundations of physical science does not contradict it. Causality follows directly for Margenau in a somewhat reconstructed way: if a result is the consequence of a law of physics represented by a mathematical equation, it is caused by the physical conditions put on the solutions of the equation. Since the time-dependent Schrödinger equation completely determines (in association with the axioms of quantum mechanics and the physical boundary conditions) the wave function, he asserts the fundamental determinism of the theory even though the observables are indeterminate. Carnap in perhaps a purer positivistic mode prefers to call the theory indeterminate despite Margenau's argument. The point, however, is that their analyses reach the same pragmatic conclusions, and one knows the basis for their metaphysical positions quite unambiguously.

Classical mechanics, which we all use successfully in the macroscopic world, is a limiting form of quantum mechanics when Planck's constant may be considered small. It is also a limiting form of special relativity when the velocity of light may be considered large, and of general relativity when masses may be considered small (the sun's mass is just large enough to produce measurable general relativistic effects, to give you the idea of the magnitudes meant – although we are reaching a level of precision in measurement that interesting effects may soon be measurable on earth). These comments illustrate a property of physical theory.

Because theory is connected to the P-plane by clear (though changeable) correspondence rules, developments in theory extend rather than replace earlier levels of development.

I would be remiss if I left the impression that there are no questions raised by physicists about quantum mechanics and its interpretation. If, as most philosophically minded physicists believe, there should be only one theoretical structure for physics, there are problems. One interpretation of certain experiments first proposed by Einstein, Podolsky and Rosen fifty years ago implies faster-than-light transmission of information between parts of the experimental system contrary to the results of special relativity. Recent versions of the experiment as actually carried out are satisfactorily consistent with the predictions of quantum mechanics but say nothing about the question of how or at what speed the information was transmitted. Part of the problem is that, epistemologically, special relativity is a classical theory, and hence it is, within that structure, appropriate to ask the question about how and at what speed the information got transmitted. But in the extended idea of reality imposed by quantum mechanics, those are not constructs and the questions cannot be answered. This leads some physicists to assert that quantum mechanics is incomplete. The debate continues, and I cannot predict the outcome.

A "Gedanken" experiment that led Schrödinger himself to question the completeness of quantum mechanics is known as the problem of Schrödinger's cat. He postulates a cat, an electronic particle counter, a piece of radioactive material, a hammer, and a vial of hydrocyanic acid enclosed in a box with opaque sides. The apparatus is arranged so that if the radioactive material decays and sends out an alpha particle that is received at the counter, an electric signal allows the hammer to fall breaking the vial. The cat dies. The problem, then, is stated as follows: we set up the apparatus, close the box, and after an interval of time, say one hour, we are to determine the condition of the cat—without opening the box. There is an interpretation of quantum mechanics that says, whether an atom of the radioactive material has decayed or not is not determinable until we measure it, i.e., that the measurement itself forces the state function into an eigen state where the decay has or has not taken place. In this case, the measurement is the opening of the box and the observation of the state of the cat. Before the box is opened, the atom has both decayed and not decayed, or, more dramatically, the cat is both alive and dead. Here is a macroscopic system significantly affected by the uncertainty principle (for energy and time).

A lot of breath has been expended and ink utilized to discuss this problem (as well as the EPR experiment mentioned above) which, as a good positivist, I think has been largely wasted. The state function is not a construct with epistemic connections to the P-plane, and hence what it says about the cat before the measurement is made is not determinable – indeed the question is outside the universe of quantum mechanical *scientific* discourse. If I wish to consign it to metaphysics, I may do so and even enjoy discussing the question – along perhaps with that dealing with the number of angels that can dance on the head of a pin.

Margenau traces a number of the debates over these questions to a confusion between the preparation of a state and a measurement. (Passing a beam of light through a polarizer prepares a state. Determing what polarization resulted is a measurement.) I would add the problem of language – one that the Viennese Circle members were so wise to raise, although not in this context. The problem is briefly stated this way: the construct immediately in the P-plane, or having only very short epistemic connections with it, are macroscopic and hence classical. Thus our ordinary words ("wave" or "particle," for example) have as their referents classical entities. Our experience, to which, in good Viennese form, all our constructs must be related by some network of connections, is intrinsically classical. When, therefore, we try to discuss non-classical constructs in terms of the only language we have, there is an automatic mismatch. Inventing a word – like Eddington's abominable "wavicle" – doesn't help. Lewis Carroll long ago showed us how to invent words without referents. The best we can do is to form constructs with *eventual* connections to the P-plane, and try to avoid the confusions that result from forgetting that this is what we have done. Logical positivism, if used, provides us with the method of classifying our statements consistently and of reminding us that we need not *expect* an answer to certain questions within the axiomatic content of a well-formed theory.

I will only inform you – without discussion – of the existence of a lot of recent pointed nonsense some writers have inferred from half-baked popular presentations of quantum mechanics and its famous puzzles (like Schrödinger's cat). I recommend science fiction instead – for it does not pretend to be what it is not.

Thus I believe quantum mechanics is complete with respect to such questions, but, there remains, in any case, the problem of bringing the theory of gravity (general relativity) and quantum mechanics together. If we are to unify physics, much less all the sciences, this is a serious defect in our current level of theory development. Einstein tried during the final years of his life to unify electromagnetism and gravity, and in the pursuit of current efforts to unify the forces of nature, some of his work and that of his contemporaries, is being reconsidered. Two forces have been added to the two with which he worked: in addition to electromagnetic and gravitational forces, there are the strong and weak nuclear forces, characterized by their very short range. It is one of the glories of the developments of theory and experiment in physics during the last fifty years that we have learned how to unify electromagnetic and weak nuclear forces, we have a good handle on bringing in the strong nuclear force, and we are at least at the stage of building an "island universe" (in the sense of the diagram with a dotted enclosure) of constructs to bring in gravity. The optimistic of us would say that we understand the development of the universe from the Planck time onward; i.e., from about 10^{-43} sec. after the Big Bang until today. It's inside the Planck time that eludes us. If the "island universe" of quantum gravity can be satisfactorily completed, and if its internally consistent constructs can be connected with others and eventually to the P-plane, we will have a "theory of everything."

There are difficulties with this scenario. The energies in question at the Planck time – and in fact well after: say at 10^{-35} sec. – are beyond our ability to reach in the laboratory. The superconducting supercollider, which is the subject of fierce competition among the states to be designated as its site, is a proposed accelerator to allow us to explore energies and times closer to the Planck time than we can now achieve, but only the universe has had the energy calculated for 10^{-43} seconds and earlier, and we shall have to develop an extended network of rules of correspondence to find effects within our ability to measure that point to conditions when all four forces were unified in nature.

I have no doubt that as we explore realms of higher and higher energy and earlier and earlier times, we shall be guided by an epistemology based on logical positivism and its developments. The spirit of the Vienna Circle, and indeed many of its ideas, still influence not only the philosophy of science in America and elsewhere, but the practice of science as well.

The Impact of the Vienna School of Medicine on Modern American Medicine

Ralph D. Parks

Da die amerikanische Medizinerausbildung bis ins späte 19. Jahrhundert viel zu wünschen übrigließ, studierten viele Amerikaner in Europa. Die stärkste Nachwirkung hinterließ dabei die Lehre der Zweiten Wiener Medizinischen Schule, die jedoch auf wichtigen Prinzipien der ersten Schule beruhte, die etwa auf führende Ärzte wie van Swieten zurückgehen. Er eröffnete eine vom Staate, also nicht mehr von der Kirche gestützte Universitätsklinik mit einem Allgemeinen Krankenhaus. Hier wurden nicht nur oft mittellose Kranke betreut, sondern es wurde auch Forschung betrieben und die medizinische Lehre an Studenten weitergegeben, die dann unter der Leitung ihrer Lehrer praktizieren mußten. Alle Universitätskliniken Amerikas sind diesem Modell nachgebaut. In der medizinischen Praxis wurden zunächst führende Ärzte wie Rokitansky, Billroth, Wagner-Jauregg, Sigmund Freud, etc. zu Vorbildern. Nach dem Zweiten Weltkrieg allerdings wurde umgekehrt die amerikanische Medizin mit ihrer auf hoher Technologie basierenden Erfahrung so führend, daß sie nun in reziproker Weise auf Europa – und somit auf Österreich ausstrahlt.

Most people do not realize how important the Vienna School of Medicine was to the development of the type of medicine and medical education that is present in the United States now. The University of Vienna was founded in the fourteenth century when modern states began in Europe. All universities had to be approved by the state. It was important to have a university and to have students. Charles IV, who was the King of Bohemia, and who became Emperor in the mid-1300s, chose Prague as his residence and founded a University there. In Vienna the second great University of Central Europe was established by Duke Rudolph IV, the son-in-law of Charles IV. Its charter was obtained from the Pope, and it already had a small medical school.

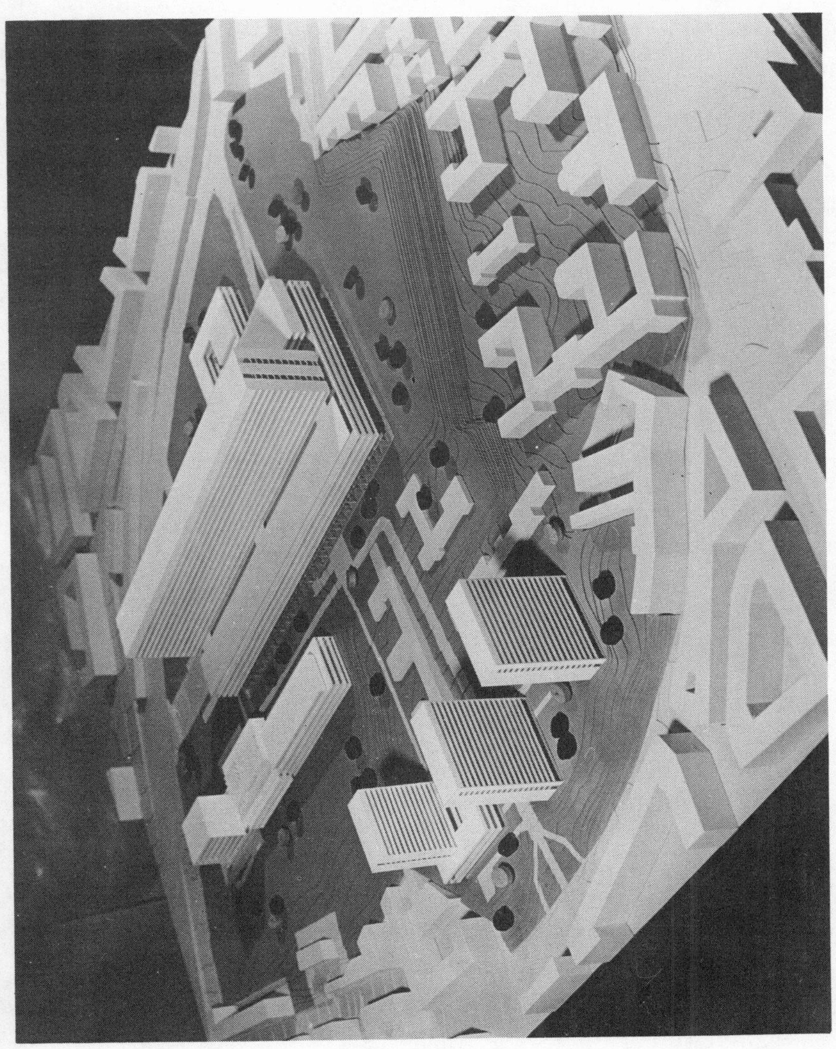

Model of the new general hospital in Vienna – "Das Allgemeine Krankenhaus." Photo VOTAVA

During the 1600s the University of Leiden (the Netherlands were part of the Holy Roman Empire) was the most important medical school in the world, and its physician Hermann Boerhaave was the most famous physician of his time. He was the first physician in the world to found a medical school, where he trained students who then went out into the world and founded other medical schools. The name Boerhaave is familiar to all physicians the world over. We still talk about Boerhaave Syndrome, for example; but the important thing about this man is that he trained other young physicians.

In 1740 Gerard van Swieten founded the first Vienna School of Medicine – "from Gerard van Swieten to Johann Peter Frank." Gerard van Swieten became physician to Empress Maria Theresia when he moved from Leiden to Vienna and soon became President of the medical faculty. An unusually talented man, van Swieten spoke nine languages, was an excellent physician, and an expert organizer. He accomplished several things – he separated the school from the influence of the Jesuits, taking the University away from the church and placing it under the control of the Empress. Professors were appointed by the Empress, salaries were paid by her, and a license to practice medicine was issued by the state. The importance of this school in Vienna was that it became a place where clinical medicine for the first time was taught, practiced, and the practice of bedside clinical diagnosis was established.

Van Swieten's successor was Anton de Haen, who again became physician to the Empress and Emperor and Chief of the First Vienna School. Later in this era the influence and support of Emperor Joseph II became markedly significant. His act of tolerance in 1782, in which he emancipated the Jews, enabling Jewish students from Germany and the rest of Europe to come to Vienna, set a precedent. Johann Peter Frank, from Baden in today's Germany, became the leading physician under Joseph II. Other doctors came from Holland, Germany, and from Austrian provinces such as Bohemia. Johann Peter Frank was another outstanding organizer. He was the first public health physician in the world. He established the principle that the governments of countries should be responsible for the health of their citizens, a concept not accepted by the rest of Europe at that time.

During the Napoleonic period of political upheaval in Europe most schools declined. Also the school in Vienna, the university, and the medical school, deteriorated and for the first half of the nineteenth century were rather mediocre. The education was poor and training of physicians was poor, and in general the quality of medicine in Europe was poor until the end of the nineteenth century when the Second School of Medicine was founded in Vienna. This became probably the most influential medical school in the world, even compared to the schools in London, Germany, and France—for several very good reasons.

The innovations established at the Second School of Vienna were to become patterns of medical education, medical training, and medical practice worldwide. Institutions in the United States and in parts of Europe took the Vienna school as a model. Essentially the credit goes to three men. Dr. Karl Rokitansky was probably the most renowned and the most productive pathologist ever. Although Rudolf Virchow in Berlin became famous because he established an institute and a journal, and published much research besides being a politician, Rokitansky in Vienna was more productive and was a greater innovator. In fact Virchow gives credit to Rokitansky. During forty-eight years as Chairman and Chief of Pathology in Vienna, Rokitansky performed over 100,000 autopsies—an average of six per day—in addition to his other duties. The method of doing autopsies today is still the Rokitansky way, including the Rokitansky incision. He was also much more than a pathologist. Rokitansky introduced microscopic pathology to the world. He was an outstanding teacher, who insisted on accurate diagnosis, both clinical and pathological.

Rokitansky attracted several other physicians to the University—among them Joseph Skoda, a Czech, who came to the University of Vienna as the first member of the non-surgical Department of Internal Medicine. Joseph Skoda was from a gifted family and had two brothers. One of his brothers became a lawyer, Joseph Skoda himself, as already stated, became the Chief of Internal Medicine in Vienna, while the third brother founded the still existent Skoda works in Czechoslovakia.

Ferdinand von Hebra was the second physician Rokitansky attracted to Vienna. He was an internist and a most outstanding dermatologist. Theodor Billroth also came to Vienna. He already had a name in Berlin and Heidelberg although originally from Sweden. He established the first surgical clinic in the world, surrounding himself with physicians from all over, particularly from the United States. These men returned to their countries, and founded surgical clinics themselves. Many of the medical students in the U.S. who went to Vienna to be trained in surgery were trained under Billroth. As one can see, this was a time in Vienna when young men, brought to the University by people like Rokitansky, then developed new fields of specialty, beginning what we now call specialty medicine. Prior to this time all physicians did everything and all professors taught everything.

The first obstetric and gynecology service in the world was established at the Second School of Medicine in Vienna and produced people like Semmelweis, who defined the cause of puerperal fever as an infection occurring after birth because the physicians did not wash their hands when going from one patient to the

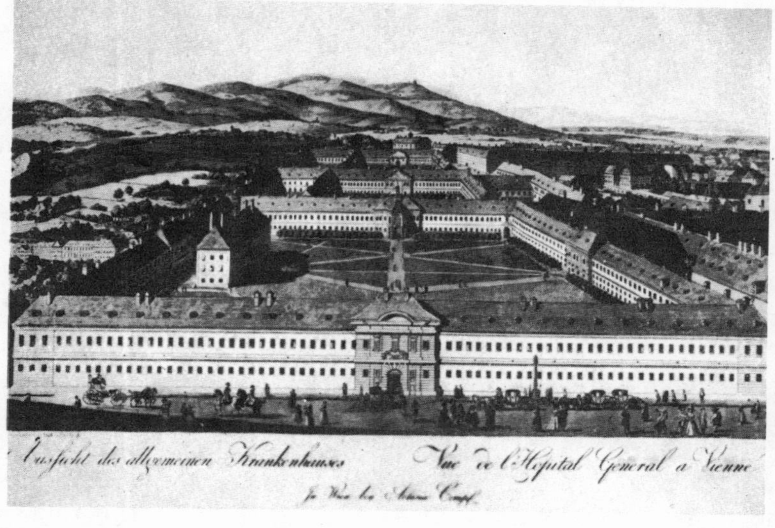

The Vienna General Hospital at the time of its foundation by Emperor Joseph II in 1783

other. Particularly, the incidence of infection was greatest in the ward when the physicians came directly from the autopsy room to the obstetrics ward. Semmelweis's findings were doubted by his colleagues and he was forced to leave Vienna. He went back to Hungary and died at the age of forty-nine in an insane asylum. His theories, however, were correct; and the influence of the School of Obstetrics and Gynecology expanded during the next fifteen to thirty years. Subsequently, the specialties of obstetrics, bacteriology, continuing pathology, and pediatrics were introduced. By the late nineteenth century the school had become the center of the most vigorous scientific activity in Europe.

Pharmacology started with Meyer and Pick, as well as Dr. Karl Landsteiner, who eventually left Vienna and came to New York. Here he created the method of testing blood groups which won him the Nobel Prize. The specialties of laryngology, opthalmology, otology and internal medicine were also created in Vienna. Accurate history, complete physical examination and clinical diagnosis became routine for the first time in the world. No more guess work!

The first psychiatric clinic was also established by Rokitansky and attracted several other well-known specialists including Meynert, Kraft-Ebing and Wagner-Jauregg. Kraft-Ebing became known for his original studies in the psychopathology of sexual disease. Wagner-Jauregg won the Nobel Prize for his fever treatment of various diseases, primarily of cerebrospinal syphilis. Wagner-Jauregg probably took care of and had more famous people die under his hands than any other physician in the history of the world, for there was no antibiotic therapy for syphilis. The psychiatric and neurology school subsequently attracted another psychiatrist, who initiated a whole new school which ended this second period, namely Sigmund Freud.

Towards the end of the nineteenth century and in the early part of this century, American medicine was of very poor quality. However, students who went from the U.S. to Vienna came back home to establish schools based on the models of Rokitansky, Skoda, von Hebra, and Billroth and their students. In addition, the role of Johns Hopkins University cannot be underestimated in the development of medical education in the U.S. Johns Hopkins University was modeled after the University of Vienna and was characterized by a fulltime faculty, a general hospital, to which patients were admitted, the association of medical care with teaching, and the attraction of young physicians who then would go elsewhere and establish similar schools. This University was also founded by several famous surgeons and an internist who were trained in Vienna – Dr. Halstead, William Osler, who later became Sir William Osler, Dr. Kelly, who founded American obstetrics, and William Welch, an American bacteriologist and pathologist. These four all had their post-graduate training in Vienna. Their students, such as Harvey Cushing and other surgeons, spread the influence of Vienna in, above all, Baltimore, New York, and Chicago. They founded large general hospitals (Philadelphia and Baltimore), Bellevue Hospital, and Cook County Hospital.

The first Chair for the history of medicine was also established in Vienna by Theodor Puschmann. Puschmann's widow founded the "Puschmann-Stiftung," which originated the Institute of the History of Medicine still present in Leipzig. The museum in Vienna, the Josephinum, is probably the most outstanding medical museum in the world, surpassing even the London museum.

Max Neuburger became the most renowned medical historian of the thirties, although he was hounded for years by the new National Socialist Party while working in Vienna and finally had to leave. He went to London where he finished out his years at the Museum of Medical History.

Students went to Vienna for several reasons. Vienna was a city that had no competition in medicine. It was where the aristocracy lived, was the capital as well as a very rich city. Germany, France, Italy and England had many schools. There were many conflicts in these countries, putting pressure on various schools to compete with each other. The problems of religion in England and France influenced the quality of the schools. For example, students went to Edinburgh because as Protestants and Quakers they simply were not accepted at Oxford and Cambridge. Primarily because of this the University of Edinburgh became the quality university that it was. The same occurred in France and to some

A 1987 aerial view of UNM Hospital as it is modeled essentially after Vienna's Allgemeines Krankenhaus. Photo by Michael Creange

extent in Germany. The influence of the Italians and the Dutch on medical schools was very important during the Renaissance. But the attraction of the city, the life in Vienna, the concentration of art, music, and literature in Vienna, in addition to the quality of the medical school made it the most attractive place at the turn of the century.

During the early part of the twentieth century, when the political and economic conditions in Europe became difficult, particularly the devastating effect of World War I on the Austrian Monarchy, was reflected in the medical school. The predominance of American medicine after World War I became quite evident, and the centers of medical education and training shifted from Europe to the United States. Being spared destruction in World War I, America had not lost significant population, and her cities were still intact. Money was there, universities were founded. "Diploma mills," where one had been able to get an easy degree, were abolished, and American medicine advanced. Medical education now is centered in the United States.

The progress of medical education and medical research has certainly changed. The influence of the University of Vienna School of Medicine on our medicine, the type of medicine, particularly medical education, and especially medicine in the U.S. cannot be overestimated. Since the mid-twentieth century the influence of medical education in the United States has been very different. The emphasis was no longer primarily on fine teachers and medical centers interested in clinical medicine, but it now has more to do with money and technology. The medical advances since the middle of this century have really been made by engineers, chemists, and biochemists–not by physicians. In summary, the influence of the School of Medicine in Vienna was the greatest of any medical school. It is interesting that there are now approximately 140 medical schools in the United States, of which the top twenty to twenty-five are still the private schools that were patterned after the Vienna medical school with a teaching hospital, faculty, clinical research, and teaching.

The Austrian Cultural Impact on America: Hollywood in World War II

Gerald D. Nash

Die durch das Naziregime exilierten Deutschen und Österreicher – unter letzteren zudem auch viele Künstler aus dem ehemaligen Österreich-Ungarn, fanden besonders in Hollywood eine Wirkungsstätte, die das amerikanische Kulturschaffen zur Weltspitze hievte. Sprachschwierigkeiten verhinderten einen wesentlichen Beitrag der Exilanten auf die amerikanische Literatur, aber umso nachhaltiger war die Wirkung in Musik, Kunst und Film. Während unter den österreichischen Schriftstellern nur Franz Werfel gewissen Erfolg hatte, waren unter den Komponisten Arnold Schönberg, Erich Korngold oder der mit Wien affiliierte Hanns Eisler, unter den Regisseuren Max Reinhardt, Josef von Sternberg oder Billy Wilder, um nur einige zu nennen, zum Teil bis heute Stützen der amerikanischen Kultur- und Filmgesellschaft.

The cultural influence of Austria on the United States has had a long history. Towards the end of the eighteenth century American liberals like Thomas Jefferson and his circle looked admiringly to European thinkers during the Enlightenment who provided them with inspiration. Along with John Locke and Jean-Jacques Rousseau the Habsburg Emperor Joseph II provided them with a model of an Enlightenment figure who was truly worthy of their admiration. His policies of religious toleration and reform, land distribution, social welfare policies, land reform, and educational innovations were carefully studied by the American Founding Fathers. In turn, European liberals viewed America as a land where their highest hopes, their seemingly impossible dreams, could be fulfilled: "We wished the Americans all success," declared the great Goethe, "and the names of Franklin and Washington began to shine and sparkle in the firmament of politics and war."[1]

As the nineteenth century drew to a close Austrian cultural

influence once more made itself felt in the New World. In the brilliant cultural renaissance of Vienna's *fin de siècle* its leading denizens exerted a strong trans-Atlantic influence, men like Gustav Mahler, Arnold Schoenberg, Sigmund Freud, Richard Strauss, Johannes Brahms, Antonin Dvorak, Franz Werfel, and Hugo von Hofmannsthal, among others. Dvorak, for example, came to the United States in 1892 to serve as director of the National Conservatory of Music in New York City and there composed his most famous work, the Symphony in E Minor, "From the New World." Freud visited the United States in 1911 as guest of the famous G. Stanley Hall, and left a lasting impact on the development of American psychology.[2]

With the growth of totalitarianism in central Europe during the 1930s Austrian influence on American culture manifested itself again, if in somewhat unexpected ways. The emergence of Hitler in 1933 in Germany and that of Dollfuß and Schuschnigg in Austria created pressures for the emigration of intellectuals opposed to Nazism and fascism, particularly Jews. The *Anschluß* of 1938 sealed their fate, for Jews were excluded from all aspects of national life and plans were made for their eventual removal and extermination. That led to a mass exodus of Jewish intellectuals and non-Jewish political refugees.

The consequent migration came to include the cream of the European intelligentsia. For Austria the emigration resulted in the elimination of a significant element from its cultural life which was to leave a vacuum in the next generation. As the historian Peter Gay wrote:

> The exile holds an honored place in the history of Western civilization. Dante and Grotius, Bayle and Rousseau, Heine and Marx did their greatest work in enforced residence on alien soil, looking back, looking back with loathing and longing to the country, their own, that had rejected them. The Greek scholars from Byzantium who flooded the Italian city-states early in the fifteenth century and the Huguenot bourgeois who streamed out of France across Western Europe late in the seventeenth century brought

> with them energy, learning, and scarce, welcome skills; New England was founded by refugees who transformed a savage wilderness into blooming civilization. But these migrations, impressive as they are, cannot compare with the exodus set in motion early in 1933, when the Nazis seized control of Germany; the exiles Hitler made were the greatest collection of transplanted intellect, talent, and scholarship the world has ever seen.[3]

Some of the refugees went to England, but the majority came to the United States, where they became carriers of German and Austrian culture. As Vienna had been the dazzling center of culture in the early twentieth century, so Vienna in exile established itself in New York and in Hollywood. These cities became the staging areas for the spread of Austrian culture in America. Although scholars have devoted much attention to the Eastern outpost, the activities of Austrians in the West also deserve attention.

The influence of the Austrian emigrés in Hollywood was diverse. In view of language problems their literary activities were understandably limited. But their impact was manifest in music, art, the movie industry, the sciences, and, of course, psychology. Humanistic studies were affected as well. A brief survey cannot do them justice but can provide a concise overview of their manifold activities.[4]

The emigration was particularly difficult for writers who were most at home in the German language. Lion Feuchtwanger, one of the best known of European novelists, expressed it well in 1943 when he said: "The author who has lost his reading public of his own land frequently loses at the same time the core of his economic existence. Very many writers of the highest talent, whose products were in great demand in their own countries, find no markets in foreign lands, either because their chief merit lies in the stylistic qualities of their language, and these qualities cannot be translated, or because their choice of subjects does not interest the foreign reader. . . . It is surprising how many authors whose accomplishments the entire world has acclaimed now stand helpless and without means."[5] Among the emigré writers in Hollywood

Thomas Mann was preeminent. He presided over salons at which colleagues such as Feuchtwanger, Vicki Baum, Erich Maria Remarque, Alfred Döblin, Bruno Frank, Joseph Wechsberg, Alfred Polgar, Bertolt Brecht, among others, were frequent guests. Of the Austrian writers Franz Werfel was the most successful. After a hectic flight from the Nazis he arrived in Los Angeles in 1941 and soon thereafter published *The Song of Bernadette*. It was a huge success in the United States once it was translated and was made into one of the most successful motion pictures of the wartime era.[6]

The language barrier was far less of an impediment for musicians and composers. Among the notable conductors in Los Angeles during these years was Bruno Walter, who although a German had spent considerable time in Vienna. Gustav Mahler had chosen him as his assistant director at the Vienna State Opera, where he served from 1901 to 1912. He returned to direct that venerable institution in 1935 but fled in 1938 because of his Jewish background. Composers as well as performers found Hollywood a congenial environment with varied employment opportunities. A number of well-known European composers came to write musical scores for motion pictures and introduced new musical patterns to American audiences. They included Friedrich Hollaender, Eugen Zador, Ernst Toch, and Werner Heyman. Of the Austrians clearly the most eminent was Arnold Schoenberg. Suffering from asthma, he left the Juliard School in New York and accepted an appointment as music professor at the University of California, Los Angeles. There he trained a group of talented students and continued his own work of composition although his scores did not as yet enjoy great popularity. Schoenberg disdained writing for the movies and turned down lucrative offers from well-known producers such as Irving Thalberg. One of Schoenberg's best known students was the German-born Hanns Eisler who became Charlie Chaplin's musical assistant and wrote scores for Hollywood productions. Best known of the Viennese composers in the movie capital was Erich Korngold who shifted from the serious compositions for which he had become well-known in Europe to writing largely for the movies. He garnered two Academy Awards during the war years, including one for *King's Row* which starred Ronald Reagan. When the one-time actor chose the music for his inauguration as President of the United States in 1981, he selected Korngold's theme as a favorite. In the postwar era Korngold's music enjoyed increasing popularity in the United States and was performed with increasing frequency.[7]

Refugees from Vienna also enriched the world of art and architecture. Some had brought valuable paintings with them but lacked space to display them. That was the case of the producer Josef von Sternberg, who lent his collection to the Los Angeles County Museum for display and helped to cultivate American tastes for modern art. The art market in the Los Angeles area was still largely undeveloped in 1940. But a group of emigrés became the pioneers in the establishment of new art galleries in the area, men like Ralph Altman, Paul Kantor, and Felix Landau. In establishing major art galleries in southern California they became the

World renowned film director Billy Wilder at a Los Angeles cocktail party with German film director Volker Schloendorff and Nikolaus Scherk, Austrian Consul General in Los Angeles, ca. 1986.

founding fathers of the art community there and important cultivators of artistic tastes. They followed in the footsteps of some of the major arbiters of architectural styles in the West, notably the Viennese Richard Neutra, who had come in 1926 to develop innovative styles, and Rudolph Schindler.[8]

Understandably, the film industry attracted some of the Viennese refugees. The great Max Reinhardt found it difficult to regain the stature he had enjoyed in Vienna and Berlin. He had come to Hollywood with high hopes in the 1930s. As he wrote to Erika and Klaus Mann: "You simply must stay here. It's going to be a new center of culture. America is going to take over the cultural heritage of Europe, and there is no more hospitable landscape . . . than the Californian. Here is a still youthful country. European and American scientists will meet to prepare a home for our old culture and for the new one that is coming into being here." But his efforts to establish legitimate theater were not successful, and in 1942 he left for New York.[9] The Viennese director, Josef von Sternberg, the man who had made Marlene Dietrich famous in *The Blue Angel* (1930), scored a number of successes in the Hollywood of this period. Another Austrian got his start as one of America's best known directors. That was Billy Wilder who because of his youth, found it easier to adapt to American styles. Of directors who also starred as notable actors Erich von Stroheim stood out, although he did not relish many of his roles in which he portrayed penultimate Nazis. In this he was not alone, for most German-speaking actors found their roles limited, although the talents of men like Peter Lorre, Conrad Veidt, Albert Basserman, Fritz Kortner, Leon Askin, and Alexander Granach were vast.[10]

Leon Askin

Austrians in the West also enriched the world of science. A brilliant group of Hungarians paced their respective fields. They included Edward Teller and Leo Szilard in physics, both of whom made substantial contributions to the development of an atomic bomb during their wartime service in Los Alamos, New Mexico. At times they were joined by one of the true mathematic geniuses of the twentieth century, John von Neumann, who worked out complicated computations needed for atomic fission. Emigrés also vitalized the field of mathematics in the West. Jerzy Neyman and Alex Tarski joined the faculty at the University of California, Berkeley, Stefan Bergman and George Polya taught at Stanford University, and Willi Birnbaum joined the mathematics faculty at the University of Washington.[11]

But the Austrian influence was especially profound in the sphere of psychology and psychoanalysis. A sizeable number of Freud's students came West to spread the master's ideas, and to establish new psychoanalytic training institutes through which they trained a whole new generation of Americans and exerted a deep influence on mental health movements in the United States. With the help of the Menninger brothers in Topeka, Kansas, the refugees came west to spread their gospel. Some, like Ernst Simmel, Otto Fenichel, and Joachim Haenel settled in Los Angeles, where they founded the Los Angeles Psychoanalytic Institute in 1942. At various times other notable Freudian refugees like Martin Grotjan, Ernst Lewy and Bernard Kamm participated in their work. In San Francisco the Viennese analyst, Siegfried Bernfeld, a favorite of Freud's, established a new training institute in that area. And one of Anna Freud's students, Edith Buxbaum, went to Seattle, Washington in 1950 to establish the first psychoanalytic training institute in that region. As a group, the Austrians had a greater influence in the United States than they might have had under more normal conditions in Europe, because Americans at this time were particularly receptive to the practical application of Freud's teachings.[12]

On a smaller scale Austrians were influential in shaping the history of science in the United States, including the philosophy of science. The Vienna School of Logical Positivism was already well established by the time of the Second World War. Many of its leading adherents found themselves among the emigrés, including Kurt Goedel, Otto Neurath, Herbert Feigl, and Carl Hempel, and also Ludwig Wittgenstein and Karl Popper. A few members of the group came to the West. Rudolph Carnap secured a teaching position at UCLA, along with Hans Reichenbach. In the same area Heinrich Gomperts introduced the philosophy of science at the University of Southern California. At a time when this field was in its infancy in the United States, and particularly the West, the Austrians had a deep influence in shaping its directions during the generation.[13]

Historical events move in mysterious ways. Who could have guessed at the time that the Nazi Holocaust would result in one of the great cultural transfers in recorded time, when the best of European civilization would impinge on an emerging American culture through the efforts of a relatively small number of fleeing refugees. The Austrian immigrants to America numbered less than 40,000, yet their cultural contributions far transcended their relatively small numbers. It was ironic that the Austrian influence on American culture, in literature, music, art and architecture, popular culture, science, social science, and the humanities, was greatest when it was born in suffering. But, whatever its origins, it made a lasting impact.

Notes

1. Goethe in his *Autobiography* as quoted in Leo Gershoy, *From Despotism to Revolution, 1763–1789* (New York, 1944), p. 217; see also Michael Kraus, "America and the Utopian Ideal of the Eighteenth Century," *Mississippi Valley Historical Review*, vol. 22 (1936), 487–504.
2. On Vienna, see Carl Schorske, *Fin-de-siècle Vienna: Politics and Culture* (New York, 1979); on Freud's influence on American psychology see John C. Burnham, *Psychoanalysis and American Medicine, 1894–1918: Medicine, Science and Culture* (New York, 1967).
3. Peter Gay, "Weimar Culture: The Outsider as Insider," in Donald Fleming and Bernhard Bailyn (eds.), *The Intellectual Migration* (Cambridge, Mass., 1970), pp. 11–12.

4. I discuss their contributions in greater detail in *The American West Transformed: The Impact of World War II* (Bloomington, 1985), pp. 186-198.
5. Lion Feuchtwanger, "The Working Problems of the Writer in Exile," in *Proceedings of the Writers Congress, Los Angeles, 1943* (Berkeley, 1944), pp. 345-348.
6. On Werfel see Lore B. Fantin (ed.), *Franz Werfel* (Pittsburgh, 1961), and Werner Braselman, *Franz Werfel* (Wuppertal, 1960), and Erich Maria Remarque, *Shadows in Paradise* (New York, 1972), translated by Ralph Manheim, pp. 228-231.
7. Bruno Walter, *Themes and Variations* (London, 1947), and Luizi Korngold, *Erich Korngold, Ein Lebensbild* (Vienna, 1967), p. 80; Dika Newlin, *Schoenberg Remembered: Diaries and Recollections 1938-1976* (New York, 1980), pp. 89-234.
8. Salka Viertel, *The Kindness of Strangers* (New York, 1969), p. 217; Nash, *American West,* pp. 192-193.
9. Quote in Erika and Claus Mann, *Escape to Life* (Boston, 1939), p. 265; see also Gottfried Reinhardt, *Der Liebhaber: Erinnerungen seines Sohnes Gottfried Reinhardt an Max Reinhardt* (München, 1973), pp. 269-270.
10. Charles Higham and Joel Greenberg, *Hollywood in the Forties* (New York, 1968), p. 92; Gunther Anders, *Die Schrift an der Wand: Tagebuecher 1951 bis 1955* (München, 1967), pp. 1-5; Darrell C. Jackman, "Exiles in Paradise: A Cultural History of German Emigres in Southern California, 1933-1950," (Ph.D. Dissertation, University of California, Santa Barbara, History, 1977), pp. 133-135, 183-187.
11. Nash, *American West,* pp. 164-167; Laura Fermi, *Illustrious Immigrants* (Chicago, 1971), pp. 180-185.
12. A detailed discussion with bibliographic references can be found in Nash, *American West,* pp. 167-173.
13. Fermi, *Illustrious Immigrants,* pp. 359-360.

Jura Soyfer

Jura Soyfer – A Writer of the Austrian 1930s Only?

Horst Jarka

Als Opfer eines tragischen Schicksals, das sein Leben im Konzentrationslager enden ließ, geriet dieser scharfsinnige Autor der österreichischen Linken länger in Vergessenheit. Erst in den letzten Jahren wird Soyfers Andenken endlich gefördert. So bemüht sich Horst Jarka um Soyfers Anerkennung in Amerika. Hier bringt er Beispiele, um Soyfers Nähe zu Karl Kraus und Ödön von Horváth zu beweisen und das Amerikabild eines österreichischen Autors der dreißiger Jahre sichtbar zu machen. Hinzuweisen ist ferner auf Jarkas Herausgabe von Soyfers Werken (englisch 1977, deutsch 1980, 1984) und auf seine Biographie *J. Soyfer, Leben Werk Zeit* (1987).

The title suggests two questions: was Jura Soyfer only an Austrian writer or does his work have a significance beyond Austrian literature? And secondly: is this significance limited to the 1930s and is his work only historically interesting or does it have something to say to us today – in Austria and elsewhere? But before I attempt to answer these questions I had better answer this one: who was Jura Soyfer? If known at all in the USA he is known only as the poet of the "Dachau-Song," a most moving, remarkable document of human strength in the face of barbarism. But what were his other works like?

Jura Soyfer's life began in the deceptive peace before World War I and ended in a German concentration camp six months before the second war broke out. He was born in 1912 in Kharkov, the capital of the Ukraine, as the son of a wealthy businessman. The Bolshevik Revolution drove the family out of Russia, and finally, in 1921, they settled in Vienna, a Vienna of inflation and economic and political uncertainty. Thus, the boy Jura was a refugee when he was eight. He attended the *Realgymnasium* in the third district, was not a brilliant student but a bright boy, and soon spoke Viennese like any old Erdberger. He was the class wit who wrote satirical sketches against school boredom. The catalyst of his integration into Viennese society was the Socialist Youth movement, which he joined shortly after the massacre on 15 July 1927. Jura was soon in the grip of Red Vienna, where vision was combined with practice. It must have been exciting, unbelievably stimulating, to live in Vienna during the time of Austro-Marxism, which Karl Popper, even as Sir Karl, recalled as an "admirable movement." Young Jura Soyfer thrived in this atmosphere, where Utopia was pulled from the skies to the ground to rise to the skies again. Every day on his way to school he passed the site where another municipal housing block was growing, tangible victory over the housing shortage and the greed of middle-class property holders and rent sharks. As a member of the Social-Democratic Youth Organization and later as a young party member, he belonged to the left opposition which criticized the party establishment's schizophrenia of verbal revolutionism and defensive tactics that made Austrian Social-Democracy retreat step by step before the advance of anti-parliamentary forces. The showdown came in the events of February 1934 which are well known.

But before I talk about Soyfer's life and work under Austro-Fascism, I would like to say a few words about his poetry before February 1934, the poems that appeared every Saturday in the *Arbeiter-Zeitung,* which at that time was of a very high quality and read by 80,000 people. To these readers Jura Soyfer had become something of an institution, and they looked forward from week to week to his witty satirical commentaries on political events, which were grim enough in those years of the Great Depression, of mass unemployment, and violent political tensions. Marxist that he was, Soyfer saw in the Austrian dilemma only the local variation of the world-wide catastrophe of capitalism in agony. Most of his poems of those two extremely tense years are set in this international context, and Soyfer expressed the collective indignation of the victims of the depression, perhaps most powerfully in his "Song of Order":

> That we go hungry is a trifling matter
> That we go begging is beside the point.

Our protests are but idle chatter.
Don't shake the order out of joint!
Whoever has not noticed, hear it now:
There is an order in this world, you bet!
We hold it up and it holds us – and how!
The order's order must not be upset!
  This planet is, from east to west,
  From Singapore to Budapest,
  Organized so well!
  Thirty million people trot
  Hunger pains is all they've got.
  He who can't go on can rot.
  The order is just swell.
  There is too much bread? Then heat with bread!
  Too many people? Shoot them dead!
  The order is God's gift to Man,
  We die like dogs to fit his plan,
  The order works like hell.[1]

In this gloomy world panorama the United States appears again and again, and the image of America in Soyfer's satires is predictably devastating. Like other left-wing writers in Europe, Soyfer saw in the U.S. the bulwark of capitalism in which the contradictions of a profit-oriented economy were most glaring. Soyfer hardly missed any of them, and he did not waste time either. On 8 January 1932 *The New York Times* reported a demonstration of 10,000 unemployed who marched from Pennsylvania to Washington, D.C. to appeal to Herbert Hoover. Two days later Soyfer attacked Hoover and linked him with the Austrian depression-Chancellor Buresch in a New Year's poem that warned those in power of the consequences of their insensitivity to the misery of the masses. In July of the same year thousands of American war veterans staged what became known as the bonus march to Washington. According to law, these veterans were entitled to bonus pay, but the payment had been delayed again and again, and now the ex-soldiers came from all over the country to claim their right. They set up camps of cardboard shacks, determined to stick it out.

But instead of the money, the government sent them troops (for the first time in history the U.S. government used armed forces against its citizens). Two veterans were killed; war cripples, women, and children were driven off with tear gas by soldiers under the command of two officers who were to make more glorious history in years to come: Douglas MacArthur and his aide Dwight D. Eisenhower. Soyfer satirizes the ingratitude of the American fatherland and urges the cannon fodder of World War I to resist a second slaughter.

There was another dark feature of the U.S. image in Soyfer's poetry. Just as he had attacked the class-specific partiality of justice in Austria, he condemned similar practices in the United States. He joined the international protests against the handling of the Sacco and Vanzetti case and against the Scottsboro trial when nine young unemployed blacks, accused of having raped a white woman, were sentenced to death. Naturally, racism was one of Soyfer's targets. In very effective emblematic satire that is in a combination of newsphoto and poem, he showed black and white unemployed waiting for a hand-out in front of an employment agency. The message was that racism only helps to concel the overall inequality in American society, and poor blacks and poor whites should unite against the common oppressor.

Soyfer spoke for the suffering millions in the richest country of the world. He castigated an economic "system" which allowed huge quantities of food to be destroyed to keep the price level up while thousands starved. To Soyfer such procedures, however, were not aberrations and contradictions but the logical consequences of an inhuman system. All of this was the stock-in-trade of Marxist propaganda; Soyfer drew his information from newspapers and not from his own experience, and his image of America was obviously one-sided, but his cticitism was, after all, based on fact. And what made his criticism more than propaganda and lifted it to the level of literature still readable today was his verbal virtuosity and wit, which place him in the tradition of Johann Nestroy and Karl Kraus.

Now let me proceed to the local level, the Viennese scene after February 1934. The victory of Austro-Fascism changed

Soyfer's life drastically. From then on he lived on two levels, so to speak, a "legal" and an "illegal" one, that is to say, he joined the left underground. At both levels he went on writing, and even at the legal level he did not give up his fight against fascism. That any criticism was possible at all shows that Austro-Fascism was by no means as totalitarian as Hitler's regime in Germany. In the *Wiener Tag,* one of the most liberal papers of the time, Soyfer published reviews and prose sketches criticizing the regime's cultural politics. These prose sketches have long been underestimated by critics; they are, in fact, excellent examples of short prose, displaying Soyfer's psychological insights into the frame of mind of so-called ordinary people, working-class people, but also of those who worked under similar conditions without thinking of themselves as workers: the petit bourgeoisie. Soyfer wanted to find out what motivated the political behavior of the man in the street; he wanted to see why fascism became more and more attractive to the lower middle class. He was a political writer with a sociologist's curiosity.

The few Schillings Soyfer made writing for the *Wiener Tag* hardly kept him going. The financial situation of his father was deterioriating from day to day, and Jura wanted nothing more than to be independent. Private lessons added a little to his meager income. Another trickle, however, came from his writings for the stage, a special kind of stage. In the Vienna of the thirties a number of little theaters sprang up, literally underground theaters in the basements of coffee houses. The origin of these theaters was partly economic – many actors lost their jobs in the depression – partly political: Hitler had driven many theater people out of Germany who now landed in these Viennese coffeehouse-theaters where at least they could act, even if they got paid hardly anything at all. For two of these theaters (the *Literatur am Naschmarkt* and especially the politically most outspoken theater, the *ABC*) Soyfer wrote a great number of sketches – most of which are lost – and six plays, of which fortunately five have been preserved.

Soyfer wrote his first play in the summer of 1936, the year when the Spanish Civil War started. Some historians have called this war the dress rehearsal for World War II, and Soyfer felt that the conflict in far-away Spain was only the beginning. He recognized the threat of war as Germany became stronger, left the League of Nations, and occupied the Rhineland. Appropriately, he called his play *The End of the World.* It is a grotesque black comedy starting out with a frame plot in the cosmos, combining echoes of Karl Kraus's *The Last Days of Mankind* and of Nestroy's *Lumpazivagabundus.* The sun and the planets condemn the world to death because the vermin man has disturbed the harmony of the spheres. Mars suggests that a comet be sent to crash into the world and that the impact should annihilate the human race. A scientist discovers the approaching comet and not only warns the world, but also develops a machine that could intercept the comet and save the world and mankind. But nobody listens to this Concerned Scientist; life goes on as usual, business goes on as usual. In fact, destruction is better business than salvation. The press is filled with trivia, polls about how prominent people will face the final hour, and what the ladies will wear. When the comet comes closer and closer and the masses rebel, they are kept in check with brute force and martial law.

At this moment the scientist with a conscience realizes that the world as we know it is condemned; his only hope is that our civilization may be preserved on another planet. And it is within this futuristic science-fiction vision that the United States appears again in Soyfer's work. The media announce that in the U.S., the country of technological progress, a spaceship has been built, which, for the trifle of a few million dollars per seat, will transport the elite of the country to the safety of another star. Our scientist pleads that the VIP in charge—whose name Rockford nicely blends Rockefeller and Ford, i.e., big money and big industry—take with him the fundamentals of western civilization: basic scientific books and essential documents like the Declaration of Human Rights. But the hold of the spaceship is full of stocks and bonds. There is no room for the scientist's impractical humanistic baggage. Soyfer's satire on the American social elite includes the stereotpyes: the millionaire, his nervous secretary, his small-brained do-gooder society wife, the glamorous movie star. Yet he adds a less usual figure: a writer who, in a travesty of cosmic expressionism, is anticipating the end of the world with only one worry: whether he should write a drama or a long poem about the final disaster. And of course there is a journalist who wants to publish a special end-of-the-world issue. She interviews Mr. Rockford, and this is how he wants to be quoted:

> Fellow Americans! We fifty persons in responsible positions unfortunately have to leave the earth before its end in order to observe the events more objectively from a higher point of view. We envy you who can stay behind for the great event! Be proud of it! Later you will be able to say to your children and your children's children: "I, too, was there!" Stick it through! You are dying for the United States of America! but as long as there is still time, buy End-of-the-World Bonds!

Soyfer is writing a cosmic farce, spiking a Raimund-like fantasy with Nestroy-like irony. The spaceship turns out to be nothing but a dummy, a hoax for which the "inventor" simply cashed in to enjoy the last days of his life. So much for American space technology 1937. Technology will not save the rich. And yet Soyfer does not allow the world to go to hell. The play ends with a tour de force. The comet does not have the heart to destroy the world. On one level this ending suggests the hope that many Austrians shared in the thirties, a hope against hope, the hope of people who clearly saw what was coming, and, to the very end, could not believe it. There is another dimension to this ending which I will discuss later.

Soyfer's next play was more realistic than the first insofar as it at least indicated what could be done to change the miserable existing situation. As the title, *Eddy Lechner's Trip to Paradise*, shows, the plot of this play was not less fantastic than that of the first one, but its theme was as serious as it could possibly be: unemployment – which in Austria in 1936, when the play was written, was still twenty-four percent. But Soyfer treated this dead-serious topic in a truly ingenious way that combined darkness of theme with lightness of touch, science fiction gags with genuine pathos, satire with human warmth, and ended in an unmistakable message of precarious hope. Eddy Lechner, a young Viennese from the second district has been unemployed for six years and wants to find out who is to blame for his misery. Of course, he blames technology, until the machine which he used to operate appears on the scene to tell him that it, too, is out of work, dismantled. Soyfer borrowed the magic wand of science fiction from H. G. Wells and from Ludwig Anzengruber, and made the machine into a time machine. Eddy, his girlfriend Fritzi, and the Machine travel back through the centuries to find the culprit who "invented" technology. But every invention and discovery is preceded by another one. The journey goes from Galvani to Galileo, from Galileo to Columbus, from Columbus to Gutenberg, and on and on. Technology is only one spark of human creativity; if you want to stop it, you have to undo man himself. When Eddy finally reaches paradise, his hopes are rekindled – paradise is a factory of creation, and workers are wanted! (To the unemployed of the depression, paradise was a place where man was allowed to earn his bread by the sweat of his brow!)[2] But alas, Eddy's trip is but human history in reverse gear and takes him beyond all beginnings. Creation hasn't started yet. The "Men wanted" sign is removed. When Eddy realizes that even in paradise there is unemployment he calls upon God to cancel the creation of man altogether. In a ballad that recalls Frans Masereel's woodcuts, Soyfer contrasts the divine plan with the human reality:

Lord, oh do not touch the clay!
You'll just get into a bind.
What your Adam will become
Won't be what you had in mind!

(A profiteer walks across the stage)

Look at Man when he's in power!
He will praise You, Lord, but say:
Is he still what You envisaged
On Creation's final day?

(An unemployed worker walks across the stage)

Look at Man without a job!
Starvation is his daily dread.
How can he obey Your order:
Labor for your daily bread?

(A mother walks across the stage)

Look! Don't turn Your face away!
See the mother worn with care.
When you told her to bear children,
Did you want her to despair? !

(A prostitute walks across the stage)

See the whore lost in the crowd!
Joy for sale! O Lord above!
Did you think of her profession
When your smile created love?

(A man with a gas mask walks across the stage)

Look at Man before his death!
Pitiless he's out to kill.
You had made him in Your image.
Is this brute Your image still?
Do not touch the clay, O Lord!
Adam will but wreck Your plan.
Or if You've already made him,
Cancel him! Unmake Your Man!

But Eddy's girlfriend opposes him and pleads for life. Man is created after all, as a mixture of Yes and No, and the responsibility for his fate is placed in his own hands. The play is a passionate plea for human self-determination and against historic determinism, a Marxist play in the spirit of Max Adler. The miracle that saved the world in Soyfer's first play now has to be brought about by man himself.

Soyfer's first two plays show how much he was indebted to the local tradition of popular comedy. And his next play, *Astoria*, again proves how much he had learned from Johann Nestroy, who had an unerring eye and ear for hypocrisy in behavior and language, the dichotomy between appearance and reality. Soyfer had read about a hoax in London where a group of bored young diplomats had invented an imaginary state by the name of Astoria, had established an embassy of that state in the West End, had given parties, even handed out decorations of a country that did not exist, and had found people who believed it all. The chimera Astoria provided Soyfer with a most fitting symbol for Austria, which in the thirties was suffering from a deep-rooted identity crisis: the Pan-Germans and the Austrian Nazis denied the independence of Austria; up to 1933 the Social Democrats were also dreaming of an *Anschluß;* the Monarchists were hoping for a restitution of the Habsburg rule; the Austro-Fascists defended an independent Austria but did so with an ideology modeled after German and Italian fascism with their anti-Marxist, anti-labor stance, which inevitably proved unable to sustain that independence. In July 1936 the Austrian Chancellor Schuschnigg declared Austria the "second German State," an unfortunate term indicating a course of compromises with the Nazis. In Soyfer's play of 1937 this precarious situation is reflected in satire ranging from the farcical to the tragicomic. The illusory state of Astoria for Soyfer was the perfect metaphor for the Austro-Fascist state, the Ständestaat (corporate state), which was always planned and promised but never came into being; the state had lots of symbols and emblems but lacked popular mass support.

German aggression became more threatening day by day. What a German takeover would mean Soyfer showed in his play *Vineta* (1937) based on the legend of the medieval town engulfed by the spring flood tide. Around the motif of the drowned city Soyfer builds a theatrical image of the stagnation and hopelessness that engulfed Vienna in the thirties. In this play Soyfer explores new literary ground. The old Viennese folk-theater tradition is still there insofar as this play, too, is a dream play, but the dream becomes a nightmare. Soyfer dramatizes the symbolic situation by presenting the attempts of *one* person to stay alive in a city of lifeless shadows, a spiritually dead community. Soyfer's plot is again constructed simply. In the frame of the play an old sailor tells the most memorable adventure of his youth. He had been a diver and was lowered to a wreck to salvage it; but the air hose got snared and he became unconscious. In this unconscious state he finds himself in the city at the bottom of the sea. The people he meets live outside time and memory, their language has no logic, his rational questions receive absurd replies. The Vinetans lead a pseudo-existence of oblivion; they have forgotten what love is, they have forgotten what hate is. They know no hope and no despair. In Soyfer's play T. S. Eliot's hollow men haunt the makeshift stage in the basement of a Viennese coffee house. To indicate another dimension: Soyfer's *Vineta* has the terrifying prophetic quality of Orwell's *1984*. Let me quote just one scene:

In a prison, Johnny, accompanied by a Guard, is visiting a Prisoner.

> JOHNNY: Speak quite openly to me. I am Senator John. I want to help you. Do you need help?
> PRISONER: No, Senator.
> JOHNNY: Are they treating you all right?
> PRISONER: Yes, Senator.
> JOHNNY: Don't you have any complaints?
> PRISONER: No, Senator.
> JOHNNY: You don't have to stand at attention for me. Sit down. Go ahead, do sit down!
> PRISONER: Yes, Senator.
> JOHNNY: What crime did you commit?
> PRISONER: Don't know, Senator.
> JOHNNY: When will your sentence run out?
> PRISONER: Yesterday, Senator.
> JOHNNY: Guard, what has this man done? When will he leave the prison?
> GUARD: Don't know. Yesterday.
> JOHNNY (to prisoner): What's your name?
> PRISONER: Don't remember.

GUARD: Don't remember.

JOHNNY: I'll tell you why I've come. Ever since I came to this town, I have been looking for life in vain. I haven't found it, not among the poor and not among the rich. I haven't got much time left. Then it occurred to me: In the days when I was young, no one loved life as much as the prisoners. That's why you are my last hope. I give you your freedom. Do you hear? You are free!

PRISONER: I hear, Senator.

JOHNNY: Repeat: I am free.

PRISONER: I am free.

GUARD: Free.

JOHNNY: What are you going to do, now that you are free?

PRISONER: Don't know.

JOHNNY: Try to remember. Isn't there anybody waiting for you, somebody you want to hug and kiss when you come out?

PRISONER: No.

JOHNNY: But there must be an enemy waiting for you somewhere, somebody you want to get even with after all these years.

PRISONER: No, Senator.

JOHNNY: Man, listen to me! There is a world that is different. A world where night follows day, and where there is spring, and storms blow, and the sun is shining. Grain is being sown and harvested and sown again, without end. Human beings are being born and grow like grain. Because they have a restless heart, they must love and hate as long as they live, and they become old and die. And new men are being born to hate and to love, to grow old and to die, without end, and all this has no other meaning than itself. But it's a great meaning, it's called life. Do you understand?

PRISONER: No, Senator.

JOHNNY: I know, it's still hard for you, but a spark of longing for all that has been alive in you all these years, hasn't it?

PRISONER: I don't remember.

Vineta was certainly the most avant-garde of Soyfer's plays. He wrote it shortly after having reviewed a surrealist play by Salacrou, which he criticized for being a game of irrelevancies to titillate an intellectual elite. In his own play Soyfer did use surrealist methods and, in the disintegration of his dialogues, he foreshadowed the technique of the absurdists after the war. But he did not write an absurdist play hinting at the mystery of human existence, or, to put it differently, hinting at some metaphysical sense behind the nonsense. Soyfer did not wait for Godot. He gave a nightmare vision to wake people up. In the last scene he takes us out of the nightmare, into the real world that has to be preserved. I shall return to this play when I talk about the meaning of Soyfer's work for us today.

The last play of Soyfer that has survived the war, was an adaptation of *Christofer Columbus* by Walter Hasenclever and Kurt Tucholsky, a very successful adaptation. The original was a not particularly spirited, rather conventional comedy on the theme that the savages are after all more civilized than their conquerors. Soyfer not only added thirteen songs to the play, he also added political fervor and wit to it and made the play an incisive critique of colonialism combined with an attack on the master-race ideology of the Nazis. Soyfer's *Broadway Melody 1492*, as he called his adaptation, is a historical play in which history is presented from the point of view of the underdog and where great men like Columbus lose their greatness. It is also a satire on the traditional history plays performed in the Burgtheater at the time. It is even more than that: Soyfer's talent, nurtured by the Austrian local theater tradition, triumphs over Hasenclever and Tucholsky, two of the biggest names in German literature of the inter-war period. Perhaps in 1992, when everybody will be commemorating the discovery of America, some American director will discover Soyfer and produce his *Broadway Melody* on, or better still, off Broadway.

The aspect of the play that concerns us here also represents the most significant difference between Soyfer's play and that by Hasenclever-Tucholsky—the difference in the image of America. Hasenclever-Tucholsky had ended their rather gentle satire on colonialism with an apotheosis of modern America. The play ends with a view of modern New York City—"Times Square with skyscrapers and fiery neon advertisements"—and Columbus's faith in the American future: "God's chosen will live in this new land. Even the poorest will be respected; none will go hungry and none will be oppressed. A statue will stand at the ocean's edge and from its mouth will issue the words: 'Give me your tired, your poor, your huddled masses yearning to breathe free.'" Whatever satire Hasenclever-Tucholsky may have implied in this ending, beyond any ambivalence they did express the hope America held for many Europeans, especially as the thirties progressed and fascism advanced. Soyfer ends his play with a similar view of New York City, but his projection into the future is a satire on all the Broadway-Melodies, those glamorous Hollywood productions that during the twenties and thirties dazzled the Europeans. In Soyfer's play Columbus's prophecy is countered with the prediction that the American dream will be perverted into a profit-oriented tinpot civilization. The argument about which prophecy will come true is not resolved in the play, but the final song shows which of the two Soyfer thought most likely to be fulfilled:

Wir steppen vorwärts und stoppen nie
Den dröhnenden Takt.
Unser Herz ist prima Stahl;
Zwar schmilzt es manches Mal,
Wenn Rührung uns packt,
doch das Hirn bleibt intakt,
Und man steppt vorwärts, und man stoppt nie
Im Takt
Der Broadway-Melodie!

Wir haben Gangster und Demokraten,
Höhlenbewohner, Filmpotentaten;
Wir lassen Kaffee auf dem Felde braten

Und löschen mit Milch den Brand,
Wir, die Vereinigten Staaten,
Gottes eigenes Land . . .

Wir steppen vorwärts und stoppen nie
Den dröhnenden Takt.
Unsre Seelen sind aus Chrom
Und singen «Old Kentucky Home»,
Wenn Rührung uns packt,
Doch das Hirn bleibt intakt,
Und man steppt weiter, und man stoppt nie
Im Takt
Der Broadway-Melodie.

Wir haben Häuser in den Himmel gebaut
Und Nigger zur Hölle geschickt,
Wir haben in dreizehn Sekunden getraut
Den ältesten Mann mit der jüngsten Braut,
Die jemals die Sonne erblickt.
Wir haben Gangster und Demokraten
Und Höhlenbewohner und Filmpotentaten,
Wir lassen Kaffee auf dem Felde braten
Und löschen mit Milch den Brand,
Wir, die Vereinigten Staaten,
Gottes eigenes Land . . .

Wir steppen vorwärts und stoppen nicht
Den stählernen Tanz.
Wir lächeln hygienisch der Not ins Gesicht
Und fordern vom Herrgott Bilanz.
Unsre Seelen sind auch Chrom
Und singen «Old Sweet Home»,
Wenn Rührung sie packt –
Aber das Hirn bleibt intakt
Und steppt immer weiter und stoppt nie
Im Takt, im Takt
Der Broadway-Melodie.

Soyfer never saw his *Broadway Melody* on the stage. Astoria-Austria finally caught up with him and involved him in a political farce that he himself could have written. The police shadowed him for weeks thinking that he was the head of the underground propaganda machine of the left. They followed him to the little theaters where his plays were performed, and what they heard and saw confirmed their suspicion. Soyfer had couched his message in fairy-tale plots that skillfully evaded the censor, but nevertheless his plays were obviously too critical, the expression of a mind that in every nation is quickly labeled subversive because it does not subscribe to uncritical self-glorifying patriotism.

But how unpatriotic was the left-winger Jura Soyfer really? A detail buried in the archives gives us some indication. Soyfer was studying German and history at the University, the very disciplines which, in those years, were especially prone to the warping influences of Nazi ideology. Those were the years when Jewish students were beaten by young Nazis while the police looked on. What Soyfer heard in the lectures of Joseph Nadler and Heinrich von Srbik must have gone against his grain often enough, and he finally gave up school because a left-wing Jew had little hope of getting a job in Schuschnigg's Austria. When he was still a student he had to fill out his registration form every semester. One of the data required was the student's ethnic affiliation – Volkszugehörigkeit. And for most students at the time there was no question that Austrians belonged to the German people. When Schuschnigg declared Austria to be the second German State, German from his point of view was an ethnic categoy, not a political one. But the left-wing student Jura Soyfer filled in the blank for ethnic affiliation with "Austrian." That is how unpatriotic he was.

In November 1937 Soyfer was arrested. The police realized soon enough that he was not the big fish they had hoped to catch, but they felt relieved when they found some underground literature in his room, reason enough to keep him behind bars for three months without trial in Vienna's largest jail, a couple of blocks away from the coffee house where his *Broadway Melody* was being performed and loudly acclaimed.

Among the papers that the police confiscated was the manuscript of a novel Soyfer had been working on since 1934. The debacle of February had caused Soyfer to write the novel, the history behind it was its theme, that is, the disintegration of Austrian Social Democracy that made it possible for the Austro-Fascists to destroy the party and outlaw it. Soyfer's manuscript, which he considered to be his most important work, was destroyed by the police before the Nazi takeover, but fortunately some friends copied chapters of the novel and preserved them. *Thus Died a Party*, as the novel is called, is a political novel but one that combines an analysis of political events with psychological insights and exemplifies sociological trends in individually conceived characters. Unlike other novels about February 1934 that were written by outsiders, Soyfer's work is especially valuable because it presents the point of view of a critical insider. He does not hide his appreciation for the party in which he had grown up; at the same time he does not hold back his disappointment, even anger at the failure of what had been an admirable political organization and the intellectual home of thousands. The book, though highly critical of Austrian Social-Democracy was also a condemnation of the reactionary forces that had undermined parliamentary government. It could never have been published in Schuschnigg's Austria. To the investigating police officer the manuscript proved once more that Soyfer was a dangerous intellectual, subversive, Marxist, and un-Austrian.

In February 1938 Schuschnigg was summoned to Berchtesgaden by Hitler and given an ultimatum, one point of which was the release of Nazis in Austrian jails. The amnesty was extended to include all political prisoners, and Soyfer was free—for twenty-five days. On March 13 he was arrested while attempting to cross the Swiss border on skis. The consequences were obvious. Soyfer was Jewish *and* had a police record for subversive left-wing activities. Either one of these "crimes" was reason enough to send him to Dachau. He died in Buchenwald in 1939—twenty-six years young.

Thus ended Soyfer's life and work in the 1930s, What did this work amount to, and what was his significance as an Austrian writer of the inter-war period? This significance is considerable indeed, and that in all three genres of his literary work. As a playwright Soyfer holds a unique position. At a time when the Austrian *Volksstück* (popular comedy) was degenerating into what the critic Oskar Maurus Fontana has called "optimistic Heurigen-parties in the theater," Soyfer revived the critical Volksstück—like Ödön von Horváth, but with an important difference: Both men were social critics, but while Horváth presented incisive diagnoses, Soyfer created dramatic parables of protest. He was a Nestroy who had read his Marx. His serious playfulness resulted in excellent theater; of all the plays written for the little theater in the Vienna of the 1930s only Soyfer's plays are being performed today.

How unique Soyfer's poetry is becomes evident if we look at the lyric anthologies of his time. The great majority of the poems considered representative reflected the concept of lyric poetry as the Romantics had developed it. It was mostly the expression of subjective experience, the experience of nature, often a kind of nature mysticism religiously toned, a poetry of "Gott und Boden" (God and Soil), one might call it. Of course there was social poetry, mostly social poetry of pity and Christian consolation. And there was realistic social poetry. The outstanding poet of this kind, and one who was not often included in those anthologies, was Theodor Kramer, the poet of those without voice, the poor and underprivileged. Kramer has often been called the poet of the fringe of society, but in the 1930s that "fringe" included thousands of unemployed and was too broad to be written off as exceptional or exotic. In his matter-of-fact presentation of the life of the victims of the depression, Kramer was indirectly also a political poet, but he was not as openly and passionately political as Soyfer was. Soyfer, like Brecht, did not believe in social poetry of the traditional type; he had little use for pity "that did not turn into indignation." He proved lyric poetry to be a legitimate expression not of private, subjective, but of public, collective emotion. His anger at social injustice, his scorn for the propagandistic theatrics of fascism, his hatred of war sparked his satire, and it was this satiric temperament that set him aside from the Austrian poets of his time. He was influenced by Karl Kraus, but as a political satirist he was closer to German writers like Mühsam,

Brecht, Kästner, and Tucholsky than to any Austrian contemporary. In none of the anthologies of Austrian poetry in the 1930s do we find any poems like Soyfer's "Song of Man Selling Himself":

The raw material prices are a-booming,
The hopeful heralds of a bullish trend.
Dow Jones is stirring, Wall Street is a-blooming,
The Stock Exchange is sprouting dividends.
One stock alone cannot keep up the pace,
One kind of merchandise is losing in this race
And stays as cheap as when all this began:
It is the reject product they call MAN.

The price of MAN in our modern age is
A couple of bucks apiece. Oh, MAN is shrewd!
Free self-delivery and starvation wages
Make him the cheapest sucker to get screwed.
MAN sells himself with all the proper wrappings,
With human dignity thrown in for trappings;
And if, dear buyer, you are low on cash,
Pay in installments for the human trash.

And if you're broke, don't think about their pay –
Just keep on buying, buy them by the herd.
Pay them with stale ideals of yesterday,
Man sells himself for any pretty word.
For of his kind there simply are too many,
He knows the market and stays cheap and meek.
He knows his value's minimal if any.
The spirit is a bargain but the flesh is weak.

(*The reply of the waiting applicants:*)

Don't get too smart, you shining business light!
You overrate your creditors' good will.
A place to live and food's a human right.
If you deny it, we present the bill.

> We've come at last to make you pay the price.
> MAN's sick and tired of being merchandise.

The special place that Soyfer merits in Austrian poetry and drama of the thirties, he also deserves in the prose of that period. As I have tried to show, his novel, even as a fragment, was a political novel of a very unique type: the novel of a political party, its structure, its function, its failures. Soyfer's achievement is all the more astounding because he had absolutely no literary model to follow. How perceptive his analysis was has been demonstrated by political scientists of our time.

No doubt Soyfer was a significant author of the 1930s, even if according to literary and political definitions of his time, his work was neither "literary" nor "Austrian." The officially recognized authors of the 1930s, those considered important enough to be awarded State prizes of Literature, i.e., authors like Waggerl, Perkonig, or Scheibelreiter were so "genuinely Austrian" that they could go on publishing after 1938, so well did they ideologically fit the new German literary canon.

The truly great writers of the time, though not officially supported, like Musil, Canetti, Broch, have long since been recognized as masters of World Literature. Soyfer can certainly not be compared with these literary giants—after all he was allowed to live only twenty-six years, and his outstanding potential was recognized by only a few, by Friedrich Torberg, for instance, who once told me: "If anybody had asked me then who was going to be the great dramatist, Soyfer or Horváth, I would have said Soyfer!" Still, Soyfer's work was of more than narrowly Austrian or regional significance. He was not only an Austrian writer of the thirties. In spite of his local roots he represented a very special kind of the often acclaimed Austrian universality. His work can very well be considered to be part of world literature if we understand by that term not the great everlasting masterworks—a sometimes dubious definition. His work belongs to the world literature of the world-wide depression, to the literature of social consciousness of a decade, when the "modern" gulf between "the people" and the writers and artists was bridged, when the fate of millions of unemployed roused the sympathy and the imagination of intellectuals in almost every country of the world.

To indicate the range of this type of world literature let me mention just the best known authors: in Germany: Brecht, above all, Anna Seghers, and Friedrich Wolf; in France, André Malraux, Louis Aragon, and André Chamson; in England: W. H. Auden, Cecil Day Lewis, and George Orwell; in Italy: Ignazio Silone, Cesare Pavese, and Elio Vittorini; in Spain: Ramón Sender; in this country: John Steinbeck, John Dos Passos, Erskine Caldwell, James T. Farrell, Richard Wright, Clifford Odets; in Chile: Pablo Neruda; in Brazil: Grazilia Ramos. Of all the Austrian writers who are specifically associated with the 1930s Soyfer comes to mind as one of such writers who in their national idiom expressed international concerns. He was one of those sons of middle-class parents who followed their conscience and took sides with the working class, with the fifty million unemployed around the world.

But here again Soyfer developed his individual style. One of the most endearing qualities of his plays is his comic spirit, which lends his work a playful lightness of touch and favorably sets them off from the left-wing plays, which, like Soyfer's, grew out of the Depression but which, like Clifford Odets's *Waiting for Lefty*, did not go beyond the heaviness of political naturalism. Soyfer left no doubt in which camp he stood in those years, and there is bitter satire and powerful indictment of social and political evils. But side by side with moral indignation and satirical wit we find genuine pathos and gentle lyricism. Side by side with the cynical bitterness of Brecht – the Brecht of the *Dreigroschenoper* – there is the wit of Nestroy and the magic of Raimund. There is political commitment and humor, a rare combination indeed in the "dirty thirties," when the radicalization of public life produced a political literature varying in color but uniform in its inhuman deadly seriousness.

I come to the last question implied in my title: was Jura Soyfer only an author of the 1930s? Or to put it differently: what is the significance of his work today? When I say "today" I can't help asking: what about Soyfer "yesterday," that is ten years ago? Twenty years ago? It took Austria forty years to remember Soyfer.

His plays were first published in 1947 by a small publisher and soon forgotten. For many years Jura Soyfer was an Austrian writer only by neglect. In 1980 his collected works were finally made accessible to the public. And even then not all the public was made aware of these works. The edition that was reviewed in twenty-seven papers and journals, including *Der Spiegel, Die Frankfurter Allgemeine Zeitung, Die Neue Zürcher Zeitung*, and *Times Literary Supplement*, was never reviewed by Austria's most prestigious paper *Die Presse* and not in Austria's oldest literary magazine *Literatur und Kritik*. I could speculate on the reasons; suffice it to say that even without such prestigious recognition, his works are becoming known again. Some of them have appeared in English, French, Italian, and Romanian translations. In recent years, his plays have been performed not only in Vienna, Salzburg, and Graz, but also in Frankfurt, Heidelberg, Zürich, and Meran. All of these productions were put on in small experimental theaters. Three of Soyfer's plays are short (though not shorter than Büchner's *Woyzeck*), but two plays are of the length traditional theater-goers expect for their money after a good supper. Maybe someday a larger stage, let us say the Volkstheater, might remember that Soyfer wrote *Volksstücke*.

Soyfer's plays are being very well received by the critics, too well perhaps. Of all his plays, *Vineta*, this haunting vision of dehumanization, has been praised for presenting a "timeless problem." What an ironic praise and what a misunderstanding. Soyfer wrote *Vineta* and his other plays in the passionate hope that the inhuman times he was presenting would be overcome at last and not be timeless.

There is no doubt that Soyfer is being read again, especially by the young generation, not by the Austrian Yuppies, the young career Austrians, but the politically conscious, ethically alive young Austrians, those who look for a link in the past to their own critical perception of the present. In Soyfer they find what they miss in the political scene today: the combination of politics and imagination, a vision instead of *Realpolitik*. For them the revival of Soyfer's work should be more than assigning him a place in a documentary museum, a place of honor of course, dignified and harmless. But Soyfer is by no means only an author for the Austrian present. Again, and more than in the thirties, perhaps, his work addresses concerns that go far beyond Austria, global concerns indeed.

Take Soyfer's *Astoria* for instance: the play, written in 1937, was a social and political satire on fascism, especially on the deceptions of fascism, the illusions kept operating by brute force. But Soyfer's political parable has an even wider dimension. Soyfer questions the idea of the state as such. Astoria is the State *an sich*, the state as complete and absolute abstraction, a state without any territory. Against this abstraction, Soyfer sets the idea of *Heimat*, not in the sense of the *Heimatkunst* that was glorified in Austrian and German literature at the time but a very different concept: the idea of a home country, or region which would overcome the alienation of living in an abstract State by a system of communal living in which the citizens would share in the decision-making. It was Soyfer's answer to the hoax of a *Volksgemeinschaft* propagated by fascism. But beyond its historic context, Soyfer's distinction points to the deep dissatisfaction with abstract and dehumanized centralization, a dissatisfaction that finds its expression in the new democratic regionalism even bioregionalism of today, in Tyrol as in Montana.

Or take Soyfer's play *Eddy Lechner's Trip to Paradise:* the play ends in a plea for human self-determination, for human freedom instead of domination by technology. But Soyfer did not overlook the difficulties of such a liberation. There is one scene in particular that strikes an uneasily present-day note. Eddy, the poor unemployed wretch on his magical journey through the past is confronted with Galileo. Eddy takes sides with the forces that say that the world does not move—with the forces of the status quo—only, as he says, "to get a job." That scene pinpoints the dilemma of the German and Austrian workers in the 1930s: the choice between starving and working, and be it for rearmament and war preparations. Hitler's miraculous abolishment of unemployment was achieved through his armament policies, and some historians say that in this country the Great Depression ended only with the war effort. (Statistics point to a macabre relationship between unemployment and war casualties. In 1932 there were five million unemployed in Germany; in 1945 there were five million dead in the same country.) Apart from all the differences between the 1930s and the 1980s, the ominous parallel exists between poor Lechner Eddy and many workers today. Again and again the arms race is defended with the argument that the arms build-up does, after all, provide jobs. Hardly any congressman can politically afford to vote against any defense project that would bring new jobs to his state. Immediate material needs, shortsightedness, refusal to rethink employment and the very concept of progress may bring us to the brink of a disaster much greater than the one Soyfer saw coming. His warnings are as relevant and as necessary today as they were then. Soyfer's cosmic farce *The End of the World* does not anticipate the lunacy of Star Wars but does imply a mentality conceivable today. In the play, the world is doomed. But as the end approaches an American invents a spaceship which promises to carry fifty people who can pay for it to safety on another planet. This rescue ship turns out to be nothing but a hoax profitable to the prepaid "inventor." We laugh at the deceived deceivers, write the ending off as a clever surprise ending, absurd and harmless as it is unrealistic. But the rescue idea as such is not unrealistic at all. The idea that a few important people might survive the destruction of the world caught on with certain people in Washington who had never read Soyfer. Last August this story went through the American press; some of you will remember it:

> The Federal Emergency Management Agency has dreamed up a 1.5 billion dollar plan to build 600 bomb shelters for use by politicians and a few other important people the administration deems worthy to survive a nuclear holocaust. FEMA's plan calls for the non-politicians and unimportant people of the nation to use "self help" to survive such an attack.

The plan was never carried out, but imagine the mentality behind it! Talking about bombshelters and the like makes me think of a passage in one of Soyfer's reportages of 1937. The title of this piece, "Be Prepared," he took not from the Boy Scout Handbook, but from the inscription above a Civil Defense display showing Salzburg under an air attack. This display in the Kärtnerstraße was supposed to lure passersby into the basement of the store to marvel at an exemplary air raid shelter,

> . . . equipped with everything to prevent suffocation as well as starvation. There are two air-regenerators: one to be operated by hand, the other one to be operated like a bicycle. Furthermore, there is a cupboard full of gas-masks and cans of food, a fire extinguisher, a special approved gas-protection-shelter-toilet complete with turf container; there are shovels for digging oneself out; there is a light generator, fed by an emergency battery in case the power plant should be destroyed, and in the eventuality of the emergency battery being buried under rubble, there are two phosphorescent boards that give a greenish glow in the dark. German patents all. And – I almost forgot – there is a telephone! In the event of a completely buried and destroyed world, we could still have the chance to put a phone call through. "Hello, is that the Stone Age? This is the Twentieth Century. We'd appreciate some technical advice for restoring peace! How's that? You are surprised that we in the technological age. . . ? But, dear friend, don't you know that our technology has other problems to work out? Almost half of our technology is busy developing means for the destruction of life; almost the other half is working hard to find the necessary counter weapons. In between there's just enough time to think up a new perfume [today we'd say deodorant, I suppose]. But to protect human life from natural forces or even to make it more worth living – really, dear friends and fellow human beings, that's not what our gas-protection-patents are for.

Reality does not have to be distorted by the satirist. Reality is the satire. That, too, Soyfer learned from Karl Kraus. And, as with Kraus, his indignation found its expression in the pathos of bitter irony. Already in 1932 Soyfer wrote his poem, "Take It Easy," a dialogue between an optimist and a *Nörgler,* as Kraus called him in *The Last Days of Mankind,* a grumbler. The optimist keeps pointing to the impossibility of war and the reassuring disarmament conferences in session. The "grumbler" keeps reminding him of the hypocrisy behind such disarmament conferences while armament is escalated. With Kraus, Soyfer knew that all he had with which to counter the madness was words, and he knew how powerless words were. Soyfer was aware of the same dilemma that besets the peace movement in our time which keeps warning the world while the world's business goes on as usual. The last lines of Soyfer's poem powerfully express this powerlessness of the word *and* the hope of making people abandon their course to destruction: "And those whom words can never teach / The calm will shock, the stillness reach! / If now no words of warning wake you, / After the storm the calm will shake you!" Soyfer belongs to the often forgotten, if not denied tradition of Austrian pacifism together with names like Berta von Suttner, Alfred Fried, Julius Braunthal, Hans Thirring, or Erich Fried in our own day. When in May 1982, 70,000 people took part in a peace demonstration in front of the Vienna City Hall, Soyfer's poems were quoted more often than those of any other Austrian writer. His "Song of the Earth" sounded as if it had been written for the occasion.

This song which ends with a triumph of hope poses a problem, however, if read in the context of the play for which Soyfer wrote it. That play was *The End of the World,* which like Kraus's *The Last Days of Mankind,* scene after scene proves that this world deserves going to hell, and yet, in contrast to Kraus's final condemnation, the world is saved, as we have seen, by nothing less than a miracle – a happy ending, but not a happy ending like one of those Nestroy tagged on to his satiric comedies. The comet that was sent out to destroy the world has fallen in love with the world, his last words are the "Song of the Earth," his declaration of love:

> I've been near this planet, this world of man,
> Much closer than you understand.

I saw it golden with fields of grain,
I saw huge shadows darken its plains,
When the bombers roared over the land,
I saw the world caught in nets of lies,
Saw poverty past comprehending.
Saw it wretched and sick—and free as the skies
With wealth and joy unending.

Full of hunger, full of bread is man's world,
Full of life, full of death is man's world,
Blessed is man's world and damned.
Infinite in misery and wealth is man's world.
Radiant with beauty and health is man's world,
And its future is glorious and grand.

This future is nearer than you understand
I've seen the new world arise.
I saw it ripening in waves of grain
Outgrowing the shadows of bombing planes,
I saw dreams repossess the skies.
The day will come when the world is well
And blessed beyond comprehending
When the world is free from its age-old spell
And enjoys its riches unending.

Full of hunger, full of bread is man's world,
etc.

The poem seems to contradict the preceding bitter play, but does it really? I think it presents two alternatives of the world and the hope that man will make the right choice after all. The two possibilities recall the words with which Sigmund Freud ended his *Civilization and Its Discontents* which appeared in 1929 and which Soyfer, who was keenly interested in psychoanalysis, probably knew:

> The question which will determine the fate of mankind seems to be whether and to what extent human culture will succeed

> in overcoming human aggression and self-destruction which disrupt human coexistence. In this regard the present time deserves special attention perhaps. In the control over natural forces, humanity has reached the point where they can annihilate each other to the last individual. They know that, and this knowledge is the reason for their present restlessness, their unhappiness, their anxiety. And now it is to be expected that the other of the two "heavenly powers," eternal eros will make every effort to assert itself in the struggle with its equally immortal opponent. But who can foresee the outcome of this conflict?

In the light of this passage the end of Soyfer's play is not simply the fairy-tale ending for which it has been criticized. It is the expression of a hope in spite of the uncertainty of the outcome. It is the same hope that triumphs in *Eddy Lechner's Trip to Paradise,* which ends with the "yes" of Eros against the "no" of self-destruction; an ending that has always reminded me of Wallace Stevens's credo: "After every no there is a yes and on that yes the future world depends." But what kind of a "yes" does Soyfer imply, imply in all of his work?

In its first issue of this year the Hamburg *Zeit* published what a number of scientists and other intellectuals gave as their answer to the question: "Hat die Hoffnung noch Zukunft?"–"Is there any future for hope?" Soyfer faced the same question in 1937. One of the answers in 1987 was given by Max Frisch, the Swiss writer who was born in 1911, a year before Soyfer, and is still alive as Soyfer could be if he had not been murdered. Max Frisch says:

> When I page through the newspapers in the morning, when I look at TV in the evening, I have no doubt that the Enlightenment, that grand experiment of the Modern Age, has failed. People do not want to know, they want to believe. Consciousness, awareness are not wanted. They only lead to responsibility. And let's face it: don't we all live better than ever before–at the expense of the Third World and at a risk that Cassandra could do nothing about. I feel

> solidarity with all those who, wherever they be in this world, resist. Resist at all levels in this world of profit maniacs. Resist with the goal that enlightenment will triumph after all . . . and that soon. There are beginnings of such resistance. Without a breakthrough to a moral reason which can only come out of resistance there won't be a twenty-first century, I am afraid. Today a call for hope is a call to resist.

Soyfer could have written that. Before 1934 he called out to resist the danger of fascism. After 1934 he called upon the audiences in the little theaters to resist apathy, the apathy of all the good people who allow the bad things to happen, the often glorified resignation of the Viennese who are proud of their motto: "Glücklich ist, wer vergißt . . ." ("Happy is he who forgets what cannot be changed.") He called out against the happy-go-lucky flirtation with disaster: as he said in one of his satirical songs in the *The End of the World:*

> Let's go dying just a little,
> Always dashing, smart and gay.
> With crash boom bang to keep your step by,
> 't won't be as bad as people say.
> First: We've always been ok.
> Secondly: to fade away
> Is about the only thing
> The underdog can do today.
> So let's try dying just a little!
> It is risky but it's fun.

His play *Vineta* ends with a plea for collective resistance against the threat of war. The sailor, having told his experience in the dead town of Wienata turns to the audience:

> Sure, I thought there is no such place as Vineta. But if one day a tidal wave should come, some big war, some big barbaric outbreak. I wonder if the whole world might not

> turn into a Vineta. But that's just in my imagination, isn't it? Because if it isn't just in my imagination, then it's a pretty serious business, isn't it? In that case all of us would have to put all our energies together, all of us and right now, and even then there might not be much time left, because no one would know when it might come, that flood. Maybe it's already quite close by now, maybe right outside the door of this hole here. And that would be something to be scared of, don't you think?

Soyfer's plea for resistance, for making the right choice before it would be too late, his hopes for a better world, were based on his faith in man's ability to shape his own fate in a rational, ethical, moral way. Looking at the world today such hopes might appear hopelessly idealistic. But let us not forget that Soyfer found the strength to believe in man even in the hell of the concentration camp. His Dachau-Song proves it. His example should prevent us from giving in to a smug and shortsightedly comfortable pessimism. And let us not forget that Soyfer's idealism was not a naive one, that it was accompanied by very realistic insights into human imperfection. His hope was the hope of a skeptic humanist who, like Max Frisch, based his precarious hope for a future on the negation of the status quo: Let me end my talk with these lines from Soyfer's "Song of the Twentieth Century Man":

> Something human struggles to be free,
> One way only that can help us know:
> All the time to ask if men we be,
> All the time to give the answer: no!
> A poor, half-finished sketch is all we are,
> A glimpse of humans in the final state.
> A tune suggested by the opening bar –
> You call us wretches human beings? –Wait!

Notes

1. All quotations are taken from *The Legacy of Jura Soyfer 1912-1939. Poems, Prose and Plays of an Austrian Antifascist.* Ed. and trans. by Horst Jarka. Montreal: Engendra Press, 1977, and *Jura Soyfer. Das Gesamtwerk.* Hrsg. Horst Jarka. Wien: Europaverlag, 1980 (paperback edition: 1984).
2. This vision also appeared in a strike song of the Textile Workers Union of America in 1947, "The Mill Was Made of Marble":

> I dreamed that I had died
> And gone to my reward – A job in Heaven's textile plant
> On a golden boulevard.
> The mill was made of marble,
> The machines were made out of gold,
> And nobody ever got tired,
> And nobody ever grew old.
> . . . .
> There was no unemployment in heaven;
> We worked steady all through the year;
> We always had food for the children;
> We never were haunted by fear.

Songs of Work and Freedom. Ed. by Edith Fowke and Joe Glazer, New York: Doubleday, 1960, p. 76f.

The Reception of Austrian Literature in the United States from 1970 to 1987

Donald G. Daviau

Der Autor beschäftigt sich unter anderem mit der Unterscheidung zwischen österreichischer und deutscher Literatur, die vielen amerikanischen Germanisten schwerfällt. Er zeigt aber auch, was für die österreichische Literatur in den USA getan wird—etwa in Fachjournalen, wie Daviaus eigenem *Modern Austrian Literature* oder in dem texanischen *Dimension* oder in *World Literature Today* aus Oklahoma. Schließlich werden Autoren mit relativ größerer Anerkennung, wenigstens in literarischen Fachkreisen, besprochen, wie Peter Handke, Elias Canetti, Thomas Bernhard, Ilse Aichinger, Ingeborg Bachmann oder Erich Fried, etc. Eine exemplarische Bibliographie über "Objekte Literatur" und einige der bekanntesten Autoren ergänzt diese Arbeit.

Literary reception is a topic that is as complicated as it is broad, and the topic of the reception of Austrian literature in the United States is no exception. Indeed, it involves one additional complicating factor not usually encountered in studying the reception of a national literature by another country, in that Austrian literature is often received under the rubric of German literature, with the English-speaking audience unaware that it is dealing with Austrian literature at all. Name identification is still a major problem, particularly in terms of the general public. Because the subject is so extensive and some of the means of mediation are so subtle and indirect that they are very difficult to document, it will not be possible to give more than a brief overview in the space available here. Nevertheless it is hoped that this survey will convey a fairly accurate understanding of the extent to which contemporary Austrian literature is presently known in the United States and the various ways in which this reception has been accomplished.

The term reception, as it is being used in this presentation, refers to the dissemination of the literature of one nation in another and its recognition, acceptance, and influence in the host country. Reception of Austrian literature in the United States occurs in two major forms: 1) academic reception, which involves awareness of the German language texts as well as reception in the form of scholarly books, articles, and reviews, papers given at conferences and other scholarly meetings, and textbooks at all levels of instruction, and 2) popular reception, which concerns works made available in English in the form of translations, along with reviews of such works in magazines and newspapers. In the following discussion both of these levels will be addressed to show which contemporary Austrian authors and works are known in the United States, how widely recognized they are, how this information has been disseminated, and the impact or influence that has resulted.

Let us first address the issues of dissemination and identification. How is Austrian literature received in the United States and to what extent is it known? The attempt to create name identification for Austrian literature is a relatively recent phenomenon, not surprising because national identification is essentially a postwar development in Austria itself. Efforts to create a national literary identity for Austria began in the late eighteenth century but were only pursued in earnest in the 1930s and 1940s by the exile writers in the United States, who emphasized the distinction between Austria and Germany in order to free Austria from the issue of war guilt. Their efforts were successful and played a major role in persuading the Allied governments to treat Austria differently than Germany after World War II.

These efforts to stress Austria's independent identity in terms of its literature aroused considerable scholarly debate as a major issue of the postwar era.[1] In earlier times, and indeed to some degree still today by diehards, Austrian literature had always been subsumed under the rubric of German literature in all university and college courses as well as in all literary histories and textbooks. Publishers too in presenting translations did not and often still do not distinguish between German and Austrian literature. There is still a long way to go in this matter of name identification, particularly in the commercial publishing business, but progress is being made steadily. For example, the situation has finally reached the point where the Modern Language Association's *Bibliography* identifies Austrian literature as such, still of course subsumed under the major heading of German literature, but at least properly identified in its own section under its own name.

In recent years a number of symposia and conferences have been devoted entirely to Austrian literature and culture, and almost all professional meetings such as the Modern Language Association (MLA), the American Association of Teachers of German (AATG), and the German Studies Association (GSA), now have a number of identifiably Austrian sections. Even in elementary language textbooks today Austrians are described as being different from Germans. Horst Jarka compiled a *Checklist of Austrian Textbooks,*[2] and at least two reading texts have been made available featuring the designation Austrian literature in the titles.[3] The vast majority of texts, however, do not single out or even identify the Austrian component, although the Austrian contribution may be substantial. Thus, in a number of ways and on a number of levels Austria and Austrian literature are increasingly establishing an individual and independent image in the academic setting. This level of mediation has not been matched by the reception of the general public, which, if it has an image of Austria at all, still has one of Lederhosen, Dirndl, Sachertorte, Strauss waltzes, and beautiful scenery as seen in the film *The Sound of Music*. Beyond this discrepancy there are still such basic problems in the minds of Americans as confusing Austria with Australia. This may sound like a joke, but unfortunately it is not.

In terms of popular reception a foreign author needs to be well established and recognized before newspaper or magazine editors will select his or her works for review. The entire reviewing system of newspapers and popular journals is so shrouded in mystery and is so subjective and eclectic that it is impossible to determine any rationale behind it. Excluding the influence of personal taste in an editor's choice of books for review, it seems fair to say on the basis of current practice that review editors are rarely interested in breaking new ground by introducing new authors but only in responding to interests which already exist. If a writer enjoys a reputation or is in the news in any way, he or she will be reviewed; otherwise the probability of selection is not great. Even acclaim at home is not necessarily persuasive. A good case in point is the extremely slow reception of Thomas Bernhard, who has only recently begun to receive some sporadic reviews in American newspapers and has yet to achieve mention in popular magazines like *Time* or *Newsweek*.

Academic reviewing is no more systematic than the popular side. Very few scholarly journals review primary literature but concentrate on secondary works. What is reviewed depends on the willingness of presses to send their books and then the cooperation of faculty members to write the reviews and deliver them in timely fashion. Many books are not reviewed simply because colleagues never submit reviews of books they are sent. Scholarly reviews also usually appear two to four years after the book has been published. Since the readers of specialty journals all know German, the reviews usually are of German versions, and translations of primary works are generally ignored. No American journal attempts to provide anything even approximating systematic coverage in the form of reviews or even lists of recently translated Austrian books. Only *World Literature Today* (*WLT*), edited by Ivar Ivask, regularly features reviews of current primary works, though not in any manner approaching comprehensiveness. It is also the only current journal that devotes attention to translations. *WLT* can claim the additional merit of bringing reviews out fairly promptly, that is, usually in the same year as the book. The only other significant source of information about new books is the Viennese journal *Literatur und Kritik*, edited by Kurt Klinger, which is read by some specialists but not widely disseminated in the United States.

It should be clear from the above that the academic reception of Austrian literature exists in a fairly advanced state and remains in a developing trend, while the popular reception is still in a state of infancy. From highschool language classes all the way through graduate courses and continuing to scholarly meetings Austrian literature is highly visible at all levels and receives proportional attention far in excess of its geographic size vis-à-vis Germany and certainly far beyond anything accorded to Switzerland. Many universities, for example, have introduced a course on turn-of-the-century Austrian culture. The efforts of the German Summer School at Taos should also be mentioned, for Austrian literature and culture have always been featured there. Generally the prominence of Austrian literature in the academic setting can be attributed to the large number of scholars who have been attracted to the field and to the various societies such as the American Council for the Study of Austrian Literature (ACSAL), the Kafka Society, and the International Arthur Schnitzler Research Association, which actively promote Austrian literature. Of primary importance to all of these endeavors is the support and encouragement of the Austrian Institute in New York. Without this assistance many of the academic efforts and projects would be hampered and certainly rendered less effective, if they could be carried out at all.

The highly positive situation in the academic sphere changes radically when one turns to the open market of popular reception. Without the impetus of special interest groups or individuals to stimulate mediation, contemporary Austrian writers on their own have not commanded widespread attention either by publishers or critics. In terms of recognition and reception in this country Peter Handke is the best-known writer on the contemporary scene by a considerable margin, followed at quite some distance by Thomas Bernhard and Elias Canetti, and at still further remove by Erich Fried, Ilse Aichinger, and Wolfgang Bauer. There has been an effort to stimulate interest in Canetti ever since he won the Nobel Prize in 1981, but, given the intellectual nature of Canetti's writings, it is unlikely that he will ever achieve broad popularity here any more than he has in Austria. For the rest there are individual volumes by a small number of writers – Fritz Hochwälder, Franz Innerhofer, Friederike Mayröcker, and Gerhard Roth – but not a sufficient quantity of work in translation to attract much attention. None of the contemporary Austrian writers has yet achieved ready name identification in the United States on the order, say, of Kafka or Freud, not surprising, when one considers that even Arthur Schnitzler, Franz Werfel, and Stefan Zweig never achieved general recognition, although they are the most frequently trans-

Modern Austrian Literature (*MAL*) with a special issue on narrative prose, after an Austrian Literature Symposium at Stanford University in 1979. The issue was put together at the German Summer School in Taos, where Austrian artist in residence Georg Eisler provided the cover drawing of "The Rockies near Taos."

lated Austrian authors. Even films made from the works of Austrian writers usually do not contribute to recognition, because they fail to identify the author more than by name in the credits, if at all. The same is true of other forms. How many opera lovers, for example, know that the libretti for the Strauss operas were written by Hugo von Hofmannsthal? Austrian plays have not yet found acceptance in American theaters, usually an effective means of reception. None of the leading contemporary dramatists, including Handke, Bernhard, Canetti, and Bauer have reached off-Broadway or even university theaters yet. Indeed, except for a few productions of Handke, Hochwälder, and Bauer, they have not been introduced into the American theater at all.

In terms of performances Handke again leads the list. The Repertory Theater of Lincoln Center in New York produced *Publikumsbeschimpfung, Selbstbezichtigung,* and *Das Mündel will Vormund sein* in 1971, and *Ritt über den Bodensee* in 1972. Also, *Kaspar* was performed at the Chelsea Theater in the Brooklyn Academy of Music in 1973. None of these productions was particularly well received, and it remained for the performance of *They Are Dying Out* (*Die Unvernüftigen sterben aus*) at the Yale Repertory Theater in 1979 to become the first successfully received presentation of a Handke play in the United States.

Another major production was the performance of Bernhard's play *Eve of Retirement* in Gitta Honegger's translation at the Guthrie Theater in Minneapolis in 1981. The performance received mixed but on balance favorable reviews, but still produced no echo; neither the Guthrie nor any other theaters continued with additional Bernhard productions. Honegger, who is a director in the Yale Repertory Theater, planned a production there and also off Broadway, but neither possibility was carried out. This situation affords striking contrast to Austria, Germany, and Switzerland, where Bernhard is a staple of the theater at the present time.

Productions of plays by other authors were even more limited: a performance of Hochwälder's *Lazaretti or the Saber-toothed Tiger* at Rockwell College in 1985, and one performance of Bauer's *Party for Six* at Stanford University in 1983, with the

DIMENSION

Contemporary German Arts and Letters / Volume 12, No. 3, 1979

Department of Germanic Languages / THE UNIVERSITY OF TEXAS AT AUSTIN

A. LESLIE WILLSON, *Editor*
HANS BENDER, *Advisory Editor*
PETER PABISCH, *Guest Editor*

SPECIAL ISSUE ON GERMAN DIALECT LYRICS (=DIE NEUE MUNDART)

Dimension, special issue on German dialect lyrics, with many examples from Austrian authors. The manuscript was finished at the German Summer School of New Mexico in Taos Ski Valley and illustrated by Austrian artist in residence Georg Eisler, Summer 1979.

author in attendance. The world première of a second Bauer play, "A Wonderful Morning in the Barber Shop," was held at the Max Kade Institute in Los Angeles in 1988, made possible by a subsidy of the Austrian Institute.

Concerning professional journals that include articles and reviews of Austrian literature, there is in addition to *The German Quarterly, Monatshefte, The German Studies Review,* and *Seminar, Modern Austrian Literature,* the only journal outside of Austria exclusively devoted to Austrian literature. In addition to the publication of articles and reviews *Modern Austrian Literature* as an Allied Organization of the MLA always sponsors two or three Austrian sections at the annual meeting, and usually sponsors a section on Austrian literature at the AATG and GSA meetings as well. Another journal which contributes to the awareness of Austrian literature by presenting translations is *Dimension,* edited by Leslie Willson. Most notable are the two issues devoted to Austrian literature, one in 1975, containing selections by all of the major contemporary writers and a number of lesser names, guest edited by Ernst Jandl and Hans P. Prokop, and another featuring translations of dialect works in 1979, guest edited by Peter Pabisch. There is also the special issue on *Contemporary German Arts and Letters* (1983), which although indicating only German in the title includes approximately fifteen Austrian writers. A more popular but important publication is *Austria Today,* which, lavishly illustrated, provides the most current information about happenings in Austria in all areas, along with feature articles.

Another organization that disseminates information about Austrian literature and culture is the American Council for the Study of Austrian Literature (ACSAL), which sponsors an annual section on "Austrian Literature in the Classroom" at the AATG meeting, coordinated by Maria-Luise Caputo-Mayr. The papers from these sections are collected and published periodically in a series called *Österreich in amerikanischer Sicht.*[4] In addition, ACSAL now sponsors an annual symposium at the University of California, Riverside,[5] the papers from which are published either as a special issue of *Modern Austrian Literature*[6] or in separate book form.[7] ACSAL also sponsors a newsletter, covering Austrian activities, meetings, reviews, and other cultural information.

Other institutions and agencies help to spread information about Austrian literature and assist in the effort to create an Austrian presence and image. The Center for Austrian Studies at the University of Minnesota, which until 1989 was directed by William Wright, disseminates information about Austria through an annual symposium. Wright continues as editor of the *Austrian History Yearbook*, which features articles and book reviews on Austrian history.

Stanford University has also become identified with Austrian studies. Each Spring semester Stanford brings an Austrian faculty member to the campus to give courses on a different specialty, such as literature, theater, or political science. Stanford has also sponsored a number of symposia, several of which have resulted in such publications as the volume edited by Kurt Steiner, *Modern Austria*, which provides a comprehensive overview of the contemporary cultural and political scene.

The University of Southern California has also helped to disseminate information about Austrian literature through its lecture series and through symposia. The director of the affiliated Max Kade Institute, Cornelius Schnauber, presents programs on Austrian, German, and Swiss writers. Other universities have contributed to creating an Austrian presence by devoting a specific symposium or conference to Austrian literature: the State University of New York at Albany under the auspices of Joseph Strelka on Celan, Kraus, Saiko, and Csokor; the State University of New York at Stony Brook through the efforts of Barbara Elling on Celan, Trakl, and Kafka; Fredonia College in New York through the efforts of Robert Rie and Marion Sonnenfeld a symposium in 1981 commemorating the 100th anniversary of Stefan Zweig; and the University of Houston in 1979 under the direction of Erika Nielson a conference titled "Finale and Prelude: Turn-of-the-Century Vienna." All of these conferences have resulted in publications, generally subsidized by the Austrian Institute. The list is not comprehensive and does not include conferences in Canada and papers given at regularly scheduled meetings, including such forums as the Kentucky Foreign Language Conference and other regional organizations. Austrian literature is also represented in all of the books, conferences, and programs dealing with exile literature, as well as at the meetings of groups such as Women in German.

Over and above the efforts of these organizations and individuals to spread awareness of Austrian literature and culture there stands the work of the Austrian Institute in New York. The Institute has created a known Austrian presence in New York through its many programs and exhibits, its newsletter, and the many speakers, writers, and artists it sponsors on American tours as well as for writers-in-residence programs. It has exerted influence throughout the United States through the subsidy of many of the symposia and the resulting publications mentioned above. A number of volumes, including translations, have also been published in recent years thanks to the financial support of the Austrian Institute. The importance of the Institute's contribution would be difficult to overestimate. Without it the Austrian activity and presence in the United States would soon be reduced to a small fraction of what it is today.

As can be seen from this overview, Austrian literature still remains largely a topic for specialists or at least for a specialized audience. This is reflected in the fact that not many commercial publishers have elected to publish translations of Austrian authors. The major firms are the Frederick Ungar Publishing Company, now absorbed into the Continuum Press with the death of Mr. Ungar, Suhrkamp, the Continuum Press, Knopf, Schocken, the Camden House Press, and the Fairleigh Dickinsen Press. During his publishing career Frederick Ungar, a native Austrian with an abiding love for Vienna, contributed more to the reception of Austrian literature in the United States than any other commercial publisher. He was willing to risk volumes that no other press would undertake, such as an abridged translation of Karl Kraus's *The Last Days of Mankind,*[8] a collection of three plays of Nestroy,[9] a volume of three plays by Fritz Hochwälder,[10] *An Austrian Literature Handbook,*[11] and biographical studies of individual Austrian writers such as Hofmannsthal and Schnitzler. He has recently edited and published a volume of poetry entitled *Austria in Poetry and History,* knowing in advance that he would lose money on such an enterprise, as he claimed he did on most of his other

Austrian publications, including the *Handbook.* As the list of his publications makes clear and as he has emphasized in the preface to *Austria in Poetry and History,* where he insists that there is no worthwhile contemporary poetry, Ungar was a traditionalist who abhorred the direction and tendencies of the modern scene both personally and from a publisher's point of view. But he was also a humane individual whose values extended beyond the balance sheet.

The record of sales for translations of Austrian literature unfortunately confirms Ungar's judgment. The results have been disappointing, and the poor profit potential has severely limited publishers' interest in undertaking translations. The Fairleigh Dickinson Press has published an *Anthology of Austrian Drama,* edited by Douglas A. Russell, as well as a volume by Beth Bjorklund entitled *Contemporary Austrian Poetry,* which takes its place alongside *Austrian Poetry Today,* edited by Milne Holton and Herbert Kuhner, published by Schocken Books. All of these works had to be subsidized by the Austrian Institute to interest publishers. Many of Ungar's books were also subsidized at least in part. The Continuum Press intends to publish a *German Library,* presenting a hundred volumes of translations of German and Austrian writers, but it is staying largely with the established writers who belong to the accepted literary canon and is not venturing to any degree into contemporary literature. Finally, Camden House Press has published a number of translations, including works of Ebner-Eschenbach (*Seven Stories*),[12] Nestroy (*Three Comedies*),[13] and Hans Weigel (*Ad Absurdum: A Hans Weigel Potpourri*),[14] along with several critical studies devoted to Otto Basil's *Plan,*[15] Heimito von Doderer,[16] and Zweig.[17] These volumes reach only primarily academic audiences, and none of these books has been reviewed in either newspapers or popular magazines. Indeed few of them have even been reviewed extensively in scholarly journals. Most of these publications were made possible by grants from the Austrian Institute, all were published in small printings, and it seems unlikely that any of them will ever enjoy a second printing. The same may be said of the Austrian volumes published by Peter Lang and by the University Press of America, most if not all of them published only with the aid of subsidies.

A volume deserving of special mention is the *Anthology of Modern Austrian Literature,* edited by Adolf Opel, containing a comprehensive introduction and translations of a large sampling of contemporary authors. It is the only commercial volume that includes a generous number of narrative prose works. The book was distributed in the U.S. by the Humanities Press and received neither reviews nor publicity. A more successful commercial anthology, *German Stories,* by Harry Steinhauer, a book often reprinted in English and as a dual language volume, contains ten stories, including four by Austrians – Stifter, Schnitzler, Kafka, and Aichinger – but without designation as such. So too the anthology of Michael Hamburger, *German Poetry 1910–1975* contains eighteen Austrian poets who are not so identified.

Turning to the individual authors, the best known of the contemporary authors in the United States, according to a check of the *1986–1987 Books in Print,* is, as mentioned, Peter Handke, who shows eleven titles currently available in English (for these references and all other mentioned translations see the bibliography in Appendix B.) Most of these works are available in paperback, showing that the publisher expects more than just sales to libraries. The runs of hardback editions are usually not extensive, ranging from five hundred to three thousand copies, while paperback editions may run to ten thousand copies. Handke has been more widely reviewed in the popular press than any of the other contemporary Austrian writers, and he has also received more attention from scholarly critics. A bibliography of Handke, Thomas Bernhard, and Wolfgang Bauer in 1981 showed approximately three times as many articles devoted to Handke than to Bernhard with the same proportion again between Bernhard and Bauer.[18] Since that bibliography appeared, Canetti, Fried, and Aichinger have replaced Bauer in number of translations and in critical attention. Despite the number of books in print and the critical reception he has been accorded, Handke still cannot be considered a well known or popular author in the United States. His plays have not yet been performed to any extent, and his films have not been brought to the United States. Having grown more conservative of late, he may yet produce a work or body of works that will command more widespread public attention here. The extensive bibliography of secondary works shows that scholars clearly regard him as a major literary figure, as he is considered in Europe, but the popular reception has been insignificant by comparison, although he is expected to be known to sophisticated readers. In a review of Gerhard Roth in 1980 John Updike felt free to make comparisons to Handke, showing that he assumed familiarity at least among readers of the *New Yorker.*[19]

Handke took the academic world here by storm, just as he did in Europe, but now that he has given up some of his fireworks and gimmickry, critics have begun to evaluate his works more critically. For example, in a recent review of Handke's newest novel, *Die Wiederholung* (1986), an appropriate title since it contains the typical Handke canon of alienation, the journey, and language, Theodore Ziolkowski upbraids him for his verbosity. "What Joyce and Hofmannsthal accomplished in a luminous paragraph or two takes Handke many pages. The occasional insights are a large price to pay for the langueurs of rustic repetition."[20]

As with Handke, Elias Canetti, the only other author to rival him in number of translations at the present time, also reveals the same sharp contrast between academic and popular reception. Much of the attention devoted to Canetti came belatedly after 1981 when he was awarded the Nobel Prize for Literature. Since then the Seabury Press has published eleven of his works, many of them in paperback, but Canetti's plays remain to be discovered by the American theater. Neither his study of eccentric behavior set against the burning of the Palace of Justice in Vienna in 1927, the novel *Die Blendung,* originally published in English as *The Tower of Babel* and now reissued as *Auto-da-fé,* nor his massive psychological study *Crowds and Power* (*Masse und Macht*), or his various books of essays, inspire little hope that he will ever attract a readership beyond academic and intellectual circles.

Thomas Bernhard, who rivals and perhaps even surpasses Handke and Canetti in popularity in Austria, is still having a difficult struggle becoming accepted in America.[21] He currently has ten titles in English translation, six novels and four plays. All of the dramas have appeared in the *Performing Arts Journal* and are thus limited in distribution. There has been only one attempt to perform a Bernhard play to date, as mentioned, and in general the status of Bernhard in this country stands in almost diametrical contrast to his reception in Austria and Germany, where he presently appears to rank above Handke. Even American scholars are not currently devoting the attention to Bernhard that one might assume he merits on the basis of his productivity and his Austrian reputation.

After Handke, Canetti, and Bernhard, the situation of contemporary Austrian literature in English translation thins out quickly. Wolfgang Bauer currently has two titles in print, *Change and Other Plays* (originally published in 1973), and *Memory Hotel,* which appeared as a stage manuscript in a publication of the Theater Communications Group in 1981. Although he is recognized in Austria as an established writer of importance, he has yet to make the transition to this country. As mentioned, a second production was scheduled in 1988 at the Max Kade Institute in Los Angeles. None of Bauer's works has been reviewed in popular magazines or newspapers, and the brief notices in *Library Journal* and *Choice* indicate that he is considered an author for academic institutions with large theater departments.

Ilse Aichinger currently has two American volumes of translations in print, *Bound Man and Other Stories,* which has gone through a number of editions, and *Selected Poetry and Prose.* Two additional volumes appeared in England, edited by James C. Alldridge: *Selected Short Stories and Dialogs* (1966, in German) and *Ilse Aichinger* (1969, in English). The latter volume appeared in a series called *Modern German Authors. Texts and Contexts,* and contains the translations found in the earlier volume along with a thirty-eight page monograph presenting Aichinger in most favorable terms. Her major novel about a young Jewish girl's tribulations and persecution during World War II, *Die grüne Hoffnung* (1946), translated as *Herod's Children* in 1963, is no longer in print. Selections of her work have appeared in some twenty-five anthologies. The approximately fifteen reviews or brief mentions of her writings have been consistently favorable.

Erich Fried, who elected to stay in England rather than return from exile to Austria after the war, but who continues to write in German, has three works in translation at the present time: *On Pain of Seeing* (1969), *One Hundred Poems Without a Country* (1980), and *Four German Poets: Günter Eich, Hilde Domin, Erich Fried, Günter Kunert,* translated and edited by Agnes Stein (1980). The reviews to date in *World Literature Today* (8), *The Times Literary Supplenent* (3), and in library journals (2) recognize Fried's leftist political activist tendencies but rate him as "a very fine poet," whose poems are intended to fight against the alienation caused by the war. He is acknowledged for his efforts to deal with the ideological and military issues in Germany, Vietnam, Chile, and Israel, as well as with such concerns as the political extremism represented by the Baader-Meinhof group. He is particularly recognized for his gifted use of the German language and for his linguistic virtuosity displayed in word play, patterns of association, and montages – the techniques of concrete poetry that make some of his works untranslatable. His linguistic craftsmanship sometimes gives reviewers the impression that he is reveling in his technical skill for its own sake, but this view could merely be a misunderstanding of the techniques of concrete poetry. He is described in reviews as a poet of wit and humor and as "one of the few contemporary German [sic] poets of commitment to have mastered the art of public poetry, of putting across a political standpoint without succumbing to the twin pitfalls of bombast and naively overstating the obvious. . . . Fried goes beyond the surface to relate issues to underlying enduring themes such as aggression, injustice, and oppression."[22] Reviewers are almost unanimous in praising the translations of Fried's works, and the only negative comment is the feeling that he publishes too much, issuing new books frequently with the same poems in different groupings. All in all Fried, like Aichinger, has been presented in English in a most positive manner.

Franz Innerhofer gained quick recognition in Austria on the basis of his first novel, *Schöne Tage,* which joined the trend of *Anti-Heimat* literature in the 1960s. This autobiographical work, depicting the hard life of a young illegitimate boy growing up virtually as an indentured servant on his father's farm, was followed by *Schattseite, Die großen Wörter,* and finally *Der Emporkömmling,* further tracing the course of the protagonist's life into factory work, the university, a beginning career as a writer, and finally back to the farm as a mature man. Of these works only *Schöne Tage* has been translated, as *Beautiful Days,* by Anselm Hollo in 1976. It was distributed without fanfare in this country by Patton Distributors. The book received only three reviews: in *Publisher's Weekly,* the *New Statesman,* and the *New York Times Book Review* section. In addition, the German version of the sequel *Schattseite* was reviewed in the *London Times Literary Supplement,* which still reviews German books while no American periodical does. *World Literature Today* also brought short reviews of the *Die großen Wörter* and *Der Emporkömmling.*

The reviews of *Beautiful Days* are generally favorable, if not overly enthusiastic. *Publisher's Weekly* describes "this unusually skillful first novel" as a "deep and brutal account of the author's childhood on an Austrian farm in the 1950s, tracing his life to age seventeen when he is finally able to leave the farm and find kindness and encouragement for the first time."[23] Richard Gilman's review in the *New York Times* goes beyond a mere plot summary to comment on Innerhofer's "hard, dry, matter-of-fact style" with only an occasional elegiac note or piece of metaphysical questioning allowed to vary its controlled icy recounting of events. The result is a novel that many readers, educated to expect and value complication, development, density of texture, will be likely to find "narrow" and "boring."[24] Gilman notes the conventionality of the book, and this same characterization is applied to *Schattseite,* which seems "more like a documentary than a novel; it reads like straight reporting."[25] At the present time *Beautiful Days* is no longer in print, and there is no indication that any of Innerhofer's other works are currently being considered for translation.

Friederike Mayröcker has been recognized as one of the leading, if not the leading poet in Austria since the 1950s, and she has been awarded every literary prize that Austria offers to substantiate her reputation. Despite her acclaim in her native country she has not yet been introduced into the English-speaking world to any corresponding extent. Her major champion in English is Beth Bjorklund through her critical studies, book reviews of Mayrocker's German writings, and translations of her poems. No entire volume of Mayröcker's poetry has yet appeared in English but only selections in the anthologies previously mentioned. Instead, Mayröcker is represented by two children's books, which have been translated and illustrated: *Sinclair Sophocles. The Baby Dinosaur* (1974), translated by Renate Moore and Linda Haywood and illustrated by Angela Kaufmann, and *Pegas the Horse*, illustrated by Angelica Kaufmann (1982).

The review of *Sinclair Sophocles* in the *Library Journal* is not favorable: "The Adventures of Boy and Dinosaur . . . are recounted in a trite, tongue in cheek manner and the ending is mushy. While there is a demand for dinosaur books at this level, this poorly written and illustrated offering has neither informational nor entertainment value."[26] The review in Wilson Library *Bulletin* is only slightly more positive.[27] The Chicago University Center for Children's Books considers *Sophocles* "an unconvincing fantasy illustrated with sophisticated, interestingly stylized pictures. The writing style is haughting and static, perhaps due to translation, but the primary weaknesses [lie] in the story line . . . meandering and pointless, the story seems only an exercise in combining impossibilities."[28] *Pegas the Horse* is considered to lack coherence in theme. The narrative is full of "private references and fragmented scenes," but this part of the book follows an introduction that invites the child to be a writer and artist.

The most noteworthy aspect of these reviews is the fact that the very qualities of "combining impossibilities and improbabilities" and "indulging in leaps of thought and word association at random" that are considered weaknesses represent the very qualities that have contributed to Mayröcker's outstanding reputation as a serious poet, at least in the eyes of academic critics to date. In the scholarly reviews Mayröcker is praised by Bjorklund for her "discerning sensibility, imaginative power, and verbal precision," which combined make her "the strongest contemporary writer in the German-speaking world."[29] Mayröcker is praised by M. Goth for her "dazzling capacity for free association" and her "poetic imagination which releases itself into an ever-flowing stream of sensitive reminiscences and images." Readers are warned that the first reading might cause "syntactic confusion and psychic puzzlement," but one is attracted to reread and expose oneself again to the "shower of colors, sounds, and movements, the sensorial potency, pictorial acuteness and dramatic mobility of the images and poetic evaluations."[30]

Thus far Mayröcker has received seven reviews of German editions of her works in *World Literature Today*, four reviews of her children's books in library journals, and one review in the *London Times Literary Supplement*, of another children's book, *Fantom Fan* (1972), which has not yet been translated. Mayröcker illustrates a commonplace, namely, that the number of translations of a poet's work stands in direct relationship to the linguistic difficulty of the texts. Because of the complexity of her works translators will always have to select carefully what is capable of adequate rendition, unless one decides merely to indulge in poetic paraphrase. The same holds true for the works of Ernst Jandl as well as of most other contemporary poets.

Gerhard Roth is probably less well known than any of the other writers discussed so far (except Innerhofer), and yet Austrian and German critics have already begun to accept him as a modern classic. Possibly they are influenced by the fact that S. Fischer in Germany has become his publisher, generally a sign of quality, for Fischer has traditionally published the best Austrian writers. Despite his reputation in Austria and Germany Roth is represented in English by only one translation, of his novel *Winterreise* (1979), translated by Joachim Neugroschel. To date Roth has received six reviews of his various works in German in *World Literature Today*. In English there have been reviews of *Winterreise* in the *New Statesman*, *The Atlantic Monthly*, the *New York Times Literary Supplement*, and the *New Yorker*. Neither the *New Statesman* nor the *Atlantic Monthly* found much that was positive in the book nor were they impressed with Neugroschel's translation. Roth's hero is described as "a provincial school teacher who suffers from the currently fashionable disease of alienation. He wanders about Italy, drinking and making love to a young woman almost as bored and ruthless as he is himself, and finally drifts, still aimless from the reader's ken. The fellow's 'nothing matters' state of mind is most convincingly presented but becomes, by its very nature monotonous. What variety the novel offers lies in the erotic gymnastics, which are frequent, explicit, and suggest copulation between animated pretzels."[31] John Updike's review in the *New Yorker*, written in the hip style of that magazine, has fun at the expense of the work but at the same time manages to present a reasonably fair appraisal. He begins by mentioning that Roth's novel won a prize for the best work "depicting with great literary seriousness the human experience of alienation."[32] offered by the German literary magazine *Südwest Funk*. The review is a detailed plot summary with Updike's breezy commentary, tracking the alienated protagonist from his bored experience as a teacher through his Italian journey, which does nothing to improve his dejected alienated spirit, to his decision finally to travel to Alaska where the climate would match his spirit and where he "hopes for nothing." The only real trouble with this book, according to Updike, besides the translation, which he feels is not always felicitous, is that the protagonist "feels too conscientiously determined to carry off the alienation prize."[33]

Finally, there are five reviews in library journals, all containing a brief plot summary and lukewarm recommendations. The translation is again faulted, with one reviewer pointing out a sentence that was translated to mean exactly the opposite of what the original had stated. Another critic writes: "Despite Roth's impressive contribution to the literature of alienation . . . Nagl's search for numbness and invulnerability is an acutely depressing experience for the reader."[34] There is one favorable review: "A characteristic piece of first rate modern European fiction . . . this is strong stuff vigorously grounded in excesses of the flesh, in hauntingly overripe landscapes both of the mind and of Mediterranean terrain, in suggestive symbolism, and in themes of alienation. It is also beautifully written and will reward sophisticated readers of current avant-garde fiction."[35]

Hans Weigel, the former cabarettist turned author, critic, and cultural commentator, is represented in English by one book, *Ad*

Absurdum. A Hans Weigel Potpourri, translated by Katharina Wilson and Robert Harrison. Since the book has appeared so recently there are no reviews yet. The book will probably be confined to an academic audience and not reach the general public, the reverse of the situation in Austria, where Weigel is largely ignored by scholars but eagerly read by the public for his wit, humor, and Krausian attacks on every manner of literary, social, and political ill or folly. Since the specialized university audience that would be interested in Weigel can read German, it would be better advised to read the texts in the original, since so much of Weigel's strength resides in his virtuoso use of language, which makes him difficult to translate well.

Weigel is an institution in Austria because of his outspokenness and because he has played a leading role as an entrepreneur and power behind the scenes since he returned from exile in Switzerland in 1946. But because of the nature of his writings Weigel is not known here to any but specialists in Austrian literature, who regard him highly for his manifold contributions to the literary scene. For example, he helped the breakthrough of young postwar poets and has continued to foster young talent. Although he has written a satirical novel *Der grüne Stern* (1946) and several plays, he is mainly known as a critic or in his words "as the proprietor in Vienna of a one-man writing factory, known throughout the city, which operates on a 24-hour-a-day, 7-day-a-week schedule, producing, as the occasion arises, works of drama, fiction, and journalism."[36] Since he deals primarily with questions of language and with the specific internal conditions in Austria from an insider's point of view, it is not readily apparent what his largely polemical and satirical writings would have to say to a general American audience.

Like Weigel, Fritz Hochwälder has received very little reception in English, despite the volume of five plays introduced by Martin Esslin, *The Public Prosecutor and Other Plays,* the translation of the *Raspberry Picker* in the volume *An Anthology of Austrian Drama,* edited by Douglas A. Russell, and the college production of *Lazaretti* at Rockwell College in 1985, in the translation by James Schmitt. Hochwälder, who died in October 1986 and was returned from his exile in Switzerland to be buried in an "Ehrengrab" in Vienna, is virtually forgotten in Austria at present in the sense that none of his plays has been performed in recent years.

This is the essential list of Austrian authors represented in English translation to date, a relatively sparse sampling when one considers that there are well over a thousand active writers in Austria today with at least a hundred of recognized stature. Many of the prominent names are available at least in a minimal sampling in the various available anthologies. For example, there are approximately fifty authors represented in Beth Bjorklund's anthology, *Contemporary Austrian Poetry*, forty-five authors in Milne Holton and Herbert Kuhner's dual language volume *Austrian Poetry Today*, and the same number in Frederick Ungar's volume *Austria in Poetry and History*. There are about sixty authors represented in Alfred Opel's *Anthology of Modern Austrian Literature* and twenty-nine in the Jandl special Austrian edition of *Dimension*. Another useful anthology containing fewer poets but more selections by each is a volume entitled *Six Major Austrian Poets: The Vienna Group*, translated and edited by Rosemarie Waldrop and Harriet Watts, which includes Friederike Mayröcker, Friedrich Achleitner, Konrad Bayer, Ernst Jandl, H. C. Artmann, and Gerhard Rühm. In terms of drama we have already mentioned the volume of Hochwälder's plays published by Ungar and the anthology of *Austrian Drama*, edited by Douglas A. Russell, containing plays by Nestroy, Grillparzer, Schnitzler, Hofmannsthal, Werfel, and Hochwälder. Since different authors are rerpesented in each of these anthologies, they provide collectively a sampling of well over a hundred writers.

To date there is no specifically Austrian literary history in English, but there are resource books containing information about contemporary writers. Ungar's *Handbook of Austrian Literature* contains brief commentaries on many of the leading twentieth-century writers, although it lacks information on recent authors since the book was published in 1973. A useful reference volume for contemporary writers is *Major Figures of Contemporary Austrian Literature*, which contains essays on Aichinger,

Artmann, Bauer, Bernhard, Canetti, Ebner, Fried, Frischmuth, Handke, Innerhofer, Jandl, Jonke, Mayröcker, Roth, and Turrini. The volume also contains an introduction and bibliography of primary and secondary works in German and English. The second volume, *Major Figures of Modern Austrian Literature,* (1989), includes essays on Ingeborg Bachmann, Hermann Broch, Christine Busta, Paul Celan, Franz Theodor Csokor, Heimito von Doderer, Albert Paris Gütersloh, Fritz Hochwälder, Christine Lavant, Alexander Lernet-Holenia, Robert Musil, Joseph Roth, George Saiko, Friederich Torberg, and Franz Werfel. There are five additional volumes in preparation, which will result in a series covering Austrian literature from approximately 1800 (Grillparzer) to the present. Another useful volume for the contemporary scene is the work of Alan Best and Hans Wolfschütz, *Modern Austrian Writing Literature and Society after 1945,* which contains essays on Hochwälder, Doderer, Gütersloh, Canetti, Saiko, Horvàth, Celan, Aichinger, Fried, Bernhard, Jandl, Handke, and Bauer along with the "Wiener Gruppe" and the "Grazer Gruppe." A good recent book by Peter Demetz, *After the Fires* contains an excellent but necessarily limited overview of postwar Austrian literature. For the earlier generation the volume of C. E. Williams, *The Broken Eagle. The Politics of Austrian Literature from Empire to Anschluß,* treats Hofmannsthal, Bahr, Schnitzler, Werfel, J. Roth, Zweig, Doderer, Musil, and Kraus.

Another reference work currently in preparation is the *Dictionary of Twentieth-Century Austrian Prose Writers* (Gale Publishing Co.), which in two volumes will contain some fifty-five essays along with complete bibliographies of primary and secondary works. Along the same lines the Salem Press is preparing a volume on European novelists entitled, *Master Plots II: World Fiction,* which will include works of approximately thirty Austrian writers. The entries, approximately eight to ten pages long, deal with individual works and provide a plot summary along with some critical commentary to make them useful to people who desire quick orientation about a specific novel.

Other volumes which have contributed importantly to the awareness of the Austrian scene and have more or less become standard reference works remain available: Carl Schorske's *Fin-de-Siècle Vienna,* which was very widely reviewed in the popular press and earned a Pulitzer Prize, William Johnston's *The Austrian Mind,* Allan Janik and Stephen Toulmin's *Wittgenstein's Vienna,* Jonathan Miller's *Freud, the Man, his World, his Influence,* and Jane Kallir's *Schoenberg's Vienna.* In this connection it might be mentioned that Schoenberg and Wittgenstein have achieved more widespread name recognition than many of the writers.

Although the popular reception of contemporary writers is still in its infancy, at the same time there continues to be considerable reception of Austrian literature through the works of older authors that are either kept in print or are just being printed for the first time. Translations of Grillparzer and Nestroy, for example, are constantly appearing, as well as books and articles about them. A number of Austrian writers are represented in the Twayne Author's Series, and writers like Kafka, Hofmannsthal, Schnitzler, Bahr, Beer-Hofmann, Joseph Roth, Musil, Rilke, Trakl, Kraus, Soyfer, Broch, Doderer, Werfel, and Zweig all have had either biographies, critical studies, or works published in English recently. Ingeborg Bachmann, Thomas Bernhard, Paul Celan, and Peter Handke are the authors who continue to receive the greatest critical attention at scholarly meetings.

In summary, it can be seen that the academic reception of Austrian writers is substantial, while the popular reception lags disappointingly behind, a faint echo of the university scene. It is particularly evident that contemporary Austrian literature has not made a serious impact or aroused any particular enthusiasm in the United States outside of the scholarly environment. The situation is not difficult to intepret. Commercial publishers, and more and more university presses, are bottom-line people, who are not concerned with breaking new ground but only with whether the book will sell. Publishing is a business and has to return a profit. Hence publishers are unwilling to risk money on the books of unknown authors, or authors perceived to hold appeal for only a limited audience. It is a chicken-and-egg situation: many more translations are needed to create an awareness of Austrian literature, while the publishers would first like to feel that the readers exist before they bring the translations. Despite the difficulties more translations are appearing all the time, and the larger number of works will help to stimulate and broaden the mediation of Austrian literature. Most of the translations continue to be published by firms more interested in Austrian literature than in profits. For example, the Overlook Press is publishing all of Joseph Roth's works in translation because the publisher admires this author. The Ariadne Press, founded to help mediate Austrian literature, has published Elisabeth Reichart's *February Shadows* (*Februarschatten*) in the translation of Donna Hoffmeister, and will bring translations of Lili Körber's "An Austrian Woman Experiences the Annexation" (*Eine Österreicherin erlebt den Anschluß*) in the translation of Viktoria Hertling, as well as of Peter Henisch's "Negatives of My Father" (*Die kleine Figur meines Vaters*) in the translation of Anne C. Ullmer. Although the experimental nature of much of current Austrian writing may act as a deterrent to broad appeal, it can also be said that publishers and reviewers have not taken the trouble to help make Austrian writers and their different tradition known to the American public by including introductory essays to provide a context. Austrian literature has been popular in the United States in the past, and it can be so again. For example, in 1943 the list of the ten best-selling books in the United States included *The Song of Bernadette* by Franz Werfel and *Beneath Another Sun* by Ernst Lothar, showing that with appropriate thematic content and suitable publicity, interest can be created. This situation has not been repeated in recent times. But to keep matters in perspective, Austrian literature, when judged in relative terms in comparison to the reception of West German, East German, and Swiss books, can be said to be faring at least as well as all others at the present time. Given the sustained growing enthusiasm for Austrian culture, the literature, in translation, should do even better in the future.

Notes

1. See the Special Issue of *Modern Austrian Literature* devoted to "Perspectives on the Question of Austrian Literature," Vol. 17, Nos. 3/4 (1984), particularly the bibliography on pp. 219-258, which contains

over 400 books and articles devoted to the question "What Is Austrian Literature? "

2. Horst Jarka. "Austrian Literature in Editions for American Undergraduate Students." *Modern Austrian Literature,* Vol. 8, Nos. 3/4 (1975); reprinted by the Austrian Institute.
3. Harry Zohn, ed. *Der farbenvolle Untergang. Österreichisches Lesebuch* (Englewood Cliffs, New Jersey: Prentice Hall, 1971) and Jürgen Köppensteiner. *Österreich erzählt: Ein Lesebuch für Deutschlernende* (Wien: Bundesverlag, 1986).
4. To date there are five volumes in print of *Österreich in amerikanischer Sicht: Das Österreichbild im amerikanischen Schulunterricht,* edited by Herbert Lederer and Maria Luise Caputo-Mayr (1980, 1981, 1984, 1987, and 1988).
5. The fourth annual symposium will be held at the University of California, Riverside from May 4 to 6, 1989 on the topic "The Contemporary Literary Scene in Austria."
6. "The Reception of Twentieth-Century Austrian Culture in the United States." *Modern Austrian Literature,* Vol. 22, Nos. 3/4 (December 1989).
7. *1938: Understanding the Past – Overcoming the Past* (Riverside: Ariadne Press, 1989).
8. Karl Kraus. *The Last Days of Mankind,* ed. Frederick Ungar (New York: Ungar, 1974).
9. Johann Nestroy. *Three Comedies,* trans. Max Knight and Joseph Fabry (New York: Ungar, 1967).
10. Fritz Hochwälder. *The Public Prosecutor and Other Plays* (New York: Ungar, 1980).
11. Frederick Ungar, ed. *Handbook of Austrian Literature* (New York: Ungar, 1973).
12. Helga H. Harriman, trans. *Seven Stories by Marie von Ebner-Eschenbach* (Columbia, S.C.: Camden House, 1986).
13. Johann Nestroy. *Three Viennese Comedies,* trans. Harrison Robert and Katharina Wilson (Columbia, S.C.: Camden House, 1986).
14. Katharina Wilson and Robert Harrison, trans. *Ad Absurdum: A Hans Weigel Potpourri* (Columbia, S.C.: Camden House, 1987).
15. Ruth Gross. *PLAN and the Austrian Rebirth* (Columbia, S.C.: Camden House, 1982).
16. Elizabeth C. Hesson. *Twentieth Century Odyssey* (Columbia, S.C.: Camden House, 1982).
17. Donald G. Daviau, Jorun B. Johns, and Jeffrey B. Berlin, eds. *The*

Correspondence of Stefan Zweig with Raoul Auernheimer and with Richard Beer-Hofmann (Columbia, S.C.: Camden House, 1983).

18. Charles A. Carpenter. "The Plays of Bernhard, Bauer, and Handke: A Checklist of Major Critical Studies." *Modern Drama,* Vol. 23, No. 4 (January 1981), 484-491.
19. John Updike. "Disaffection in Deutsch." Review of *Winterreise* by Gerhard Roth. *The New Yorker,* Vol. 56 (April 1980), 130.
20. Theodore Ziolkowski. Review of *Die Wiederholung* by Peter Handke. *World Literature Today,* Vol. 61, No. 2 (Spring 1987), 284.
21. See Donald G. Daviau. "The Reception of Thomas Bernhard in the United States." Special Thomas Bernhard Issue, *Modern Austrian Literature,* Vol. 21, Nos. 3/4 (December 1988), 243-276.
22. "Bowels of Compassion." Review of *Die Freiheit den Mund aufzumachen. Times Literary Supplement* (23 March 1973), 319.
23. *Publishers Weekly,* Vol. 210 (16 August 1976), 120.
24. Richard Gilman. Review of *Beautiful Days* by Franz Innerhofer. *The New York Times Book Review* (23 January 1977), 7.
25. John Neves. "Life in the Kulturstaat." Review of *Schattseite* by Franz Innerhofer. *Times Literary Supplement* (17 September 1976), 1184.
26. *Library Journal,* Vol. 99, No. 16 (15 September 1974), 2252.
27. Wilson Library *Bulletin,* Vol. 57 (September 1982), 58-59.
28. Chicago University Center for Children's Books–*Bulletin,* Vol. 28 (September 1974), 13.
29. Beth Bjorklund. Review of *Gute Nacht, guten Morgen: Gedichte 1978-1981* by Friederike Mayröcker. *World Literature Today,* Vol. 57, No. 2 (Spring 1983), 280-281.
30. M. Goth. Review of *rot ist unten* by Friederike Mayröcker. *World Literature Today,* Vol. 52, No. 4 (Autumn 1978), 628-629.
31. *Atlantic Monthly,* Vol. 245 (March 1980), 102.
32. John Updike. "Disaffection in Deutsch." See note 19 above.
33. Ibid.
34. *Publishers Weekly,* Vol. 216 (3 December 1979), 46.
35. *Booklist,* Vol. 76 (15 March 1980), 1031.
36. Katharina Wilson and Robert Harrison, trans. *Ad Absurdum: A Hans Weigel Potpourri,* p. 13.

Amerikanisch-österreichische Texte

Burghild Nina Holzer

Als Österreicherin, die in die Vereinigten Staaten einwanderte, wurde die Dichterin zweisprachig. Holzers Gedichte und Texte reflektieren das Doppelerlebnis zweier Heimatbereiche.

Brief aus Aztlan

Die zu Hause geblieben sind
wissen wenig von uns
auch wenn wir zurückkehren,
sie sagen "so, bist du wiedereinmal da? "
Sie wissen nicht vom Geruch ihrer nassen Erde,
sie schauen mich an, die trockene Erde rieselt mir aus den Kleidern,
sie flüstern, und der Regen fällt
und Aztlan klumpt sich zu meinen Füßen.

Die zu Hause geblieben sind
wissen nicht vom Gewicht ihrer Sprache,
in Aztlan fällt die nasse Erde aus den Briefen
ich bücke mich, hebe sie auf
aber sie stockt mir im Mund.

Morgan Hill, California 1981

*

I am a guest at someone's house
looking through the window
I see snow has fallen on the mountains
down near where I live
but I am not there

and I know my house stands in a spring of green fields
and I know, were I there
I could not see the snow mountains from my living room

Mama writes: “die Ingeborg Bachman ist einen
schrecklichen Tod gestorben”

she means to say: “why take the risk”
she means to say: “artists pay for it” as if
entering the life force that deeply must surely
be punished by death

the snow mountains from the distance
appear as pure winter
my house in the green fields
is lush spring

today I am a guest at someone else’s house
the windows open up to large perspectives
the room is warm
I come to no conclusions

Kafka writes about his disease: “these discussions
between my brain and lung which went on without my knowledge
may have been terrible”

Morgan Hill, California 1981

*

Großer Gott

I was in the parking lot of the shopping center, walking
from the college to the car to drive home, to correct papers,
to get up, to teach, to drive home to prepare, to

at the eating troughs of the shopping center I had bought
myself some coffee

I ignored the choices of international feed that are standard
for every California shopping center – you can eat Mexican,
Chinese, Pizza, or Hofbrau, all tasting exactly like cardboard

I had drowned myself in coffee to stay awake, to drive home,
to correct papers, to get up, to teach, to

and when the coffee was in me something happened, I was in
Austria in a coffeehouse and der Ober serviert schon den Kuchen
und ein Kind kriegt Schokolade mit Schlagobers, und die alte Dame
beim Fenster hält die Gabel mit ganz feinen Fingern, und die
Leute gehen ein und aus wie aus einem Haus

I am thinking about Kafka and Milena, a student asked me "what
happened when they met in Vienna?" he was upset, the letters we
are reading are not like a novel, they didn't say what happened
(because when you are together you don't need to write)
and I said I didn't know what happened (although I was tempted
to make it up because that is what writers do all the time)
but I said, letters are fragments, isn't it lovely, so much
space in between
but he looked at me and his eyes said "you are the teacher"
and I said "you get to fill it in"

anyway, I was sitting in the coffeehouse in Austria saying
"what happened, someone fill it in"

but the woman behind me said "excuse me, do you know what time
it is" and I was furious, how dare she interrupt me, here I was
back with the multicultural eating troughs, and I don't remember
what I was just going to say, I was going to . . . "I don't know
what happened"
she said "excuse me, do you know . . ." and I said "I don't know
what happened, I don't know"
she brushed her coat against me and I hated her
ich wollte den Ober fragen ob . . . but it was too late for that,
it was definitely too late for that

so I walked across the parking lot to the car, to drive home to
correct papers, to get up to teach, to
and I was singing right along with it,
what it?

I am singing
the chimes from the church are playing something
plastic church by the parking lot, some national anthem,
cardboard, cardboard, why are you singing this
no wait, this is not, this is
from early, early
then it comes to me, breaks out of my
mouth

Großer Gott wir loben dich
Herr wir preisen deine Stärke

I am trembling, I am covered with sweat, I am standing in the Stonestown shopping center, and the rocks are breaking out of my mouth, loud, I am hurling them over the cars

vor dir neigt die Ende sich
und bewundert deine Werke

and the people are looking at me, or maybe no one is looking,
and I am alone, and crawl into my car and begin to drive,
begin to cry as I move along the freeway

I am sitting in church next to my father
and as the organ begins to play – he stands up,
looking way beyond the windows,
he stands straight up and begins to sing

my father never sang, he went to church only when there was no sermon, no fuss, I liked to go with him, silently

I am sitting in church and my father is rising next to me,
he is rising and singing full strength, looking way beyond,
and I am rising, I am standing straight up, looking way up,
way beyond the light, and I am singing full strength, trembling
inside

wie du warst vor aller Zeit
so bleibst du in Ewigkeit

once when we were in the mountains, I was singing by myself,
and he said "if you are going to sing, sing as loud as you
can"
and I sang, and he was silent

but maybe that is not true, maybe I filled all that in, maybe
I sang another time, by myself, not daring to shout out loud,
wishing that someone would stand with me, and we would sing
together "vor dir neigt die Ende sich . . ."

what happened, I don't know, words like jewels out of my
mouth, words like rocks

San Francisco, California 1981

*

the reservoir

we are sitting by the edge of the reservoir in the late
afternoon, the bottle of wine between us
the wind has come up curling the water into a crisp surface
of streaked light, behind us the hills bake in orange heat,
in the little cove the water is calm,
a deep muddy calm, almost black
and a tree trunk rolls in it as if
in black oil

He has asked me "why don't you go back? " The inevitable question, and I don't know what to say without talking for hours, I don't know what to say. But then he says "you know, I have been away for long periods of time but I always loved to come home." I don't know what to say. In the small cove the tree trunk is rolling and rolling as if in black oil. I want to explain, how if the beginning is sound it is easy to come back. But there is

a break in my line of thought as if someone had chopped it off
with one quick hack of the blade. I try it over and over, in
the beginning . . . in the beginning . . . but I do not get beyond,
there is the tree trunk turning with its slippery surface.
I put my hands over my face and say "there was too much pain."

He takes the bottle of wine, then I take it, then he takes it.
I am anxious, I want him to understand. He is waiting for me to
say more so it would make sense. I want to put the sentences
together, a clear sequence of cause and effect but the blade
rotates, each stalk chopped off, dislocated several feet further.

I look out over the water. Around the water the round hills
are like animals resting in the purple afternoon and the large
oaktrees are standing securely from root to crown, limbs stretched out
to embrace. I belong here, and I tell him "I love to live here,
I love this place."

He looks at me, he takes the bottle of wine, then I take it.
Then he says "but you are not here, you are always there."

I take the bottle of wine, I say "that is true." The water
in the cove is dark, and the tree trunk is turning and turning.

Morgan Hill, California 1981

*

Gregor Samsa

This morning I threw Gregor Samsa out of the house; I killed him several days ago late at night, while grading piles and piles of student papers. I looked down and there from the pile of papers crawled the black beetle, calmly onto my living room rug. His shinyness crunched when I hit him, it cracked and it crunched. I let him die there and went to bed.

Today I found him again, I threw him over the balcony, and
still his black impertinence, the shiny beetle coat, it
crunched as I pushed him over.

Mama writes: "Ich bin so traurig, daß du uns heuer nicht besuchen
kommst,
du bist schon vierzig Jahre alt und hast immer noch keine
gesicherte Existenz."

I push the black beetle over the balcony, I sit on my back
steps smelling the sweet peas in the garden, drinking the
bitter coffee

I don't have a job for fall, in the living room are the last
stacks of graded papers. The chairman looked at me and he assured
me it was the budget, it was the budget . . .
A student comes to me, tells me that I changed her life, books
will never be the same to her . . .

Mama sends a picture, a circle of women in a green meadow, their
children around them: my sister, my sister in law, her mother,
my mother, lots of children.

The dry winds come down from the hill behind my house, the grass
is yellow now, the rains are gone.

Mama writes: "one day you will come back here" she says "they
all come crawling back." She tells a story of a friend from Brazil
and how she came crawling back.

I push the beetle over the balcony, God help me not to crawl,
God help me.

Morgan Hill

*

Prinz Eugen

it is early morning, I am sitting on the porch and the radio
is playing a tune. The sprinkler is watering the rosebush
and the humming bird comes close to my face as if I were a flower
to be kissed.
I feel green this morning, it is not hot yet, I feel green
sitting behind the green leaves of the grape vines on the porch.
And the radio is playing a tune very gently,
and I am humming it.
I am humming it, it seems to make me happy,
I am humming it trying to remember where it belongs.
Then I recognize it as from "back home," no words,
I reach for words, no words.
I feel the feeling inside me that the song brings forth,
try to place it, as if matching one color to the next.
I am in church singing, it is morning – the feeling does not match.
I am in a garden, grandmother's garden, the flowers are
up to my nose – the feeling does not match.
All right then, I am older, I am in the mountains with friends,
or I am in the woods, I am walking in the fields – it does not
match.
Maybe not outdoors then, not the garden of childhood, not
in the village, there were times in the city,
perhaps in Innsbruck, the way an old house looked at me with its
tall windows, a courtyard opening up – none of it matched.
What then?
Love? Memories of love. I search for them. Months and months of
waiting for that boy, if he would ever notice me, and then one
winter night he lies down next to me in the snow, no words.
The feeling does not match the song. And the radio has stopped
playing the song and has switched to something else. I turn off
the radio, try to hold onto the tune, it still makes me happy
when I hum it, but no words, no memory. Then I begin to doubt
myself, I begin to doubt the origin of this feeling. Maybe it
is not from "there," maybe it is from "here." I match this thought
to the feeling I have when I hum the song and it seems incongruous,

nothing comes, no memories at all. This makes me wonder about myself. Why this attachment to memories from "there." I begin to explain this to myself, I say: "Maybe it is because your far-sighted eyes can see "there" better, while everything from "here" gets blurred.

I hum the song to myself, the feeling it produces is not blurred, it is clear and intensely "at home." It is as clear and at home as this cool morning on my porch, the cool morning in this hot country, the green edge between garden and house, the pleasure I feel from the sound of water in this dry season.

I hum the song, and then suddenly the first words are here: "ließ eine Brücke schlagen . . . ," what is it, what Brücke? "ließ eine Brücke schlagen . . ." again and again the words are here, what words, I get up, grow restless, walk down the stairs of the cool porch out into the hot garden. I look up at the yellow parched California hills, I look at the tall redwood trees beside my house, for a moment they look like Tannenbäume – "ließ eine Brücke schlagen. . . ." the words come faster now and more urgent, and suddenly I understand. I stand in my California garden and understand my task. . . . ich muß eine Brücke schlagen, von der einen Sprache in die andere, von der einen Landschaft in die andere. . . .

I stand in my hot garden, facing east, singing das Prinz Eugen Lied

"Er ließ schlagen eine Brücke
daß man konnt hinüberrücken
mit d'r Armee
wohl für die Stadt"

I don't like this language, the words come like soldiers out of my mouth, I have not used this language for so long, it hurts, I want to speak English. I try to say the song in English, it is not possible. And all day long, the words are after me "ließ schlagen eine Brücke." Am Abend gebe ich endlich nach, wie ein erschöpftes Kind, ich schreibe in mein Tagebuch "ich muß eine Brücke schlagen."

Morgan Hill, California 1981

*

Am Abend gehe ich über eine Wiese mit Platanen, mit der Sonne
wie schräges
Gold auf dem Gras, und wo das Grün am goldensten ist, da steht
ein Pilz.
Ein Schirmpilz im Park am Pazifik.

Da leg ich mich hin mit Decke und Kissen, da leg ich mich hin
neben den Pilz,
der so riecht wie Zimt.

Dann riech ich ihn, den Pilz neben mir, da riech ich die Wiesen
in einem
anderen Land, da riech ich die Hände des Vaters: "dort, wenn
das Gras so lang ist,
auf dem Hang, unter solchen Bäumen, dort schau." Dann
riech ich wenn er
abbricht ein Stück, reibt zwischen den Händen, sagt "riech."

Ich riech hier am Pazifik, leg mich in das Gras am Abend, streichle
sanft
den Pilz, pflück ihn nicht, schlafe ein eine Weile mit dem Licht.

Oregon 1987

*

Schwäne, die nicht im Wasser sitzen
sondern plötzlich schlagen
mit riesigen Flügeln sich abheben
und fliegen!
über dem Fluß, über mir
die weiten Schwingen gegen den Himmel
wie mystische Urvögel
fliegen sie gegen die blauen Hügel des Abends
wie Ewigkeit denke ich,
drunter die Traun mit Seidenwasser
und jeder Stein am Grund sichtbar
oben die Himmelstöne der riesigen Schwingen
das Licht im Zeitalter des Herbstes
ich sitz am Fluß
in einem fremden Land
wo ich geboren bin.

Salzburg 1987

The most prominent Austrian "Liedermacher" since 1970 – André Heller
Photo: API

American Elements in Austrian *Liedermacher* Songs

Richard J. Rundell

Amerikanische Musik ist bei den Europäern seit den frühen Tagen des Jazz oder den späteren des Rock-and-Roll sehr beliebt, so auch bei den Österreichern. Ihre Liedermacher haben seit den sechziger Jahren Texte eher österreichspezifischer Thematik mit amerikanischen Melodien begleitet, so daß ihre Produkte eine völkerverbindende Mischung ergeben. Zuweilen sind auch ihre Texte englisch. Die meisten dieser Lieder sind satirisch und gesellschaftskritisch, wobei selbst Amerika öfters scharf zur Rede gestellt wird, wie die angeführten Textbeispiele zeigen.

The United States has sent forth two expeditionary forces in the twentieth century which were not military but rather musical: jazz in the twenties and rock and roll in the fifties. The long-term impact of American music on Europeans in general and Austrians in particular can hardly be overestimated, and with the massive influence of American popular music has come American popular culture, the values and concerns of everyday life in the USA. Motion pictures and television have visually reinforced what popular music conveyed aurally; the electronic media and the commercial recording industry guarantee a steady flow of American culture which washes over not only sophisticated Viennese but rustic inhabitants of rural Alpine valleys, for better or for worse.

In the eyes of the Austrian *Liedermacher,* active like their West German counterparts since the sixties, the American influence has been largely a negative one, one which has tended to dehumanize and commercialize traditional European spiritual and intellectual values. This disdain for Coca Cola imperialism is shared by the artistic and literary intelligentsia all over Western Europe (and much of the rest of the world), so there is nothing novel in the viewpoints of the Austrian *Liedermacher;* the USA makes a massive and temptingly easy target for cultural pessimism. The

Liedermacher or political singer-song writers are a cultural phenomenon of the affluent postwar era, although many of their roots are to be found in earlier socially conscious musical forms such as the cabaret chansons of the turn of the century and between the wars, folk music (especially Anglo-Irish songs), and that democratic stream of German-language folk song untainted by National Socialism. Those *Liedermacher* in Austria whose names are well-known through their recordings and concerts are mainly children of the late forties and fifties, that is, the years of the Allied occupation of Austria up to the signing of the State Treaty in 1955. Five of them will be discussed here: Georg Danzer (born in Vienna in 1946), Rainhard Fendrich (Vienna, 1955), André Heller (Vienna, 1947), Ludwig Hirsch (Vienna, 1946), and the somewhat lesser-known Rolf Schwendter (Vienna, 1939). There are at least a dozen more, many of them artistically impressive and musically engaging, but with few or no songs involving American elements, and some with strong American connections, such as Wolfgang Ambros (Vienna, 1952) with his powerful Viennese dialect renditions of several of Bob Dylan's songs.

In Austria as in West Germany, Switzerland, and, to a more limited extent, East Germany, the *Liedermacher* have seen themselves as critical gadflies, a kind of nagging national conscience working in tandem with the politically engaged (almost exclusively Left), socially critical authors, artists, and film makers who are intent upon following through on the democratic and revolutionary impulses of 1776, 1789, 1848, 1918, and, finally, 1945. The battle against intolerance serves as a kind of umbrella for many of the songs written, composed, played, and sung by the *Liedermacher*, and it is often the social consciousness of their songs which sets them apart from other strands of the popular music industry; there are also cross-overs, particularly from rock music.

There are three principal American elements to be found in Austrian *Liedermacher* songs, two of which are of interest here; the third, namely melodic borrowings and American musical accompaniments (especially blues), is dependent upon recordings for a meaningful interpretation. The other two are specific references in *Liedermacher* song texts to aspects of U.S. life such as personalities, places, events, and institutions, on the one hand, and ideological critiques of U.S. cultural influence on Austria, on the other. In a few instances Austrian *Liedermacher* have even composed parody versions of well-known American songs, of which one of the more memorable is Rolf Schwendter's "Yankee Doodle" of 1968, written at the height of European opposition to America's involvement with Vietnam and student revolts in much of Western Europe, to the familiar tune:

Yankee Doodle

(1) Der Yankee Boy ist hübsch und rank,
ansonsten auch sehr nett, Sir.
Er schießt die Völker alle krank,
frißt sich an ihnen fett, Sir.

Refrain: Yankee Doodle, ohne Schmerz,
wir haben von dir genug.
Liebst die Musik und den Scherz,
Gewalt und den Betrug.

(2) Der Yankee Boy ist voll Moral,
dahinter steckt Zynismus,
hält viel vom Tod am Marterpfahl,
das ist sein Hedonismus.

(3) Der Yankee Boy ist mild gestimmt
vom weiblichen Gewissen,
doch will er, wenn er Geld einnimmt,
seinen Profit nicht missen.

(4) Der Yankee Boy denkt nichts dabei,
tut er die Leute töten.
Doch wenn sein Trieb sich regt im Mai,
dann tut er hold erröten.

Rolf Schwendter

It is a brutal, avaricious, bloodthirsty Yankee of whom Schwendter insists an unspecified "we" has had enough. This image of an ugly American, generalized with pointed finger to condemn U.S. warmongering in Asia and the profit-oriented preoccupations of the mecca of capitalism, is varied in verses two and four to include rejections of an American self-righteous morality behind which hides a hypocritical cynicism, and of the Puritan heritage of anti-sexualism and denial of natural urges. The tone is bitter and harsh, not to mention militantly one-sided, but there is, as with all generalizations, a kernel of validity to each of the characteristics Schwendter condemns. That one might recite this litany of numerous other nations with few or no variations is clearly of little consequence to Schwendter. The refrain makes apparent that "we" reject the Yankee mixture of glossy exterior and rotten core.

Georg Danzer offers his critique of America in less frontal form but resorts to English to underscore his point, in a song from 1984 entitled "Spaceinvaders":

Spaceinvaders

mir ist kalt
sie spielen krieg
töten zum spaß

wir leben im herzen einer toten welt

I am cold
I am freezing
children playing in the park
spaceinvaders in the dark
we are living in the heart of a dead world

New York City
wargames
killing for fun
summer in the city

mir ist kalt
unser wahnsinn hat methode
und methode führt zum ziel
alles nur ein spiel

I am cold

Georg Danzer

The image of the arcade video game, where children destroy imaginary aggressors for twenty-five cents on a screen, is a metaphor for the extent to which Americans, but not only Americans, have become inured to the horrors of war and killing by having trivialized them. Danzer does not stand above that which he criticizes but expresses his sense of freezing cold, an absence of humanizing warmth, and alludes, like Schwendter, to an undefined "we," in which he clearly includes Europeans; New York City is merely a preview of things to come, the heart of a dead world. The musical accompaniment to this song is mechanical and lifeless, and the text is sung in a correspondingly monotonous *Sprechgesang.* Danzer free-associates in this bleak text from the video-game image and comes to the disturbing conclusion that the purposeful method to urban civilization's madness is to make a game of everything.

André Heller, in a song entitled "Das berühmte Jean Harlow-Lied vom 4. Oktober 1970," focuses his attention on the Hollywood dream to a rather tinny tune sung as if through a twenties Rudy Vallee-style megaphone.

das berühmte jean harlow-lied vom 4. Oktober 1970

guten morgen, jean harlow! wie war die nacht?
hat man zwischen orchideen geweint oder gelacht?
war der himmel über hollywood schwarz oder rot?
wars champagner oder kokain was man bot?
gesegnet sei dein lamettadekollete
und die marabustola aus chicago!
In deinen hüften wiegt sich die ganze welt!
guten morgen, jean harlow! bei mir!

The Jazz Age illusion which culminated in the glitter of such escapist motion-picture fare as Jean Harlow's (1911–1937) best-known films, "Platinum Blonde" (1931), "Red Dust" (1932), and "Bombshell" (1933), has a magic attraction for Heller's fey perspective. Formulated as a greeting, much as an attentive servant might greet the sensational sex star upon her waking, this song evokes an image of thirties Hollywood which, with its sex and drugs, seems not to have changed much in half a century. Heller's lyrical imagery in his description of Harlow's dress, which he pronounces as a blessing, is followed by a peculiarly powerful sex-goddess–as–earth-mother formulation which reminds one of Schiller's "Diesen Kuß der ganzen Welt" from "An die Freude." Heller does not condemn; on the contrary, he seems to adulate the wise-cracking platinum blonde who died at twenty-four. This, too, is an American image which had a charismatic appeal all over the world through the medium of film and seems harmonious with the persistently self-delusive mien with which one associates Belle-Epoque Vienna, again the shiny shell with a decomposing interior.

Motion pictures account for numerous American elements in Austrian *Liedermacher* songs, some of them treated with slightly more humor and nonchalance than the first songs cited above. Rainhard Fendrich's 1980 "Mundgeruch" pokes fun at that characteristically American preoccupation with hygiene which dictates odorlessness from mouth and underarms: bad breath as the worst imaginable social sin.

Mundgeruch

Ich bin ein Wunder der Natur
von höchst athletischer Figur
und für mein Alter noch dazu intelligent.
Auch mein Physiognomie
erfreut sich höchster Sympathie,
ich bin ein Mann, wie man ihn nur aus Filmen kennt.
Ich pflege mich stets mit der Frische von Lemonen,
um meine herbe Männlichkeit noch zu betonen.
Ich bin viel schöner als der "Dean",

wißt's eh, der James, der aus'm Film,
und trotzdem hab' ich bei den Frauen kan Erfolg.

Denn ich hab' Mundgeruch,
das stört mich so, wenn ich bei Damen Anschluß such.
Ich hab' schon all's probiert,
doch hab' ich bis jetzt noch kan Weg gefunden, der
mich zum Erfolge führt.

Bei mir hat alles keinen Sinn,
nicht einmal Hexachlorophen,
das Klumpert bleibt in seinen roten Streifen drin.

Ich tät so gern mit manchem schönen Mäderl knutschen
anstatt allanich dauernd scharfe Zuckerln lutschen.
Was nützt an seine Männlichkeit,
man ist gestraft für alle Zeit
wenn ana so wie i aus seiner Pappn fäut.

Was nutzen an die Körperformen von Adonis,
wenn ana jeder Frau nach zwei Minuten schlecht is.
Ich kann's nicht ändern mit Gewalt,
die letzte Möglichkeit bleibt halt,
daß ich mein ganzes Leben lang de Gosch'n halt

Rainhard Fendrich

The "ich" of Fendrich's wry portrait is the advertising agency's picture of perfection in all aspects save one, the dreaded halitosis, which his repeated efforts cannot eradicate. In reality Fendrich is a strikingly handsome man with a sizable female following in German-speaking Europe, and he is not exaggerating, however vain it may sound, when he states that he is much better-looking than James Dean – but outer appearances do not suffice. This is an interesting and lightly accented variant of the gleaming-outsides/decaying-insides metaphor for America which other *Liedermacher* have found apt. The ironic conclusion to the song, whereby the subject sees as his last option the necessity of keeping his trap shut all his life, draws a parallel between emitting bad breath and not speaking, lest the visual beauty be seen as deceptive and false.

Ludwig Hirsch, in his song entitled "1928" from the year

1979, constructs an elaborate fiction to make his point relating to the influence of America on the world, saving for the very end an explanation of the significance of the song's title: the birth year of Mickey Mouse.

1928

Eines Abends setzte sich ein alter Mann zu mir
und erzählte:

"Weißt Du, mein Sohn, irgendwann einmal,
kurz nach diesem gewaltigen, allerletzten Knall,
wenn's auf der Erde nur mehr große, nackte
Steine gibt,
mit einer fettigen, schwarzen Rußschicht bedeckt,
wird ein großes, weißes, strahlendes
Raumschiff landen.
Irgendwo zwischen dem ehemaligen Los Angeles
und dem verdampften Schwarzen Meer."

"Und diese fremden, hochgewachsenen Wesen
werden Pillen an Bord haben,
die sie uns Menschen als Geschenk
überreicht hätten,
so wie man immer, wenn man irgendwelche
Wilde besucht,
ihnen kleine Geschenke überreicht.
Pillen gegen die Traurigkeit hätten sie uns
geschenkt,
wenn wir noch dagewesen wären,
Stell Dir vor, mein Sohn –"
sagte der alte Mann ganz traurig –
"wunderbare, kleine Pillen gegen die Traurigkeit."

"Und diese fremden, hochgewachsenen Wesen
werden ihr Raumschiff verlassen,
sie werden sich umsehen und sofort wissen,

daß hier vor kurzem ein gewaltiger,
ein allerletzter Knall war.
Und dann werden sie sich kopfschüttelnd
zwischen die großen, nackten Steine setzen
und schwer durchatmen.
Und jeder von ihnen wird schnell
eine Pille gegen die Traurigkeit schlucken.
Einer von ihnen wird sogar mit dem Finger
in die fettige, schwarze Rußschicht an einem
großen, nackten Stein schreiben:
"Wir hätten so gerne gewußt, wie Du bist!
Wie Du aussiehst! Wie Du sprichst!
Mensch!"

"Und dann plötzlich wird einer von ihnen
was rufen,
er wird rufen, daß er was gefunden hat.
Und das wird ein alter, verbeulter, kleiner
Filmprojektor sein,
mit einem eingespannten Film.
"Ja, warum nicht," sagte der alte Mann.
"Und sie werden sich freuen,
die hochgewachsenen fremden Wesen,
sie werden warten, bis es dunkel ist
und den Film auf ihr strahlendes, weißes
Raumschiff projizieren.
Und sie werden sehr staunen,
denn sie werden einen Micky Maus-Film sehen.
Einen Micky Maus-Film, mit Donald Duck.
Kater Carlo und Goofy.

Und diese fremden, hochgewachsenen Wesen
werden in ihr Raumschiff steigen und sagen,
sie waren lustig, diese Menschen.
Sie haben lustig ausgesehen,
sie haben lustig gesprochen,
wir hätten unsere Pillen gegen die Traurigkeit
völlig umsonst überreicht."

Diese Geschichte hat mir der alte Mann erzählt.
Ich habe nachgedacht und folgende Zeilen
aufgeschrieben.

An einem bestimmten Tag, im Jahr 1928,
standen sich plötzlich links,
der seine Pflicht tuende Mond, und rechts,
der ihre Pflicht tuende Sonne,
am selben Himmel gegenüber.
Erschreckt starrten sie sich an
und in diesem kurzen Schreckensmoment
vergaßen beide
für Bruchteile von Sekunden ihre Pflicht zu tun.
Die Folgen waren verheerend.
Bitte, dieser Tag sei an alle Ewigkeit verflucht!
An diesem Tag wurde die Micky Maus geboren.

Ludwig Hirsch

Rather than a song, this is more a poem or narrative with musical accompaniment in the style of a film score, lacking distinct rhythms but providing an emotional underlayer to the text. The story belongs to the tradition of the negative utopia, a popular staple of science fiction in this century. The mixture of a world after a nuclear holocaust, in which a spaceship lands somewhere between what used to be Los Angeles and the vaporized Black Sea (i.e., USA and USSR have mutually destroyed one another and everything else on earth), is Hirsch's device for setting up his punch line, to the effect that aliens would not pity us if all they saw of our culture were Disney cartoons—and we would be deserving of their pity. The final passage centers on a moment of such import that even sun and moon stood still, with the devastating consequence of the birth of Mickey Mouse. This disturbing vision of the beloved Disney characters illustrates in yet another variation the Austrian allergy to American imports, in Hirsch's view, not because Mickey Mouse and Donald Duck are themselves harmful or ideologically dangerous, but because of the cultural banality they are thought to symbolize, as well as the commercialized trivialization of traditional high-cultural values. One is provoked to interpret Hirsch's ending in opposition to the apparent inconsequentiality of the creation of a cartoon figure fifty years ago.

These five texts by Viennese *Liedermacher* are neither characteristic of all *Liedermacher* songs – the spectrum is far broader – nor a definitive cross-section of contemporary attitudes toward the USA and American culture, although disdain for Disney superficiality is widespread. The *Liedermacher* are availing themselves of the means of popular musical culture to construct a systematic critique of popular culture in its American guise of film and pop/rock music. These *Liedermacher* are implicitly advocating a more selective integration of American cultural influences into Austrian life and exhorting their listeners (a principally young audience) to resist being overwhelmed by the bedazzling American juggernaut. Their struggle does not look promising.

The large Austrian industrial plant "Chemie Linz AG" in 1976.

Der Marshall-Plan und Österreichs Wirtschaft

Jürgen Kullnigg

Without the help of America's Marshall Plan Europe's economy could hardly have recovered after World War II; that was particularly but not only true for the former Hitler countries, Austria among them. Thanks to the industrial know-how of Austrian economists and engineers this country recovered relatively fast. The available Marshall funds financed the restoration of many industrial plants and Austria's entire economic infrastructure. Because the money did not have to be paid back directly its interest and otherwise acquired reserves have helped Austria's economy to this day.

Abhandlungen und Referate mit historischer Thematik werden oft durch Beschreibung der Ausgangssituation, durch geschichtliche Bestandsaufnahmen eingeleitet. Nun, der politische Zustand, die wirtschaftliche Lage Europas nach sechs Jahren Krieg sind hinlänglich bekannt, eine Beschreibung daher überflüssig. Selbst wirtschaftsstatistische Daten, so präzise sie auch sein mögen, sind in diesem Fall zu abstrakt, um das Ausmaß der europäischen Katastrophe ausreichend zu verdeutlichen.

Sieger und Verlierer in Europa lagen gleichermaßen darnieder und nur der kühnste Optimist konnte glauben, in absehbarer Zeit wieder den ohnehin bescheidenen Lebensstandard der Vorkriegsjahre zu erreichen. Die Realisierung dieses Vorhabens schien unmöglich, wenn sie auf eigener Kraft basieren mußte.

Zwei Jahre waren seit der bedingungslosen Kapitulation Hitler-Deutschlands vergangen, zwei Jahre, in denen das hungernde Europa bereits Hilfsgüter im Wert von über acht Milliarden US$ aus den USA erhalten hatte.

Glaubte man zunächst, daß diese Unterstützung, großteils in Form von Lebensmittelsendungen, ausreiche, um die Staaten

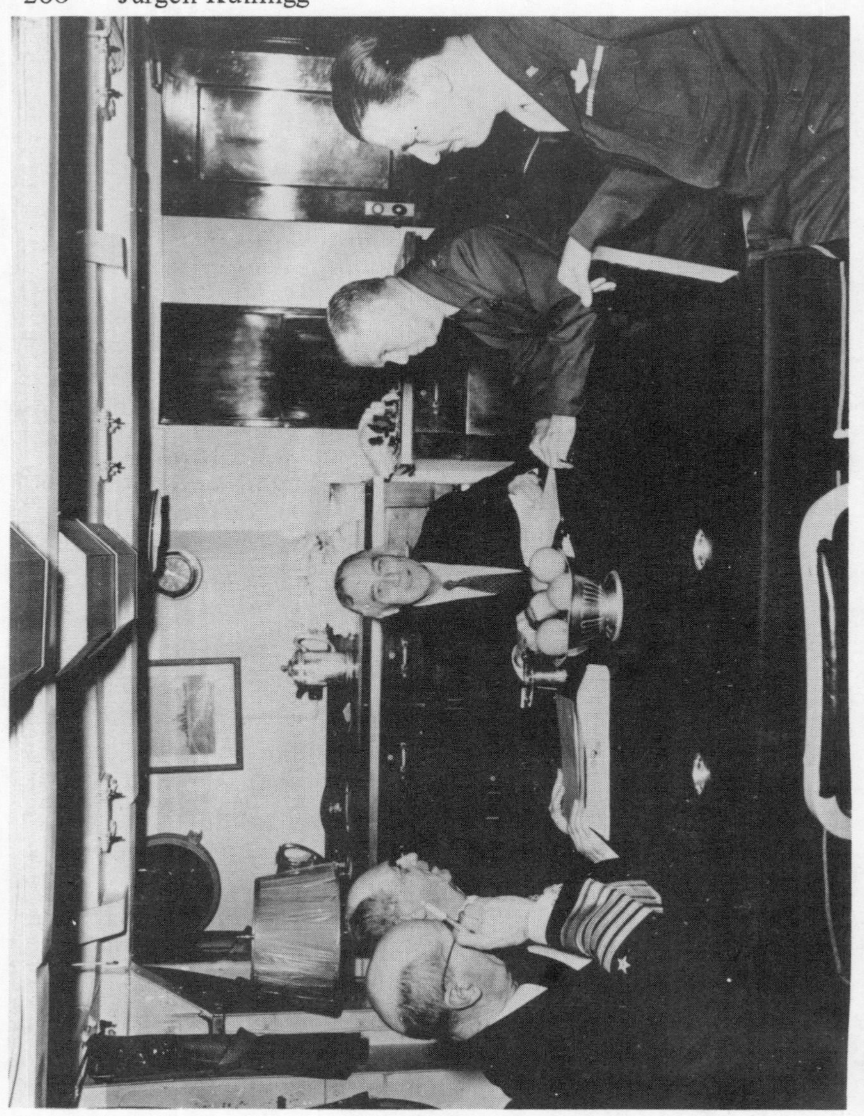

From the left: Admiral E. J. King, Admiral W. M. Leahy, President F. D. Roosevelt, General G. C. Marshall, and Major General L. S. Kuter in conference aboard a warship. Malta, 2 February 1945.

Special Collections Department – General Library
The University of New Mexico

General George C. Marshall Photo by U.S. Army Signal Corps

Europas wieder zu lebensfähigen Wirtschaftseinheiten zu machen, so zeigte sich doch bald, daß dieses "Durchfüttern Europas" allenfalls Linderung, nicht jedoch die dringend nötige Heilung bringen konnte.

Der drohende wirtschaftliche Zusammenbruch mit seinen unübersehbaren weltpolitischen Folgen konnte die verantwortlichen Kräfte in den USA nicht unberührt lassen. Ein Umdenkprozeß hatte eingesetzt, der eine amerikanische Politik des konstruktiven Engagements in Europa einleitete.

Herausragender Proponent dieser neuen Politik war der damalige Außenminister George Catlett Marshall. Seine Rede vom 5. Juni 1947 an der Harvard University ist wohl mit Recht als Initialzündung für den Wiederaufbau Europas zu bezeichnen. "Ziel der amerikanischen Bemühungen müsse es sein," so George C. Marshall, "den Glauben der europäischen Völker in die wirtschaftliche Zukunft ihrer Länder sowie Europas in seiner Gesamtheit wieder herzustellen." Und "abgesehen von der demoralisierenden Wirkung auf der ganzen Welt und der Möglichkeit der Entstehung von Unruhen als Folge der Verzweiflung der betroffenen Völker sind die Folgen für die Wirtschaft der Vereinigten Staaten offenkundig. Logischerweise müssen die Vereinigten Staaten alles, was in ihrer Macht steht, unternehmen, um zur Rückkehr normaler wirtschaftlicher Verhältnisse beizutragen, denn ohne diese sind eine politische Stabilität und ein gesicherter Friede unmöglich."

In den USA stieß die Idee einer großangelegten Hilfsaktion nicht auf ungeteilte Zustimmung. Nachdem in verschiedenen Gremien Vor- und Nachteile dieses Projekts analysiert und diskutiert worden waren, sprach sich besonders der Harriman-Ausschuß in seinem Bericht gegen das Marshall-Konzept aus, da eine wiedererstarkte europäische Wirtschaft einerseits mittel- bis langfristig ersthafte Konkurrenz auf dem US-Binnenmarkt darstellen würde, andrerseits durch den zu erwartenden großen Nachfrageschub aus Europa kurzfristig mit steigenden Inflationsraten zu rechnen sei.

Letztendlich setzte sich die Idee George C. Marshalls gegen protektionistische und isolationistische Tendenzen durch und Präsident Truman konnte am 3. April 1948 den "Economic Cooperation Act" unterzeichnen. Dieses Gesetz bildete den Rahmen für ein "European Recovery Program" und schuf somit das Fundament für die wirtschaftliche Entwicklung und Integration Europas. Bevor ich mich meinem eigentlichen Thema "Der Marshall-Plan und Österreichs Wirtschaft" widme, seien zum besseren Verständnis die organisatorischen und institutionellen Grundlagen bzw. Strukturen dieses Hilfsprogramms skizziert:

George C. Marshalls Absicht war es, sämtliche europäische Staaten in den von Amerika unterstützten Wiederaufbauprozeß einzubeziehen. Im Juli 1947 luden daher die Außenminister Großbritanniens und Frankreichs alle Staaten Europas – mit Ausnahme des faschistischen Spaniens – zu einer Wirtschaftskonferenz nach Paris ein. Zweck dieses Treffens war eine gesamteuropäische Bestandsaufnahme, auf deren Basis eine Art Wunschzettel zusammengestellt wurde. Weiteres Ergebnis dieses Treffens war die Schaffung eines "Committee of European Economic Cooperation." Neun Monate später, im April 1948, gründeten die achtzehn Marshallplan-Teilnehmer (einschließlich westdeutscher Bizone und dem Freistatt Triest) – der Osten hatte das amerikanische Hilfsangebot abgelehnt – die "Organization for European Economic Cooperation," die in Zusammenarbeit mit Washington die Durchführung des "European Recovery Programs" leiten sollte. Das Pariser Abkommen vom 16. April 1948 zwischen den USA und den einzelnen Teilnehmerstaaten bildete schließlich die vertragliche Grundlage zur Verwirklichung des Marshall-Plans.

In kurzer Zusammenfassung kann gesagt werden, daß sich die europäischen Teilnehmerländer vier Hauptziele gesetzt hatten: Vorrangig war eine drastische Produktionssteigerung in allen Industriebereichen. Die Schaffung und Aufrechterhaltung innerer finanzieller Stabilität sollte den Aufschwung absichern. Weiters sollte die wirtschaftliche Zusammenarbeit innerhalb Europas gefördert werden und nicht zuletzt, als Lösung des Problems der Dollardefizite gegenüber den USA, mußten die Exporte nach den Vereinigten Staaten gesteigert werden.

Insgesamt hatte der US-Kongreß Direkthilfen in Höhe von $13 Milliarden bewilligt, teils auf Kreditbasis, den überwiegenden Teil jedoch als Geschenk. Weitere $4 Milliarden wurden auf dem

Wege indirekter Unterstützung als Ziehungsrechte unter Einschaltung der Bank für Internationalen Zahlungsausgleich genehmigt.

Auf Österreich entfiel der überproportional hohe Anteil von $670 Millionen Direkthilfe, das sind 5% des gesamten ERP-Volumens, sowie $284 Millionen in Form indirekter Hilfe, womit die Gesamtunterstützung zwischen Juli 1948 und Dezember 1953 rund $960 Millionen betrug. Herauszustreichen ist, daß Österreich jene ERP-Mittel zur Gänze als Geschenk zur Verfügung gestellt wurden. An dieser Stelle gilt es nun zu erläutern, wie Österreich diese Unterstützung zum Wiederaufbau einsetzte, welche Ziele verfolgt und welche erreicht wurden.

Die Verwendung der Marshall-Plan-Hilfsmittel ist zeitlich in zwei Phasen zu trennen, in einen Abschnitt zwischen 1948 und 1962, sowie in jene Zeit seit dem Inkrafttreten des Bundesgesetzes über die Verwaltung der ERP-Counterpartmittel (ERP-Fondsgesetz). Ich sprach jetzt eben von Counterpartmitteln oder auch Schillinggegenwertmitteln, wie die viel weniger gebräuchliche deutsche Übersetzung lautet, und muß diesen Begriff doch näher erklären, da er zum Verständnis der österreichischen Spielart der Marshallplanhilfe wesentlich ist und die Counterpartmittel als deren Herzstück zu betrachten sind.

Wenn auch der Staat Österreich die ERP-Unterstützung als Geschenk erhielt, so bedeutete dies jedoch nicht, daß dieses Geschenk direkt an die österreichische Wirtschaft weitergegeben wurde. Wollte ein Industriebetrieb z.B. eine Maschine kaufen, die jedoch nur im Ausland gegen Bezahlung in US$ erhältlich war, so konnten ERP-Mittel zur Begleichung der Importrechnung herangezogen werden, während das österreichische Unternehmen, das in der Regel nicht über Hartwährungsbestände verfügte, den festgesetzten Schillinggegenwert auf ein bei der Nationalbank eingerichtetes Konto der österreichischen Bundesregierung einzahlte. Die so angesammelten Counterpartmittel konnten wiederum zur Investitionsfinanzierung in Österreich vergeben werden. Die Abwicklung dieser innerösterreichischen Finanzierung erfolgte dann durch Einschaltung des Kreditapparates. Durch den ständigen Rückfluß fälliger Kredite konnte so ein Kreislauf geschaffen werden, der die österreichische Wirtschaft in der Zeit von 1948 bis 1962 mit rund 20 Milliarden Schilling (= ca. US$20 Millionen) versorgte.

In der Anfangsphase der Counterpartmittel-Vergabe war es notwendig, erhebliche Mittel als *Subvention* zum Aufbau der Infrastruktur aufzuwenden. Die Möglichkeit, aus ERP-Mitteln Bundesschulden abzudecken, war zeitlich begrenzt. In erster Linie waren die "am Aufbau der österr. Wirtschaft aktiven Kräfte zu fördern." Anders formuliert, diese Mittel wurden nicht zum Stopfen von Budgetlöchern, sondern für produktive Zwecke vergeben. Der zahlenmäßig größte Anteil an diesen Subventionen, die sich insgesamt auf rund 7 Milliarden Schilling beliefen, entfiel auf Lebensmittelverbilligungen, gefolgt von Investitionen in den Ausbau der Verkehrswege sowie Maßnahmen zur Unterstützung der Landwirtschaft. Geförderte Projekte waren Bahn-, Post- und Schulbauten, Subventionen zur Wildbach- und Lawinenverbauung, sowie der Wiederaufbau des Fremdenverkehrs, um nur einige Beispiele zu nennen. Auch die ersten Bemühungen der österreichischen Exportförderung wären ohne den Rückgriff auf Counterpartmittel nicht möglich gewesen.

Neben der Subventionierung öffentlicher Investitionen war die *Vergabe von Krediten* das zweite wichtige Element des österreichischen Wiederaufbaus. Von den insgesamt gewährten 13 Milliarden Schilling entfielen rund 6 Milliarden Schilling auf verschiedene Industriezweige, sowie 3,5 Milliarden Schilling auf den Energiesektor. Diese Zahlen verdeutlichen, daß in den ersten Jahren der Counterpartmittel-Vergabe verhältnismäßig hohe Beträge für den Ausbau der Energiequellen und der Grundstoffindustrie aufgewendet werden mußten. Erst nachdem diese einigermaßen tragfähig waren, konnte der Investitionsschwerpunkt mehr auf den Halbzeug- bzw. Fertigwarensektor verlagert werden.

Besondere Erwähnung verdienen jene 560 Millionen Schilling, die der Fremdenverkehrswirtschaft zur Verfügung gestellt wurden. Der Bettenbestand betrug im Jahre 1948 rund 120.000 und ermöglichte Deviseneinnahmen in Höhe von 400 Millionen Schilling (ca. $16 Millionen). Das Ziel der ERP-Investitionspolitik war, den Bettenbestand zu erhöhen und die Betriebe zu renovieren bzw. zu modernisieren. Bereits im Jahre 1963 war der Bettenbestand auf 390.000 gestiegen, die Deviseneinnahmen aus dem Fremdenverkehr näherten sich zehn Milliarden Schilling (ca. $400 Millionen). Die für Österreichs Wirtschaft lebenswichtige Bedeutung der Counterpartmittel in der Zeit von 1948 bis 1962 ist an deren Anteil an den Bruttoinvestitionen zu erkennen. Dieser Anteil lag 1948 bei 25%, erreichte 1950 den Höchstwert von 32%, fiel aber durch das Erstarken der österreichischen Eigenleistung auf 3% im Jahr 1958.

Der Beginn der sechziger Jahre markiert einen Einschnitt in der österreichischen Marshallplan-Geschichte. Dokumentiert wird diese Zäsur durch ein Abkommen zwischen den Vereinigten Staaten und Österreich vom 29. März 1961, in dem Österreich das alleinige Verfügungsrecht über die Counterpartmittel zugestanden wurde. Das daraufhin beschlossene "Bundesgesetz vom 13. Juni 1962 über die Verwaltung der Counterpartmittel" ist bis zum heutigen Tag die Grundlage für den Einsatz jener Mittel, die ihren Ursprung in den späten vierziger Jahren hatten. Aufgrund der Bedeutung dieses Gesetzes und des darin verankerten ERP-Fonds, ist eine detailliertere Behandlung, soweit sie dieser Rahmen zuläßt, gerechtfertigt.

Paragraph 1 des Gesetzes steckt den Aufgabenbereich des Fonds ab, indem er normiert, daß der Ausbau, die Rationalisierung und Produktivität der österreichischen Wirtschaft zu fördern seien und dadurch auch zur Erhaltung der Vollbeschäftigung sowie zur Erhöhung des Sozialproduktes unter Bedachtnahme auf die Stabilität des Geldwertes beizutragen sei. Die volkswirtschaftlich relevante Aussage wird durch das Gesetz ergänzt, wonach der Fond seine Mittel nach wirtschaftlichen Grundsätzen zu verwalten habe und keine Leistungen zugunsten von Gebietskörperschaften erbringen dürfe. Diese Untersagung von Leistungen zugunsten von Gebietskörperschaften verbietet nichts anderes als die Heranziehung von ERP-Geldern zur Abdeckung von Haushaltsdefiziten.

Im Gesetz werden die einzelnen Kredite angeführt, welche aus dem Fonds-Vermögen vergeben werden können, wobei die Zinssätze so festzusetzen sind, daß sie jenen des Kapitalmarktes nahekommen. Vor der Festsetzung des Zinssatzes ist die Nationalbank zu hören. Für bestimmte Arten von Investitionen, z.B. in strukturschwachen Regionen, kann ein abweichender Zinssatz festgesetzt werden, wenn der Ertrag dieser Investitionen marktähnliche Kapitalkosten nicht zuläßt.

Wesentlich für die wirtschaftspolitische Wirksamkeit des Einsatzes der ERP-Counterpartmittel sind naturgemäß die Entscheidungsgremien des Fonds und deren Zusammensetzung. Die ERP-Kreditkommission und deren einzelne Fachkommissionen werden von der Bundesregierung bestellt, wobei das Kräfteverhältnis der im Nationalrat vertretenen Parteien zu berücksichtigen ist. Nachdem ich bereits über die Auswirkungen der Marshallplan-Hilfe in den Aufbaujahren der zweiten Republik gesprochen habe, will ich abschließend die Entwicklung seit dem Inkrafttreten des ERP-Fondsgesetzes beschreiben.

Eine detaillierte Analyse der einzelnen ERP-Jahresprogramme, wie sie die Geschäftsführung des Fonds der Bundesregierung vorzulegen hat, ist schon aus zeitlichen Gründen nicht möglich. Enzelne Fallbeispiele für den ablauf- und ordnungspolitischen Einsatz von ERP-Mitteln sollen daher ausreichen, um sich ein Bild über deren gegenwärtige Verwendung zu machen.

Der erste Rückblick fällt auf das Wirtschaftsjahr 1966/1967, das nach den Hochkonjunkturjahren in der ersten Hälfte der sechziger Jahre einen wirtschaftlichen Einbruch brachte, der von geringer Investitionsbereitschaft begleitet wurde. Durch eine Ausdehnung des Kreditrahmens und durch Sonderprogramme – man könnte von einer Politik des billigen Geldes sprechen – sollten Anreize zu konjunkturbelebenden Investitionen geschaffen werden. Bereits in der folgenden Wirtschaftsperiode war das gewünschte Ansteigen der Konjunktur erreicht, wobei zur Klarstellung der Relationen zu sagen ist, daß die ERP-Fonds-Politik nur eine die Wirtschaftspolitik der Bundesregierung begleitende Funktion ausüben konnte und keinesfalls als einziges Instrument zu verstehen ist.

Ein gegenläufiger Trend war in den Jahren 1970–1972 zu registrieren, in denen eine übergroße Kreditnachfrage zu einer Überhitzung der Konjunktur zu führen drohte; im Herbst 1971 wurde sogar eine Annahmesperre für Kreditanträge seitens des ERP-Fonds verhängt.

Eingefrorene Mittel wurden in den Jahren 1973/1974 dann zur Finanzierung von Sonderprogrammen eingesetzt, die in erster Linie die Schaffung von Arbeitsplätzen in strukturschwachen Grenzgebieten zum Ziel hatten. Als herausragendstes Projekt des ERP-Fonds ist die Zinsenstützungsaktion des Jahres 1976 hervorzuheben.

Fünfhundert Millionen Schilling wurden zur Kreditverbilligung zur Verfügung gestellt, um eine 5%-ige Zinsenstützung zu ermöglichen und somit die antizyklischen Effekte der Wirtschaftspolitik zu verstärken. Zu Beginn der achtziger Jahre wurde wiederum verstärktes Augenmerk auf Sonderprogramme zur Förderung strukturschwacher Regionen gelegt, wobei besonders das Krisengebiet der Obersteiermark gestützt wurde.

All diese Beispiele dokumentieren die Bedeutung des ERP-Fonds als parafiskalisches Instrument der Wirtschaftspolitik bis in die Gegenwart.

Im Laufe des nunmehr vierzigjährigen Einsatzes von Counterpartmitteln konnten der österreichischen Wirtschaft rund 60 Milliarden Schilling zur Verfügung gestellt werden und somit ein entscheidender Beitrag zum Aufbau Österreichs als modernen Industriestaat geleistet werden. Diese finanzielle Unterstützung, gepaart mit dem unbedingten Willen zum Wiederaufbau, machte es möglich, daß aus dem Bittsteller von 1948 ein Staat werden konnte, dessen wirtschaftliche Leistung heute weltweit Anerkennung findet.

Mögen Kritiker den Marshall-Plan als politische Waffe im Kalten Krieg und in ihm die Festschreibung der Teilung Europas sehen, er bedeutete für Österreich den ersten Schritt in eine hoffnungsvollere Zukunft. Der Grundstein war am 5. Juni 1947 gelegt worden.

Der Staatsvertrag 1955 und die Vereinigten Staaten

Nikolaus Scherk

Although the United States held Austria also responsible for the atrocities of the Third Reich it understood the historical fact that this small country was the first victim of Hitler's aggressive expansion politics. The USA therefore supported the restoration of Austria's sovereignty according to the Moscow Declaration of 1943. It emphasized the need for an expedient conclusion of Austria's postwar occupation status, and sought a limitation of Soviet influence upon Austria during and, definitely, after the occupation. Due to a brief thawing period during the Cold War after Stalin's death America's diplomacy contributed to the final liberation of Austria a decade after World War II.

Mit der Befreiung vom Nazismus im Frühjahr 1945 kam für Österreich noch lange nicht die Freiheit, sondern das Land mußte vorerst noch eine Besatzung durch die vier Siegermächte – die Sowjetunion, die Vereinigten Staaten von Amerika, Großbritannien und Frankreich – akzeptieren, die zehn Jahre lang dauern sollte. Während die Alliierten mit den anderen Staaten, die an der Seite Hitler-Deutschlands gegen sie Krieg geführt hatten, nämlich Italien, Ungarn, Bulgarien, Rumänien und Finnland, relativ rasch in den Jahren 1946 und 1947 Friedensverträge abschlossen, konnte Österreich seine Souveränität und volle Freiheit erst nach langwierigen, zähen Verhandlungen und vielen Rückschlägen im Jahre 1955 erreichen.

Allerdings unterschied sich die Situation Österreichs von jener der genannten Staaten. Österreich war, wie in der Moskauer Deklaration der Allierten vom 1.11.1943 ausdrücklich festgestellt worden war,[1] ein gewaltsam besetztes und nun befreites Land. Der sowjetische Außenminister Molotow erklärte auf der Außenministerkonferenz in Paris im April 1946, daß Österreich eine

15 May 1955 – Austria's State Treaty is signed by the four allied powers. U.S. State Secretary John Foster Dulles at the table second from the left.

Photo "Bundespressedienst"

besondere Stellung einnehme, da es weder Krieg erklärt, noch als Staat Krieg geführt habe. Andrerseits habe Österreich einen Teil Deutschlands gebildet.

Somit war Österreich weder ein Feind- noch ein Siegerstaat, sondern ein Sonderfall. Die Zwischenstellung Österreichs kam u.a. darin zum Ausdruck, daß der abzuschließende Vertrag über die zukünftige internationale Stellung des Landes von Anfang an nicht als Friedensvertrag sondern als *Staatsvertrag* bezeichnet wurde.

Die neue österreichische Bundesregierung, die im Laufe des Jahres 1945 von allen vier Besatzungsmächten anerkannt worden war, war von Anfang an bestrebt, den Staatsvertrag möglichst rasch abzuschließen, um schnell den Abzug der Besatzungstruppen und die volle Unabhängigkeit zu erreichen. Sie konnte sich dabei auf die schon erwähnte Moskauer Deklaration berufen, in welcher dies als eines der Kriegsziele der Alliierten bezeichnet worden war.

Die Politik der Vereinigten Staaten gegenüber Österreich nach Kriegsende verfolgte drei wesentliche Ziele:

– die Wiederherstellung der Unabhängigkeit Österreichs im Einklang mit der Moskauer Erklärung,
– die baldige Beendigung der Besatzung des Landes, d.h. Abzug der eigenen und vor allem auch der sowjetischen Truppen,
– die Einschränkung des sowjetischen Einflußes in Österreich, da sie das Land grundsätzlich zum westlichen Einflußbereich zählten.

Schon kurz nach der Bildung der aus den Wahlen vom Dezember 1945 hervorgegangenen Bundesregierung am 2. Februar 1946 übermittelte Außenminister Gruber den politischen Vertretern der USA und Großbritanniens einen ersten Vorentwurf für einen "Vertrag zur Wiederherstellung der Rechtsstellung Österreichs." Die amerikanische Seite griff die Anregung auf und unterbreitete mit Rat der Außenminister der Vier Mächte ihrerseits Ende Mai 1946 einen Vertragsentwurf, der ihren Wunsch dokumentierte, die österreichische Frage schnell zu bereinigen. Dabei ging es ihr, wie erwähnt, einerseits um die baldige Rückführung der eigenen Truppen (1946 dachte noch niemand an die dauernde Stationierung von amerikanischen Streitkräften in

Europa) und andrerseits um die Verhinderung des Verbleibs sowjetischer Truppen in Rumänien und Ungarn. Durch den gleichzeitigen Abschluß der Friedensverträge mit diesen Staaten und des Vertrags mit Österreich wäre nach Auffassung der US-Regierung die Verankerung jener Bestimmungen in den Friedensverträgen mit Ungarn und Rumänien entbehrlich geworden, welche die Stationierung sowjetischer Truppen in diesen Ländern für die Dauer der Besatzung Österreichs zur Aufrechterhaltung der Verbindungslinien vorsahen.

Auf der Außerministerratstagung in Paris im Juni 1946 kam es noch zu keiner Debatte über Österreich und auch auf den folgenden Ministertreffen der Vier Mächte brachte sie kein Ergebnis. Zu groß waren die Meinungsunterschiede, im besonderen hinsichtlich zweier Problemkreise:

1. Die Gebietsansprüche Jugoslawiens:

Die Siegermächte waren sich zwar seit langem einig gewesen, daß Österreich in den Grenzen von 1937 wiederhergestellt werden sollte, aber Jugoslawien stellte Ansprüche auf die von der slowenischen Minderheit bewohnten Gebiete in Kärnten, und zwar maximale Forderungen. Offenbar hoffte man auf jugoslawischer Seite, schließlich als Kompromiß einen Teil dieser Gebiete zugesprochen zu erhalten. Die Sowjetunion unterstützte diese Forderungen im Laufe des Jahres 1947; die Westmächte wandten sich entschieden dagegen, zumal sich die Bewohner Südkärntens schon 1921 in einer Volksabstimmung mit großer Mehrheit für einen Verbleib bei Österreich ausgesprochen hatten. Nach dem Bruch Titos mit Stalin rückten die Sowjets ebenfalls von den Gebietsansprüchen Jugoslawiens ab. Stalin gab sie 1949 ganz auf, offenbar, um seine eigenen wirtschaftlichen Forderungen umso besser durchzubringen, nämlich seine Ansprüche auf

2. Das sogenannte "deutsche Eigentum":

Auf der Potsdamer Gipfelkonferenz im Sommer 1945 hatten sich die Sieger geeinigt, keine Reparationsforderungen an Österreich zu stellen. Es wurde aber vereinbart, jedem der vier Mächte quasi als Anzahlung auf die von Deutschland zu leistenden Reparationen den Zugriff auf das Eigentum deutscher Staatsangehöriger ("German assets") in ihrer jeweiligen Besatzungszone in Österreich zu gestatten.

Dabei hatten die Westmächte vernachlässigt, den Begriff "German assets" näher zu definieren. Es stellte sich die Frage, ob damit das "deutsche Eigentum" zum Zeitpunkt des Einmarsches Hitlers in Österreich gemeint war oder auch die während der deutschen Besetzung aufgebauten Industrien (z.B. die riesigen Reichswerke Hermann Göring), das vom Deutschen Reich mehr oder minder zwangsweise erworbene Eigentum von Staatsbürgern von Drittstaaten (darunter ein Großteil der Erdölquellen in Niederösterreich) und schließlich das Vermögen, das Deutsche durch Arisierung oder sonstwie illegal von Österreichern erworben hatten. Die Sowjetunion verlangte eine möglichst umfassende Definition, die Westmächte eine möglichst enge, um zu verhindern, daß Österreich – wie es der amerikanische Außenminister Marshall ausdrückte – wirtschaftlich eine "Marionette" der Sowjetunion werde (Außenministertagung in Moskau, 18. April 1947).

Denn die Frage des "Deutschen Eigentums" in der Sowjetischen Zone betraf (nach Außenminister Grubers Schätzung) 10–15 Prozent des gesamten Industriepotentials des Landes, vor allem im Bereich der Grundstoff- und Schwerindustrie. Wie in den von ihnen besetzten Balkanstaaten, schlugen die Sowjets vorerst die Gründung gemischter österreichisch-sowjetischer Gesellschaften zur Verwaltung dieser Industriebetriebe vor. Die USA sprachen sich im Einklang mit der österreichischen Bundesregierung entschieden dagegen aus, da der Sowjetunion damit ein entscheidender Einfluß auf die österreichische Wirtschaft gesichert worden wäre. Daraufhin beschloß das österreichische Parlament im Jahre 1946 die Verstaatlichung der Betriebe. Dabei wurde argumentiert, daß es sich um das unveräußerliche Eigentum des österreichischen Volkes handelte und die Verstaatlichung eine Garantie gegen eine neuerliche Veräußerung der Betriebe an das Ausland bieten würde. Paradoxerweise bezeichneten die Sowjets das Verstaatlichungsgesetz als ungültig (weil den Potsdamer Beschlüssen widersprechend), während die USA diese Maßnahme unterstützten. Im übrigen übergaben die Westmächte des "deutsche Eigentum" in ihren Besatzungszonen der treuhänderischen Verwaltung der Republik Österreich.

Eine Lösung der dornigen Frage der "German assets" zeichnete sich erst 1948/1949 ab, als der französische General Cherrière ihren *Rückkauf* durch Österreich vorschlug. Auf der Grundlage dieser Idee (Cherrière-Plan) konnten erfolgreiche Verhandlungen geführt werden. Schiffe der Donaudampfschiffahrtsgesellschaft (DDSG) und Erdöl sollten in natura der Sowjetunion abgetreten werden, das übrige "deutsche Eigentum" in der sowjetischen Zone sollte um $150 Millionen in konvertierbarer Währung, damals ein enormer Betrag, abgelöst werden.

Österreich war in den Jahren 1947–1949 begierig, den Staatsvertrag abzuschließen, und hätte auch sehr schwere wirtschaftliche Belastungen auf sich genommen, um die Teilung des Landes nach deutschem Muster zu vermeiden. John F. Dulles schrieb 1947: "[Gruber] is so eager to get out the Soviet troops that I think he would accept almost any economic terms."

Die Vereinigten Staaten lehnten aber bilaterale Abkommen zwischen Österreich und der Sowjetunion über das "deutsche Eigentum" kompromißlos ab, insbesonders hinsichtlich der Erdölquellen, auf die auch amerikanische Gesellschaften Ansprüche erhoben. Überhaupt hielt die US-Regierung in jenen Jahren nicht viel vom raschen Abschluß des Staatsvertrags, da sie der Auffassung war, daß ein Vertrag, der nicht die wirtschaftliche Unabhängigkeit Österreichs garantierte, schlechter gewesen wäre als gar kein Vertrag.

Dazu kam, daß das Pentagon in den Jahren 1948–1949 angesichts des kommunistischen Putschs in der Tschechoslowakei auch aus strategischen Gründen den Abzug der US-Truppen aus Österreich nicht wünschte. Die amerikanischen Militärs waren besorgt, daß Österreich sich selbst nicht gegen eine kommunistische Machtübernahme verteidigen könnte, da es keine Armee hatte.

Im Sommer 1949 schien ein Vertragsabschluß auf der Grundlage der eben erwähnten wirtschaftlichen Regelung zum Greifen nahe. Die amerikanische Seite zeigte sich zurückhaltend und die österreichische Regierung drängte Washington zum Einlenken. Das "US Department of State" trat aus allgemeinpolitischen Erwägungen für den Vertragsabschluß ein, das Pentagon machte aber Bedenken gegen die damit verbundene Räumung Westösterreichs geltend. Schließlich entschied Präsident Truman am 26.10.1949 persönlich zugunsten des Vertragsabschlusses. Inzwischen war die (vielleicht nur vermeintliche) Bereitschaft der Sowjets allerdings bereits geschwunden.

Tatsächlich kam es von 1950 bis 1954 geradezu zu einem Einfrieren der Staatsvertragsgespräche, wobei die Sowjetunion die österreichische Frage eng mit der deutschen verknüpfte, d.h. den Abschluß des Vertrages vor einer Friedensregelung mit Deutschland ablehnte.

Im März 1952 versuchten die Westmächte, die Verhandlungen wieder in Gang zu bringen, indem sie den Abschluß eines Kurzprotokolls und den Verzicht aller Vier Mächte auf das "deutsche Eigentum" vorschlugen. Die Sowjetunion lehnte aber ab, darüber auch nur zu sprechen.

Erst nach dem Tode Stalins 1953 trat ein Tauwetter ein. Der neue Bundeskanzler Raab suchte aktiv eine Verständigung mit der Sowjetunion; von sowjetischer Seite wurden einige Verbesserungen des Besatzungsregimes zugestanden.

Anfang 1954 stand die österreichische Frage wieder auf der Tagesordnung der Außenministerkonferenz in Berlin. Die Sowjetunion bot dabei der österreichischen Regierungsdelegation den Staatsvertrag an, verlangte aber, daß ihre Truppen bis zum Abschluß des deutschen Friedensvertrags in Österreich bleiben sollten. Einen Vertrag ohne Abzug der Besatzungstruppen mußte die österreichische Delegation aber ablehnen.

Als zweite Bedingung hatten die Sowjets verlangt, daß sich Österreich verpflichten solle, keinerlei Koalitionen und Militärbündnisse abzuschließen. Die Westmächte waren mit der Aufnahme eines solchen Bündnisverbots in den Vertrag nicht einverstanden, weil es mit der Souveränität eines freien Staates nicht vereinbar wäre. In Wirklichkeit scheinen sie aber eine Präjudiz für Deutschland befürchtet zu haben.

Im Rahmen der Berliner Konferenz erklärte Außenminister Dulles, daß die zum Unterschied mit einer durch andere Staaten auferlegten Neutralität, eine frei gewählte Neutralität wie jene der

Schweiz durchaus ehrenhaft sei und die USA eine solche Wahl Österreichs respektieren würden.

Die Enttäuschung über das Scheitern der Berliner Verhandlungen war in Österreich sehr groß, aber ein Jahr später, im Februar 1955, erklärte der sowjetische Außenminister Molotow vor dem Obersten Sowjet, vorerst noch in verschlüsselter Form, daß die Sowjetunion zum Abschluß des Staatsvertrags *vor* dem Friedensvertrag mit Deutschland bereit wäre, wenn ausreichende Garantien gegen einen neuen Anschluß geboten werden und daß sich Österreich zur Bündnisfreiheit verpflichten müsse.

Die österreichische Regierung verlangte unverzüglich Klarifikationen, und im April 1955 reiste eine Delegation, bestehend aus Bundeskanzler Raab, Vizekanzler Schärf, Außenminister Figl und Staatssekretär Kreisky, nach Moskau. Die Westmächte waren von der russischen Initiative überrascht, gaben der österreichischen Regierung aber "grünes Licht." Für die amerikanischen Militärs war eine Unterbrechung der Nord-Süd-Verbindung der neugegründeten NATO von Deutschland nach Italien sicherlich nicht erwünscht, aber der österreichische Botschafter in Washington, Gruber, vertrat die Ansicht, daß die USA "eine wirkliche und praktische Lösung aus militärischen Gründen im Gegensatz zur Ansicht der Bundesregierung" nicht einfach zurückweisen könnten. So kam es auch. Die offenen Fragen konnten in den Moskauer Verhandlungen rasch geklärt werden.

Auch die so schwierigen Vermögensfragen konnten zu einem einvernehmlichen Abschluß gebracht werden. Österreich erreichte schließlich, die Erdöllieferungen an die Sowjetunion zu reduzieren und statt Ablösezahlungen für die Industriebetriebe in konvertibler Währung Warenlieferungen über zehn Jahre zu vereinbaren, was eine bedeutende Erleichterung darstellte.

Im politischen Bereich akzeptierte Österreich die Verpflichtung, keine politische und wirtschaftliche Vereinigung mit Deutschland einzugehen. Das Anschlußverbot wurde als Artikel 4 in den Staatsvertrag aufgenommen.

Darüberhinaus übernahm die österreichische Regierungsdelegation bei den Verhandlungen in Moskau die politische Verpflichtung, eine international bindende Neutralitätserklärung

Just having signed the State Treaty (15 May 1955) Austrian Foreign Minister Leopold Figl and the foreign ministers of the four allied powers appear on the balcony of Belvedere Castle in Vienna before a large crowd of people in the garden below. US State Secretary John Foster Dulles to the very right.

Photo by "Bundespressedienst"

abzugeben. Das erfolgte am 26. Oktober 1955, nach dem Abzug aller ausländischen Truppen, in Form eines vom Parlament einstimmig beschlossenen Verfassungsgesetzes.

Die Delegation konnte sich dabei zweifellos an die Erklärung von John F. Dulles in Berlin erinnern, daß eine *freiwillig* gewählte Neutralität achtbar sei. Österreich legt Wert auf die Feststellung, daß seine Erklärung der immerwährenden Neutralität freiwillig erfolgt ist, da dieser Status seiner geographischen und politischen Lage angemessen ist.

Die Vereinigten Staaten erhoben daher gegen die Neutralitätserklärung keine Einwände und haben sie seither stets als wichtigen Faktor der Stabilität und des Friedens in Europa respektiert und anerkannt.

In Moskau war Vizekanzler Schärf für die Verwendung des Ausdrucks "Bündnisfreiheit" eingetreten, um den militärischen und nicht ideologischen Charakter der Neutralität zu unterstreichen und um die Vereinigten Staaten nicht vor den Kopf zu stoßen. Die Sowjetunion bestand aber auf das Wort "Neutralität." Schließlich einigte man sich auf die Formel "eine Neutralität, wie sie von der Schweiz gehandhabt wird." Der Hinweis auf das Vorbild der Schweiz hat für Österreich den großen Vorteil der klaren Abgrenzung der sich aus dem Neutralitätsstatus ergebenden Verpflichtungen. Im Neutralitätsgesetz vom 26.10.1955 wurde der militärische Inhalt der Neutralität übrigens klar dargelegt.

Die Regelung der österreichischen Frage durch die Unterzeichnung des "Staatsvertrags über die Wiederherstellung eines unabhängigen und demokratischen Österreich" am 15. Mai 1955 war für die Sowjetunion keine isolierte diplomatische Aktion und wurde von den Vereinigten Staaten auch nicht als solche verstanden. Offenbar wollte Chruschtschow seit 1954 u.a. aus wirtschaftlichen Erwägungen eine gewisse Détente einleiten und durch ein Einlenken in der österreichischen Frage seine Verhandlungsbereitschaft generell signalisieren. Die Standhaftigkeit der Österreicher in den Jahren seit 1945 hatte ihm wohl die Hoffnung genommen, daß das Land auf friedlichem Wege in das kommunistische Lager eingegliedert werden könnte. Immerhin trieb der Abzug der Westmächte aus Westösterreich einen Keil zwischen die

NATO Nord- und Südflanken. Schließlich konnte die österreichische Neutralität immer wieder als Beispiel und Lockmittel für Bündnispartner der USA herangezogen werden.

Zusammenfassend muß anerkannt werden, daß die grundsätzlich stets positive Haltung der Vereinigten Staaten zu den österreichischen Bemühungen um Wiedererlangung der Unabhängigkeit und ihre konstante Unterstützung auf politischem und wirtschaftlichem Gebiet die erfolgreiche Verhandlungsführung der österreichischen Regierung erst ermöglicht hat. Der Abschluß des Staatsvertrags 1955 ist somit nicht nur eine Sternstunde Österreichs gewesen, sondern auch ein großer diplomatischer Erfolg der USA.

Note

1. In der Moskauer Deklaration der Außenminister der Vereinigten Staaten, Großbritannien und der Sowjetunion vom 1.11.1943 hieß es:
   - Österreich, das erste Land, das der typischen Angriffspolitik Hitlers zum Opfer fiel, soll befreit werden;
   - die Besetzung Österreichs durch Deutschland ist null und nichtig;
   - die Wiederherstellung eines freien unabhängigen Österreich ist ein Kriegsziel der Alliierten;
   - Österreich trägt eine Verantwortung für die Teilnahme am Kriege an der Seite Hitler-Deutschlands. Bei der endgültigen Abrechnung wird Bedacht darauf genommen werden, wieviel es selbst zu seiner Befreiung beigetragen haben wird.

Das österreichische Erziehungswesen nach 1945 im Einfluß der USA

Gerhard H. Weiss

Several educational ideas had already crossed the Atlantic from Austria to the U.S. in the twenties and thirties. Particularly the school reforms of social-democratic Vienna with their emphasis on individualistic education found quick adoption in the New World. It seems almost ironical that these methods were brought back to Vienna as American ideas. Nonetheless, the American occupation forces never played a dictatorial, only an advisory role. Yet they insisted on the redemocratization of the Austrian school system, still maintained today.

Das hier formulierte Thema verspricht etwas, was es nicht halten kann. Es klingt, als ob es sich um einen verkappten oder gar nicht so verkappten Bildungsimperialismus handeln solle, als ob etwa das österreichische Erziehungswesen durch einen "geistigen Marshall-Plan" aus seiner "selbstverschuldeten Unmündigkeit" durch amerikanische Hilfe zur Erkenntnis der Wahrheit geführt worden sei. Dem ist nicht so. Erziehungssysteme gehören in die Intimsphäre einer jeden Gesellschaft und lassen sich nur sehr begrenzt von außen beeinflussen. Und was von außen kommt wird gewogen, geformt, verändert, bis es in das eigene System paßt. Es wird zum Eigentum, dem man den fremden Ursprung oft nicht einmal mehr ansehen kann. Um es vorwegzunehmen: das österreichische Erziehungswesen hat vor und nach 1945 sowohl gegeben als auch genommen, aber es ist (mit Ausnahme der Anschlußjahre) immer sehr betont ein österreichisches System gewesen und geblieben.

Gerade das macht eine Untersuchung der österreichischen Schule so besonders interessant – denn die Entwicklung dieses Schulsystems ist ein klarer Spiegel der gesellschaftlichen, politischen und historischen Entwicklung des Landes Österreich, ist Teil des sich immer stärker ausprägenden "Österreichbewußtseins." Sollten wir uns hier nur auf amerikanische Einflüsse beschränken, wären wir mit unserer Weisheit bald am Ende. Im Gegensatz zur Bundesrepublik Deutschland hat nicht einmal die Besatzungszeit auf die Schulen bleibend eingewirkt. Wollen wir von Österreich sprechen, müssen wir die gesamte schulische Entwicklung seit etwa 1918 skizzieren, weil man dadurch eine wechselseitige Befruchtung erkennen kann, die für Österreich und die USA wichtig gewesen ist. Wir sollten daher unserem Thema eine andere Zielrichtung geben und es umnennen in "Das moderne österreichische Erziehungswesen in seinen Wechselbeziehungen zu den USA."

Zunächst ein paar kurze historische Hinweise. Die schulpolitischen Pole Österreichs in neuerer Zeit sind getragen von zwei Hauptströmungen, der katholisch-konservativen und der sozialistisch-reformfreudigen. Diese beiden ideologischen Richtungen (heute getragen durch die ÖVP und die SPÖ) haben seit 1918 das Erziehungswesen des Landes bestimmt, wobei in Wien die reformfreudige und in vielen Teilen des restlichen Österreich die konservativere Auffassung vorherrschte und vorherrscht. Diese Gegensätzlichkeit, die oft zu bitteren Kämpfen Anlaß gegeben hat, reflektiert auf das genaueste den Klimaunterschied Wien und Provinz.

Die grundsätzlichen Unterschiede zwischen, grob gesagt, "schwarz" und "rot" lassen sich nicht leicht auf einfache Formeln bringen. Aus unserer Sicht ist die "alte Schule" den elitären Vorstellungen des alten deutschen Schulsystems ähnlich. Die "neue Schule" wiederum entspricht mehr den Formen, die wir in den USA kennen. Die "alte Schule" machte einen Übergang von einem Schulzweig zum anderen fast unmöglich, während die "neue Schule" den Übergang und das Weiterlernen förderte. Die alten Schulen bewahrten den Status quo, die neuen erlaubten Beweglichkeit. Das alte System forderte den obligatorischen Religionsunterricht und die tarifgemäße Bezahlung von Priestern, Pfarrern und anderen Religionslehrern. Es verlangte auch die staatliche Subvention der Konfessionsschulen. Die neue Schule hingegen proklamierte strikte Trennung von Kirche und Staat. Es ist ein Beweis für den positiveren Geist der zweiten Republik, daß nach hartem Ringen in den sechziger und siebziger Jahren Kompromisse möglich geworden sind, aus denen Schulgesetze entstehen konnten, wie sie noch vor vierzig Jahren kaum zu erhoffen waren. Die neuen Schulgesetze sind verfassungsgebunden und können nur durch eine 2/3 Mehrheit geändert werden. Das gibt der heutigen österreichischen Schule eine politische Stabilität, die ihr früher fehlte.

Doch zurück zum Jahre 1918 und der darauf folgenden Epoche wirtschaftlicher und politischer Not. In einer Zeit, da das alte Österreich zerbrochen war, da die alten Werte in Frage gestellt wurden, begann eine entscheidende Reformarbeit, die aus dem traditionellen, autoritären Schulsystem ein neues, freiheitliches Programm erschaffen wollte, dessen Ziel es war, das Kind zum verantwortlichen Staatsbürger zu erziehen und gleichzeitig auf die Eigenart des Kindes in seiner Begabung und Entwicklung einzugehen. Psychologie und Pädagogik sollten eng miteinander verbunden werden und gut geschulte Lehrer (die es nur begrenzt gab) hatten die Aufgabe, das Kind bis zum höchstmöglichsten Punkt seiner Entwicklung zu fördern. Diese Reformbewegung, die mit dem Namen Otto Glöckel verbunden ist, verarbeitete die Ideen und Modelle vieler Pädagogen und Philosophen aus den verschiedensten Ländern, aus Deutschland, Schweden, der Schweiz, aus Amerika (William H. Kilpatrick vom Columbia Teachers College, John Dewey, der Kinderpsychologe G. Stanley Hall) und den Wiener Psychologen und Pädagogen wie Freud, Adler, Karl und Charlotte Bühler, August Aichinger und anderen mehr. Aus den Vorstellungen der besten und fortschrittlichsten Erzieher entwickelte Glöckel sein Programm, das er in Rohform schon 1917 vorlegte.[1] Dieses Konzept deckt sich in vielem mit der amerikanischen Schulreform, ja nimmt manches voraus, was später in den USA als "neu" gepredigt wurde. Die Grundziele der Glöckelschen Schulerneuerung wollten die Richtung weisen von der "Buchschule" zur "Arbeitsschule" und können wie folgt formuliert werden. Zunächst muß die Schule von der Tyrannei des Stoffes und des Lehrers befreit werden. Die Bildung entwickelt sich aus dem "arbeitenden Handeln in Freiheit." Soziale Arbeitsformen (z.B. Gruppenarbeit) müssen für die Schule fruchtbar gemacht werden. Die Selbsttätigkeit und Schüleraktivität ist das oberste pädagogische Prinzip. Alle Unterrichtsvorgänge müssen lebensgemäß und lebensecht sein.[2]

Mit diesen strukturellen und kurrikularen Konzepten (die nur zum Teil verwirklicht werden konnten) ging Hand in Hand die Internationalisierung der österreichischen Schule. Die ersten Austauschprogramme wurden entwickelt, Schulheime zur internationalen Begegnung entstanden und schließlich, im Jahre 1926, das *Austro-American Institute of Education* in Wien, das von Paul Leo Dengler bei seinem Amerikabesuch konzipiert worden war als ein Beitrag "zur Erziehung der Nationen zum globalen Denken" und als ein neuer Weg, "ihr brennendes Interesse am Mitmenschen" wachzurufen. Denglers Manifest, unter dem Titel "International Good Will," proklamierte folgendes:

> War je eine Zeit größer als die unsere? War es je interessanter, auf dieser schönen, wunderschönen Erde zu leben? Wir sind es satt, stets alte Zeiten gepriesen zu hören. Täglich von neuen Wundern der Technik umringt, nehmen wir teil an der Entfaltung einer neuen Epoche. Ihr Ideal ist übernationale Vereinigung der Menschheit. Nicht nur die Völker des Westens suchen heute einander, die Bewegtheit der abendländischen Kultur hat auch die ruhenden Kulturen des Ostens ergriffen. Es bereitet sich ein Spannungsausgleich zwischen Menschheitsgebieten vor, wie ihn die Welt noch nie erlebt hat, noch nie erleben konnte, da die technischen Voraussetzungen fehlten. . . . In unsere täglichen Sorgen verstrickt, wurden wir uns nur selten dieser großen Menschheitsbewegung bewußt. Unser Land, losgerissen aus dem großen Zusammenhang, lag bisher abseits vom großen Strom des Erlebens.
>
> Österreichs Flüsse und Bäche in diesen Strom überzuführen ist Ziel und Sinn des Amerika-Institutes. Starke Bindungen mit den Vereinigten Staaten sollen auf allen Gebieten der Wissenschaft, Wirtschaft und Kunst geschaffen werden, dazu viele menschliche Bindungen – ein Arbeitsfeld für viele Jahre.

> Das Amerika-Institut will dazu beitragen, den "International Good Will"–die gegenseitige verständnisvolle Duldung und Anerkennung–zu festigen, denn keine andere Macht der Erde wird neue Weltbrände verhindern können als eine internationale Armee des Geistes, der jeder Krieg als ein Bruderkrieg gilt.[3]

Die Entwicklungen in Österreich und besonders in Wien hatten Weltformat. Von überall kamen Experten, um das Experiment (trotz seiner Unvollständigkeit) zu beobachten. So verzeichnet das Besucherregister der Wiener Schulen in den Jahren der Reform 490 Fachleute aus dem Deutschen Reich und, an zweiter Stelle, 373 aus den Vereinigten Staaten. Dagegen steht die Tschechoslowakei (ein Nachbarland!) mit 111 Besuchern an dritter Stelle. In den pädagogischen Fachzeitschriften der USA sind für die Zeit von 1922 bis 1934 27 Aufsätze verzeichnet, die sich mit der Reformpädagogik in Österreich befassen! Österreich beeinflußte eindeutig Amerika, und nicht umgekehrt.

Nach 1929 wurden die Reformen mehr und mehr zurückgesteckt. Als 1934 der Ständestaat das demokratische Regime ablöste, wurde auch das neue Schulsystem fast ganz abgeschafft. Man griff auf die Zeit vor 1918 zurück, man restaurierte das alte Elitesystem, man stellte in vielen Landesgebieten die katholische Bekenntnisschule wieder her (so z.B. 1935 im Burgenland). Der schöne Traum schien ausgeträumt.

Nach dem Anschluß von 1938 wurden die Schulen "eingedeutscht," um die Ostmärker zu braven Bürgern des Großdeutschen Reiches zu erziehen. Die fortschrittlichen Ideen der österreichischen und internationalen Pädagogen, der Nachdruck auf die liebevolle Unterstützung des Kindes, mußten den harten und brutalen Forderungen des neuen Regimes weichen, das mit dieser dekadenten Weichheit aufräumte.

Schulpläne, Schulbücher, Lehrer und Kinder wurden "auf Vordermann" gebracht, das österreichische Schulkonzept hatte aufgehört zu bestehen. Manche Lehrer wurden entlassen, viele akkomodierten sich mit den neuen Richtlinien und machten mit. Gerade die Volksschullehrer zeigten besonders wenig Charakterstärke.[4]

Von den Planern und Denkern, die die Konzepte der Reformpädagogik formuliert hatten, gingen viele in die Emigration. Sie haben dort auf das pädagogische Denken in den Gastländern eingewirkt. Die Vereinigten Staaten waren für sie ein besonders fruchtbarer Boden, deckten sich doch ihre Ideen mit den Vorstellungen der amerikanischen Reformer. Karl und Charlotte Bühler z.B. arbeiteten als klinische Psychologen an der University of Southern California, wo Charlotte Bühler das Werk *Childhood Problems and the Teacher* verfaßte, das jahrelang als Grundwerk der amerikanischen Lehrerausbildung galt. Siegfried Bernfeld, Bruno Bettelmann und viele andere beeinflußten das amerikanische Denken, besonders auf dem Gebiet der "Educational Psychology."

Als im April 1945 der Zusammenbruch kam, stand man auch vor dem Bankrott der Schule. Das durch die provisorische Regierung Renner proklamierte wiedererstandene Österreich hatte deutsche Schulen mit deutschem Lehr- und Lernmaterial. Doch die neue Republik wollte sofort an den Wiederaufbau gehen. Noch in den letzten Kriegstagen übernahm Ernst Fischer das Staatssekretariat für Schule und Erziehung, ohne aber viel Einfluß auf die realen Verhältnisse zu haben. Der Krieg hatte die Schulen zerstört, Schulbücher waren stark nationalsozialistisch gefärbt, Lehrer waren entweder Opfer des Krieges, oder sie waren als ehemalige Parteigenossen nicht mehr zulaßbar. Papier fehlte, Heizungsmaterial war nicht vorhanden, Kinder und Lehrer waren unterernährt, es fehlte an Kleidung – es fehlte an allem. Dennoch bedeutete die Tatsache, daß eine österreichische Regierung existierte, die eigene Vorstellungen hatte und Vorschläge machen konnte, daß die Entwicklung im befreiten Österreich andere Wege gehen konnte als in den Besatzungszonen des Deutschen Reiches. Grundsätzlich war es das Anliegen der Österreicher, zur Reformzeit der zwanziger Jahre zurückzukehren, was aber sofort wieder die bitteren Kontroversen zwischen Schwarz und Rot hervorrief.

Selbstverständlich hatten auch die Besatzungsmächte gewisse Vorstellungen von einer neuen österreichischen Schule. Daß es grundsätzliche Unterschiede zwischen den Besatzungszonen gab, war zu erwarten. Zum Teil drehte sich die Diskussion um die schwerwiegende Frage, ob Englisch oder Russisch die erste Fremdsprache sein sollte. Fragen dieser Art hinderten lange die Möglichkeit einer gesamtösterreichischen Lösung.

Im Rahmen unseres Themas ist das Verhältnis der US-Besatzungsmacht zum österreichischen Erziehungswesen von besonderem Interesse.[5] Das *Handbook, Joint Chiefs of Staff, Military Government Austria* setzte als oberstes Ziel die Ausschaltung jeglichen nationalsozialistischen Einflusses auf Schulen und Erziehungswesen. Das bedeutete praktisch, daß die Schulgesetzgebung von vor 1934 wieder eingesetzt wurde. Im Juni 1945 erhielt General Mark Clark zusätzliche Anweisungen von Washington, in dem Programm der "reorientation" die Entwicklung demokratischen Ideengutes an den österreichischen Schulen besonders zu fördern.

Im großen und ganzen war die Zusammenarbeit der Amerikaner mit den lokalen Schulbehörden positiv und konstruktiv. Die Amerikaner sahen die Einzelheiten der Kurrikulumplanung als interne Sache der österreichischen Regierung an, in die sie sich nicht einmischen wollten. Das bedeutete nicht, daß den Amerikanern die neuen Lehrpläne vom pädagogischen Standpunkt besonders zusagten. Sie diskutierten darüber mit den Beamten des Unterrichtsministeriums jedoch nur "informally" und "unofficially." Ihr Grundsatz wurde von C. J. Fry bei einer Sitzung der Besatzungsmächte im Jahre 1950 so formuliert: "We believe that Austrians should be allowed to run their own affairs. We believe in cooperating and helping and not interference and dictation. Further, we believe that the Austrians have demonstrated their own ability and should be left alone."[6]

Obwohl die Amerikaner nicht direkt eingriffen, benutzten sie verschiedene Mittel der "gentle persuasion," um den Demokratisierungsprozeß zu stärken. So wurden von der Education Division der US Army Vortragsserien zum Thema Demokratie angeboten, es wurden "workshops" organisiert (eine bis dahin eigentlich unbekannte Arbeitsmethode), und schließlich erschien ab 1948 die Zeitschrift *Erziehung,* auch von den Amerikanern herausgegegeben. Hier hatte man bewußt auf eine gleichnamige Zeitschrift der zwanziger Jahre zurückgegriffen, die als Sprachrohr der großen Reformideen gegolten hatte. Die Auflage des von der "Education

Division" herausgegebenen Blattes erreichte eine Ziffer von 35 000. Die Zeitschrift wurde den Lehrern kostenlos zugestellt, finanziert vom *Wiener Kurier.* In dieser Zeitschrift wurden die österreichischen Lehrer, von denen man meinte, sie seien "typische Provinzler," mit amerikanischen Erziehungsmethoden vertraut gemacht. *Erziehung* war aufgebaut nach Art eines *Digest* und brachte Auszüge aus amerikanischen pädagogischen Fachschriften. Ein weiteres Ziel dieser Zeitschrift war es, die österreichische Einstellung zu bekämpfen, daß die amerikanischen Besatzer kulturell unterlegen seien.

Auch amerikanische Lernmuster und Lehrbücher wurden den Österreichern als Anregung zur Verfügung gestellt. Der US-Sender strahlte besondere Bildungsprogramme aus (z.B. "Rot-Weiss-Rot Hochschule für Jedermann"), die auf ursprünglich amerikanische Sendungen zurückgriffen und für den österreichischen Bedarf abgeändert worden waren.

"Dependent Schools," zu denen österreichische Lehrer und Schulleiter oft eingeladen wurden und an denen auch Österreicher unterrichteten, galten als Direktmodell für demokratische Erziehungsmethoden. Dieses Direktverfahren wurde erweitert durch "Schuladoptionen," bei denen Schulen in den Vereinigten Staaten die Patenschaft für österreichische Schulen übernahmen. Leitende Schulpersönlichkeiten wurden in die USA eingeladen, um dort den Unterrichtsbetrieb kennenzulernen. Schließlich wurden auch Sommerseminare für Lehrer eingerichtet, die seit 1949 von der Education Division geleitet worden sind. Das Schwergewicht lag bei diesen Seminaren auf der demokratischen Gruppenarbeit.

Es wurde auch Kritik am österreichischen System geübt. Die Amerikaner waren für die Einheitsschule, um die soziale Struktur aufzulockern, sie waren gegen die Drill-Schule, sie waren für die Einführung eines fünften Hauptschuljahres, sie übten Kritik am Geschichtsunterricht, und sie meinten, daß zu viel österreichische Geschichte, Kunst- und Literaturgeschichte und zu wenig Verfassungs- und Wirtschaftsgeschichte gebracht werde.[7] Außerdem wollten sie die Eltern zur aktiven Mitarbeit am Schulleben heranziehen. Diese Kritik wurde jedoch nur in Form von Vorschlägen vorgebracht in der Hoffnung, die Schulbehörden überzeugen zu

An American classroom scene, here in Albuquerque, New Mexico, as it differs in no way from a modern Austrian scene – a friendly school ambiente, activated participating students, coeducation and the teaching with many visual aids. Photo by Rudolfo Gaitan Serrano

können. Was der "Education Division" wahrscheinlich nicht bekannt war, war die Tatsache, daß so manche dieser "amerikanischen" Vorschläge schon in Glöckels Reformpädagogik Ausdruck gefunden hatten. Sie kehrten aus der "Emigration" in ihr Ursprungsland zurück.

Was ist von all dem geblieben? Eigentlich nicht sehr viel. Gewiß, der Nachdruck auf "staatsbürgerliche Erziehung" ist von den Amerikanern gefördert worden. Er bestand aber schon in der Zeit der Reform. Die Gründung eines "Psychologischen Dienstes" für Schulbesucher und des Institus für Erziehungshilfe in Wien-Heiligenstadt als österreichische "Child Guidance Clinic" basiert auf amerikanischen Anregungen, setzt aber auch eigenständige Versuche fort, die in die zwanziger Jahre zurückgehen. Das Schulsystem, das nach 1955 in einem freien Österreich geformt wurde und gesetzlich 1962 festgelegt werden konnte, reflektiert die Erfahrungen der Vergangenheit, auch der Besatzungszeit. Von einer direkten Übernahme amerikanischer Modelle kann aber nicht die Rede sein, auch von keinem direkten Einfluß. Das Schulsystem der Bundesrepublik Österreich ist ein System, das eine westliche, demokratische Gesellschaftsordnung widerspiegelt, es ist ein System, das durch und durch österreichisch ist. Auf dem Gebiet des Erziehungswesens sind die Vereinigten Staaten und Österreich gleiche Partner, die viel von einander gelernt haben, aber dennoch ihre eigenen Wege gegangen sind.

Anmerkungen

1. Ernst Papanek, *The Austrian School Reform* (New York: Fell, 1962), S. 4-6.
2. Erik Adam, *Die österreichische Reformpädagogik 1918-1938* (Wien: Böhlau, 1981), S. 14-15.
3. Paul Leo Dengler, *Erziehung zum globalen Denken* (Salzburg: Bergland Buch, 1968), S. 49.
4. Dieter Stiefel, *Entnazifizierung in Österreich* (Wien: Europa Verlag, 1981), S. 162.
5. Im folgenden beziehe ich mich auf den Aufsatz von Helmut Engelbrecht, "Die Eingriffe der Alliierten in das österreichische Schul- und

Erziehungswesen nach 1945" in *Umerziehung und Wiederaufbau,* Die Bildungspolitik der Besatzungsmächte in Deutschland und Österreich. (Stuttgart: Klett-Cotta, 1981), S. 278-306.

6. Engelbrecht, S. 296-297.
7. Ibid., S. 302-303.

Die österreichisch-amerikanischen Beziehungen in der Ära Kreisky (1970-1983)

Wolfgang Petritsch

When Bruno Kreisky, as Austria's Chancellor, brought a check for a million dollars to the University of Minnesota as a present from the Austrian people he wanted more than to symbolize his perception of good relations between the two countries or to celebrate the American Bicentennial. The money was meant to establish a chartered Center for Austrian Studies, which still exists and flourishes in Minneapolis.

For Kreisky Austria's good relations with the United States were tantamount to a guarantee of his country's economic and political status quo under the democratic principles of the free West. He understood the Marshall Plan as America's declaration of solidarity and moral support for Austria; yet he did not abstain from criticizing the United States for mistakes made in foreign policy vis-à-vis the Middle East. Henry Kissinger once called Kreisky an important European politician whose capacity and impact far exceeded the dimensions of the country he represented.

Kontinuität und Innovation

Es gibt wohl keinen anderen Abschnitt in der jüngsten österreichischen Geschichte, der so sehr mit dem Namen einer Persönlichkeit verbunden ist, wie die siebziger Jahre. Der Zeitraum 1970 bis 1983, die Ära Kreisky, von der hier die Rede sein soll, war eine Epoche umwälzender innenpolitischer Reformen und starker internationaler Präsenz Österreichs.

Während innenpolitisch u.a. auf dem Gebiet der Straf- und Familienrechtsreform wichtige neue Akzente gesetzt wurden und Österreich an den westeuropäischen Standard herangeführt wurde, ist die Außenpolitik dieser Periode doch auch von einer Kontinuität und Kohärenz der Themen bestimmt, die für die Außenpolitik der 2. Republik insgesamt charakteristisch sind.

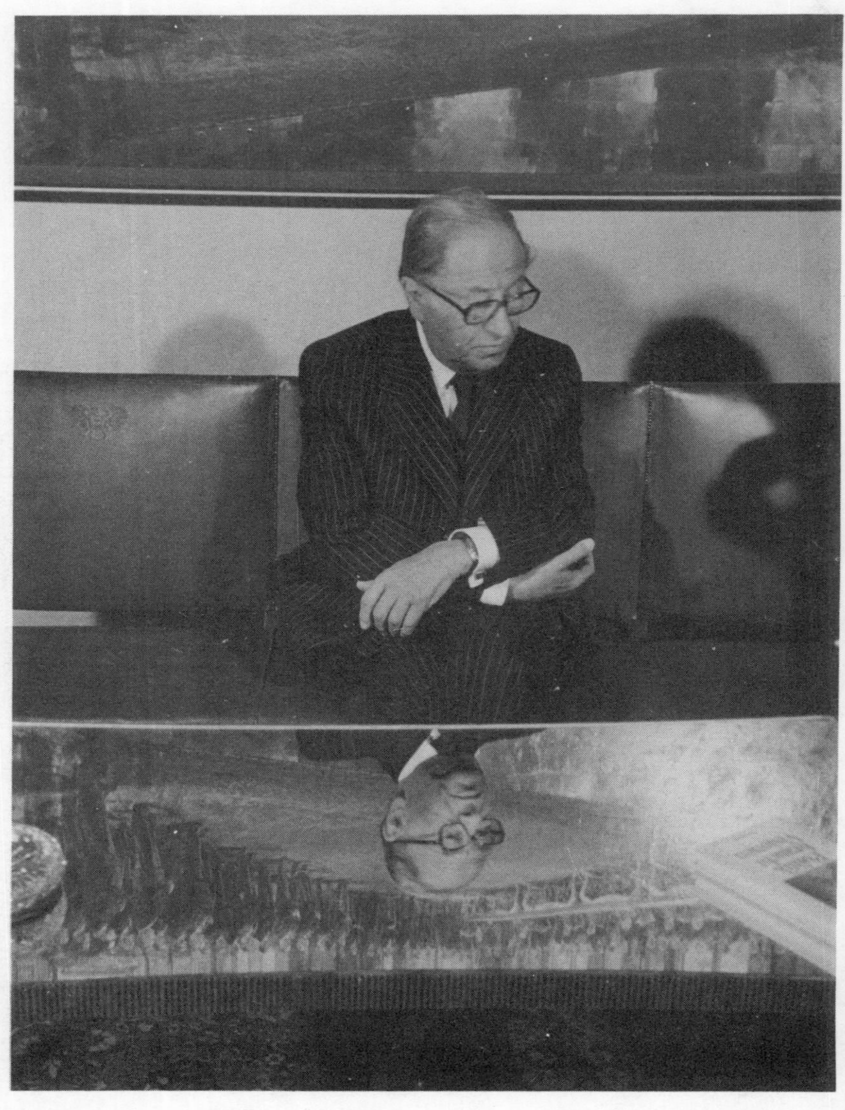

Bruno Kreisky in 1983 at the end of his service as Federal Chancellor, which had lasted since 1970. His mirror image is embellished by a painting that shows the scene of the signing of Austria's State Treaty, which he had brought about among others as well. Photo by Eugen Freund

Then Austrian State Secretary Bruno Kreisky with US President John F. Kennedy in Vienna 1961, where Kennedy met Nikita Khrushchev during a summit conference. Photo by "Bundespressedienst"

In diesem Zusammenhang ist es interessant festzuhalten, daß die Außenbeziehungen Österreichs seit Beginn der Zweiten Republik ganz klar eine Domäne des Regierungschefs sind. (Das Außenministerium als eigene Organisationseinheit gibt es erst seit 1959.) Dies läßt sich historisch wohl damit erklären, daß die Hauptziele der österreichischen Außenpolitik unmittelbar nach 1945, die Wiederherstellung Österreichs und der Abschluß des Staatsvertrags im Jahre 1955, von so vitaler Bedeutung für Österreich waren, daß sie die volle Autorität des Regierungschefs beanspruchten.

Außenpolitisches Fundament der 2. Republik

Das Wiedererstehen Österreichs in seinen Vorkriegsgrenzen wurde von den Kriegsalliierten 1943 in der "Moskauer Deklaration" festgeschrieben. Der Staatsvertrag, den Österreich 1955 mit eben diesen Kriegsalliierten und Frankreich abschloß, ist ein wesentlicher Faktor der Identität der 2. Republik.

Der Staatsvertrag definiert Österreich als souveränen und gleichberechtigten Partner im westlich-pluralistischen Gesellschaftssystem. Die Sicherung und Vertiefung dieser Identität stellt das erste Ziel der österreichischen Außenpolitik dar. (Der Staatsvertrag enthält – wie oft fälschlich angenommen wird – keine Bestimmungen über Österreichs Neutralität. Der Entscheidung, eine militärische immerwährende Neutralität zu verfolgen, wurde vom österreichischen Parlament mehrere Monate nach Abschluß des Staatsvertrags und nachdem der letzte ausländische Soldat das Bundesgebiet verlassen hatte, beschlossen.)

Westintegration

Die weltanschaulich-politische Integration Österreichs in das westliche System wurde durch den Marshall-Plan ökonomisch abgesichert. Die österreichische Volkswirtschaft wurde durch diesen historischen Akt amerikanischer Solidarität gleichsam gezwungen, vom fruchtlosen Bilateralismus vergangener Depressionszeiten in den wirtschaftlichen Multilateralismus überzuwechseln.

Einleitend läßt sich also zusammenfassend sagen, daß die Beziehungen Österreichs zu den Vereinigten Staaten von Amerika vor dem Hintergrund zweier geschichtlicher Fakten zu sehen sind:

– dem Willen der Kriegsalliierten und späteren globalen Konkurrenten, Österreich als einen der wenigen Staaten Zentraleuropas aus dem Griff des Kalten Krieges in die volle Souveränität zu entlassen;
– der ökonomischen Hilfe des Marshall-Plans.

Darüber hinaus wurden die österreichisch-amerikanischen Beziehungen jedoch von allem Anfang von der bereitwilligen Aufnahme des "American Way of Life" in Österreich gefärbt. Die ideologische Vorbildfunktion der USA und das Bewußtsein der Bedeutung eines "special relationship" zwischen den USA und Österreich ruhen auf einem breiten gesellschaftlichen Konsens in Österreich.

Kreiskys Amerika-Bild

Zwei Elemente der amerikanischen Außenpolitik der unmittelbaren Nachkriegszeit hat Kreisky in zahllosen Reden und Statements – zuerst als junger Staatssekretär, später als langjähriger Außenminister und schließlich als Regierungschef – immer wieder thematisiert:

– die "Policy of Containment" und die daraus resultierenden Chancen einer Entspannungspolitik (lediglich in einer Epoche der Entspannung ist auch für Staaten wie Österreich die Chance zu größtmöglicher außenpolitischer Entfaltung gegeben); und
– die Rolle des "European Recovery Program," des Marshall-Plans, für den Aufbau des demokratischen Europa.

Die von George Kennan entwickelte Bollwerkspolitik ist für Kreisky der "konstruktivste Beitrag der Vereinigten Staaten zur Erhaltung des Weltfriedens." "Trotz der Polarisationsprozesse in der internationalen Politik ist kein Quadratmeter eines demokratischen Landes in Europa mehr verlorengegangen, seit diese Politik begann," sagte er 1963.

Détente

Der Entspannungsprozeß – die Détente – steht in den siebziger Jahren im Zentrum von Kreiskys politischen Reflexionen.

Die Détente beginnt seiner Meinung nach mit dem Abschluß

des österreichischen Staatsvertrages. Ihre erste Phase endet mit der Unterzeichnung der Schlußakte von Helsinki im Jahre 1975, die er "den Abschluß einer ersten, aber sehr entscheidenden Phase der Einleitung und Vorbereitung der Entspannungspolitik" nennt. Von dieser Konferenz an, meint Kreisky, "muß erst die Entspannungspolitik beginnen, sie muß nun sichtbare und substantielle Resultate zeigen."

Die Einigung von Helsinki, so erklärt er 1975 in der finnischen Hauptstadt, sei nur möglich geworden, "weil der Präsident der Vereinigten Staaten, Gerald Ford, trotz aller Fährnisse die Entspannungspolitik zwischen den beiden großen Mächten in so konsequenter Weise weitergeführt hat."

An diese offensichtliche Übereinstimmung westeuropäischer und amerikanischer Politik muß gerade heute erinnert werden, wo sich der Eindruck und die Befürhrchtung verstärken, daß Westeuropa und die Vereinigen Staaten auseinanderdriften.

Marshall-Plan

Der Marshall-Plan nimmt in Kreiskys politischem Denken ebenfalls eine zentrale Position ein.

Immer wieder erinnert er daran: "Der Marshall-Plan ist ... letzten Endes eine großartige Solidaritätsaktion des amerikanischen Volkes für die europäischen Demokratien gewesen."

Kreisky sieht die historische Leistung in der Schaffung einer internationalen wirtschaftlichen Zusammenarbeit der westlichen Industrieländer, wie sie heute in der OECD institutionalisiert ist.

Die Idee des Marshall-Plans hat im übrigen der österreichischen Außenpolitik einen der originellsten Gedanken geliefert: nämlich Kreiskys Vorschlag eines "Marshall-Plans für die Dritte Welt." Kreisky hat diesen Gedanken immer wieder vorgetragen, am deutlichsten wohl im Zuge der Vorbereitungen für die Nord-Süd-Konferenz in Cancún im Oktober 1981.

Wissenschaftliche Beziehungen

Der 200. Jahrestag der amerikanischen Unabhängigkeitserklärung im Jahre 1976 bot der damaligen österreichischen Regierung unter Kreisky Gelegenheit, das besondere und enge Verhältnis zwischen

Österreich und den Vereinigten Staaten in einer konkreten Aktion zum Ausdruck zu bringen: die österreichische Öffentlichkeit wurde zu Spenden aufgerufen, die sozialdemokratische Bundesregierung verdoppelte den namhaften Spendenbetrag und aus dem Erlös wurde an der "University of Minnesota in Minneapolis" das "Center for Austrian Studies" sowie an der Stanford University ein Österreich-Lehrstuhl eingerichtet.

Austrian Federal Chancellor Bruno Kreisky is testing the peace pipe. A scene at the Center for Austrian Studies, which Kreisky had helped to found, with University of Minnesota President Peter Magrath on 16 March 1977.

Photo by William E. Wright

Diese Aktion bewies, daß sich die Österreicher sowohl ihrer Dankesschuld gegenüber den Vereinigten Staaten als auch der Notwendigkeit bewußt waren, in Zukunft die Beziehungen mit der Führungsmacht des Westens möglichst eng zu gestalten.

Politische Beziehungen

Ich will hier nicht die wichtige Frage erörtern, ob ein Staat von der Größe Österreichs der Supermacht USA überhaupt gleichberechtigt begegnen kann. Gerade die Ereignisse der vergangenen zwei Jahre zeigen schmerzlich, daß dies – jedenfalls in der politischen Praxis – nicht der Fall ist. Bei Österreich müssen weder ökonomische noch bündnispolitische Rücksichten angestellt werden, denn Österreich ist bekanntlich kein Wirtschaftsgigant wie Japan und auch nicht Mitglied der NATO.

Diese Feststellungen galten natürlich theoretisch bereits in den siebziger Jahren. Es hat sich die Situation jedoch seither graduell zu ungunsten Österreichs verändert. Trotz weiterbestehender Gemeinsamkeiten der Grundwerte gestaltet sich die Erarbeitung gemeinsamer Positionen zunehmend schwieriger.

In ganz Westeuropa wird ein zunehmendes Unverständnis der USA für europäische Belange beklagt. Gore Vidal hat dies in einem bemerkenswerten Beitrag im *Corriere della Sera* analysiert und ist zu dem Ergebnis gekommen – das man teilen mag oder nicht –, daß die europäisch-amerikanische Entfremdung primär auf sich verändernde Bildungsideale zurückzuführen sei.

Politik der siebziger Jahre

Während in den siebziger Jahren in Österreich die Ära Kreisky (und damit Kontinuitität) herrschte, fand in den USA ein reger Wechsel zwischen demokratischen und republikanischen Administrationen statt.

Dennoch gab es zwischen Österreich und den USA im Rückblick einigermaßen überraschend friktionsfreie und freundschaftliche Beziehungen. Ob der amerikanische Präsident Richard Nixon, Gerald Ford oder Jimmy Carter hieß, das Verhältnis zwischen ihrer Administration und der österreichischen Bundesregierung war im Grund – trotz der auch in Österreich teilweise heftigen Vietnam-Demonstrationen – problemlos.

Nixon, Ford and Carter besuchten Österreich und etablierten gute persönliche Beziehungen zu österreichischen Politikern, insbesondere zu Kreisky.

Die österreichisch-amerikanischen Beziehungen auf Regierungsebene erreichten zweifellos Mitte der siebziger Jahre – also am Höhepunkt der Détente – ihre größte inhaltliche Übereinstimmung. Die Unterzeichnung der Schlußakte der Konferenz für

Sicherheit und Zusammenarbeit in Europa (KSZE) in Helsinki 1975 ist das sichtbare Zeichen dieses Prozesses.

Weitere wichtige Stationen sind ohne Zweifel das Treffen Carter–Breschnew 1979 in Wien, das für Österreich, unbeschadet der globalen Relevanz der SALT-Abkommen, gleichsam die Bestätigung der Richtigkeit seines außenpolitischen Kurses zwischen den Blöcken brachte, sowie der Besuch des österreichischen Bundeskanzlers in Washington, ebenfalls im Jahre 1979.

Die beiden Ereignisse schienen die Kreiskysche Maxime "so nahe wie unbedingt notwendig zur Sowjetunion und so eng wie nur möglich mit den USA" augenfällig zu verwirklichen.

Die Ära Reagan

Der Wahlsieg Ronald Reagans und damit eines Neokonservativismus besonderer Prägung im November 1980 brachte jedoch eine nachhaltige Veränderung in den österreichisch-amerikanischen Beziehungen, ja im transatlantischen Dialog insgesamt.

Im Wahlsieg Reagans erblickte Kreisky ". . . eine fundamentale Veränderung . . . über deren Ausmaß man sich in Europa und vor allem im sozialdemokratischen Lager nicht genug Rechenschaft ablegt." Den aufflammenden Patriotismus und Fundamentalismus interpretierte er als "eine Art Rückkehr zum wahren Amerikanismus," eine Hinwendung ". . . zu jenen Auffassungen, die weit zurückreichen in die Zeit vor Roosevelt." Kreisky meinte damit in der Wirtschaft die Lehren des Monetarismus und die Theorien der "Supply Siders" vom Schlage Gelders. Er antizipierte aber bereits damals auch den ideologischen Fundamentalismus, der ihm im totalen Gegensatz zu den ursprünglichen Werten der amerikanischen Demokratie zu stehen scheint.

Dennoch warnt Kreisky vor dem enttäuschten Rückzug Europas aus dem transatlantischen Dialog. Im Gegenteil, Kreisky fordert, man müsse der neuen Administration deutlich vor Augen führen, daß "auch wenn sie unsere Auffassungen nicht teilen, diese doch von Leuten kommen, die echte, verläßliche Vertreter demokratischer Gedankengänge sind, und daß wir uns hier nicht anschicken wollen, die amerikanische Administration nur zu kritisieren."

In Anspielung auf den damals in Österreich geführten Disput, wonach die Regierung Kreisky – so jedenfalls der Vorwurf der konservativen Opposition – antiamerikanisch sei, da sie in manchen Fragen eine von den USA abweichende Position einnehme, sagte Kreisky in der vorhin zitierten Rede: "Die Konservativen reden ihnen (gemeint ist die Reagan Administration) ohnehin nach dem Mund, sie bezeichnen die amerikanische Politik heute als die große Offenbarung und wollen sie nach Möglichkeit überall nachmachen." Damit apostrophierte Kreisky wohl in erster Linie die sogenannte "Politik der Wende" in der Sozial- und Wirtschaftspolitik. Gemeint hat Kreisky aber auch die Mittelamerika-Politik der USA (Nikaragua), das Aufziehen eines neuen Kalten Krieges (im Zuge dessen Präsident Reagan bekanntlich die Sowjetunion als "Reich des Bösen" charakterisierte) und die Belastung der europäisch-amerikanischen Allianz durch die These der "Begrenzbarkeit des Atomkrieges."

Im multilateralen Bereich gelangen der österreichischen Diplomatie trotz der genannten Konfliktbereiche zwei bemerkenswerte Vorstöße, die auf die konsequente und unabhängige außenpolitische Linie dieser Ära zurückzuführen sind:

– die Nord-Süd-Konferenz von Cancún und
– der österreichische Beitrag zum Nahostproblem.

Die Nord-Süd-Konferenz von Cancún

Die Nord-Süd-Konferenz von Cancún kam im Oktober 1981 auf Initiative Kreiskys und des mexikanischen Präsidenten Lopez Portillo zustande. Diese Konferenz brachte im mexikanischen Badeort Cancún 22 Staats- und Regierungschefs zusammen, darunter so unterschiedliche Politiker wie Ronald Reagan und François Mitterand, Indira Gandhi und Ferdinand Marcos. Sie bot Gelegenheit, in ungezwungener Atmosphäre wirtschaftliche Probleme, vor allem Finanz- und Agrarfragen, die den Norden und den Süden verbinden, zu diskutieren.

Dieser erste Versuch eines Nord-Süd-Gipfelgesprächs hat nach dem Rücktritt Kreiskys kein "follow-up" erlebt; ein solches wäre wohl in den folgenden Jahren angesichts der Konfrontation zwischen Ost und West sowie der Krise der UNO auch schwer möglich gewesen.

Kreiskys Beitrag zur Behandlung des brennenden Problems des Nord-Süd-Dialogs war es, im Norden wie im Süden Mißtrauen gegen eine Initiative zu überwinden, die sich deutlich vom Format bisheriger, meist unproduktiver Nord-Süd-Konferenzen abheben sollte. Sein Verdienst war es insbesondere, die USA überzeugt zu haben, mit ihrem Präsidenten an der Konferenz teilzunehmen.

Mit der Organisation von Cancún wurden neue Maßtäbe im Nord-Süd-Dialog gesetzt und das Problem des Nord-Süd-Gefälles wurde auf die höchste Ebene der Weltpolitik gehoben. Seit dieser Konferenz ist klar, daß Probleme des Nord-Süd-Verhältnisses zu den wichtigsten Fragen heutiger Weltpolitik gehören.

Naher Osten

Ein weiterer Krisenbereich, wo die österreichische Außenpolitik der siebziger Jahre wichtige Impulse und Ideen produzierte, die sodann von den USA für eine gewisse Zeit aufgenommen worden sind, war der Nahe Osten.

Das Nahostproblem und mögliche Lösungen sorgten seit dem Ende des Yom-Kippur-Krieges 1973 für Auffassungsunterschiede zwischen Westeuropa und den USA.

Bruno Kreisky hatte zur Nahostfrage bereits als Außenminister in den sechziger Jahren eine sehr eigenständige Meinung entwickelt, die von seinen westlichen Kollegen nicht sofort geteilt wurde. Er erkannte früher als andere, daß die Palästinenser–Frage im Zentrum des gesamten Nahostkonfliktes steht. Ohne eine befriedigende Lösung für die nationale Selbstbestimmung des palästinensischen Volkes könne es keinen Frieden im Nahen Osten und daher keine Sicherheit für Israel geben, sah Kreisky.

Diese These setzte sich in Westeuropa relativ spät durch. 1979 anerkannte aber auch die Europäische Gemeinschaft in ihren Beschlüssen von Venedig das Selbstbestimmungsrecht der Palästinenser.

Dieser Überlegung schlossen sich die Vereinigten Staaten faktisch nur sehr zögernd und niemals formell an. 1982 kam es dann jedoch zur Präsentation des sogenannten Reagan-Friedensplanes für den Mittleren Osten. Dabei ist interessant für unser Thema, daß der Vorschlag des amerikanischen Präsidenten Ele-

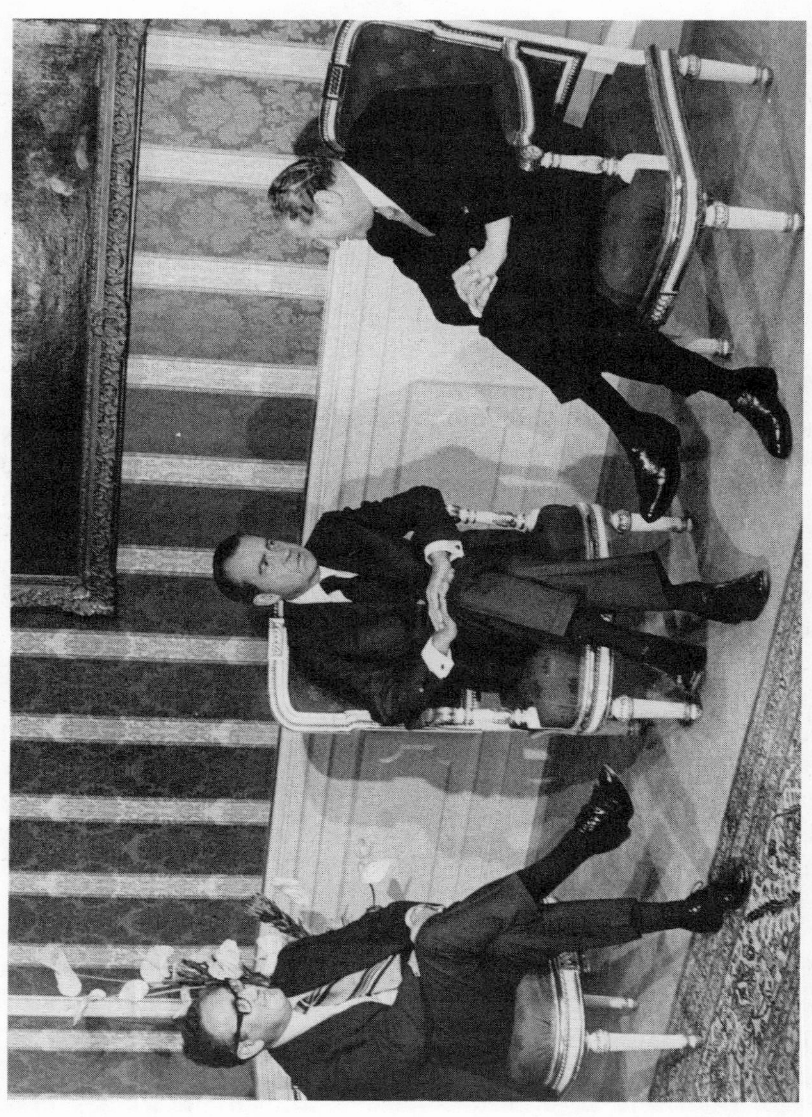

Austrian Chancellor Bruno Kreisky meets U.S.-President Richard Nixon and U.S. Secretary of State Henry Kissinger in Vienna in the early seventies.

Photo VOTAVA

mente enthält, die Österreich und seit 1979 auch die EG als Möglichkeit für eine alle Seiten befriedigende Lösung präsentiert hatten.

Dies hervorzustreichen ist umso wichtiger, als ein Vorwurf lautet, Österreichs sozialdemokratische Regierung habe die USA in der Nahostpolitik desavouiert, die USA seien irritiert über die österreichischen Kontakte mit Persönlichkeiten wie Arafat oder Gaddafi und Österreich bekäme deshalb nun im Zusammenhang mit der "causa Waldheim" den Zorn der USA zu spüren.

In der Tat gab es in den siebziger Jahren einige Ereignisse, die als "Sekundärerscheinung des Nahostkonflikts" die Beziehungen zwischen den USA und Österreich belasteten.

Die terroristische Eskalation des Nahostkonflikts nach Westeuropa machte auch vor Österreich nicht halt. Im September 1973 kam es kurz nach dem Grenzübergang nach Österreich zu einem Attentat auf eine Gruppe sowjetischer Emigranten. Ein Palästinenser-Kommando überfiel den Chopin-Expreß und nahm sowjetische Juden als Geiseln. Die Verhandlungen mit den Terroristen führten zur Schließung des jüdischen Durchgangslagers Schönau in der Nähe Wiens, was international einen Sturm der Entrüstung hervorrief. Die amerikanischen Medien kritisierten die Entscheidung Kreiskys und eine erste Trübung des Verhältnisses zwischen den USA und Österreich trat ein.

Freilich war, was als Nachgeben gegenüber Terroristen interpretiert wurde, lediglich der – durch das Ereignis beschleunigte – Nachvollzug einer längst notwendigen Maßnahme. Die Schließung des Lagers beeinträchtigte in keiner Weise Österreichs Rolle als Transitland für sowjetische Juden; im Gegenteil, die von Kreisky vertretene Regelung führte sogar zu einer Beschleunigung des Transits jüdischer Emigranten durch Österreich. Nach wie vor ist Österreich das einzige westliche Land, in das sowjetische Juden auf ihrem Weg in die Freiheit erste Station machen können. Mehr als 280.000 sowjetische Juden sind in den vergangenen 20 Jahren über Österreich nach Israel, in die USA oder in ein anderes Land ihrer Wahl ausgewandert.

Auch die Begegnungen Kreiskys mit Arafat und Gaddafi haben das Bild Österreichs in den amerikanischen Medien negativ

Austrian Chancellor Bruno Kreisky is received by U.S. President Jimmy Carter in the White House in the late seventies. Photo–UPI

beeinflußt. Die hinter den Begegnungen stehende politische Grundauffassung Kreiskys, nämlich den Dialog mit allen involvierten Parteien zu suchen, wurde jedoch von vielen ernstzunehmenden Beobachtern des Nahostkonflikts durchaus richtig verstanden.

Gerade Kreiskys Engagement im Nahostkonflikt bewog Henry Kissinger zu seiner anerkennden Charakterisierung des österreichischen Regierungschefs. In seinen politischen Memoiren schreibt der frühere amerikanische Außenminister:

> Nixon had a meeting with Austria's shrewd and perceptive Chancellor Bruno Kreisky, who had parlayed his country's formal neutrality into a position of influence beyond its strength, often by interpreting the motives of competing countries to each other. That he could bring off this balancing act was a tribute to his tact, his intelligence, and his instinct for the scope – and the limits – of indiscretion. He was much traveled; his comments on trends and personalities were invariably illuminating. He had a great sense of humor and far more geopolitical insight than many leaders from more powerful countries. One of the asymmetries of history is the lack of correspondence between the abilities of some leaders and the power of their countries. . . . Kreisky and Nixon exchanged good-humored reflections on the international situation. As a practicing politician Kreisky could not help admiring a man who stakes his election on a bold move and brings it off. Nixon remarked later that he wished Kreisky could change places with some of the Socialist leaders in larger European countries whose insight and sturdiness Nixon rated less highly.

Kreiskys Verhältnis zu Präsident Richard Nixon und seinem Außenminister Henry Kissinger war bekanntermaßen besonders eng. Alle drei sind Anhänger einer globalen politischen Betrachtungsweise, die der Außenpolitik ihrer – so verschiedenen – Länder einen je entsprechenden Stellenwert einräumte.

Nicht viel anders war das Verhältnis zum demokratischen Präsidenten Jimmy Carter – auch mit ihm verband Kreisky eine ähnliche Sicht des Nahostproblems.

Die Beziehungen kühlten sich unter der Präsidentschaft Reagans merklich ab. Im Nahen Osten verfolgten die beiden Politiker – zumindest anfangs – jedoch ähnliche Ziele. Ich zitiere aus einem bisher unveröffentlichten Brief Ronald Reagans vom 28. September 1982, also nach der Publikation des Reagan-Plans:

> Dear Chancellor Kreisky: It is good to hear that our countries are pursuing complementary policies on several questions in recent days. Your efforts in support of the United States peace initiative for the Middle East are greatly appreciated and I urge you to continue your efforts to persuade others to work with us. I pray that we may be successful in ending the division which tears this troubled region.

Technologie-Transfer

Die beiden soeben beschriebenen Bereiche betreffen internationale Probleme und illustrieren Österreichs Politik der guten Dienste.

Lassen Sie mich nun kurz ein Problem der internationalen Beziehungen skizzieren, das auch ein bilaterales Problem zwischen den USA und Österreich darstellte: die Frage des Technologietransfers.

Im Dezember 1982 berichtete die konservative Wiener Tageszeitung *Die Presse,* der Unterstaatsekretär im US-Verteidiungsministerium Fred Iklé habe Österreich mit Sanktionen gedroht, falls es die "illegale Weitergabe" – wie er es nannte – von Technologie an den Osten nicht stoppt. Zwar sei das neutrale Österreich kein Alliierter der USA, aber "Teil der westlichen Welt, der an Ideen, Erfindungen, gemeinsamen Errungenschaften und Industrievorhaben Anteil hat." Iklé weiter: "Wenn irgendwo Barrieren durchlässig werden und zusammenbrechen, dann müssen wir die Grenzen enger ziehen und Einschränkungen verhängen." Dies gelte vor allem für elektronische Technologie, da über 100 österreichische Unternehmen Zugang zu US-Datenbanken und Technologie hätten.

Kreisky reagierte sofort, obwohl zum damaligen Zeitpunkt

die ideologisch-politische Dimension noch nicht erkannbar war.

In langwierigen Verhandlungen, die insbesonders auf den neutralitätspolitischen Status Österreichs Rücksicht nehmen mußten – Österreich ist nicht Mitglied des NATO-nahen Kommitees für die Überwachung von Hochtechnologieexporten (COCOM) – wurde schließlich im Jänner 1985 eine Novelle zum österreichischen Außenhandelsgesetz in Kraft gesetzt, das die von den USA monierte Lücke schließt.

Mehr als die nunmehr aufgelisteten Fakten der amerikanischen Beschwerde störte und verstörte in Österreich der Einsatz politischen Drucks gegenüber einem amerika-freundlichen Land, zumal man auch in der US-Administration wissen mußte, daß die wirklich großen Fische woanders durchs Netz schwimmen.

Im Herbst 1987 hat eine weitere Novelle auch die – bisher – letzte offene Frage, und zwar jene des Transits von High-Tech durch Österreich in den Osten, einer hoffentlich auch die US-Administration voll befriedigenden Regelung zugeführt.

"The Widening Atlantic"

Warum, muß man fragen, geriet Österreich so sehr ins Visier der Reagan-Administration? Sind es "nur" die Falken aus dem Pentagon, oder steckt dahinter eine größere Konfliktdimension, die weit über die österreichisch-amerikanischen Kalamitäten hinausreicht?

Ich vertrete die Meinung, es ist letzteres. Die USA sehen sich einer mehrfachen, nachhaltigen Verschiebung der weltpolitischen Gewichte gegenüber:

- Im Politischen wird die "Pax Americana" der Nachkriegszeit zunehmend durch eine multipolare Struktur ersetzt.
- Im Wirtschaftlichen kann Ähnliches beobachtet werden.
- Militärisch ist die globale Dominanz der USA längst einer (auch nur noch bedingt gültigen) Bi-Polarität gewichen.

Dies hat Auswirkungen auf Europa. In den vergangenen Jahren hat sich denn auch in den europäisch-amerikanischen Beziehungen das Schlagwort vom "widening Atlantic" herausgebildet.

Dieser Begriff scheint angesichts der Intensität der Kommunikation, wie sie noch vor wenigen Jahren unvorstellbar war, paradox. Während die verfügbaren Informationen ein nie gekanntes

Ausmaß erreicht haben, scheint jedoch der Stand des gegenseitigen Verstehens abzunehmen.

Das Auseinanderdriften der beiden Machtblöcke Westeuropa – USA hat zweifellos faktische Ursachen. Lassen Sie mich ein paar Beispiele anführen:

- Seit 1983 ist der US-Handel mit Westeuropa bereits geringer als mit der pazifischen Region;
- der Prozentsatz der amerikanischen Bevölkerung in den westlichen Bundesstaaten und im Südwesten hat sich seit dem Zweiten Weltkrieg verdoppelt; dies bringt auch eine Verlagerung der ökonomischen und kulturellen Gewichte in Richtung Pazifik mit sich;
- während in den vierziger Jahren noch jeder vierte Amerikaner europäischer Herkunft war, ist es heute nur noch jeder zehnte.

Am europäischen Ufer des Atlantiks wiederum werden die Vereinigten Staaten nicht mehr, wie noch Jahre nach dem Krieg, als das Vorbild für alle Lebensbereiche angesehen. Westeuropa – und damit auch Österreich – ist selbstbewußter und auch kritischer geworden. Hinzu kommt, daß die Europäische Gemeinschaft (EG), bei allen Detailproblemen, doch so etwas wie eine neue europäische Identität zu schaffen im Begriffe ist.

Das Gemeinsame pflegen

Dennoch gibt es auf anderen, weniger leicht faßbaren Ebenen, noch genügend Gemeinsamkeiten, die nicht zu bloßen Versatzstücken mit Erinnerungswert reduziert werden dürfen.

Da ist vor allem das Bekenntnis zu den Grundwerten unserer Politik, das gemeinsame kulturelle Erbe, der bürgerliche Demokratie-Begriff mit seinen humanistischen Werten von individueller Freiheit und gesellschaftlicher Verpflichtung.

Daran sollte gerade 1987 erinnert werden, da die Beziehungen zwischen den USA und Österreich von einer längst überwunden geglaubten tragischen Vergangenheit überschattet werden.

Wie sehen die Deutschen das Verhältnis USA-Österreich

Walter Picard

The author, a former CDU Member of the West-German Parliament, believes that Austria's president Kurt Waldheim was treated in violation of international law when his name was put on the watch list by the so called Meese decision. He warns of a dangerous move into isolationism on the part of the USA, because this world power is neglecting European sentiments. Larger European contries could draw consequences counter to the policies of Western détente should such short-sighted decisions become routine.

Obwohl es reizvoll wäre und vielleicht sogar unerläßlich, die Geschichte Österreichs eingehender und durch die Jahrhunderte zu verfolgen, muß das aus zeitlichen Gründen unterbleiben. Nur so viel: Österreich, das jahrhundertelang die Hausmacht des deutschen Kaisers war, und das heraufkommende Deutsche Reich unter der Führung Preußens waren bis 1806 eine Union, die spätestens 1866 in der Schlacht von Königgrätz endgültig zerbrach. Dennoch war auch nach Entstehung des deutschen Nationalstaates das Ziel Bismarcks eine enge Zusammenarbeit, die beide ehemaligen Rivalen durch Bündnisse aneinanderband.

So ist auch nach dem ersten Weltkrieg eine enge Verbindung, ja Zusammenarbeit das Ziel des nun auf seinen deutschen Kernbestand reduzierten Österreich und der Weimarer Republik gewesen. Nach dem verlorenen Weltkrieg hatten sowohl Deutschland wie Österreich gehofft, daß, wie in den 14 Punkten des US-Präsidenten Wilson aufgeführt, in Verfolg des Selbstbestimmungsrechtes, das zur Bildung der ehemals zu Österreich-Ungarn gehörenden Nationalstaaten führte, die deutschsprachige Bevölkerung in einem Staat vereinigt würde. Die Verhandlungskommission Österreichs unter Staatskanzler Karl Renner hatte die 14 Punkte

Wilsons als Richtschnur genommen, um den Anschluß Österreichs an Deutschland zu erreichen. Dieses Ziel wurde nicht erreicht. Der Friedensvertrag von St. Germain verbot den Anschluß.

Dennoch hielt sowohl in Österreich wie in Deutschland kaum ein Politiker dies für das letzte Wort. Beide Seiten arbeiteten auf den Anschluß hin, der für Österreich allein aus wirtschaftlichen Gründen für lebensnotwendig gehalten werden mußte. Zitat von Jedlicka:

> Die Weimarer Republik hat im Spiel um Österreich seit dem Jahre 1919 zunächst auf dem Gebiet der Propaganda und der Wirtschaft, später aber aktiv über österreichische Parteien und politische Wehrverbände eingreifend, immer den Standpunkt vertreten, daß der in den Verträgen von St. Germain verbotene Anschluß Österreichs an das Deutsche Reich kommen müßte. Es gab kein Gebiet des öffentlichen Lebens in Österreich, das nicht versteckt oder offen auf diesen kommenden Anschluß vorbereitet wurde. Österreichische Politiker aller Parteien priesen die Weimarer Verfassung als das beste Verfassungswerk, und die Durchdringung der österreichischen Wirtschaft durch deutsches Kapital wurde nicht nur gefördert sondern sogar gewünscht (S. 144).

Zitat Bruno Kreisky: "Eine der stärksten Triebkräfte des Anschlußgedankens war die österreichische Sozialdemokratie. Otto Bauer hat sich immer nur als österreichischer Deutscher verstanden" (S. 43). Er trat übrigens als Staatssekretär zurück (im Außenamt) und schied aus der Regierung aus, als "die Verhandlungskommission das Anschlußverbot akzeptieren mußte." Kreisky schreibt weiter: "Aber das Thema kam zurück wie ein Bumerang. Als Hitler 1938 Österreich okkupierte, wollten alle Sozialdemokraten von Otto Bauer Antwort darauf, wie man sich jetzt verhalten solle." Bauers Antwort war lapidar: "Die Parole, die wir der Fremdherrschaft der faschistischen Eroberer aus dem Reich über Österreich entgegensetzen, kann nicht die reaktionäre Parole der Wiederherstellung der Unabhängigkeit Österreichs sein, sondern nur die revolutionäre Parole der gesamtdeutschen Revolution . . . ." Sieben Jahre später sah das allerdings anders aus.

Karl Renner, nach 1945 Kanzler und dann Bundespräsident, glaubte nicht, daß Österreich je wiederhergestellt werden könne, und nahm den Anschluß resignierend hin.

Der Anschluß von 1938 entsprach nicht den Vorstellungen von 1919 und bedeutete auch keineswegs Erfüllung der Bemühungen der zwanziger Jahre. Man muß sich aber darüber klar sein, daß er auf beiden Seiten von weiten Teilen der Bevölkerung nicht als Willkürmacht oder gar Eroberung empfunden wurde, sondern als die endliche Herbeiführung eines eigentlich längst fälligen Zustandes. Die politisch Weiterblickenden waren wie immer und überall eine kleine Minorität.

Das bittere Schicksal eines selbstverschuldeten verlorenen Krieges traf Deutschland und Österreich in gleichem Maße. Im Gegensatz zu 1918/1919 war nun kein Gedanke mehr an einen auch noch so zaghaften Versuch, beieinanderzubleiben, zumal die Alliierten die Wiederherstellung Österreichs als Ziel erklärt hatten.

Von manchem deutschen Politiker wurde die Nachkriegesentwicklung Österreichs aufmerksam verfolgt. Es war aber ein Irrtum, an dem Schicksal Österreichs eine mögliche Entwicklung für Deutschland ablesen zu können. Die Legende 1952, das angebliche Angebot der Wiedervereinigung Deutschlands gegen dessen Neutralität – hat mit dem Staatsvertrag von 1955 nichts Vergleichbares (Notenwechsel und Literatur darüber, bes. Prof. Grewe). Natürlich gibt es noch und immer wieder Träume, die den Neutralismus Deutschlands für den Zauberschlüssel zum Tor der Einheit und einer friedlichen Welt halten. Vielleicht haben die Sowjets beim Staatsvertrag eine solche Wirkung auf die öffentliche Meinung in Deutschland ins Kalkül gezogen.

Das Verhältnis USA-Österreich hat sich ähnlich dem deutsch-amerikanischen entwickelt, mit dem Unterschied, hier Neutralität eines westlichen, freiheitlichen Staates, dort Einbindung in die NATO bzw. den Warschauer Pakt; hier Wiederherstellung des vorherigen Staatsgebietes, dort Verlust von 25% desselben mit Flucht und Vertreibung seiner Bevölkerung unter unsäglichen Härten und Verlusten. Manche Deutsche könnten Österreich beneiden, wenn es den gewaltsamen Anschluß nicht vor Augen hätte.

Es gibt, soweit mir bekannt, keine entsprechende Umfrage, aber man kann sagen, daß die Deutschen das Verhältnis USA-Österreich bis in die jüngste Zeit hinein als problemlos, gut und vertrauensvoll ansahen. Das gilt, was Österreich angeht, auch heute noch, wie sich beim Besuch des österreichischen Bundeskanzlers Kreisky in USA gezeigt hat. Daran besteht wegen der engen Verbindung zwischen unseren beiden Ländern, der Gleichartigkeit der politischen, sozialen und wirtschaftlichen Lage ein großes Interesse. Es sei nur darauf hingewiesen, daß unser Handel mit Österreich weitaus bedeutender ist als mit der Sowjetunion und den mit der Schweiz fast erreicht. Jede Verschlechterung des Klimas zwischen Österreich und den USA wirkt sich negativ auf das deutsch-amerikanische Verhältnis aus. Ebenso hat eine Veränderung der Beziehungen USA-Deutschland Auswirkungen auf die zwischen USA-Österreich.

Für Deutschland ist es von hohem Wert, daß Österreich, dessen Sprache und Kultur deutsch ist, eine gar nicht zu überschätzende Wirkung ausübt, man denke nur an Komponisten wie Haydn, Mozart, Bruckner, Mahler, an Dichter wie Musil, Zweig, Roth oder auch an Sigmund Freud. Allerdings ist, wie Kreisky schreibt, diese kulturelle Vielfalt und Fruchtbarkeit mit dem Ende der Donaumonarchie dahingeschwunden, weil der Nährboden und die kulturelle Mannigfaltigkeit des Vielvölkerstaates nicht mehr vorhanden sind. Seiner Meinung nach war übrigens die Auflösung der Donaumonarchie eine Fehlentscheidung, die vermeidbar gewesen wäre, sozusagen eine Dummheit, die mehrere Väter hat.

So ist der größere Bruder Deutschland als Ganzes (Kulturnation) gewissermaßen Nutznießer des kleineren. Ich hoffe, daß das auch umgekehrt so empfunden wird. Jedenfalls ist wirtschaftlich und kulturell, aber auch politisch, das Verhältnis Österreich-Bundesrepublik ohne Probleme – und das ungeachtet der jeweiligen politischen Mehrheiten.

Selbstverständlich führt die Sympathie Deutschlands dazu, daß man bei uns alles, was Österreich betrifft, mit größter Aufmerksamkeit verfolgt und daran Anteil nimmt, als beträfe es uns selbst. Das wird bei der Lektüre deutscher Zeitungen und Zeitschriften sofort deutlich.

Meine Herren, stoppen Sie sofort die Offensive–ich kriege sonst später großen Ärger!

Frankfurter Allgemeine Zeitung–Freitag, 12. Februar 1988, Nr. 36/S. 3.–Politik

Nun heißt nicht nur der übergreifende Titel dieser Woche "von Wilson bis Waldheim," beide Namen umspannen einen Zeitraum vom Beginn des Verhältnisses USA-Österreich überhaupt – vorher gab es Österreich nicht, von dem wir reden – bis zu einem kritischen, d.h. entscheidenden Punkt. Dieser kritische Punkt berührt die USA und nicht Österreich, oder er sollte sie wenigstens berühren.

1919 fing das Verhältnis mit einer Enttäuschung an. Der Rückzug der USA vom europäischen Kontinent in den Isolationismus ist zum wesentlichen aus innenpolitischen Gründen, aber auch aus Unkenntnis der komplexen europäischen Verhältnisse erfolgt. In der amerikanischen Außenpolitik und ihren Einzelentscheidungen fällt immer auf, heute nicht weniger als vor mehr als zwei Generationen, wie groß die Abhängigkeit von der Innenpolitik ist, wie stark der Einfluß innenpolitischer, regionaler, provinzieller Interessen. Da alle vier Jahre der Präsident gewählt wird, alle zwei Jahre das ganze Haus und 1/3 des Senats, ist schon allein deshalb mit Kontinuität amerkanischer Außenpolitik nicht zu rechnen. Sie wird zusätzlich erschwert durch den permanenten Machtkampf zwischen Kapitol und dem Weißen Haus. Eine vergleichbare Situation gibt es in keinem westlichen Land.

Von diesem Hintergrund ist das Verhältnis USA-Österreich, repräsentiert in seinem Bundespräsidenten, zu sehen, wie es sich seit dem Wahlkampf vor gut einem Jahr (1986) entwickelt hat. Was bei der Zeitungslektüre auffällt, ist die gleiche Unkenntnis, die von Fahrlässigkeit und vielleicht sogar Böswilligkeit nicht frei ist, wie sie auch in der Berichterstattung der amerikanischen Medien anläßlich des Reagan-Besuchs um den 8. Mai 1985 bestimmend war. Anders ist diesmal die Übereinstimmung zwischen veröffentlichter Meinung und Regierung. Ob die eigentliche öffentliche Meinung in den USA so wie damals anders als die veröffentlichte ist, weiß ich nicht.

Die öffentliche und gleichzeitig veröffentlichte Meinung in Deutschland, soweit sie als unvoreingenommen angesehen werden kann, ist eindeutig. Es gibt kein Verständnis, noch weniger eine Entschuldigung für den Mißgriff, Bundespräsident Waldheim auf die "watch list" zu setzen. Wohl gibt es dafür eine Erklärung. Was aber müssen wir Deutsche von einem Präsidenten und einer Regierung halten, die sich aus innenpolitischer Rücksichtnahme (das ist der mildeste Ausdruck, den ich finde) zu einer solchen Fehlentscheidung und Brüskierung bewegen lassen? Man möge sich nicht täuschen hierzulande. Diese Entscheidung hat weit über Österreich hinaus eine negative Wirkung und dem Ansehen, der Glaubwürdigkeit und dem Vertrauen in die Rechtsstaatlichkeit der USA großen Schaden zugefügt. Daß dieser Akt, der nach allen zur Verfügung stehenden Informationen als Willkürakt angesehen werden muß, wonach gegenüber dem österreichischen Bundeskanzler mit der lapidaren Feststellung erklärt wurde, nach hiesiger Auffassung bedürfe es keiner Beweise gegen Leute, die in Verbrechen verwickelt gewesen seien, ist ein Skandal.

Der Skandal wird noch größer dadurch, daß bis heute Akteneinsicht verweigert wurde. Gibt es überhaupt welche, die die Bezeichnung Akte verdienen? Der österreichische Bundeskanzler Vranitzky hat übrigens sein Land bei seinem kürzlichen Besuch mit Würde, Takt und Selbstbewußtsein vertreten.

Diesen Punkt abschließend zitiere ich Professor Ernst Topitsch, Ordinarius für Philosophie an der Universität Graz: "Wo überhaupt kein Belastungsmaterial aufzutreiben ist, dort hilft die Umkehrung der Beweislast. Nicht der Ankläger hat die Schuld des Angeklagten nachzuweisen, sondern dieser seine Unschuld, wobei die Bedingungen dafür so festgesetzt werden, daß ihm dies nur schwer oder überhaupt nicht möglich ist. Wer kann etwa – wie im sogenannten Fall Waldheim – nach mehr als 40 Jahren noch beweisen, daß er einen Akt begangen oder Zeitungsartikel nicht gelesen hat. So sind einst die Hexenrichter verfahren und später Stalins "Säuberer." Wenn so etwas Schule macht, ist es mit der Rechtsstaatlichkeit bald vorbei." (Zitat aus "Die deutsche Neurose" in *Criticon* 100/101.)

Österreich ist in seiner Haltung angesichts der willkürlichen Mißhandlung und Diffamierung zu bewundern. Wir Deutsche können diese Affaire nur als ein Zeichen der Mißachtung kleiner befreundeter Staaten ansehen. Wir sind damit selbst betroffen. Ein in Gang gekommener Umdenkungsprozeß, der das deutsch-amerikanische Verhältnis betrifft, wird davon beeinflußt.

Austria and the United States as Seen by the Respective Media

A Summary Based on a Talk by Ulf Pacher

Während die Presse und die Medien in den Vereinigten Staaten in der Regel sehr wenig über Österreich berichten, was über Touristisches hinausgeht, ist die österreichische Presse von Meldungen aus den USA geradezu überschwemmt. Eine Ausnahme zur geringen Beachtung Österreichs in Amerika stellte die Waldheim-Affäre der Jahre 1986 bis 1987 dar. Sobald sie aber abgeflaut ist, wird man wieder zum Gewohnten zurückkehren.

Three predicaments offer themselves when evaluating press and media reports on Austria in the United States or, vice versa, on the United States in Austria. One is methodology: how do we evaluate the quality of this material? Second, and that is even worse, there is often very little information that could be considered hard scientific data on Austria, and practically none with regard to the Austrian press on the United States. Yet there is some semi-scientific material, one could say, with regard to the American press in its description of Austria. When we talk about the press or the media we are referring strictly to the print media, because there is no systematic analysis of either American television and how it treats Austria nor of Austrian television and how it covers the United States.

The third predicament is the problem of time reference. One could say, as a footnote, that Austria started out on the wrong foot in the American movie and public perception, largely but not exclusively because somehow the Austro-Hungarian Empire (1866 /67–1918) did not have a very good press, to put it mildly, in the young democratic and revolutionary America. Many descendants of people who came originally from the Slavic or Hungarian parts of Austria still had a perception of the Empire as a prison of people or "Völkerkerker." America is primarily and especially in its early stages a Protestant country; Austria was and is predominantly Catholic and supported the absolute monarchy until relatively late into the nineteenth century, a situation that did not help to create a favorable picture in the American press.

On the other extreme, in recent months (1986/1987) we cannot take the Waldheim "affair" as a typical press situation because it was carried out so one-sidedly. Yet for the post-World-War-II situation I have selected an example of press coverage taken from a study made by the Austria Press and Information Service in New York (APIS) that was intended to establish what had happened in the United States in 1982 in this regard. The result portrayed a picture that had been stable since 1962, when Austria's occupation and immediate postwar construction was sufficiently remote in time and the Waldheim controversy did not yet exist.

We had a clipping service at the APIS which was asked to consider every single article on Austria that had appeared in the United States, including daily newspapers, weekly newspapers, magazines, and journals. We decided to take material from the East, the South, the Middle West, and everything west of the Rockies. To demonstrate the magnitude of this task, there were in 1982 about 1780 dailies and approximately 4000 weeklies and magazines (even ten thousand other things which we did not attempt to cover). In addition there were about 2000 television and 8000 radio stations. And our findings from all that material? The breathtaking result was that in 1982 there were merely 3492 articles about Austria in the American press!

What were the topics? The most favorable topic was "culture" with 37.5% of the articles referring to Austrian matters. Second came "tourism" with 22.6%, probably attributable in part to the efforts of the Austrian tourist promotion. Topical events such as "Breshnev in Vienna" followed third with 9.7%. As to articles on Austrian affairs, 8% were devoted to general affairs, 7.7% to politics, and 5.5% to economics.

In terms of the individual items on Austrian culture the Viennese Choir Boys were by far the leading topic with 399 articles, followed by the Spanish Riding School, and thirdly (before the

Austrian wine scandal) came Wine. Other topics were "Kadafi in Vienna" or "Refugees from Poland in Austrian Camps." Reports on the sciences and technology amounted to no more than half a percentage point.

Which states published the most articles on Austria in 1982? New York was, as always, unchallenged in first place, followed by California, New Jersey, Pennsylvania, and Florida. Of all of the articles, 65% were in dailies, 18.8% in weeklies, and 16.2% in magazines and journals. According to not always reliable statistics, in 1982 40 million Americans got their information about Austria from dailies and roughly 30 million from magazines and journals.

Another item of interest is that in all of the articles about Austria Vienna was covered in 50 of them, Salzburg in 10 and Innsbruck in 3. American papers which had more than 20 articles on Austria in 1982 were the *New York Times* (far ahead with 150), *The Washington Post* (61), *Los Angeles Times* (55), *The Wall Street Journal* (43), *Chicago Tribune* (33), *The Boston Globe* (31), *USA Today* (25), *The Christian Science Monitor* (25).

After 1955, the year of the Austrian State Treaty with the Allies, a recognizable and drastic reduction of articles about Austria occurred in the United States, obviously because the "problem" had been solved. Another study shows that Austria has had an identifiable image in America, as in the world, since 1955 and it can be summarized as follows: culture and classical music, good cuisine, beautiful scenery, and winter sports. These aspects of the Austrian image are universal.

As to personalities, "the old age sun king" Bruno Kreisky led in the American press from the seventies to 1986, followed by W. A. Mozart, Kurt Waldheim (as U.N. Secretary General), Sigmund Freud, Maria Theresia, Kaiser Franz Joseph I, Gustav Klimt, and Egon Schiele. In 1986, as a sudden and atypical change, 94% of all articles regarding Austria in the *New York Times* and the *International Herald Tribune* were published on President Waldheim and "Austria During the Third Reich."

If we turn now to what the Austrian press thinks about the United States, we must first state that there is no doctoral dissertation available on this topic. One of the reasons for this neglect might stem from the fact that, except for the Waldheim issue, there was very little controversy regarding the United States in Austrian politics. The images are mostly positive since the United States protected Austria against the Soviet Union and granted economic help through the Marshall Plan. On the negative side there was criticism because of the Vietnam War – from leftist groups, mainly students. Once Vietnam was resolved the press went back more or less to pre-Vietnam sentiments, except for some harsher criticism of the Reagan government's one-sided involvement in Central and South America.

With the Waldheim affair matters changed decisively. According to new studies by serious opinion polls in 1987, 65% of the Austrians thought there had been a deterioration of relations between the United States and Austria. Suddenly, 37% of the Austrians agreed to improved relations with the Russians. Yet during the Reagan era 43% of all West Europeans thought that the relations of their countries with the United States had gone sour. Once the Waldheim controversy has calmed down – and that time should not be too far off – we will go back to normal, unless something unusual should happen again.

(Summary, using Mr. Pacher's wording, by Peter Pabisch)

An official photograph of Austrian Federal President Kurt Waldheim who was elected to office in 1986. Photo by the Austrian Press and Information Service

Der Österreichische Weg – Dr. Kurt Waldheim

Ferdinand Trauttmansdorff

Trauttmansdorff, staff member of the Austrian Embassy in Washington, D.C., was delegated to the Taos Workshop to represent President Waldheim's view. In this essay, however, a fair degree of objectivity is attempted and achieved. It also mentions mistakes and shortcomings on Waldheim's side during his election campaign for Austria's presidency in 1985/1986. On the other hand Waldheim's major achievements for Austria and himself, not least of all his holding the prestigious position of Secretary General of the United Nations for a whole decade, are stressed as favorable factors. Furthermore it is made clear that Waldheim comes from an anti-Nazi family whose members, such as his father, were persecuted for their political views. Since the end of World War II Waldheim has been a top official in Austria's diplomatic service as well as a respected member of the Austrian government during the late sixties.

Bevor ich in die Substanz meines Themas eintrete, das in den letzten Monaten so viele Gemüter erregt hat, halte ich es für zweckmäßig, einige Bemerkungen zu meiner persönlichen Position zu machen, damit Sie meine folgenden Überlegungen zum Zweck der akademischen Auseinandersetzung noch klarer an dem bei mir vorauszusetzenden Denkschema zu messen vermögen.

Ich war gerne bereit, mich im Herbst 1985 für die Mitabeit in Dr. Waldheims Wahlbüro zur Verfügung zu stellen, da ich erwartete, in diesem Wahlkampf als Parteiloser für einen parteilosen, aber zugleich wie ich der christlichen Weltanschauung anhängenden Kandidaten im Sinne meiner Weltanschauung politisch tätig werden zu können. Dies war eine in Österreich seltene Gelegenheit, da das politische Leben in unserem Land nach wie vor von den politischen Parteien beherrscht wird.

Meine persönliche Einstellung zu Dr. Waldheim als Person ist von neun Monaten engster Zusammenarbeit unter höchst spezifischen Bedingungen geprägt. Ich stehe nach wie vor zu ihm als Person, und zwar sowohl aus staatsbürgerlicher Loyalität als auch aus persönlicher Überzeugung. So fühle ich mich auch zum Teil für die Fehler mitverantwortlich, die während des Wahlkampfes gemacht wurden. Ich stehe nämlich nicht an zu bekennen, daß vor, während und nach dem Wahlkampf eine Reihe von Mißgeschicken passiert sind, die Dr. Waldheim und seiner Umgebung zuzurechnen sind. Viele dieser Fehler entstanden aus dem Zwang der Umstände und aus dem schweren Druck übertriebener, bzw. den Tatsachen nicht entsprechender, aber von der internationalen Medienszene begierig aufgegriffener Angriffe der Kritiker Dr. Waldheims. Diesen kommt daher zumindest eine Mitverantwortung für eine Reihe ungünstiger Entwicklungen im Zusammenhang mit der Kontroverse um die Kriegsvergangenheit des derzeitigen österreichischen Bundespräsidenten zu.

Eine der entscheidendsten weltanschaulichen Grundfragen meiner Jugend war und ist nach wie vor: wie konnte es zu den Verbrechen des Nationalsozialismus kommen, wie konnten diese Verbrechen von Menschen wie "du und ich" ausgeführt werden? Mitausgelöst wurde die Auseinandersetzung mit diesen Fragen durch das *Tagebuch der Anne Frank*, das mir mein Vater im Alter von zehn oder elf Jahren zu lesen gab. Dieses Buch über das tragische Schicksal eines jüdischen Mädchens im zweiten Weltkrieg hinterließ auf mich einen unauslöschlichen Eindruck, den ich bis heute nicht ganz verarbeitet habe.

Dr. Waldheim wird heute von seinen Kritikern gerne als Symbol bezeichnet. Damit konnten sich zunächst jene, die ihn weiterhin als Zielscheibe benützen wollen, der immer schwieriger werdenden Aufgabe entziehen, Dr. Waldheim konkreter Verfehlungen während des Zweiten Weltkrieges anzuklagen; die inzwischen vervollständigten Dokumente und sonstige Beweislage machen es nämlich auch für Unbelehrbare immer schwerer, eine persönliche, objektive Schuld Dr. Waldheims zu konstruieren, denn die harten Beweise sprechen dagegen.

Die Bezugnahme auf Dr. Waldheim als Symbol erfolgt in verschiedener Weise. Im negativsten Sinne wird Dr. Waldheims

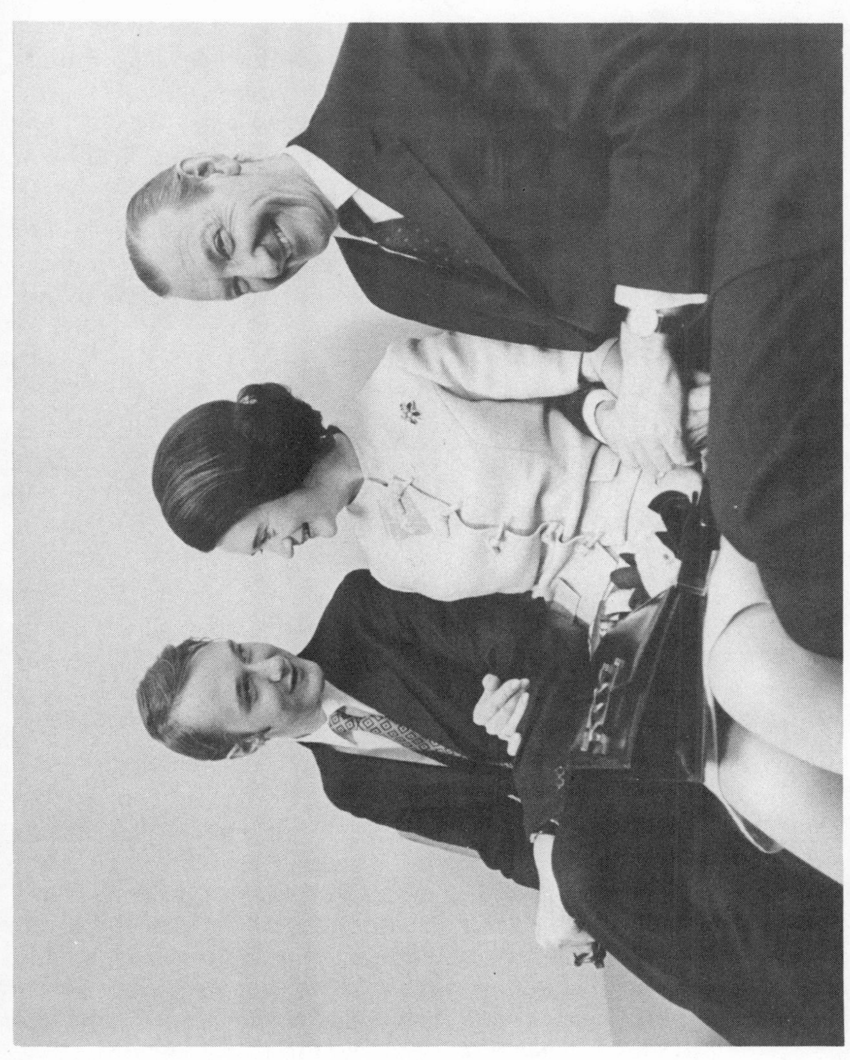

Kurt Waldheim of Austria as newly appointed Secretary-General with Mrs. Waldheim and their son Gerhard on 23 December 1971. He began his office with the New Year in 1972. At that time he was 53 years old and his country's Permanent Representative at the United Nations.

Photo by UN/Y. Nagata/ARA

Verhalten im Zweiten Weltkrieg, aber auch danach – implizit oder explizit – als symbolisch für Unwertbegriffe wie Unaufrichtigkeit und Lüge, Vergessen und Verdrängung des Holocaust, Opportunismus, Pflichterfüllung im Dienste Hitlers, Antisemitismus, Nationalsozialismus und Involvierung in oder zumindest Wissen über Kriegsverbrechen hingestellt. Zugleich wurden diese Unwerte wiederholt mit dem österreichischen Volkscharakter in Beziehung gebracht. Gegen diesen Gebrauch des Symbolbegirffes verwehre ich mich auf das Entschiedenste, da er auf unrichtigen oder entstellenden Medieninformationen beruht oder auf unsauberen moralisierenden oder hypokritischen Analysen eines angeblichen und in der Form keineswegs erwiesenen Verhaltens des österreichischen Bundespräsidenten.

Auf der anderen Seite ist Dr. Waldheims Person und sein Lebensweg so weit mit einer ganzen Generation von Europäern und – vor allem – seinem Land verknüpft, daß er tatsächlich zur Symbolgestalt geworden ist. Ja, sein Leben ist mit dem österreichischen Weg seit dem Zusammenbruch der Monarchie schlechthin aufs engste verbunden: Dr. Waldheim wurde praktisch zusammen mit der ersten Republik geboren. Nach dem Anschluß an Hitlerdeutschland teilte er das Schicksal unseres Landes mit Millionen seiner Landsleute. Nach dem Wiedererstehen unseres Landes wirkte er von Anfang an mit, Österreich wieder als vollwertiges Mitglied in die Völkergemeinschaft einzugliedern. Als die Vereinten Nationen als Hauptbühne der österreichischen Außenpolitik angesehen wurden, waren viele Österreicher auf ihn als Generalsekretär der Vereinten Nationen stolz. Jetzt, wo sich unser Land gemeinsam mit ihm der vielleicht größten internationalen Kritik in der Geschichte unseres jungen Landes ausgesetzt sieht, würden viele Österreicher – unter dem Eindruck eines niederschmetternden Medienechos – sich dieses Symbols allzugerne entledigen in der Hoffnung, daß ein solches "Schlachtopfer" die innere Selbstreinigung bewirken und den internationalen Klischeeglitzerschein der Insel der Seligen wieder herstellen würde. Andere wiederum wenden sich wehklagend von der bösen Welt ab, pflegen unser beleidigtes Selbst- und Nationalbewußtsein und verkriechen sich in authistischem Chauvinismus, oft mißverstanden als – aber auch vermischt mit – Antisemitismus.

Ich möchte hier im Gegensatz dazu den Versuch machen, uns dieser symbolhaften Verflechtung zwischen unserem Land, seiner jüngsten Geschichte und der Person unseres derzeitigen Staatsoberhauptes offen und selbstbewußt zu stellen. Keine politische Kraft in Österreich kann sich der im Lebensweg Dr. Waldheims wiederspiegelnden Geschichte unseres Landes entziehen. Die Diskussion um den Herrn Bundespräsidenten hat Grenzen und Tabus aber auch Illusionen der österreichischen Selbstdarstellung gesprengt, zugleich aber ein Feld der Selbstbetrachtung und Selbstbestimmung eröffnet, wie dies vielleicht noch nie der Fall war. So schmerzlich dieser Prozeß auch scheinen mag, liegt darin doch eine große Chance für die Zukunft unseres Landes.

1918-1938 – Die erste Republik–Die ersten beiden Lebensjahrzehnte Kurt Waldheims

Die Geburt Dr. Waldheims fällt mit den Geburtswehen Österreichs in seiner heutigen geographischen Gestalt zusammen. Dr. Waldheim wurde am 21. Dezember 1918, einen Monat nach dem Ende des Ersten Weltkrieges, in die vielleicht ärgste Not hineingeboren, die unser Land je durchleiden mußte. Das durch den Krieg ausgeblutete Kernland Österreichs war von seinen wirtschaftlichen und Ernährungsgrundlagen abgeschnitten. Die Not und Verzweiflung der Menschen war unvorstellbar. Es fehlte am Allernotwendigsten, an Nahrung und Heizung.

Die Mutter Dr. Waldheims war zwar die Tochter eines wohlhabenden Bauern, dieser mußte jedoch noch während des Ersten Weltkrieges krankheitsbedingt seine Wirtschaft aufgeben. Das durch den Verkauf der Liegenschaft erworbene Vermögen wurde durch die Geldentwertung nach Kriegsende rasch aufgezehrt.

Der Vater Dr. Waldheims wurde nach dem Krieg angesehener Lehrer an mehreren Orten in Niederösterreich, konnte jedoch von seinem damaligen Gehalt seiner Familie gerade das Überleben sichern. Die Familie Dr. Waldheims – sie war mittlerweile auf drei Kinder angewachsen – ließ sich ständig in Tulln nieder, wo der Vater Dr. Waldheims schließlich die wichtige Position eines Bezirksschulinspektors erlangte.

Österreich war damals ein Staat, "an den niemand glaubte," vielmehr noch als "ein Staat, den niemand wollte," wie Helmut Andics die Erste Republik charakterisierte.

Die ersten von der provisorischen und konstituierenden Nationalversammlung, d.h. von den ersten gesetzgebenden Körperschaften der jungen Republik erlassenen Gesetze über die Staats- und Regierungsform nannten Österreich "Deutschösterreich" und sagten unmißverständlich "Deutschösterreich ist ein Bestandteil des Deutschen Reiches."

Die durch den mangelnden Glauben an die Lebensfähigkeit Österreichs motivierte und in vielen Bevölkerungsschichten währen der Ersten Republik vorhandene Bereitschaft zum Anschluß an die demokratische Weimarer Republik muß daher insbesondere für amerikanische Augen vom 1938 erzwungenen Anschluß an Hitler-Deutschland streng unterschieden werden. Der Anschlußgedanke war in Österreich lange vor der Machtübernahme Hitlers lebendig.

Sehr wohl war dieser latente Anschlußgedanke, wie es der große Österreicher Karl Renner einmal bemerkte, weit eher ein Ausdruck des Verlassenseins der Österreicher als ein Glaube an die deutsche Herrenrasse. Es kann allerdings kein Zweifel sein, daß diese Einstellung den Widerstand gegen den von Hitler 1938 erzwungenen Anschluß vor allem unter dem Eindruck der deutschen Propagandamaschinerie nachhaltig schwächte. Denn international war Österreich zu dieser Zeit tatsächlich verlassen, nicht nur von den Westmächten, sondern schließlich auch vom Italien Mussolinis, dessen ursprüngliche Unterstützung gegen Hitler einen früheren Anschluß zu verhindern half.

Zunächst wurde jedoch Österreichs politische Landschaft in der ersten Republik durch die zunehmende Lagerbildung gekennzeichnet. Der scharfe Gegensatz zwischen Sozialdemokraten und Christlich-Sozialen kam immer stärker zum Tragen. Die in den frühen und mittleren Zwanzigerjahren gebildeten paramilitärischen Verbände begannen zu marschieren. Zusammenstöße wurden zunehmend unvermeidlich.

Dr. Waldheim war neun Jahre alt, als im Juli 1927 infolge eines von der Arbeiterbewegung als ungerecht empfundenen Justizurteils die aufgebrachten Mengen nicht mehr zurückgehalten werden konnten und der Justizpalast in Wien angezündet wurde und in Flammen aufging.

Der in Klosterneuburg die Mittelschule besuchende Kurt Waldheim erlebte immer bewußter mit, was Lagerbildung, Haß und Intoleranz schon unter Schülern bewirken konnte. Als Hitler im Jahre 1933 in Deutschland die Macht übernahm – Kurt Waldheim befand sich in seinem 15. Lebensjahr – trat auch in Österreich eine einschneidend gesellschaftspolitische Veränderung ein. Der im Mai 1932 mit der Regierung betraute Kanzler Engelbert Dollfuss nutzte eine Parlamentskrise, um die parlamentarische Demokratie auszuschalten. Immerhin wurden in Österreich als erstem Land die nationalsozialistische Partei ebenso wie die kommunistische Partei verboten. Dollfuss begründete die "Vaterländische Front," in der er versuchte, die politischen Kräfte des Volkes auf möglichst breiter Ebene einzubinden. Die Sozialdemokraten versagten freilich dem nunmehr diktatorisch regierenden Kanzler ihre Unterstützung. Im Februar 1934 kam es sodann zu bewaffneten Auseinandersetzungen zwischen dem im Untergrund weiter tätigen Schutzbund, der Exekutive und dem Bundesheer, die zu hunderten von Toten und Verletzten führten.

Im Juli 1934 kam es zu einem Putschversuch der Nationalsozialisten, der mit der Ermordung von Bundeskanzler Dollfuss am 13. Juli 1934 endete. Dem kaum 16jährigen Kurt Waldheim führte die Ermordung von Engelbert Dollfuss drastisch vor Augen, daß das bis dahin einzige Land, das Hitler aktiv und gewaltsam Widerstand leistete, dies mit dem Tod seines Regierungsschef bezahlen mußte. Es zeigte aber auch, daß Opferbereitschaft und Bestimmtheit gegenüber den Nazis zum Erfolg führen konnten, solange Österreich nicht völlig auf sich allein gestellt war.

Dollfuss' Nachfolger Kurt Schuschnigg gelang kein Ausgleich der verfeindeten österreichischen Kräfte, sondern er führte in strenger und unflexibler Weise den totalitären Ständestaat weiter. Wohl trat nach Ausschaltung der sozialdemokratischen Partei und damit der Opposition eine aufgezwungene Konsolidierung innerhalb Österreichs ein. Da der entscheidende Fehler gemacht wurde, auch die Sozialdemokraten in die Illegalität zu drängen, fehlte es Österreich jedoch trotz relativer äußerer Stabilität an der inneren Kraft, derer es bedurft hätte, dem zunehmenden Druck Hitler-Deutschlands und der Nationalsozialisten Stand zu halten.

In Österreich wurde die nationalsozialistische Agitation immer brutaler. Nationalsozialistische Schlägerbanden und Terroristengruppen schreckten vor Gewalt- und Bluttaten nicht zurück. Die Fäden zog der in München stationierte Landesleiter der Nationalsozialistischen Partei Österreichs, der Reichsdeutsche Theo Habicht. Die Zeit der wachsenden politischen Auseinandersetzungen bewog auch Kurt Waldheim, sich aktiv zu seiner christlichen Weltanschauung zu bekennen und an einem christlichen Mittelschülerverband mitzuwirken. Im Jahre 1936, während der Regierungszeit Schuschniggs, beendete Dr. Waldheim seine Mittelschulzeit und maturierte in Klosterneuburg.

Als sich abzeichnete, daß auch Italien nach dem Abessinien-Debakel Österreichs Unabhängigkeit gegenüber Hitlerdeutschland nicht mehr länger unterstützen wollte, mußte die österreichische Regierung im Jahre 1936 zur Selbsthilfe greifen: Bundeskanzler Schuschnigg führte zur Erhaltung der Unabhängigkeit Österreichs die "Allgemeine Dienstpflicht," d.h. de facto die Wehrpflicht ein, obwohl diese nach wie vor unter dem Friedensvertrag von Saint Germain verboten war. Es war der weitgehenden Handlungsunfähigkeit des Völkerbundes zu verdanken, daß Österreich im Frühjahr 1936 sozusagen auf schleichendem Wege entgegen den Friedensvertragsbestimmungen die allgemeine Wehrpflicht einführen konnte.

Im Rahmen dieser allgemeinen Wehrpflicht wurde auch Dr. Waldheim nach seiner Matura im Jahre 1936 als Einjährig-Freiwilliger zum österreichischen Bundesheer eingezogen. In seiner Liebe zu Pferden meldete er sich zur Kavallerie und rückte zum Dragonerregiment nach Stockerau bei Wien ein. Noch vor dem Anschluß brachte er es zum Zugführer der Reserve, die Voraussetzung für eine militärische Laufbahn als Reserveoffizier.

In Bezug auf die Wahl seines Studiums lehnte sich Kurt Waldheim gewissermaßen gegen den Willen seines von ihm hochrespektierten Vaters auf, der sicherlich lieber gesehen hätte, daß sein älterer Sohn Medizin studiert. Kurt Waldheim träumte schon als Mittelschüler von einer Karriere als Diplomat. Er entschied sich daher im Herbst 1937 für das Jus-Studium und inskribierte gleichzeitig an der damaligen Wiener Konsularakademie, die seinerzeit als Ausbildungsstätte für Diplomaten weltbekannt war.

Was die politische Einstellung des jungen Kurt Waldheim betraf, folgte er wie sein Bruder getreu den Spuren seines Vaters. Walter Waldheim war als Bezirksschulinspektor im Bezirk Tulln eine hochangesehene und – wie ich mich selbst während des Wahlkampfes wiederholt persönlich überzeugen konnte – weithin beliebte Persönlichkeit. Er stand fest im christlich konservativen Lager und unterstützte daher auch die "Vaterländische Front." Er war ein typischer Vertreter jener konservativen österreichischen Patrioten, die den Kommunismus ebenso entschieden und vehement ablehnten wie den Nationalsozialismus. Ganz im Sinne ihres Vaters betätigten sich daher auch die Söhne politisch, wobei sie in tatkräftigen Gegensatz zu den im Tullner Bereich tätigen nationalsozialistischen Gruppen gerieten. Dies sollte für die beiden nicht nur blaue Flecken bedeuten, die sie in einer Schlägerei mit nationalsozialistischen Schlägerbanden abbekamen, sondern sollte ihnen natürlich nach dem Anschluß entsprechende Schwierigkeiten bereiten.

Inzwischen bewegten sich die politischen Ereignisse unaufhaltsam auf den Anschluß zu. Der österreichische Bundeskanzler mußte sich am Berghof von Hitler wie ein Schulknabe abkanzeln lassen. In seiner Verzweiflung versuchte Schuschnigg der Welt nochmals im Rahmen einer Volksabstimmung zu beweisen, daß die Mehrheit der Österreicher Patrioten seien. Aber die Welt schien sich mit dem Verschwinden Österreichs von der Landkarte schon abgefunden zu haben, bzw. glaubte, wie das Münchner Abkommen später zeigte durch begrenzte Zugeständnisse den Expansionismus Hitlers eindämmen zu können.

Am Wochenende des 12. und 13. März 1938 war es soweit. Hitler kam der geplanten Volksabstimmung durch Einmarsch der deutschen Truppen zuvor. Österreich wurde von deutschen Truppen besetzt und unmittelbar danach von der Landkarte gelöscht. Die Welt schwieg. Lediglich Mexiko protestierte gegen den Einmarsch. Tausende österreichische Juden, tausende Politiker und öffentliche Funktionäre, tausende Patrioten, die sich den Nationalsozialisten aktiv entgegengestellt hatten, hatten nur wenig Zeit, ihrer unsicheren Zukunft mit Bangen entgegenzusehen. Bereits Stunden und Tage nach dem Anschluß fanden sich tausende Österreicher in Gefängnissen wieder und bald danach in Konzentrationslagern.

Es konnte daher nicht verwundern, daß auch der Vater Dr. Waldheims alsbald verhaftet und verhört, allerdings bald wieder entlassen wurde. Gleich darauf verlor er als Regimegegner jedoch seine Anstellung und wurde mit einem Minimalgehalt frühpensioniert. Die Familie Waldheim verlor damit ihre wirtschaftliche Lebensgrundlage. Walter Waldheim fügte sich in sein Schicksal, in seinem unerschütterlichen Glauben an Österreich war er jedoch offensichtlich überzeugt, daß die nationalsozialistische Herrschaft nur von begrenzter Dauer sein könne. Aus dieser Zukunftsperspektive lag es an seinen Söhnen zu versuchen, trotz ihrer ungünstigen Lage, über diese Zeit möglichst ohne Schaden hinwegzukommen und sich, soweit wie möglich, auf ein Leben danach vorzubereiten.

In diesem Sinne setzte Dr. Waldheim seine Studien an der Universität und an der Wiener Konsularakademie fort.

Die Verhältnisse hatten sich jedoch ziemlich dramatisch verändert. Alsbald wurde nicht nur die Führung der Konsularakademie nationalsozialistischer Kontrolle unterworfen, indem dem Direktor ein standfester Nationalsozialist zur Seite gestellt wurde. Auch unter den Studenten befanden sich solche, die glaubten, die Gelegenheiten nützen und sich im Angesicht der neuen Machthaber in Szene setzen zu müssen. Jene Studenten, die sich dem nationalsozialistischen Gedankengut in keiner Weise verbunden fühlten und es daher auch nicht über sich brachten, sich mit den neuen Machthabern umgehend zu arrangieren, waren nun vor ein schweres Dilemma gestellt.

Vor genau einem solchen Dilemma stand der 19jährige Kurt Waldheim: Offener Widerstand gegen die Agitation der Nationalsozialisten an der Konsularakademie hätten seine sofortige Entlassung zur Folge gehabt, somit das Ende seiner Träume von einer diplomatischen Karriere bedeutet. Dazu kam, daß er den Nazis –

ebenso wie sein Vater – bereits als Gegner bekannt war. Er entschied sich dafür zu versuchen, sich über die verbleibenden 15 Monate seines Studiums an der Konsularakademie hinwegzuretten, indem er sich politisch abstinent verhielt. Der in allen Bereichen einsetzenden Unterwerfung des öffentlichen Lebens unter die Organisierung im Rahmen der NSDAP versuchte sich Kurt Waldheim dadurch zu entziehen, daß er an Studentenveranstaltungen, die von NS-Aktivisten veranstaltet wurden, teilnahm. Leicht fiel ihm als passioniertem Reiter die Mitwirkung an einer Reitertruppe, die – von Studenten der Konsularakademie organisiert – in der Reitschule Rasumofskigasse in Wien Übungen abhielt. Auf diese Weise gelang es ihm, das Studium an der Konsularakademie zu beenden, ohne irgendeiner NS-Organisation beizutreten, was alsbald für den Verbleib an der Konsularakademie praktisch Voraussetzung bildete. So brauchte er auch seine österreichische katholische Gesinnung nicht über Bord zu werfen, um seinen persönlichen Berufswünschen dienen zu können, obwohl seine Stellung durch seine den NS-Behörden bekannten Anti-NS-Aktivitäten und die Opposition seines Vaters gegenüber dem NS-Regime äußerst verwundbar war. Viele Österreicher traten damals so obskuren Organisationen wie dem Reichskolonialbund bei, um sich dem Druck zum Beitritt zu echten NS-Organisationen zu entziehen. Ein jüdischer Mitstudent Dr. Waldheims, der sich bald nach dem Anschluß der NS-Verfolgung ausgesetzt sah und die Konsularakademie verlassen mußte, konnte sich noch sehr gut daran erinnern, daß Dr. Waldheim sein freundschaftliches Verhalten ihm gegenüber nicht wie so viele andere Mitstudenten unmittelbar nach dem Anschluß änderte. Dieser jüdische Mitstudent ist heute einer der bekanntesten Verleger Englands. Dasselbe gilt für eine holländische Mitstudentin, die während des Krieges dem holländischen Widerstand gegen die Nazis angehörte und die heute zu den vehementesten Verteidigern Dr. Waldheims gegen ungerechtfertigte Vorwürfe zählt.

Diese Teilnahme an Veranstaltungen im Rahmen der Konsularakademie sollte jedoch für Dr. Waldheim bereits kurz nach Kriegsende 1945 unangenehme Folgen zeitigen. In seinen Personalunterlagen, die von seinem späteren Gerichtsdienst beim

Landesgericht Wien stammten, fand nämlich auf bisher nicht gänzlich geklärte Weise diese Teilnahme offensichtlich in Form von Eintragungen Niederschlag, die eine Mitgliedschaft Kurt Waldheims beim nationalsozialistischen Studentenbund und bei der SA Reiterstanderte 5/90 samt angeblichen – übrigens unwahrscheinlichen – Eintrittsdaten angaben. Letztere Eintragung wäre nach dem nationalsozialistischen Verbotsgesetz von 1945 einer Aufnahme in den öffentlichen Dienst im Wege gestanden, falls sich erwiesen hätte, daß sie der Wahrheit entsprach. Dr. Waldheim, der sich freilich nie entsinnen konnte, bei irgendeiner Organisation Mitglied geworden zu sein, hatte daher unmittelbar nach dem Krieg zu beweisen, daß diese Mitgliedschaftseintragungen nicht der Wahrheit entsprachen, was ihm bekanntlich auch gelang.

Die angebliche – wenn auch bereits 1945 widerlegte – Mitgliedschaft des jungen Kurt Waldheim zu NS-Studenten- und Reiterorganisationen wird ihm von Kritikern als Ausdruck einer damaligen nationalsozialistischen Gesinnung oder zumindest als Opportunismus ausgelegt. Die Dokumentenlage und glaubhafte Zeugenaussagen sprechen eindeutig dagegen.

Unter Berücksichtigung der damaligen Umstände wäre der Opportunismusvorwurf selbst dann nur bedingt zu erheben, wenn die Mitgliedschaft Kurt Waldheims bei den genannten Organisationen erwiesen gewesen wäre. Die bestehende Dokumentenlage spricht jedoch trotz der erwähnten Eintragungen vielmehr dafür, daß der junge Kurt Waldheim derartigen Mitgliedschaften bewußt aus dem Wege gegangen ist. Sein Verhalten an der Konsularakademie nach dem Anschluß daher als opportunistisch zu bezeichnen, setzt einen moralischen Standard voraus, der mangelndes Verständnis für diese so unerhört schwierige Zeit aufbringt.

Kriegszeit – Wehrdienst 1938-1945

Im August 1938 wurde der damals neunzehneinhalbjährige Kurt Waldheim nach Absolvierung seines ersten Studienjahres zum Militärdienst bei der deutschen Wehrmacht eingezogen. Wie schon beim österreichischen Bundesheer wurde er wieder der Kavallerie in Stockerau bei Wien zugeteilt. Bereits im September wurde er im

Zuge seiner Fortbildung als Offiziersanwärter noch aus dem österreichischen Bundesheer auf eine Kavallerieausbildung nach Norddeutschland geschickt. Kurz darauf machte er seinen ersten Einsatz bei der deutschen Besetzung des Sudetenlandes im Oktober 1938 mit. Nach diesem militärischen Zwischenspiel wurde er wieder in die Reserve zurückversetzt und konnte sein zweites Jahr an der Wiener Universität bzw. an der Konsularakademie absolvieren. Im Sommer 1939 schloß er die Konsularakademie mit Auszeichnung ab. Kurz darauf wurde er endgültig zum aktiven Dienst in der Wehrmacht eingezogen, wo er bis zu Kriegsende im Mai 1945 mit Ausnahme seiner Lazarettaufenthalte, Studien- und Erholungsurlaube verblieb.

Was die eigentlichen Details seiner Kriegszeit angeht, ist soviel mehr oder weniger Ernstzunehmendes darüber geschrieben worden, daß dies bereits eine kleine Bibliothek füllen würde. Lassen sie mich zusammenfassen:

Nach einem Einsatz im Frankreichfeldzug praktisch ohne Feindberührung im Frühjahr und im Sommer 1940 kam es zu seinem einzigen echten Fronteinsatz während des Rußlandfeldzuges, den er als Zugskommandant bei den berittenen Schwadronen der "Aufklärungsabteilung 45" mitmachte, bis er im Winter 1941 nahe Orel verwundet wurde.

Nach seiner Verwundung in Rußland im Jahre 1941 konnte Leutnant Waldheim die Zeit seiner Rekonvaleszenz im ersten Viertel des Jahres 1942 praktisch dazu benutzen, sein Jus-Studium an der Wiener Universität fortzusetzen. Im Frühjahr 1942 wurde er wieder in den aktiven Dienst eingezogen, war jedoch aufgrund seiner Verletzung nicht mehr an der Front einsetzbar. Offensichtlich wegen seiner italienischen Sprachkenntnisse wurde er im Frühjahr 1942 dem in Belgrad stationierten "Armeeoberkommando 12" als Dolmetscher zur Verfügung gestellt.

Zunächst wurde er einem Verbindungsstab bei der sogenannten Kampfgruppe Bader zugeteilt, wo er als Dolmetscher helfen sollte, die Verbindung zwischen der deutschen Führung dieser Kampfgruppe und der ihr unterstellten italienischen Division "Pusteria" zu halten. Er wurde beim Hauptquartier der Pusteria eingesetzt. Bei den konkreten Kampfhandlungen und den mit den

Partisanenkämpfen leider so oft einhergehenden Übergriffen gegen Zivilisten kam der junge Offizier offensichtlich nicht zum Einsatz, zumal die italienische Division sich nur marginal an dem von der Kampfgruppe durchgeführten sogenannten Säuberungsaktionen gegen Partisanen beteiligte.

Bei der in der Folge in Westbosnien durchgeführten großangelegten Aktion gegen Partisanen im Bereich des sogenannten Kozara-Gebirges beteiligten sich die italienischen Divisionen nicht mehr. Dr. Waldheim wurde daher der dort gebildeten Kampfgruppe nicht als Dolmetscher zugeteilt, sondern in einer Hilfsfunktion im Versorgungsbereich, da Dr. Waldheim aufgrund seiner Verletzung nicht an der Front eingesetzt werden konnte, er jedoch andererseits für qualifizierte Stabsfunktionen keine geeignete Ausbildung besaß. Im Rahmen der äußerst grausamen Kampfhandlungen im Kozara-Gebiet kam es auch zu Massendeportationen von Zivilisten und massiven Übergriffen gegen diese, was neben der unmenschlichen Härte der deutschen Kriegsführung gegen Partisanen besonders auch der kroatisch-serbischen Todfeindschaft zuzuschreiben war. Auch mit diesen Operationen kam Leutnant Waldheim – und die wenigen vorhandenen Unterlagen sprechen dafür, daß er in die Kriegsrechtsverstöße und Verstöße gegen die Menschlichkeit persönlich nicht eingeschaltet war – nur am Rande in Berührung. Seitens der Kritiker Dr. Waldheims wurden jedoch – ausgehend von der routinemäßigen Verleihung eines kroatischen Ordens – Spekulationen angestellt, die bishin zum Vorwurf einer direkten Verwicklung des jungen Leutnants in massive Verstöße gegen die Menschlichkeit reichten. Diese Spekulationen sind jedoch durch keinerlei handfeste Fakten erhärtet und stützen sich darauf, daß die unvollständige Aktenlage Raum für phantasievolle Konstruktionen um die Person des jungen Leutnants lassen.

Im Spätsommer 1942 wurde Leutnant Waldheim – nun wiederum in seiner Eigenschaft als Dolmetscher – dem Stab des "Armeeoberkommandos 12" (nunmehr "Heeresgruppe E") zugeteilt. Als Dolmetscher kam er dabei naturgemäß im Stab der Feindnachrichtenabteilung (Ic) zum Einsatz. Im Winter 1942 bis Frühjahr 1943 erhielt Leutnant Waldheim nochmals einen ausgedehnten Studienurlaub, den er zu einer Fortsetzung seiner

Studien bis zum Referendar-Examen nutzte. Inzwischen zum Oberleutnant befördert, kam er im April 1943 wieder zum Stab der "Heeresgruppe E" zurück, wurde jedoch sofort zu einem Verbindungsstab nach Albanien versetzt, wo er bis zum Sommer 1943 verblieb. In diese Zeit fiel eine eintägige Verwendung als Dolmetscher bei einer Besprechung in Podgoriza von der das berühmte Bild auf dem Flugfeld stammt, um das sich die abenteuerlichsten Spekulationen einschließlich der abwegigen Idee seiner Zugehörigkeit zu einer SS-Einheit rankten.

Im Sommer 1943 kam Leutnant Waldheim bei einem größeren Verbindungsstab in Athen zum Einsatz, dem in der Folge die heikle Aufgabe zukam, nach dem "Abfall" der Italiener die Übergabeverhandlungen mit der elften italienischen Armee zu führen. In dieser Verwendung kam Obleutnant Waldheim zum ersten Mal als Ordonanzoffizier zum Einsatz. Er hatte dabei während eines Monats das Kriegstagebuch des Verbindungsstabes zu führen, weshalb sich auf einer Reihe von Dokumenten seine Paraphe findet. Besonders böswillige Kritiker nahmen die von Oberleutnant Waldheim zur Ablage im Kriegstagebuch paraphierten Dokumente zum Anlaß, ihn mit den darin beschriebenen Aktionen, von denen einige sowohl militärische als auch bedrückende massive zivile Opfer forderten, in Verbindung zu bringen. Darunter befindet sich auch ein Dokument, das eine Bezugnahme auf die jüdische Gemeinde von Joannina enthält, die später einem grausamen Schicksal entgegenging. Daraus wurde von entweder schlecht informierten oder übelwollenden Kritikern sogar eine Involvierung in Deportationen von Juden abgeleitet, wobei die tatsächlichen Ereignisse auf den Kopf gestellt werden. Aus späteren Dokumenten, die zur Zeit der Vorbereitungsmaßnahmen für den Abtransport von Italienern aus Griechenland entstanden sind und auf Oberleutnant "W." Bezug nehmen, wurde in Verzeichnung der Tatsachen eine ins Gewicht fallende persönliche Mitwirkung am Transport von Italienern in deutsche Internierungslager abgeleitet.

Aus Athen wurde Oberleutnant Waldheim im Oktober 1943 nach Arsakli zur Feindnachrichtenabteilung des Führungsstabes der "Heeresgruppe E" versetzt, wo er bis zum Kriegsende verblieb. Er nahm dort die Aufgaben eines Ordonanzoffiziers, d.h.

eines Hilfsoffiziers des für Feindnachrichten zuständigen Generalstabsoffiziers (sog. Ic) wahr und zeichnete in späterer Folge für die Erstellung der Morgen- und Abendmeldungen für den Generalstab und weitere Aufgaben wie Lageübersichten und Tätigkeitsberichte verantwortlich. Es stellte sich aufgrund der Dokumentenlage heraus, daß Mitglieder dieser Abteilung in späterer Folge auch in Einzelfällen Gefangenenvernehmungen von hochrangigen Gefangenen bzw. alliierten Kommandoangehörigen durchführten. Keine der außergewöhnlich reichlich vorhandenen Unterlagen über die damalige Tätigkeit Dr. Waldheims spricht jedoch für seine Beteiligung an diesen Vernehmungen oder für einen Einfluß das jungen Oberleutnants auf das weitere Schicksal der Vernommenen. Zu Ende des Jahres 1943 und Beginn des Jahres 1944 erhielt er nochmals zweimal kurz hintereinander Heimat- bzw. Krankenurlaub, den er zur Fertigstellung seiner Dissertation benutzte. Im April 1944 – nach seiner Promotion – kehrte Dr. Waldheim zu seiner Einheit nach Arsakli zurück. Mit Ausnahme von weiteren Urlauben anläßlich seiner Eheschließung im August 1944 und kurz vor Kriegsende verblieb Dr. Waldheim sodann als "03" zuständig für Feindnachrichten und erlebte in dieser Position die Zeit mit, in der sich die deutschen Truppen auf dem Balkan und in Griechenland auf dem Rückzug vor den Alliierten befanden und die von ihnen besetzten Gebiete einem ständigen Druck durch Partisanenverbände ausgesetzt waren. Über diese Tätigkeit gibt es eine Unzahl von Dokumenten, da Dr. Waldheim die jeweiligen Meldungen paraphierte bzw. selbst abzeichnete. Freilich war diese Tätigkeit von Relevanz für die Aktivitäten der Führung der "Heeresgruppe E," für die sie Teil der Entscheidungsgrundlage bildete. Auf diese Tatsache sowie auf den Umstand, daß auch die mit heikleren und kriegsrechtlich bzw. menschenrechtlich bedenklicheren Aufgaben befaßte Abwehr-Abteilung der Heeresgruppe dem Vorgesetzten Dr. Waldheims unterstand, gründeten sich viele der gegen ihn erhobenen Vorwürfe. Daraus versuchte man, angebliche Beteiligung an von den deutschen Truppen auf dem Balkan verübten Verstößen gegen das Kriegsrecht und die Menschlichkeit – allerdings in historisch und rechtlich unvertretbarer Weise – abzuleiten.

Beim Versuch, die Dienstzeit Dr. Waldheims auf dem Balkan

zu rekonstruieren, wurden und werden folgende historisch und juristisch nicht zu rechtfertigenden Fehler gemacht, die grundsätzlich zulasten Dr. Waldheims gehen:

1) Oberleutnant Waldheims Paraphe bzw. Unterschrift findet sich auf einer Reihe von Berichten über militärische Vorgänge, die seinerseits auf Informationen von anderen, meist untergeordneten Stellen beruhen. Dr. Waldheim wird nunmehr aufgrund dieser Tatsache nicht nur von seinen Kritikern, sondern auch von ernstzunehmenden Historikern mit den tatsächlichen Ereignissen in eine Art schuldhafte Verbindung gebracht. Die Abfolge der Ereignisse, die tatsächliche Möglichkeit Oberleutnant Waldheims, auf diese Ereignisse einzuwirken, kriegsrechtliche Kriterien und ungenügend definierte Moralvorstellungen werden miteinander in eine nebulose Beziehung gebracht, die Dr. Waldheim in eine schuldhafte Relation zu den bedauerlichen Vorgängen auf dem Balkan bringt ("Guilt by Association"). Im besonderen wird immer wieder für den Beweis einer schuldhaften Verstrickung als genügend erachtet, der "Einheit" Dr. Waldheims (das geht bis zur "Heeresgruppe E" mit einer Mannstärke etwa der US-Armee in Vietnam) die Verantwortung für Kriegsverbrechen nachzuweisen, um ihn in eine "schuldhafte" Nähe zu solchen Verstößen gegen die Menschlichkeit zu bringen (siehe die "Watch-List"-Entscheidung des US *Department of Justice*).

Diese Vorgangsweise erbringt zwar ein erhebliches Potential politisch oder medial nutzbarer Kritik gegenüber dem jetzigen Bundespräsidenten Österreichs, trägt jedoch wenig zur Klarstellung jener Fakten und Verantwortlichkeiten bei, die zu den tragischen Kriegsereignissen auf dem Balkan geführt haben.

2) Die Position Dr. Waldheims im Stab der "Heeresgruppe E" war naturgemäß in der Nähe der Entscheidungsgewalt der deutschen militärischen Führung auf dem Balkan angesiedelt. In der Beschäftigung mit der ihn betreffenden Dokumentenlage – sozusagen durch das Vergrößerungsglas – wird jedoch seine Position als im Verhältnis zur Führung untergeordneter Offizier aus dem Zusammenhang gerissen. Ihr wird perspektivisch eine überdimensionale Bedeutung für Vorgänge auf dem Balkan zugewiesen, die sich historisch nicht rechtfertigen läßt. Dadurch entsteht der

Eindruck, der junge Offizier Waldheim hätte auf die Vorgänge ungleich mehr Einfluß nehmen können, als er seine untergeordnete Position und mangelnde Befehlsgewalt tatsächlich zuließen. Hier wird offensichtlich die politische Bedeutung der Position des Generalsekretärs der Vereinten Nationen in eine geschichtliche Situation vor einem halben Jahrhundert zurückprojiziert und dabei die tatsächliche Position des damaligen jungen Offiziers aus den Proportionen und den Zusammenhängen gerissen. Dieser Fehler passiert, wohl gemerkt, auch ernstzunehmenden Historikern.

3) Vom Beginn der Anschuldigungen gegen Dr. Waldheim bis zur sogenannten "Watch-List"-Entscheidung spielten Vorwürfe eine primäre Rolle, wonach Dr. Waldheim selbst aktiv oder durch Befehlsgehorsam sich am Holocaust – im besonderen der Deportation von Juden aus Griechenland – beteiligt hätte. Obwohl nach allen Unterlagen diese Anschuldigungen die absurdesten und weitest hergeholten sind, werden sie immer wieder in den Vordergrund geschoben. Es vergißt praktisch keine Bezugnahme in den Medien auf die Kriegsvergangenhait Dr. Waldheims, auf diese Anschuldigungen hinzuweisen. Ohne die psychologischen Hintergründe dieses Phänomens vollständig ergründen zu können, dürfte es auf folgende Gründe zurückzuführen sein:

Zunächst ist der Holocaust *de facto* als auch perspektivisch das mit Abstand größte Gesamtverbrechen, das von den Nationalsozialisten verübt wurde. Anschuldigungen von der Intensität, wie sie gegen Waldheim geführt wurden, würden eine ganz andere Qualität erhalten, wenn auch nur irgendeine konkrete Verbindung zum Holocaust hergestellt werden kann. Nachforschungen und Spekulationen gingen daher von Anfang an in diese Richtung.

Genährt wurden diese Spekulationen dadurch, daß Dr. Waldheim die für uninformierte Personen schwer verständliche Feststellung machte, von den Deportationen aus Saloniki (etwa 60.000 Juden) nicht einmal gewußt zu haben, obwohl seine Dienststelle nur wenige Kilometer entfernt war. Mittlerweile ist bekannt, daß Oberleutnant Waldheim während der gesamten Periode der Deportationen aus Saloniki an anderen Dienststellen tätig oder auf Studienurlaub war. Dennoch hat diese Feststellung zusammen mit dem frühen Glaubwürdigkeitsproblem besonders für amerikanische

Augen den Eindruck entstehen lassen, daß Dr. Waldheim hier etwas Besonderes zu verbergen hätte.

4) Mit dem Abbröckeln der Anschuldigungen gegen Dr. Waldheim betreffend eine angebliche persönliche Verwicklung in Kriegsverbrechen und Verstöße gegen die Menschlichikeit konzentrierte sich die Diskussion neben der Frage der Glaubwürdigkeit insbesondere auf die Frage, was der seinerzeitige Leutnant Waldheim als Dolmetscher und Informationsoffizier über derartige Rechtswidrigkeiten gewußt haben mußte. So konzentrierte sich die historische Beweisführung zwar weitgehend auf den relativ einfach zu führenden Nachweis, über welche Ereignisse Dr. Waldheim zumindest in militärisch-abstrakter Form informiert gewesen sein mußte. Diese Beweisführung ließ jedoch bisher eine klare Aussage über die Relevanz dieser Informationen für die Klärung der Frage einer tatsächlichen oder moralischen Schuld Dr. Waldheims vermissen. Offensichtlich wird hier implizit auf den strafrechtlich relevanten Tatbestand der Mitwisserschaft abgestellt, was jedoch bei der Frage einer persönlichen Schuld eines Offiziers in einer Kriegssituation vollkommen ins Leere geht. Es wäre daher zunächst zu definieren, ob bzw. unter welchen Umständen das Wissen über militärische Vorgänge für die Beurteilung einer rechtlichen oder moralischen Schuld relevant ist, im besonderen für einen Informationsoffizier, dessen Aufgabe es ist, Informationen über militarische Vorgänge zu sammeln. Eine solche allgemein gültige Definition wurde jedoch bisher nicht erbracht. Für die Beurteilung einer Schuld Dr. Waldheims unter rechtlichen oder moralischen Kriterien kann das Wissen über bestimmte Vorgänge wohl nur dann relevant sein, wenn ihm damit die tatsächliche Möglichkeit in die Hand gegeben worden wäre, konkrete Kriegsverbrechen oder Verstöße gegen die Menschlichkeit zu verhindern.

* * *

Soweit ich die Situation aufgrund der qualifizierten Informationen beurteilen kann, die ich über die Kriegsvergangenheit Dr. Waldheims besitze, erscheint der Kriegsdienst des Herrn Bundespräsidenten symptomatisch für den Kriegsdienst von Millionen jener Österreicher zu sein, die zwangsweise zum Militär eingezogen wurden und – wenn auch für den falschen Herrn und für das falsche Ziel – so doch redlich versucht haben, ihren Kriegsdienst ohne rechtswidriges Verhalten hinter sich zu bringen. Rechtskonformes Verhalten hieß, Verstöße gegen die Regeln des Kriegsrechts, des internationalen Strafrechts oder die Menschlichkeit durch eigenes Verschulden ebenso zu vermeiden, wie Verstöße gegen jene anderen Regeln, denen die Soldaten der Deutschen Wehrmacht zu dieser Zeit unterworfen waren.

Nach den mir zu Verfügung stehenden Unterlagen ist der Kriegsdienst Dr. Waldheims durchaus innerhalb der vorerwähnten Regeln durchgeführt worden. Dr. Waldheim ist weder nach dem damals herrschenden, noch nach dem heutigen Recht persönlich schuldig geworden. Die Frage einer persönlichen Schuld Dr. Waldheims ebenso wie hunderttausender anderer, noch lebender Kriegsteilnehmer kann daher nur in der Frage nach einer Gesamt- oder Kollektivschuld derer gestellt werden, die unfreiwillig für Hitler und seine unrechtmäßigen Ziele ihren Militärdienst versehen haben. Jedoch auch die schärfsten Angreifer Dr. Waldheims lehnen den Begriff der Kollektivschuld ab.

Die Zweite Republik (1945 bis heute)

Kurz vor Kriegsende sollte Dr. Waldheim nochmals an die Front – und zwar in die Nähe von Triest – versetzt werden. In den Wirren der letzten Kriegstage konnte er jedoch das ihm befohlene Ziel nicht mehr erreichen und versuchte daher, zu seiner Frau in der Ramsau in der Steiermark zu gelangen, die in den Tagen kurz vor Kriegsende von ihrer ersten Tochter entbunden wurde. Tatsächlich langte er dort etwa zu Kriegsende ein, mußte jedoch seine Frau nochmals für einen mehrwöchigen Aufenthalt in einem US-Kriegsgefangenenlager in Bad Tölz (Bayern) verlassen, um die erforderlichen Entlassungspapiere zu erhalten.

So wie Dr. Waldheim in die bitterste Not zu Ende des Ersten Weltkriegs hineingeboren wurde, wurde auch seine älteste Tochter in die bittersten Tage unmittelbar nach dem Zweiten Weltkrieg hineingeboren. Die Familie Waldheim hatte zwar im großen und ganzen den Krieg – im Gegensatz zu hunderttausenden anderen österreichischen Familien – mehr oder wenig unbeschadet überstanden, dennoch mußte sie, wie fast alle, neu beginnen.

Unmittelbar nach seiner Entlassung aus Bad Tölz konnte Dr. Waldheim von seinem während des Krieges beendeten Studium profitieren und am Bezirksgericht in Baden seinen Gerichtsdienst beginnen. Damit war sein unmittelbares Überleben gesichert. Dennoch gab der Absolvent der Konsularakademie seine Hoffnung nicht auf, schließlich im Außenministerium aufgenommen zu werden. So stand er im Herbst 1945 in einer schlechtsitzenden Knickerbocker vor dem damaligen Sekretär des Außenministers Karl Gruber, Fritz Molden, und erkundigte sich über die Möglichkeiten einer Aufnahme im Außenministerium. Außenminister Gruber, der gerade einen Sekretär suchte, und im vom Nachwuchsmangel geplagten Kanzleramt/Außenamt keinen geeigneten Kandidaten finden konnte, nahm den offensichtlich begabten jungen Mann in sein Kabinett. Damit war Dr. Waldheim nach den Gesetzen der Ministerialbürokratie die Chance für eine brilliante Außenamtskarriere eröffnet.

Für eine Aufnahme in den Bundesdienst mußte Dr. Waldheim durch ein Verfahren nach dem NS-Verbotsgesetz gehen, das auch Minderbelasteten aus der NS-Ära einen Staatsdienst verbot. Trotz der dubiosen Eintragungen einer angeblichen Mitgliedschaft in NS-Organisationen ergab das Verfahren keine derartige Belastung. Er wurde daher zu Ende 1945 formell in den Außendienst aufgenommen. Auch diese Zeit versetzte am Lebenslauf Dr. Waldheims interessierte Journalisten und Historiker ins Jagdfieber: die Verbindung mit Außenminister Gruber und dem bekannten Widerständler und vormals Verbindungsmann zum amerikanischen Geheimdienst, dem Schwiegersohn von Allen Dulles, Fritz Molden, gab Anlaß zu allerlei Spekulationen, wonach Dr. Waldheim Verbindungen zum amerikanischen Geheimdienst unterhalten hätte.

Das Auftauchen von jugoslawischen Anschuldigungen gegen Dr. Waldheim in den UN-Kriegsverbrecherakten andererseits ließen andererseits Vermutungen aufkommen, daß dieses von den Jugoslawen seinerzeit offensichtlich aus außenpolitischen Gründen und ohne konkrete Grundlagen fabrizierte Belastungsmaterial von der sowjetischen Besatzungsmacht benützt wurde, um Dr. Waldheim ihrerseits anzuwerben. So aufregend diese Spionage-Geschichten im Wien des "Dritten Mannes" anmuten mögen, gibt es keinen konkreten Anhaltspunkt dafür, daß Dr. Waldheim von einem der beiden Geheimdienste tatsächlich angeworben worden wäre. Zwar scheint ein Dr. Waldheim betreffender Akt beim CIA noch heute zu bestehen, was jedoch über eine konkrete Anwerbung durch den amerikanischen Geheimdienst wenig aussagt. Für eine Tätigkeit für den sowjetischen Geheimdienst fehlt außer Spekulationen schon gar jede dokumentarische oder sonstige Grundlage.

Im Frühjahr 1948 wurde Dr. Waldheim als Legationssekretär nach Paris versetzt. Die nunmehr begonnene brilliante Außenamts-Karriere von Kurt Waldheim machte ihn zum Personalchef, zum österreichischen Vertreter bei der UNO, zum Botschafter in Kanada, zum Politischen Direktor, nochmals zum UNO-Botschafter, zum Außenminister, zum Präsidentschaftskandidaten und schließlich zum Generalsekretär der Vereinten Nationen.

Nach dem Ende seiner zweiten Amtsperiode als Generalsekretär der Vereinten Nationen wurde Dr. Waldheim Vorsitzender eines Rates früherer Staatsmänner, dem unter anderen der frühere Bundeskanzler Helmut Schmidt, der japanische Premierminister Fukuda und der Schweizer Bundespräsident Furggler angehörten.

Während seiner Karriere hat Dr. Waldheim an der Lösung vieler wichtiger außenpolitischer und internationaler Fragen mitgewirkt und personifizierte neben Bundeskanzler Kreisky wie kein anderer die Öffnung Österreichs als neutraler Staat für eine aktive Rolle im Rahmen der UNO-Weltorganisation. Der kleine Staat, der mit Neutralitätserklärung und Staatsvertrag ein neues Selbstverständnis erhalten hat, sah die Vereinten Nationen als die geeignete Bühne für eine Politik an, die für alle Zukunft das Schicksal verhindern sollte, das der Ersten Republik zuteil wurde.

Die Karriere Dr. Waldheims nach dem Krieg war eng verwoben mit dem neuen Selbstverständnis und dem neuen Nationalbewußtsein, mit dem Österreich aus der Katastrophe des Zweiten Weltkrieges hervorging. Der Wille zur Eigenstaatlichkeit und zur völligen Unabhängigkeit unseres Landes wuchs in den Konzentrationslagern, den Gefängnissen, der Emigration, in den Luftschutz-

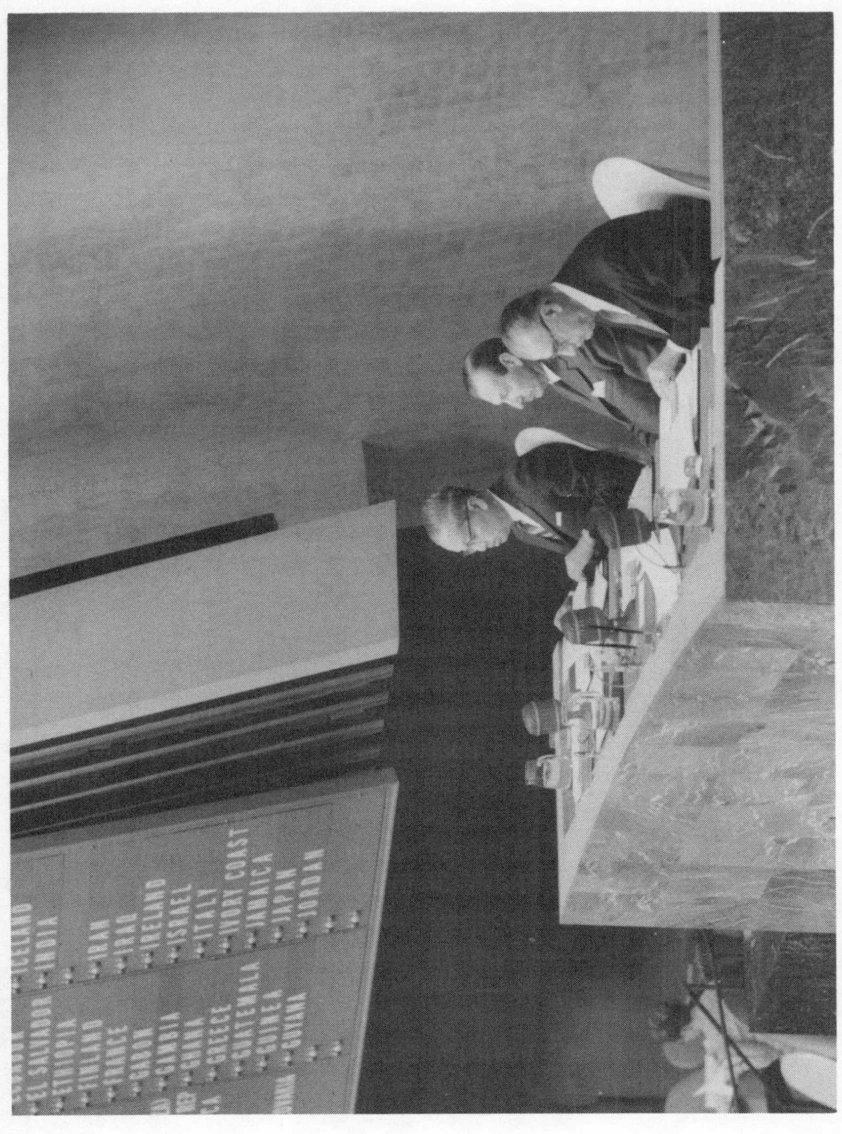

Kurt Waldheim presiding the General Assembly of the United Nations in New York.
Photo by Max Machol

kellern, in den Schützengräben und in zehn Jahren Besatzung durch die vier Siegermächte. Diese Unabhängigkeit wurde 1955 durch unseren Staatsvertrag wiederbegründet und die aus freien Stücken erklärte immerwährende Neutralität unseres Landes machte die Erhaltung der Unabhängigkeit und territorialen Integrität Österreichs zur ersten Maxime der gesamten österreichischen Politik.

Österreich hatte den Zweiten Weltkrieg als ursprünglicher Teil des Deutschen Reiches mitgemacht. Österreicher haben ebenso zu den Verbrechen des NS-Regimes beigetragen, wie hunderttausende Österreicher ihre Opfer wurden. Millionen Österreicher überstanden diese Zeit mehr oder weniger unbeschadet und hatten zu Kriegsende nichts anderes im Sinn, als Österreich aus den Trümmern als neues Staatswesen aufzubauen, dem das Schicksal der dreißiger Jahre und die Schreckensherrschaft des NS-Regimes für alle Zukunft erspart bleiben sollte. Hiezu wandten sich die meisten Österreicher bewußt von ihrer unmittelbaren Vergangenheit ab, ließen sie hinter sich und investierten ihre ganze Kraft in die Zukunft. Dem kam zugute, daß Österreich die NS-Verbrechen nicht in der Form zu verantworten hatte wie Deutschland und daß für Österreich dieses traurige Kapitel seiner Geschichte spätestens mit dem Staatsvertrag und dem Abschluß der Entnazifizierungsverfahren formell abgeschlossen war. Dazu kam, daß die führenden Köpfe, die Österreich in die Zweite Republik führten, zum überwiegenden Teil den Opfern des NS-Regimes bzw. seinen aktiven Gegnern angehörten. Die feste Grundlage der Zweiten Republik beruht auf dem gemeinsamen Schicksal, das die wichtigsten Führer der Zweiten Republik in den KZ's und der Emigration teilten. Wenn diese Österreich in eine neue Zukunft führten, warum sich dann quälenden Fragen darüber stellen, wie es zur Katastrophe des Zweiten Weltkrieges und den Verbrechen der NS-Herrschaft kommen konnte und welche Rolle Österreicher dabei spielten?

Damit zogen sich die Österreicher vielleicht etwas zu schnell aus der Affäre und haben – wie sich heute zeigt – die tragischen Jahre, denen die erfolgreiche Zweite Republik ihre Existenz verdankt, in ungenügender Weise aufgearbeitet. Im nachhinein zeigte sich, daß dieser Prozeß spätestens mit dem Abgang jener

Generation fällig war, der die Kriegsverbrecher, die willigen und begeisterten Unterstützer des NS-Regimes ebenso angehörten wie die Opfer des NS-Terrors, Emigranten, die KZ-Insassen, die Flüchtlinge, die sonstigen Kriegsgeschädigten und die Widerstandskämpfer.

Dieser geschichtlich offensichtlich notwendige Prozeß für unser Land wurde mehr zufällig als geplant während des Präsidentschaftswahlkampfes 1986 mit den Anschuldigungen gegen den jetzigen österreichischen Bundespräsidenten eingeleitet. So unfair und unwahr diese Anschuldigungen sein mögen, so schwer es für den Betroffenen selbst und viele Österreicher sein mag, diese ungerechten Beschuldigungen zu ertragen, so müssen wir doch im nachhinein denjenigen, die die Anschuldigungen gegen unser Staatsoberhaupt erhoben haben, gewissermaßen auch dankbar sein. Es zeigt sich immer mehr, daß dieser Prozeß, uns unserer tragischen Vergangenheit der dreißiger und vierziger Jahre zu stellen, für die Reife unserer Republik, unserer Demokratie von größter Bedeutung ist. Nur wenn wir die Weltoffenheit aufbringen, diesen Prozeß auch vor der Welt und mit der Welt erfolgreich abzuschließen, haben wir die Reifeprüfung für die Zukunft bestanden. Bereits jetzt zeigt sich, daß zumindest die österreichische Jugend immer offener über Dinge zu debattieren versteht, die über Jahrzehnte als tabu gegolten haben. Darunter fällt besonders auch die Verarbeitung der dreißiger Jahre und der blutigen Gegensätze zwischen den Kräften, die sich zu Beginn der Zweiten Republik zusammengefunden haben, ein blühendes Staatswesen auf die Beine zu stellen. Nur wenn wir uns der inhärenten Gegensätze und der Möglichkeiten ihrer erfolgreichen Überwindung für alle Zukunft bewußt sind, wird dieses Miteinander auch weiterhin auf einer gesunden Basis beruhen.

Die mit der Debatte um die Kriegsvergangenheit Dr. Waldheims ebenfalls vom Zaun gebrochene Diskussion um den latenten Anti-Semitismus in Österreich ist andererseits jener Teil der Reifeprüfung, der Österreich die erwähnte Weltoffenheit attestieren soll. Sie ist notwending, um auch in Zukunft in der Völkerfamilie als wertvolles und von allen anerkanntes Mitglied bestehen zu können. Ich sehe beruhigend viele Anzeichen, die darauf hindeuten, daß Österreich diese Reifeprüfung bestehen wird.

Exkurs: Die Verschweigung des Kriegsdienstes?

Vieles in der Diskussion um den Kriegsdienst Dr. Waldheims drehte sich darum, ob er absichtlich einen Teil seines Kriegsdientes verschwiegen hat oder nicht. Es steht außer Diskussion, daß Dr. Waldheim in seinem Buch *Im Glaspalast der Weltpolitik* oder *In the Eye of the Storm* auf seinen Kriegsdienst im Balkan nicht weiter eingegangen ist. Daraus wurde der für das angelsächsische Rechtsverständnis fast zwingende Schluß gezogen, daß Dr. Waldheim damit persönliches schuldhaftes Verhalten auf dem Balkan verbergen wollte. Dieser Schluß ist nach europäischem Rechtsverständnis nur dann zulässig, wenn es konkrete Beweise für schuldhaftes Verhalten gibt. Bei Dr. Waldheim fehlen sie nach wie vor.

Unter seinen verschiedenen Kriegseinsätzen nannte Dr. Waldheim ausdrücklich nur seinen Einsatz in Rußland und dort primär den Umstand seiner Verwundung. Tatsächlich wurde diese Verwundung für ihn zu einem Schlüsselerlebnis, nicht nur weil sie sicherlich mit der abenteuerlichsten Zeit seines Kriegseinsatzes verbunden war, sondern auch weil diese Verwundung – fast ein klassischer "Heimatschuß" – ihm die Fortsetzung seines Studiums ermöglicht hat, was bei einem Verbleib an der Front praktisch ausgeschlossen war. In den jeweiligen Dolmetscher- und Stabspositionen, in denen er in der Folge auf dem Balkan diente, bekam er innerhalb von zwei Jahren über ein halbes Jahr Urlaub, was ihm genügte, sein Studium bis zum Frühjahr 1944 vollständig abzuschließen. Unter dem Gesichtspunkt einer Vorbereitung auf seine Zukunft nach der NS-Zeit besteht kein Zweifel, daß er mit der Hervorhebung seiner Verwundung und seines Studiums in den biographischen Angaben das Bild seines Wehrdienstes zwar unvollständig, aber – subjektiv gesehen – richtig dargestellt hat. Dies umsomehr, als es – zumindest in Europa – bei biographischen Hinweisen unüblich ist, im Detail auf den Kriegsdienst einzugehen.

Die in vieler Hinsicht vor allem medial ausufernde Diskussion um seine Kriegsdienstzeit hat überdies gezeigt, daß eine wie üblich kursorische Darstellung seines Kriegsdienstes auf dem Balkan, ohne in alle Details auführlich einzugehen, bereits früher ähnliche Reaktionen bewirkt hätte. Schlampige Hinweise auf seinen Dienst am Balkan hätten nicht nur Dr. Waldheims vorsichtigem Charakter und seiner langjährigen diplomatischen Erfahrung widersprochen, sondern auch der typisch österreichischen Maxime, unötigen Kontroversen aus dem Weg zu gehen.

Damit ist lediglich eine Erklärung, aber sicherlich noch keine Rechtfertigung für die mangelnde Darstellung seiner Aktivitäten auf dem Balkan während des Krieges gegeben. Diese stellte sich *im nachhinein* schlicht und einfach als politisches Versäumnis heraus. Dies insbesondere im Lichte der moralischen Sensibilität, die an die Position des Generalsekretärs der Vereinten Nationen geknüpft ist und der Tatsache, daß Dokumente über diese Aktivitäten existierten, die allerdings erst im Jahre 1986 der Öffentlichkeit, aber auch ihm selbst bekannt wurden.

Die Verhaltensweise Dr. Waldheims ist im Kern typisch für die österreichische Kriegsgeneration, die meint, ihren Kriegsdienst zwar für den falschen Herren, aber nach allen Regeln korrekt durchgeführt zu haben. Viele Augehörige dieser Generation haben – in der überwiegenden Mehrheit gegen ihren Willen in den Krieg getrieben – an den Fronten ihren Kopf hingehalten und zu hunderttausenden ihr Leben gelassen; Sie haben in den Fliegerangriffen ihre Familie und ihr Heim verloren. Dafür sollten sie die alleinige Verantwortung tragen, nicht nur für die Verbrechen und Übergriffe während des Krieges –, ohne gleichzeitig auch über das von der Gegenseite angerichtete ebenfalls unfaßbare menschliche Leid zu urteilen, – sondern die Verantwortung auch für die unsagbaren Verbrechen Hitlers und seiner Schergen, mit denen sich spätestens nach Eintritt einer ersten Ernüchterung die überwiegende Mehrheit nie identifizieren konnte? Dies können viele nicht akzeptieren.

The Controversy over Austria's President-
Myth and Facts

A Summary by Peter Pabisch, Moderator

The four panelists, Ulf Pacher, Gerald Nash, Horst Jarka, and Ferdinand Trauttmansdorff, each introduced his basic viewpoints in five-minute statements which were followed by an hour-long question and answer period. The entire discussion was taped and is available on cassette. Despite their contrasting viewpoints the panelists observed fair presentation standards.

Ferdinand Trauttmansdorff spoke in favor of Kurt Waldheim but did not refrain from expressing his own personal view, thereby defending the President more convincingly. He summarized the situation by insisting on Waldheim's personal innocence. Waldheim is definitely *not* anti-Semitic and had no part in any deportations or other war crimes. On the other hand, Waldheim referred to himself as no hero in World War II. That he should now stand symbolically for an era that belonged to the worst in modern human history has to be accepted as fact. Yet it is an unfair proposition because Waldheim certainly cannot be compared to any of the masterminds of the Third Reich; he was not even a member of the Nazi party and its organization and never in his life showed any sympathy for the Nazi ideology.

That Waldheim tended to forget his war service has to be considered a subjective move on his part, one that is psychologically understandable: no one likes to remember bad times. Here we may find a mistake in his thinking, which he tried to correct during his election campaign and thereafter. Waldheim has acknowledged that we can only learn from history if we discuss it so that its events do not recur. That the American government put Waldheim's name on the watch list of persons unwanted in the United

States has to be seen as an act of American internal politics without any legal or factual justification.

Gerald Nash was asked to represent the Jewish viewpoint. In comparing Kurt Waldheim to German Federal President Richard von Weizsäcker, Nash pointed out that the latter has tried to bring about an awareness of the German Nazi past. Although von Weizsäcker was a member of the Nazi party, the Jewish community is willing to accept him as a believable leader in the Germans' efforts to overcome the past. Waldheim, by distorting, shielding, and even denying Germany's, Austria's, and his own past, has maneuvered himself into a behavior that is typical for many war criminals much more eminent than he ever could have been. Because he has sought and found the highest office in his country he is blamed symbolically for anything Austria stood for politically during the war years. Many people in the Jewish community do not belong to the World Jewish Congress, which started the confrontation, but are grateful that the matter has been brought to light. The German and Austrian Jews were decimated during the holocaust, and Waldheim attracted many votes from Austrians who were affiliated with the era and sympathized with it. Many of these Austrians are anti-Semitic, a sentiment that has returned more openly in recent months. Waldheim's acceptance of invitations to Jordan and the Vatican did not help to diminish the doubts about him in the Jewish community because both states have not yet accepted Israel as a state.

Horst Jarka discussed the variety of opinions voiced in Austria regarding the Waldheim controversy. Many Austrians refer to the watch list as the "Watschenliste" and call Waldheim a "Justamentpräsident" who was elected only to oppose the world opinion against him. Yet others have called for "Trauerarbeit," i.e., to discuss Austria's past and make plans for the future. Jarka even introduced a tape recorded in Vienna during the weeks of "Mahnwache" (June 1987), when thousands of Austrians met in front of St. Stephan's Cathedral to debate the past in Hydepark-fashion. The generation gap surfaced prominently during these spontaneous sessions, but the learning process produced positive effects.

Ulf Pacher enlightened his audience about anti-Nazi demonstrations in Austria, which were not a new occurrence. He himself had led some of them in his student days three decades ago, when the infamous Taras-Borodajkewicz-case caused students to demonstrate in Vienna against a University of Vienna history professor who retained Nazi ideals even after the war. Pacher charged that the American side had blown the Waldheim affair and Austrian anti-Semitism out of proportion, leaving the basically uninformed American viewers and readers with a one-sided picture. The present uneasiness in Austria has to be seen rather as a complex process of a basically democratic Austrian society. Yet Pacher too welcomed the learning experience accompanying the Waldheim controversy because it could bring about a new awareness in the Austrians' understanding of their own history.

Some key questions and answers regarding the formal presentations pinpointed several issues. Why did Waldheim become a symbolic figure for Austria's Nazi past (Picard)? Nash replied: because anti-Semitism is still present. Trauttmansdorff countered that the World Jewish Congress may have instigated the surfacing of real and apparent anti-Semitic reactions through its leaders' unfair attacks on Waldheim.

Martin Ögg asked whether it was unfair to put Waldheim on the watchlist. Nash thought it was proper because Waldheim served in an army group that deported Jews and other unwanted people. Pacher questioned the legality of this American governmental decision.

Ruth Lorbe doubted the timeliness of the learning process for Waldheim, but Trauttmansdorff asked whether any learning process could ever be too late. Horst Jarka questioned the validity of this hypothesis when stating that any ethical consequences in Austria were lost to the "Justamentstandpunkt" displayed by many Austrians in electing Waldheim.

Petritsch stated that the Waldheim controversy afforded the country an occasion for renewing its endeavors to take a hard look at Austria's complex history and at the roles (ranging from resistance fighter to collaborator) Austrians had played while their country was occupied by Nazi Germany.

Burghild Holzer wanted to know more about the Austrian

politics that had led to Waldheim's election. Pacher pointed to the conflicts within the Socialist Party which suffered from a leadership dilemma after fifteen years of governmental responsibilities. The opposing conservative party sought re-entrance into the political arena, a move which has in the meantime taken place to some degree within the grand coalition. Before the offensive of the World Jewish Congress, Waldheim was the conservatives' most reputable asset as former Austrian State Secretary and Secretary General of the United Nations.

Thus initially even potential socialists might have elected Waldheim as President. The Jewish issue split the camps into other fractions, strengthening the Waldheim camp and dividing the socialists, thereby weakening them and their candidate, Dr. Steyrer. The confusion is also documented by two election dates following each other within a few weeks. When many socialists did not vote the second time, Waldheim was assured an absolute majority.

Trauttmansdorff stated finally that Waldheim will not step down from his presidency because he was and is hopeful of being able to convince the world of his innocence with what he believes to be the truth.

The discussion ended on a moderate note, although without any consensus. However, it was important to have debated the issue thoroughly and openly in front of American and Austrian students.

For additional reactions of the students please see the summaries of the student reports in Appendix I.

Conclusion

Most of the events and the time period addressed in this book excited the world some time ago; today even the Waldheim controversy has lost most of its sting. It stirred world opinion for a short time and caused more light to be shed on an era that involved Austria and her people so adversely – the era of the Third Reich. When I organized the Third Taos Workshop in 1987 I had in mind to bring some semblance of order to the mass of rumors and sensationalism surrounding this case. In order to do this I required a group of scholars and a span of time that would make possible detailed discussion of a wide spectrum of viewpoints. I therefore invited some twenty experts from various professional and academic fields, people knowledgeable about both Austria and the United States, who could draw valid comparisons from specific perspectives within the period 1917 to 1987.

I am grateful that *ALL* these experts and workshop participants agreed to take part and that they urged the publication of the findings in book form. This is that book.

In looking over the manuscripts, as editor, I am exceedingly satisfied not only that it will go into print, but also that the volume will appear in timely fashion after the Workshop. The book is intended to demostrate that where goodwill is paramount, even the most controversial topic can be handled with dignity and consideration. My only regret is that there was not enough time during the Workshop nor enough space in this book, to cover every important aspect and facet of our time period. However, I do believe that we have managed to contribute a clearer picture of Austro-American relations over the past seven decades.

Peter Pabisch

Selected Bibliography by Topic

1. Austrian Studies (Nollendorfs)

German Studies Association. German Studies; Guidelines for Curricular Organization at American Educational Institutions, 1987.

Koppensteiner, Jürgen. Austria = Österreich: Ein landeskundliches Lesebuch. München: Verlag für Deutsch, 1983.

Steiner, Kurt (ed.). Modern Austria. Palo Alto, California: Sposs, 1981.

2. History and Politics (McClelland, Pabisch, and Scherk)

Adamovich, Ludwig & Bernd-Christian Funk. "Österreichisches Verfassungsrecht." 3. Auflage. In: *Springers Kurzlehrbuch für Rechtswissenschaft.* Wien: 1985.

Andics, Hellmut. Der Staat, den keiner wollte: Österreich 1918 bis 1938. Wien: Herder, 1962.

———. 50 Jahre unseres Lebens: Österreichs Schicksal seit 1918. 2. Auflage. Wien: Molden, 1968.

Bader, William B. *Austria between East and West 1945–1955.* Stanford, California: Stanford University Press, 1966.

Drimmel, Heinrich. *Vom Kanzlermord zum Anschluß–Österreich: 1934–1938.* Wien/München: Amalthea, 1987.

Heer, Friedrich. *Der Kampf um die österreichische Identität.* Wien: Böhlau, 1981.

Jedlicka, Ludwig. *Vom alten zum neuen Österreich.* St. Pölten: Niederösterreichisches Pressehaus, 1975.

Johnston, William M. *Österreichische Kultur- und Geistesgeschichte: Gesellschaft und Ideen im Donauraum 1848–1938.* Wien: Böhlau, 1984.

Österreich: Freies Land, Freies Volk. Bundesministerium für Unterricht (Dokumente). Wien: Bundesverlag, 1957.

Ringel, Erwin. *Die österreichische Seele: 10 Reden über Medizin, Politik, Kunst und Religion.* Wien: Böhlau, 1984.

Schmidt, Elfriede. *1938...und was dann? Fragen und Reaktionen.* Thaur, Tirol: Österreichischer Kulturverlag, 1988.

Simon, Walter B. *Österreich 1918-1938–Ideologien und Politik.* Wien: Böhlau, 1984.

Stearman, William Lloyd. *The Soviet Union and the Occupation of Austria* (An Analysis of Soviet Policy in Austria, 1945-1955). Bonn/Wien/ Zürich: Siegler & Co. Verlag für Zeitarchive, 1961.

Stourzh, Gerald. *Geschichte des Staatsvertrages 1945-1955; Österreichs Weg zur Neutralität.* Graz/Wien/Köln: Verlag Styria, 1980.

Waechter-Böhm, Liesbeth. *Wien 1945: Davor/Danach.* Wien: Brandstätter, 1985.

3. Economics (Kullnigg)

Achterberg, Erich. *General Marshall macht Epoche.* Frankfurt am Main: Ullstein, 1964.

Butschek, Felix. *Die österreichische Wirtschaft im 20. Jahrhundert.* Stuttgart: G. Fischer, 1985.

Heissenberger, Franz. *The Economic Reconstruction of Austria 1945-1952.* Washington: Library of Congress, 1953.

Hoscher, Dietmar. *America Changes the Course of History–The Marshall Plan in Austria from 1948 to 1953.* Wien: Österreichische Nationalbank, 1988.

Knapp, Horst. "In Memoriam Marshallplan." In: *Finanznachrichten* 38/1985. Wien: 1986.

4. Medicine (Parks)

Lesky, Erna & Adam Wandruszka. *Gerard van Swieten und seine Zeit.* Wien: Böhlau, 1973.

Probst, Chr. "Der Weg des ärztlichen Erkennens am Krankenbett: Herman Boerhaave und die ältere Wiener Medizinische Schule." In: *Sudhoffs Archiv,* Beiheft 15. Wiesbaden: 1973.

5. Education (Weiss)

Adam, Erik. *Die österreichische Reformpädagogik 1918-1938.* Symposiumsdokumentation. Wien: Böhlau, 1981.

Bader, William. *Austria between East and West, 1945-1955.* Stanford: Stanford University Press, 1966.

Bamberger, Richard und Franz Maier-Bruck, (eds.) *Österreich-Lexikon.* Wien: Verlag für Jugend und Volk, 1966.

Brusatti, Alois; Karl Gutkas; Erika Weinzierl. *Österreich 1945-1970.* 25 Jahre Zweite Republik. Wien: Bundesverlag für Unterricht, Wissenschaft und Kunst, 1970.

Dengler, Paul Leo. *Erziehung zum globalen Denken.* Autobiographie eines fliegenden Professors. Salzburg: Bergland Buch, 1968.

Fischer, Ernst. *Das Ende einer Illusion.* Erinnerungen 1945-1955. Wien: Fritz Molden Verlag, 1973.

Heinemann, Manfred (ed.). *Umerziehung und Wiederaufbau.* Die Bildungspolitik der Besatzungsmächte in Deutschland und Österreich. Stuttgart: Klett Verlag, 1981.

Hiller, Alfred. *Amerikanische Medien- und Schulpolitik in Österreich (1945-1950).* Dissertation. Wien, 1974.

Hiscocks, Richard. *The Rebirth of Austria.* London: Oxford University Press, 1953.

Klemperer, Lily von. *Austria.* A Survey of Austrian Education and Guide to the Academic Placement of Students from Austria. World Education Series, n.pl., 1961.

Papanek, Ernst. *The Austrian School Reform.* New York: Frederick Fell, 1962.

Robinson, Saul B. *Schulreform im gesellschaftlichen Prozeß.* Ein interkultureller Vergleich. Stuttgart: Klett Verlag, 1975. [Band 2.]

Schärf, Adolf. *Österreichs Erneuerung, 1945-1955.* Wien: Verlag der Wiener Volksbuchhandlung, 1955.

Schmitt, Hans (ed.). *US Occupation in Europe after World War II.* Papers and Reminiscences from the April 23-24, 1976, Conference Held at the George C. Marshall Research Foundation. Lawrence: Regents Press of Kansas, 1978.

Siegler, Heinrich. *Österreichs Weg zur Souveränität, Neutralität, Prosperität 1945-1959.* Bonn: Siegler & Co., 1959.

Stiefel, Dieter. *Entnazifizierung in Österreich.* Wien: Europa Verlag, 1981.

Weinzierl, Erika and Kurt Skalnik (eds.). *Das neue Österreich.* Geschichte der zweiten Republik. Graz: Verlag Styria, 1975.

6. Philosophy (Hull)

Achinstein, Peter and Stephen Barker (eds.). *The Legacy of Logical Positivism.* Baltimore: Johns Hopkins, 1969.

Ayer, A. J. (ed.). *Logical Positivism.* Glencoe, IL: The Free Press, 1959.

Carnap, Rudolph. *Philosophical Foundations of Physics.* New York: Basic Books, 1966.

Kraft, Victor. *The Vienna Circle.* New York: Philosophical Library, 1953.

Margenau, Henry. *The Nature of Physical Reality.* New York: McGraw Hill, 1950.

Northrup, F.S.C. *The Logic of the Sciences and the Humanities* New York: Macmillan, 1947.

Waismann, Henry (Brian McGuiness, ed.). *Wittgenstein and the Vienna Circle.* Oxford: Blackwell, 1979.

7. Physical Education (Moolenijzer)

Blackman, S., M. Owens and S. Rockett. *Every Child a Winner: A Practical Approach to Movement Education.* Atlanta: Georgia Department of Education, 1974.

Brown, Margaret C. and Betty K. Sommers. *Movement Education: Its Evolution and a Modern Approach.* Reading, MA: Addison Wesley, 1969.

Cassidy, Rosalind. "The Cultural Definition of Physical Education." *Quest* (Spring 1965).

Diem, Carl. *Weltgeschichte des Sports und der Leibeserziehung.* Stuttgart: Cotta, 1960.

Gaulhofer, Karl und Margarete Streicher. *Grundzüge des österreichischen Schulturnens.* Wien: Jugend und Volk, 1922.

———. *Grundzüge der österreichischen Schulturnens.* Wien: Jugend und Volk, 1950.

———. *Natürliches Turnen I.* Wien: Jugend und Volk, 1949.

———. *Natürliches Turnen II.* Wien: Jugend und Volk, 1949.

Groll, Hans. "Gaulhofer Gedenkfest." *Leibesübung und Leibeserziehung,* XV (December 1961).

Kerstges, Ulrike. "The Concept of 'Natural' in the Educational Philosophies of Pestalozzi and Guts Muth and its Impact on the Emphasis on Physical Education in the Curriculum of the Roundhill School." Unpublished Ph.D. Dissertation, University of New Mexico, Albuquerque, 1987.

Moolenijzer, Nicolaas J. "Implications of the Philosophy of Gaulhofer and Streicher for Physical Education." Unpublished Master's Thesis, University of California at Los Angeles. 1956.

———. "The Concept of 'Natural' in Physical Education: Johann Guts Muths–Margarete Streicher." Unpublished Ph.D. Dissertation, University of Southern California, Los Angeles, 1965.

Streicher, Margarete. "Systematik und Bewegungslehre." *Festschrift Diem.* Wien: Limpert, 1962.

Van Dalen, D. and B. Bennett. *A World History of Physical Education.* Englewood Cliffs: Prentice-Hall, 1971.

Van Vliet, M. L. *Physical Education in Canada.* Scarborough, Ontario. Prentice-Hall, 1965.

Wood, T. D. and R. F. Cassidy. *The New Physical Education.* New York: Macmillan, 1927.

8. Waldheim (Trauttmansdorff)

Born, Hans Peter. *Für die Richtigkeit–Kurt Waldheim.* München: Schneekluth, 1987.

Cohen, R. and L. Rosenzweig. *Le Mistère Waldheim.* Paris: Gallinard, 1986.

Gruber, Karl, Ralph Scheide, Ferdinand Trauttmansdorff (eds.). *Kurt Waldheim's Wartime Years–A Documentation.* Wien: Gerolds, 1987.

Herzstein, Robert. *Waldheim–The Missing Years.* New York: Arbor House/William Morrow, 1988.

Kohl, A., Th. Faulhaber, G. Ofner (eds.). *Die Kampagne–Kurt Waldheim: Opfer oder Täter?* München/Berlin: Herbig, 1987.

Maleta, A., and H. Haselsteiner (eds.). *Der Weg zum "Anschluß" 1938: Daten und Fakten.* Wien: Karl von Vogelsang-Institut, 1988.

Palumbo, Michael. *The Waldheim Files: Myth and Reality.* London/Boston: Faber & Faber, 1988.

9. Kreisky (Petritsch)

Kreisky, Bruno. *Zwischen den Zeiten.* Erinnerungen aus 5 Jahrzehnten. Berlin: Siedler, 1986.

Lucbert, Manuel, Hrsg., *Bruno Kreisky: Die Zeit in der wir leben: Betrachtungen zur internationalen Politik.* Wien: Molden, 1978.

Rathkolb, Oliver and Irene Etzersdorfer. *Der junge Kreisky: Schriften, Reden, Dokumente: 1931-1945.* Wien/München: Jugend und Volk, 1986.

10. Literature (1970–1987) (Daviau)

A. Selected General Works

Amann, Klaus. *Der Anschluß österreichischer Schriftsteller an das Dritte Reich.* Frankfurt am Main: Athenäum, 1988.

Amann, Klaus and Albert Berger (eds.). *Österreichische Literatur der 30er Jahre.* Wien: Böhlau, 1985.

Arnold, Heinz Ludwig (ed.). *Kritisches Lexikon zur deutschsprachigen Gegenwartsliteratur.* München: text und kritik, 1978ff.

Aspetsberger, Friedbert (ed.). *Österreichische Literatur seit den zwanziger Jahren. Beiträge su ihrer historisch-politischen Lokalisierung.* Wien: Österreichischer Bundesverlag, 1979.

———. *Staat und Gesellschaft in der modernen österreichischen Literatur.* Wien: Österreichischer Bundesverlag, 1977.

———. *Traditionen in der neueren österreichischen Literatur.* Wien: Österreichischer Bundesverlag, 1980.

———. *Literarisches Leben im Austrofaschismus.* Königstein, Ts.: Hain, 1980.

Best, Alan and Hans Wolfschütz (eds.). *Modern Austrian Writing. Literature and Society after 1945.* London: Oswald Wolff, 1980.

Bullivant, Keith (ed.). *The Modern German Novel.* New York: St. Martins Press, 1987.

Crankshaw, Edward. *The Fall of the House of Habsburg.* New York: Viking, 1971.

Daviau, Donald G. (ed.). *Major Figures of Contemporary Austrian Literature.* New York: Peter Lang, 1987.

———. *Major Figures of Modern Austrian Literature.* Riverside: Ariadne, 1988.

———. *Modern Austrian Literature.* Special issue: "Perspectives on the Question of Austrian Literature." Vol. 17, nos. 3/4 (1984).

Demetz, Peter. *After the Fires. Recent Writing in the Germanies, Austria, and Switzerland.* New York: Harcourt Brace Jovanovich, 1986.

Goldner, Franz. *Die österreichische Emigration: 1938–1945.* Wien: Herold, 1970.

Gross, Ruth. *Plan and the Austrian Rebirth.* Columbia, South Carolina: Camden House, 1982.

Janik, Alan and Stephen Toulmin. *Wittgenstein's Vienna.* New York: Simon & Schuster, 1973.

Johnson, Lonnie. *Introducing Austria.* Riverside: Ariadne, 1989.

Johnston, William M. *The Austrian Mind. An Intellectual and Social History 1948–1938.* Berkeley: University of California Press, 1972.

Luft, David S. *Robert Musil and the Crisis of European Culture 1880–1942.* Berkeley: University of California Press, 1980.

McVeigh, Joseph. *Kontinuität und Vergangenheitsbewältigung in der österreichischen Literatur nach 1945.* Wien: Braumüller, 1988.

Nagl, Johann Willibad, Jakob Zeidler und Eduard Castle (eds.). *Deutschösterreichische Literaturgeschichte.* Bd. IV. Wien: Fromme, 1937.

Patsch, Sylvia M. *Österreichische Schriftsteller im Exil in Großbritannien.* Wien/München: Brandstätter, 1985.

Pauley, Bruce. *Hitler and the Forgotten Nazis. A History of Austrian National Socialism.* Chapel Hill: University of North Carolina Press, 1981.

Rabinbach, Anson (ed.). *The Austrian Socialist Experiment. Social Democracy and Austromarxism, 1918–1934.* Boulder/London: Westview Press, 1985.

Rozenblit, Marsha L. *The Jews of Vienna, 1867–1914: Assimilation and Identity.* Albany: State University of New York, 1983.

Schorske, Carl E. *Fin-de-siècle Vienna. Politics and Culture.* New York: Knopf, 1981.

Spalek, John and Joseph Strelka. *Deutsche Exilliteratur. Kalifornien.* 2 vols. Bern/München: Francke, 1976.

Spiel, Hilde (ed.). *Die zeitgenössische Literatur Österreichs.* Zürich/München: Kindler, 1976.

Steiner, Kurt (ed.). *Modern Austria.* Palo Alto, California: Sposs, 1981.

Weinzierl, Ulrich (ed.). *Österreicher im Exil. Frankreich 1938–1945.* Wien: Österreichischer Bundesverlag, 1986.

———. *Österreichs Fall. Schriftsteller berichten vom Anschluß.* Wien/München: Jugend und Volk, 1987.

Williams, Cedric E. *The Broken Eagle. The Politics of Austrian Literature from Empire to Anschluß.* London: Paul Elek, 1974.

Willson, Leslie A. (ed.). Guest editors Ernst Jandl and Hans F. Prokop. *Dimension.* [Special dual-language issue devoted to contemporary Austrian literature.] Vol. 8, nos. 1 and 2 (1975).

———. Guest editor Peter Pabisch. *Dimension.* [Special dual-language issue devoted to Austrian dialect poetry.] Vol. 12, no. 3 (1979).

Wischenbart, Rüdiger. *Literarischer Wiederaufbau in Österreich 1945–1949.* Königstein, Ts.: Hain, 1983.

B. Anthologies

Bjorklund, Beth (ed.). *Contemporary Austrian Poetry: An Anthology.* Rutherford/Madison/Teaneck, New Jersey; Fairleigh Dickinson University Press, 1986.

Holton, Milne and Herbert Kuhner (eds. and trans.). *Austrian Poetry Today* New York: Schocken Books, 1985.

Jandl, Ernst and Hans F. Prokop (eds.). *Dimension,* Vol. VIII, nos. 1/2 (1975).

Opel, Adolf (ed.). *Anthology of Modern Austrian Literature.* London: Oswald Wolff, 1981.

Pabisch, Peter (ed.). *Dimension,* Vol. 12. no. 3 (1979).

Russell, Douglas A. (ed.). *An Anthology of Austrian Drama.* Rutherford/ Madison/Teaneck, New Jersey: Fairleigh Dickinson University Press, 1982.

Ungar, Frederick (ed.). *Austria in Poetry and History.* New York: Frederick Ungar, 1984.

Viebahn, Fred (ed.). *Dimension,* Special Issue 1983.

Waldrop, Rosemarie and Harriett Watts (eds.). *6 Major Austrian Poets.* New York: Station Hill Press, 1985.

C. Bibliography of Selected Individual Writers (in chronological order)

Ilse Aichinger

Translations in English

The Bound Man and Other Stories, trans. Eric Mosbacher. New York: Noonday Press, 1956; London: Secker & Warburg, 1956).

Allridge, James C. (ed.). *Ilse Aichinger: Selected Short Stories and Dialogs.* Oxford/New York: Pergamon Press, 1966.

———. *Ilse Aichinger* (Modern German Authors: Texts and Contexts, 2). Chester Spring, Pennsylvania: Dufour Editions, 1969.

The Rain Mouse. New York: F. Watts, 1970.

The Bound Man and Other Stories, trans. Eric Mosbacher. Freeport, New York: Books for Libraries Press, 1971.

Herod's Children, trans. Cornelia Schaeffer. New York: Atheneum, 1963.

Selected Poetry and Prose, trans. Allen H. Chappel. Durango, Colorado: Logbridges-Rhodes, 1983.

Secondary Literature in English

Bedwell, Carol B. "Who Is the Bound Man? Towards an Interpretation of Ilse

Aichinger's *Der Gefesselte.*" *German Quarterly,* Vol. 38 (1965), 30-37.

Allridge, James D. (ed.). "Introduction in J. C. Allridge (ed.). *Ilse Aichinger: Selected Short Stories and Dialogs.* New York: Pergamon, 1966, pp. 1-9.

Livingstone, Rodney, "German Literature from 1945." *Periods in German Literature.* Ed., J. M. Ritchie. London: Wolff, 1966, pp. 283-303.

Bedwell, Carol B. "The Ambivalent Image in Aichinger's *Spiegelgeschichte.*" *Revue des Langues Vivantes,* Vol. 33 (1967), 362-368.

Pickar, Gertrude B. "'Das Feuermal'–Mark of Life and Death." Interpretative Comments to Ilse Aichinger's 'Das Plakat.'" *Xavier University Studies,* Vol. 10, no. viii (1971), 20-27.

Langer, Lawrence. *The Holocaust and the Literary Imagination.* New Haven: Yale University Press, 1975. (Treats *Herod's Children* extensively.)

Lautenschlager, Wayne. "Images and Narrative Techniques in the Prose of Ilse Aichinger." Dissertation, Washington University, 1976.

Resler, W. Michael. "A Structural Approach to Aichinger's *Spiegelgeschichte,*" *Unterrichtpraxis,* Vol. 12, no. 1 (1979), 30-37.

Haas Stanley, Patricia. "Ilse Aichinger's Absurd 'I,'" *German Studies Review,* Vol. 2 (1979), 331-350.

Wolfschütz, Hans, "Ilse Aichinger: The Skeptical Narrator." In: Alan Best and Hans Wolfschütz (eds.). *Modern Austrian Writing: Literature and Society after 1945.* London: Oswald Wolff; Totowa, New Jersey: Barnes & Noble, 1980), pp. 156-180.

Lorenz, Dagmar C. G. *Ilse Aichinger.* Königstein, Ts.: Athenäum, 1981.

Langer, Lawrence. "Introduction," *Ilse Aichinger: Selected Poetry & Prose.* Ed. and trans. Allen H. Chappel. Durango, Colorado: Logbridge-Rhodes, 1983, pp. 7-15.

Vinke, Hermann. "An Interview with Ilse Aichinger about Sophie Scholl.. Trans., Hedwig Pachter. In: *The Short Life of Sophie Scholl.* New York: Harper and Row, 1984), pp. 205-216.

Ratych, Joanna M. "Ilse Aichinger." In: *Major Figures of Contemporary Austrian Literature.* Ed., Donald G. Daviau. New York: Peter Lang, 1987, pp. 25-45.

Gerlach, U. Henry. "The Reception of the Works of Ilse Aichinger in the United States." *Modern Austrian Literature,* Vol. 20, nos. 3/4 (1987). (The bibliography includes a listing of works in English by Ilse Aichinger included in anthologies).

Reviews of English Translations

The Bound Man and Other Stories (1956)

Commonweal, Vol. 64 (1956), 354.

Saturday Review, Vol. 39, no. 25 (16 June 1956), 25, 50.

San Francisco Chronicle, 15 July 1956, p. 22.

Times Literary Supplement, 16 September 1955, p. 546.

Kirkus Reviews, Vol. 24 (1 May 1956), 319

Herod's Children (1963)

Book Week, Supplement of New York Herald-Tribune), 17 November 1963, p. 6.

Saturday Review, Vol. 46, no. 38 (28 December 1963), 37-38.

Library Journal, Vol. 88 (1963), 4661.

Congress Bi-Weekly. A Review of Jewish Interests (New York), Vol. 30 (1963), 23-24.

Time (Chicago), Vol. 82 (25 October 1963), 109-110.

New York Times Book Review, 24 November 1963.

Bestsellers, Vol. 23 (1963-1964), 274.

Virginia Quarterly Review, Vol. 40, no. 1 (1964), xvi.

The Humanist (Yellow Springs, Ohio), Vol. 24 (1964), 201-202.

Christian Science Monitor, 8 January 1964.

Curriculum Review, Vol. 17 (1978), 344.

Ilse Aichinger: Selected Short Stores and Dialogs. Ed., James C. Allridge (1966)

Modern Language Journal, Vol. 52 (1968), 249.

Selected Poetry and Prose (1983)

Library Journal, Vol. 108 (1983), 2334.

Choice, Vol. 21, no. 7 (1984), 982-983.

Field (Oberlin, Ohio), No. 30 (Spring 1984), 64.

Review of Other Works by Ilse Aichinger in German

Der Gefesselte, Books Abroad, Vol. 28 (1954), 183.

Wo ich wohne, Books Abroad, Vol. 38 (1964), 396.

Eliza Eliza, Books Abroad, Vol. 40 (1966), 305.

Schlechte Wörter, World Literature Today, Vol. 51, no. 2 (1977), 268.

Verschenkter Rat: Gedichte, World Literature Today, Vol. 54, no. 1 (Winter 1980), 98.

Zu keiner Stunde: Szenen und Dialoge, World Literature Today, Vol. 55 (1981), 463-464.

Wolfgang Bauer

Translations in English

Microdramas. Trans. Rosemarie Waldrop. *Dimension,* Vol. 5, no. 1 (1972), 106-131.

Change and Other Plays. Trans. Martin and Renata Esslin, Herb Greer (New York: Hill and Wang, 1973), XII.

"All Change" and Other Plays. Trans. Martin and Renata Esslin, Herb Greer (London: Calder and Boyers, 1973).

Memory Hotel. Trans. Renata and Martin Esslin (New York: Theater Communications Group, 1981).

Secondary Literature in English

Esslin, Martin. "Introduction: The Absurdity of the Real." In: *Change and Other Plays.* Trans. Martin and Renate Esslin and Herb Greer (New York: Hill and Wang, 1973), pp. vii-xii.

Haberland, Paul M. "Duality, the Artist, and Wolfgang Bauer." *Modern Austrian Literature,* Vol. 11, no. 2 (1978), 73-86.

Rorrison, Hugh. "The 'Grazer Gruppe.' Peter Handke and Wolfgang Bauer." In: *Modern Austrian Writing, Literature and Society after 1945.* Ed., Alan Best and Hans Wolfschütz (London: Oswald Wolff; Totowa, New Jersey: Barnes and Noble, 1980), pp. 252-266.

Carpenter, Charles A. "The Plays of Bernhard, Bauer, and Handke: A Checklist of Major Critical Studies. *Modern Drama,* Vol. 23, no. 4 (January 1981), 484-491.

Koppensteiner, Jürgen. "Wolfgang Bauer." *Major Figures of Contemporary Austrian Literature.* Ed., Donald G. Daviau (New York: Peter Lang 1987), pp. 67-88.

Reviews of Wolfgang Bauer's Works in English

Saturday Review, Vol. 52 (26 April 1969), 37.

Modern Language Journal, Vol. 55 (January 1971), 43.

Choice, Vol. 10 (December 1973), 1555.

Drama, The Quarterly Theater Review (Winter 1973), 83.

Library Journal, Vol. 98 (15 December 1973), 3650.

America, Vol. 136 (4 June 1977), 509.

Kirkus Reviews, Vol. 44 (1 November 1976), 1191.

Christian Century, Vol. 94 (23 March 1977), 283.

Choice, Vol. 14 (May 1977), 432.

New York Book Review, Vol. 24 (29 September 1977), 15.

Drama: The Quarterly Theater Review (Autumn 1977), 78.

Encounter, Vol. 50 (May 1978), 64.
Pacific Affairs, Vol. 51 (Spring 1978), 108.

Thomas Bernhard

Works in English Translation

"In the Poorhouse," excerpt from *Frost.* Trans. Helene Scher. In: *Postwar German Culture: An Anthology* (New York: E. P. Dutton, 1974), pp. 238–242.

Gargoyles. Trans. Richard and Clara Winston (New York: Knopf, 1970).

The Lime Works. Trans. Sophie Wilkins (New York: Knopf, 1973).

The Force of Habit. Trans. Neville and Stephen Plaice (London: Heinemann Educational for the National Theatre, 1976).

Correction. Trans. Sophie Wilkins (New York: Knopf, 1979).

Eve of Retirement. Trans. Gitta Honegger (New York: Kurt Bornheim, 1979).

The Hunting Party. Trans. Gitta Honegger. *Performing Arts Journal,* Vol. V, no. 1 (1980), 101-131.

The President and *Eve of Retirement.* Trans. Gitta Honegger (New York: Performing Arts Journal Publications, 1982).

Appearances are Deceiving. Trans. Gitta Honegger. *Theater* (Yale), Vol. 15, no. 1 (Winter 1983), 31-51.

Gathering Evidence (A Child, An Indication of the Cause, The Cellar: An Escape, Breath: A Decision, In the Cold). Trans. David McLintock (New York: Knopf, 1985).

Reviews of English Translations

Gargoyles (1970)

Kirkus Reviews (15 July 1970), 760.
Publisher's Weekly, Vol. 198, no. 1 (6 July 1970), 56.
Library Journal, Vol. 95 (1 November 1970), 3903.
Book World (3 January 1971), 6.
Choice, Vol. 8, no. 2 (April 1971), 232.
Antioch Review, Vol. 30, nos. 3/4 (Fall/Winter 1970/1971), 459.

Das Kalkwerk (1970)

The Booklist, Vol. 67, no. 12 (15 February 1971), 478.
Kirkus Reviews, Vol. XLI, no. 17 (1 September 1973), 981.
Publisher's Weekly, Vol. 204, no. 16 (15 October 1973), 59.
Library Journal, Vol. 98 (1 November 1973), 3390.
Choice, Vol. 11, no. 3 (May 1974), 441-442.
Bookworld, Vol. 7 (23 December 1979), 4.

Die Jagdgesellschaft (1975)

Booklist, Vol. 71, no. 22 (15 July 1975), 1166.

Ja (1979)

Booklist, Vol. 75, No. 19 (1 June 1979), 1482.

Correction (1979)

Booklist, Vol. 75, No. 19 (1 June 1979), 1478.

Publisher's Weekly, Vol. 215, no. 11 (12 March 1979), 62.

Kirkus Reviews (1 March 1979), 276.

Choice, Vol. 16, No. 9 (November 1979), 1178.

The President and *Eve of Retirement* (1982)

Library Journal, Vol. 107 (July 1982), 1342.

Choice, Vol. 20, no. 2 (October 1982), 272.

Reviews of Books in German

Die Macht der Gewohnheit. Books Abroad, Vol. 49, no. 3 (1975), 537.

Die Ursache. Books Abroad, Vol. 50, no. 3 (1975), 658.

Die Berühmten. World Literature Today, Vol. 51 (Summer 1977), 436.

Der Keller. World Literature Today, Vol. 52 (Winter 1978), 105-106.

Immanuel Kant. World Literature Today, Vol. 53 (Spring 1979), 283.

Der Atem. World Literature Today, Vol. 53 (Summer 1979), 505.

Der Stimmenimitator. World Literature Today, Vol. 53 (Summer 1979), 496-497.

Vor dem Ruhestand: Eine Komödie von deutscher Seele. *World Literature Today,* Vol. 55 (Winter 1981), 92.

Die Kälte. World Literature Today, Vol. 56 (Spring 1982), 326.

Über allen Gipfeln ist Ruh: "Ein deutscher Dichtertag um 1980.' *World Literature Today,* Vol. 56 (Spring 1982), 329.

Ein Kind. World Literature Today, Vol. 57 (Spring 1983), 283-284.

Secondary Literature in English

Stern, Guy. "Trends in the Present-day German Novel." *Books Abroad* (1969), 334-335.

Haberl, Franz P. Review of *An der Baumgrenze,* by Thomas Bernhard. *Books Abroad* (1970), 656.

Craig, D. A. "The Novels of Thomas Bernhard–A Report." *German Life and Letters,* Vol. XXV, no. 4 (4 July 1972), 343-353.

Schumann, Thomas B. "Bibliographie zu Thomas Bernhard." *Text und Kritik,* Heft 43 (Juli 1973), 50-55.

Bakx, Hans W. "Over Thomas Bernhard." *Revisor,* Vol. 3, no. iv (1976), 58-66.

Chambers, Helen. "Theatre Checklist no. 12–Thomas Bernhard." *Theatrefacts,* Vol. IV, no. 3 (1976), 2-11.

Latimer, Renate. "Thomas Bernhard's Image of Women." *Germanic Notes,* Vol. 8 (1977), 25-27.

Esslin, Martin. "Contemporary Austrian Playwrights." *Performing Arts Journal,* Vol. 3, nos. i–ii (1978), 93-98.

May, Terrill J. "Thomas Bernhards *Der Ignorant und der Wahnsinnige:* An Analysis of Dramatic Style." *Modern Language Studies,* Vol. 9, no. 1 (1978-1979), 60-72.

Barthofer, Alfred. "The Plays of Thomas Bernhard–A Report." *Modern Austrian Literature,* Vol. 11, no. 1 (1978), 21-48.

Dierick, A. P. "Thomas Bernhard's Austria: Neurosis, Symbol, or Expedient?" *Modern Austrian Literature,* Vol. 12, no. 1 (1979), 73-93.

McLintock, D. R. "Tense and Narrative Perspective in Two Works of Thomas Bernhard." *Oxford German Studies,* Vol. 11, no. ii (1980), 1-26.

Thorpe, Kathleen. "The Autobiographical Works of Thomas Bernhard." *Acta Germanica,* Bd. 13 (1980), 189-200.

Esslin, Martin. "Ein neuer Manierismus? Randbemerkungen zu einigen Werken von Gert F. Jonke und Thomas Bernhard. *Modern Austrian Literature,* Vol. 13, no. 1 (1980), 111-128.

Honegger, Gitta. "Thomas Bernhard: An Introduction." *Performing Arts Journal* Vol. V, no. 1 (1980), pp. 96-101.

Hannemann, Bruno. "Totentanz der Marionetten: Monotonie und Manier bei Thomas Bernhard." *Modern Austrian Literature,* Vol. 13, no. 2 (1980), 123-150.

Mauch, Gudrun. "Thomas Bernhards Biographie des Schmerzes–'Die Ursache,' 'Der Keller' und 'Der Atem.'" *Modern Austrian Literature,* Vol. 13, no. 1 (1980), 91-110.

Wolfschütz, Hans. "Thomas Bernhard: The Mask of Death." In: *Modern Austrian Writings. Literature and Society after 1945.* Ed., A. Best and H. Wolfschütz (London: Wolff; Totowa, New Jersey: Barnes and Noble, 1981), 214-235.

Honegger, Gitta. "How German Is It? Thomas Bernhard at the Guthrie." *Performing Arts Journal,* Vol. VI, no. 1 (1981), 1-17.

Hirschbach, Frank. "Victims and Hangmen." *The Guthrie* (October 1981), 65-66.

Gross, Robert F., Jr. "The Greatest Uncertainty: The Perils of Performance in Thomas Bernhard's *Der Ignorant und der Wahnsinnige.*" *Modern Drama,* Vol. 23, no. 4 (January 1981), 385-392.

Carpenter, Charles A. "The Plays of Bauer, Bernhard and Handke: A Checklist of Major Critical Studies." *Modern Drama,* Vol. 23, No. 4 (January 1981), 484-491.

Esslin, Martin. "A Drama of Disease and Derision: The Plays of Thomas Bernhard." *Modern Drama,* Vol. 23, No. 4 (January 1981), 367-384.

Hoover, Marjorie L. Review of *Die Billigesser,* by Thomas Bernhard. *World Literature Today,* Vol. 55 (Spring 1981), 302-303.

Sharp, F. M. "Literature as Self-Reflection: Thomas Bernhard and Peter Handke." *World Literature Today,* Vol. 55, no. 4 (Autumn 1981), 603-607.

Dittmar, Jens, "'Die verrückte Magdalena'–An Early Short Story by Thomas Bernhard." *German Life and Letters,* Vol. XXXV, no. 3 (April 1982), 267-271.

Godwin-Jones, Robert. "The Terrible Idyll: Thomas Bernhard's *Das Kalkwerk.*" *Germanic Notes,* Vol. 13, no. 1 (1982), 8-10.

Thomas, Noel L. "The Structure of Nightmare: Autobiography and Art in Thomas Bernhard's *Der Keller. Quinquereme,* Vol. 6 (1983), 155-166.

Honegger, Gitta. "Wittgenstein's Children: The Writings of Thomas Bernhard." *Theater* (Yale), Vol. 15, no. 1 (Winter 1983), 58-62.

"The Plays of Thomas Bernhard." A Photo Portfolio. *Theater* (Yale), Vol. 15, no. 1 (Winter 1983), 52-57.

Federico, Joseph A. "Millenarianism, Legitimation, and the National Socialist Universe in Thomas Bernhard's *Vor dem Ruhestand.*" *Germanic Review,* Vol. 59, no. 4 (Fall 1984), 142-148.

Fetz, Gerald A. "The Works of Thomas Bernhard: 'Austrian Literature'? *Modern Austrian Literature,* Vol. 17, nos. 3/4 (December 1984), 171-192.

Eben, Michael C. "Thomas Bernhard's *Frost:* Early Indications of an Austrian Demise." *Neophilologus,* Vol. 69, no. 4 (October 1985), 591-613.

Honegger, Gitta, "Acoustic Masks: Strategies of Language in the Theater of Canetti, Bernhard, and Handke." *Modern Austrian Literature,* Vol. 18, no. 2 (1985), 57-66.

Articles in Books

Schwedler, Wilfried. "Thomas Bernhard." *Handbook of Austrian Literature.* Ed., Frederick Ungar (New York: Frederick Ungar Publishing, 1973), pp. 26-27.

Jones, D. C. *Modern German Drama* (New York/Cambridge: Arno, 1979).

"Thomas Bernhard." *Gale Contemporary Authors,* Vols. 85-88 (1979), 55.

Gross, Robert Francis, Jr. "The Main Text in Contemporary Drama: Osborne, Bernhard, Handke, and Bond." Dissertation, University of North Carolina, 1979.

Innes, C. D. *Modern German Drama: A Study in Form* (Cambridge: Cambridge University Press, 1979), pp. 254-259.

Wolfschütz, Hans. "Thomas Bernhard: The March of Death." *Modern Austrian Writing: Literature and Society after 1945* (London: Oswald Wolff, 1980), pp. 214-235.

Fetz, Gerald A. "Thomas Bernhard und die österreichische Tradition." *Österreichische Gegenwart: Die moderne Literatur und ihr Verhältnis zur Tradition.* Ed., Wolfgang Paulsen (Bern/München: Francke, 1980, S. 189-205.

Schmidt-Dengler, Wendelin. "Contemporary Literature in Austria." *Modern Austria.* Ed., Kurt Steiner (Palo Alto, California: Society for the Promotion of Science and Scholarship, 1981), pp. 409-429.

Honegger, Gitta. "The Theatre of Thomas Bernhard." In: *The President & Eve of Retirement by Thomas Bernhard* (New York: Performing Arts Journal, 1982), pp. 9-16.

Demetz, Peter. "Thomas Bernhard: The Dark Side of Life." In: *After the Fires: Recent Writing in the Germanies, Austria and Switzerland* (New York: Harcourt Brace Jovanovich, 1986), pp. 199-212.

Brokoph-Mauch, Gudrun. "Thomas Bernhard." *Major Figures of Contemporary Austrian Literature.* Ed., Donald G. Daviau (New York: Peter Lang, 1987), pp. 89-115.

Fetz, Gerald. "Thomas Bernhard and the Modern Novel." In: Keith Bullivant, (ed.). *The Modern German Novel* (New York: St. Martins, 1987), pp. 89-108.

Reviews in Popular Magazines and Newspapers

Gargoyles

Saturday Review. Vol. 53 (31 October 1970), 34, 39.

The Lime Works

Kennedy, William. "Many Metaphors." *The New Republic,* Vol. 169 (15 December 1973), 28-30.

De Feo, Ronald. "Terror Expression." *National Review,* Vol. 26 (1 February 1974), 152-153.

Correction

Demetz, Peter, "Tales of An Austria the Tourists Never See." *Christian Science Monitor* (August-September 1979).

Rexer, Lyle. *Chicago Tribune* (9 September 1979), Section 7, pp. 3-4.

Park, Clara Claiborne. *The Hudson Review,* Vol. 32, no. 4 (Winter 1979-1980), 582.

Gilman, Richard. "The Eloquent Compromise with Silence." *The Nation,* Vol. 231 (19-26 July 1980), 85-88.

Falkenberg, Betty. "Thomas Bernhard." *Partisan Review,* Vol. 47, no. 2 (1980), 269-277.

Rexer, Lyle. "Bernhard's Inferno." *New Boston Review,* Vol. 5 (June/July 1980), 17-18.

Concrete

Rechy, John. Review in *Los Angeles Times* (17 June 1984).

Simon, John. "The Sun Never Rises on Rudolf." *New York Times Book Review* (1 July 1984), 9.

Updike, John. "Thomas Bernhard's 'Concrete,'" *The New Yorker* (4 February 1985), 97-111.

Das Kalkwerk

"Among the Ruins of Civilization." *Times Literary Supplement* (London (12 February 1971), 174.

Tempel, Gudrun. "German fiction: two real voices among all the notebooks." *The Times* (London) (4 February 1971), 136.

"Death in Austria." Review of *Der Italiener, Midland in Stilfs,* and *Gehen,* by Thomas Bernhard. *Times Literary Supplement* (London) (29 September 1972), 1139.

Steiner, George. "Conic Sections." Review of *Korrektur,* by Thomas Bernhard. *Times Literary Supplement* (London) (13 February 1976), 158.

Vivis, Anthony. "Laments for Humanity." Review of *Ein Fest für Boris, Der Ignorant und der Wahnsinnige, Die Macht der Gewohnheit,* and *Die Jagdgesellschaft,* by Thomas Bernhard. *Times Literary Supplement* (London) (11 June 1976), 711.

Steiner, George, "Asking for an Apocalypse." Review of *Der Weltverbesserer, Vor dem Ruhestand,* and *Der Stimmenimitator,* by Thomas Bernhard. *Times Literary Supplement* (London) (29 February 1980), 238.

Steele, Mike. "Bernhard Play Brings Gloomy German Humor to Guthrie Stage." *Minneapolis Tribune* (20 September 1981), 1a, 14a, 15a.

Steele, Mike, "'Eve of Retirement' Takes Unrelenting Look at Nazism." *Minneapolis Tribune* (27 September 1981), 2b.

Plaice, S. N. "Disturber of the Peace." Review of *Ein Kind,* by Thomas Bernhard. *Times Literary Supplement* (London) (1 October 1982), 1083.

Elias Canetti

Translations into English

Auto-da-fé. Trans. C. V. Wedgwood (London: Jonathan Cape, 1946). Published in 1947 by Alfred A. Knopf, New York under the title *Tower of Babel.*

Auto-da-fé. Trans. Joachim Neugroschel (New York: Seabury Press, 1979).

Auto-da-fé. (New York: Farrar Straus Giroux, 1984).

The Numbered: A Play (Oxford: The Playhouse, 1956).

Kafka's Other Trial: The Letters to Felice. Trans. Christopher Middleton (London: Calder and Boyars, 1974; New York: Schocken, 1978).

Crowds and Power. Trans. Carol Steward (New York: Seabury, 1978).

Crowds and Power (New York: The Viking Press, 1963; New York: Farrar Straus Giroux, 1984).

The Human Province: Notes, 1942–1972. Trans. Joachim Neugroschel (New York: Seabury, 1978).

The Voices of Marrakesh: A Record of a Visit. Trans. J. A. Underwood (New York: Seabury, 1978).

The Voices of Marrakesh (New York: Farrar Straus Giroux, 1984).

The Conscience of Words. Trans. Joachim Neugroschel (New York: Seabury, 1979).

Earwitness: Fifty Characters. Trans. Joachim Neugroschel (New York: Seabury, 1979; New York: Continuum, 1979).

The Tongue Set Free: Remembrance of a European Childhood. Trans. Joachim Neugroschel (New York: Seabury, 1979; New York: Continuum, 1980).

A Torch in My Ears (New York: Farrar Straus Giroux, 1982).

Comedy of Vanity and Life Terms. Trans. Gitta Honegger with introduction by Klaus Völker (New York: Performing Arts Journal Publications, 1986).

The Plays of Elias Canetti (New York: Farrar Straus Giroux, 1984).

Secondary Literature in English

Strachey, Julia. "Elias Canetti: *Auto-da-fé.*" *Horizon,* Vol. 85 (1946), 60–63.

Fiedler, Leslie A. "The Tower of Babel." *Partisan Review,* Vol. 3 (1947), 316–320.

McFarlane, J. W. "The Tiresian Vision." *The Durham University Journal,* Vol. XLIX, no. 3 (1956), 109–115.

Parry, Idris, F. "Elias Canetti's Novel 'Die Blendung.'" In: F. Normn (ed.), *Essays in German Literature,* Vol. I (London: London University, 1965), pp. 145–166.

Sacharoff, Mark. "Grotesque Comedy in Canetti's *Auto-da-fé.*" *Critique: Studies in Modern Fiction,* Vol. 14, no. 1 (1972), 99-112.

Roberts, D. "The Individual and the Crowd: Canetti's Novel *Die Blendung.*"

Thomson, Edward. "Elias Canetti's *Die Blendung* and the Changing Image of Madness." *German Life and Letters,* Vol. 26 (1972), 38-47.

Barnouw, Dagmar. "Doubting Death: On Elias Canetti's Drama *The Deadlined.*" *Mosaic,* Vol. 7, no. 2 (1974), 1-23.

Sokel, Walter H. "The Ambiguity of Madness: Elias Canetti's Novel *Die Blendung.*" *Views and Reviews of Modern German Literature:* Festschrift für Adolf D. Klarmann. Ed., Karl S. Weimar (München: Delp, 1974), pp. 181-187.

Russell, Peter. "The Vision of Man in Elias Canetti's *Die Blendung.*" *German Life and Letters,* Vol. 28 (1974-1975), 24-35.

Wiley, Marion E. "Elias Canetti's Reflective Prose." *Modern Austrian Literature,* Vol. 12, no. 2 (1979), 129-139.

Durzak, Manfred. "From Dialect-Play to Philological Parable: Elias Canetti in Exile." Trans. David Scrase. In Joseph P. Strelka, ed. *Protest – Form – Tradition: Essays on German Exile Literature* (University: University of Alabama Press, 1979), pp. 35-36.

Turner, David. "Elias Canetti: The Intellectual as King Canute." In: *Modern Austrian Writing: Literature and Society after 1945.* Eds., Alan Best and Hans Wolfschütz (London: Oswald Wolff; Totowa, New Jersey: Barnes and Noble, 1980), 214-235.

Stenberg, Peter. "Remembering Times Past: Canetti, Sperber and 'A World that is no More.'" *Seminar,* Vol. 17, no. 4 (November 1981), 296-311.

Bartscht, Waltraud. "Five New Translations of Elias Canetti's Works." *Translation Review,* Vol. 8 (1982), 14-19.

Seidler, Ingo. "Who is Elias Canetti?" *Cross-Currents:* A Yearbook of Central European Literature (1982), 107-123.

Rosenfeld, Sidney. "1981 Novel Laureat Elias Canetti: A Writer Apart." *World Literature Today,* Vol. 56, no. 1 (Winter 1982), 5-9.

Barnouw, Dagmar. "Mind and Myth in 'Masse und Macht." *Modern Austrian Literature,* Vol. 16, nos. 3/4 (1983), 65-79.

Demet, Michel-François. "The Theme of Blood in Elias Canetti's 'Die Blendung.'" *Modern Austrian Literature,* Vol. 16, Nos. 3/4 (1983), 147-153.

Hinderburger-Burton, Tania. "The Quixotic in Canetti's 'Die Blendung.'" *Modern Austrian Literature,* Vol. 16, nos. 3/4 (1983), 165-176.

Karst, Roman. "Elias Canetti's 'Die Blendung': A Study in Insanity." *Modern Austrian Literature,* Vol. 16, nos. 3/4 (1983), 133-145.

Schmidt, Hugo. "Narrative Attitudes in Canetti's 'Die Blendung.'" *Modern Austrian Literature,* Vol. 16, nos. 3/4 (1983), 93-109.

Zorach, Cecile C. "The Outsider Abroad: Canetti in Marrakesh." *Modern Austrian Literature,* Vol. 16, nos. 3/4 (1983), 47-64.

Honegger, Gitta. "Acoustic Masks: Strategies of Language in the Theater of Canetti, Bernhard, and Handke." *Modern Austrian Literature,* Vol. 18, no. 2 (1985), 57-66.

Gould, Robert. "Die gerettete Zunge an Dichtung und Wahrheit": Hypertextuality in Autobiography and its Implications. *Seminar,* Vol. 21, no. 2 (May 1985), 79-107.

Barnouw, Dagmar. "Elias Canetti–Poet and Intellectual." In: *Major Figures of Contemporary Austrian Literature.* Ed., Donald G. Daviau (New York: Peter Lang, 1987), 117-141.

Reviews of Canetti's Works

Die gespaltene Zukunft: Aufsätze und Gespräche (1972)
Books Abroad, Vol. 48, no. 4 (1973), 767.

Der Ohrenzeuge: Fünfzig Charaktere (1974)
Books Abroad, Vol. 49, no. 4 (1975), 769.
Times Literary Supplement (10 January 1975), p. 38.

Kafka's Other Trial: Letters to Felice (1974)
Library Journal, Vol. 99, no. 16 (15 September 1974), 2157.
Atlantic Monthly, Vol. 234 (December 1974), 128.
Publishers Weekly, Vol. 206 (29 October 1974), 47.
Times Literary Supplement, (28 February 1975), p. 231.
Modern Fiction Studies, Vol. 28 (Winter 1982), 694-697.
Publishers Weekly, Vol. 221 (5 February 1982), 386.

Das Gewissen der Worte: Essays (1975)
World Literature Today, Vol. 51, no. 1 (1977), 95.

Die gerettete Zunge: Geschichte einer Jugend (1977)
World Literature Today, Vol. 52, no. 1 (1978), 106.

Crowds and Power (1978)
World Literature Today, Vol. 53, no. 2 (1979), 290.

The Voices of Marrakesh: A Record of a Visit (1978)
World Literature Today, Vol. 53, no. 2 (1979), 290.
Library Journal, Vol. 103, no. 21 (1 December 1978), 2422.
The Listener, Vol. 99 (15 June 1978), 769.
British Book News (February 1983), 74.

The Human Province (1978)
World Literature Today, Vol. 53, no. 2 (1979), 290.

Booklist, Vol. 75, no. 2 (15 September 1978), 131.
Library Journal, Vol. 103, no. 18 (15 October 1978), 2103.
Saturday Review, Vol. 5 (December 1978), 54.

The Conscience of Words (1979)
World Literature Today, Vol. 53, no. 4 (1979), 680.
Booklist, Vol. 75, no. 16 (15 April 1979), 1268.
Library Journal, Vol. 104, no. 6 (15 March 1979), 730.
Choice, Vol. 17 (April 1980), 207.

Earwitness: Fifty Characters (1979)
World Literature Today, Vol. 53, no. 4 (1979), 680.
Booklist, Vol. 75, no. 19 (1 June 1979), 1474.
Library Journal, Vol. 104, no. 14 (August 1979), 1566.
Choice, Vol. 17 (April 1980), 226.

Auto-da-fé (1979)
Bestsellers, Vol. 39, no. 4 (August 1979), 155.

Die Fackel im Ohr: Lebensgeschichte 1921-1931 (1980)
World Literature Today, Vol. 55, no. 2 (1981), 310.
Times Literary Supplement (9 January 1981), 28.

The Tongue Set Free: Remembrance of a European Childhood (1981)
World Literature Today, Vol. 55, no. 2 (1981), 313.
The Nation, Vol. 229 (29 December 1979), 696.
Library Journal, Vol. 105, no. 1 (1 January 1980), 95.
Western Humanities Review, Vol. 37 (Spring 1983), 75.
Booklist, Vol. 76 (1 December 1979), 533.

The Torch in My Ear (1982)
Choice, Vol. 20 (January 1983), 708.
Booklist, Vol. 78 (July 1982), 1413.
Publishers Weekly, Vol. 222 (16 July 1982), 68.
The Economist, Vol. 287 (23 April 1983), 107-108.
Library Journal, Vol. 107 (August 1982), 1453.

Das Gewissen der Worte (1983)
World Literature Today, Vol. 59, no. 1 (Winter 1985), 88.

Review Articles

Wood, Michael. "The Precise Exaggerator." *New York Times Book Review* (29 April 1979), 11.

Burke, Jeffrey. "Finding Elias Canetti." *Harper's Magazine,* Vol. 260 (January 1980), 82-87.

Parry, Idris. "Elias Canetti: The Forms of Power." *Times Literary Supplement* (23 October 1981), 1236.

Steiner, George. "A Tale of Three Cities." *New Yorker,* Vol. 58 (22 November 1982), 186, 188, 191–195.

Erich Fried

Translations in English

Arden Must Die: An Opera on the Death of the Wealthy Arden of Faversham. Trans. Geoffrey Skelton (London: Schott; New York: Associated Music Publishers, 1967).

Last Honours. Trans. Georg Rapp (London: Turrett, 1968).

On Pain of Seeing. Trans. George Rapp (Chicago: Swallow Press, 1969).

100 Poems without a Country. Trans. Stuart Hood (London: J. Calder, 1978).

100 Poems without a Country (New York: Red Dust, 1980).

Four German Poets: Günter Eich, Hilde Domin, Erich Fried, Günter Kunert. Trans. and ed. Agnes Stein (New York: Red Dust, 1980).

Secondary Literature in English

Last, Rex. "Erich Fried: Poetry and Politics." In: *Modern Austrian Writing: Literature and Society after 1945.* Eds., Alan Best and Hans Wolfschütz (London: Oswald Wolff; Totowa, New Jersey: Barnes and Noble, 1980), pp. 181–196.

Kane, Martin. "From Solipsism to Engagement: The Development of Erich Fried as a Political Poet." *Forum for Modern Language Studies,* Vol. 21, no. 2 (April 1985), 151–169.

Glenn, Jerry. "Erich Fried." In: *Major Figures of Contemporary Austrian Literature.* Ed., Donald G. Daviau (New York: Peter Lang, 1987), pp. 163–183.

Reviews of English Translations

On Pain of Seeing (1970)

Library Journal, Vol. 95, no. 8 (15 April 1970), 1486.

100 Poems without a Country (1978)

Books and Bookmen, Vol. 23 (August 1978), 36–37.

Times Literary Supplement (13 October 1978), 1168.

Library Journal, Vol. 105 (15 November 1980), 2417.

Four German Poets (1980)

Choice, Vol. 18 (January 1981), 666.

Library Journal (15 November 1980), 2417.

Reviews of Erich Fried's Works in English Periodicals

Die Freiheit den Mund aufzumachen (1973)
Times Literary Supplement (23 March 1973), 319.
Gegengift (1974)
Times Literary Supplement (4 October 1974), 1090.
Fast alles Mögliche: Wahre Geschichten und gültige Lügen (1975)
World Literature Today, Vol. 51 (Winter 1977), 86.
100 Gedichte ohne Vaterland (1978)
World Literature Today, Vol. 53 (Spring 1979), 291.
Liebesgedichte (1980)
Times Literary Supplement (10 October 1980), 1155.
Warngedichte, 2nd ed. (1980)
World Literature Today, Vol. 56, no. 1 (Winter 1982), 110.
Befreiung von der Flucht: Gedichte und Gegengedichte, 3rd ed. (1983)
World Literature Today, Vol. 57, no. 4 (Autumn 1983), 634.
Das Unmass aller Dinge: Erzählungen (1982)
World Literature Today, Vol. 57, no. 2 (Spring 1983), 276.
Das Nahe suchen (1982)
World Literature Today, Vol. 57, no. 3 (Summer 1983), 450.
Beunruhigungen (1984)
World Literature Today, Vol. 59, no. 3 (Summer 1985), 426.
Zeitfragen und Überlegungen: 80 Gedichte sowie ein Zyklus (1984)
World Literature Today, Vol. 59, no. 4 (Autumn 1985), 593.

Peter Handke

Translations in English

Kaspar and Other Plays. Trans. Michael Roloff (New York: Farrar, Straus and Giroux, 1970); *Kaspar.* Trans. Michael Roloff (London: Metheun, 1972).

Offending the Audience and Self-Accusation. Trans. Michael Roloff (London: Metheun, 1971).

The Goalie's Anxiety at the Penalty Kick. Trans. Michael Roloff (New York: Farrar, Straus, and Giroux, 1972).

The Ride across Lake Constance. Trans. Michael Roloff (London: Metheun, 1973).

The Innerworld of the Outerworld of the Innerworld. Trans. Michael Roloff (New York: Farrar, Straus, and Giroux, 1974).

Short Letter, Long Farewell. Trans. Ralph Manheim (New York: Farrar, Straus, and Giroux, 1974).

A Sorrow beyond Dreams: A Life Story. Trans. Ralph Manheim (New York: Farrar, Straus, and Giroux, 1975).

"The Ride across Lake Constance" and Other Plays: Prophecy. Calling for Help. My Foot My Tutor. Quodlibet. They Are Dying Out. Trans. Michael Roloff in collaboration with Karl Weber (New York: Farrar, Straus, and Giroux, 1976).

Nonsense and Happiness. Trans. Michael Roloff (New York: Farrar, Straus, and Giroux, 1976).

A Moment of True Feeling. Trans. Ralph Manheim (New York: Farrar, Straus, and Giroux, 1977).

Three Novels by Peter Handke. The Goalie's Anxiety at the Penalty Kick. Short Letter, Long Farewell. A Sorrow beyond Dreams. Trans. Michael Ralph Manheim (New York: Farrar, Straus, and Giroux, 1976).

The Left–Handed Woman. Trans. Ralph Manheim (New York: Farrar, Straus, and Giroux, 1978).

Two Novels by Peter Handke. A Moment of True Feeling and *The Left-Handed Woman*. Trans. Ralph Manheim (New York: Farrar, Straus, and Giroux, 1979).

The Weight of the World. Trans. Ralph Manheim (New York: Farrar, Straus, and Giroux, 1984).

Slow Homecoming. The Long Way Around. The Lesson of Mont Sainte-Victoire. Child Story. Trans. Ralph Manheim (New York: Farrar, Straus, and Giroux, 1985).

Books on Handke in English

Hern, Nicholas. *Peter Handke: Theatre and Antitheatre* (London: Wollf, 1971; New York: Frederick Ungar, 1972).

Schlueter, June. *The Plays and Novels of Peter Handke* (Pittsburgh: University of Pittsburg Press, 1981).

Klinkowitz, Jerome and James Knowlton. *Peter Handke and the Post-Modern Transformation: The Goalie's Journey Home* (Columbia, Mo.: University Press of Missouri, 1983).

Secondary Literature in English

Heissenbüttel, Helmut. "Peter Handke and His Writings." *Universitas,* Vol. 12 (1970), 243-251.

Willson, Leslie. "Peter Handke: The Critic On-Stage." In: *Saga of Sprak:* Studies in Language and Literature. Ed. John M. Weinstock (Austin: Pemberton, 1972), pp. 301-319.

Zipes, Jack D. "Contrary Positions: An Interview with Peter Handke." *Performance,* Vol. 1, no. 4 (1972), 63-65, 68.

Preller, Arno G. "Handke's Publikumsbeschimpfung: A New Concept of Language and Theater." *Pacific Northwest Conference on Foreign Languages.* Proceedings, Vol. 23 (1972), 165-167.

Taylor, Karen M. "Two Kaspars by Peter Handke and the Open Theater." *Performance,* Vol. 1, no. 6 (1973), 29-37.

Gilman, Richard. "Peter Handke." *American Review* (17 May 1973), 206-228.

———. "Peter Handke." In: *The Making of Modern Drama:* A Study of Büchner, Ibsen, Strindberg, Chekhov, Pirandello, Brecht, Beckett, Handke (New York: Farrar, Straus, and Giroux, 1973), pp. 267-288.

White, J. J. "Signs of Disturbance: The Semiological Import of Some Recent Fiction by Michael Tournier and Peter Handke." *Journal of European Studies,* Vol. 4 (1974), 223-254.

Lederer, William L. "Handke's Ride." *Chicago Review,* Vol. 26 (1974), 171-176.

Kermode, Frank. "The Model of a Modern Modernist." *New York Review of Books* (1 May 1975), 20-23.

McAuley, Gay. "The Problem of Identity: Theme, Form, and Theatrical Method in *Les Negres, Kaspar,* and *Old Times.*" *Southern Review* (Adelaide), Vol. 8 (1975), 51-65.

Gugelberger, Georg M. "Endlessly 'Describing' Novel Experiences: Peter Handke's Translations in/and America." *Dimension* (1975), 180-190.

Hill, Linda. "The Struggle against Language and Behavior Patterns: Handke's Kaspar." In: *Language as Aggression: Studies in the Postwar Drama* (Bonn: Bouvier, 1976), pp. 164-194.

Marranca, Bonnie. "The Sprechstück: Peter Handke's Universe of Words." *Performing Arts Journal,* Vol. I, no. 3 (1976), 52-62.

———. "Peter Handke's My Foot My Tutor: Aspects of Modernism." *Michigan Quarterly Review,* Vol. 16 (1977), 272-279.

Whaley, Michael. "Handke in the Melting Pot." *Y/Traethodydd,* Vol. 8, nos. 2-3 (1977), 148-151.

Schlueter, June. "Peter Handke's *The Ride across Lake Constance:* The Illusion of Self-Sufficiency." *Comparative Drama,* Vol. 11 (1977), 113-126.

Hill, Linda. "Obscurantism and Verbal Resistence." *The Germanic Review,* Vol. 52, no. 4 (1977), 304-315.

Taëni, Rainer. "On Thin Ice: Peter Handke's Studies in Alienation." *Meanjin,* Vol. 36 (1977), 29-37.

Hauptmann, Ira. "[Aspects of Handke:] A Play [The Ride Across Lake Constance]. *Partisan Review,* Vol. 45 (1978), 95-123.

Klinkowitz, Jerome. "Aspects of Handke: The Fiction." *Partisan Review,* Vol. 45 (1978), 416-424.

Mount, Ferdinand. "Peter Handke and 'Alienation Fiction': The Sorrows of Young Outsiders." *Encounter* (March 1978), 33-37.

Finger, Ellis. "Kaspar Hauser Doubly Portrayed: Peter Handke's *Kaspar* and Werner Herzog's *Every Man for Himself and God against All.*" *Literature/Film Quarterly,* Vol. 7 (1979), 233-243.

Schlueter, June. "An Interview with Peter Handke." *Studies in Twentieth Century Literature,* Vol. 4, no. 1 (Fall 1979), 63-73.

Schlueter, June. "Metafictional Theater: Handke's *The Ride across Lake Constance.*" (New York: Columbia Press, 1979), pp. 105-119.

Innes, Christopher. "Peter Handke." *Modern German Drama: A Study in Form* (Cambridge: Cambridge University Press, 1979), pp. 235-255.

Hayman, Ronald. "Peter Handke and the Sentence." *Theatre and Anti-Theatre: New Movements since Beckett*" (New York: Oxford University Press, 1979), pp. 95-123.

Miles, David H. "Reality and the Two Realisms: Mimesis in Auerbach, Lukacs and Handke." *Monatshefte,* Vol. 71, no. 4 (Winter 1979).

Schlueter, June. "'Goats and Monkeys' and the 'The Idiocy of Language': Handke's *Kaspar* and Shakespeare's *Othello.*" *Modern Drama,* Vol. 23 (1980), 25-32.

Rorrison, Hugh. "The 'Grazer Gruppe,' Peter Handke and Wolfgang Bauer." In: *Modern Austrian Writing: Literature and Society after 1945.* Eds., Alan Best and Hans Wolfschütz (London: Oswald Wolff, 1980), pp. 252-266.

Sharp, Francis Michael. "Literature as Self-Reflection: Thomas Bernhard and Peter Handke." *World Literature Today,* Vol. 55 (Autumn 1981), 603-607.

Critchfield, Richard. "Parody, Satire, and Transparencies in Peter Handke's *Die Stunde der wahren Empfindung.*" *Modern Austrian Literature,* Vol. 14, nos. 1/2 (1981), 45-61.

Nägele, Rainer. "Peter Handke: The Staging of Language." *Modern Drama,* Vol. 23, no. 4 (1981), 327-338.

Kersten, Lee. "Film Reference as an Imaginative Model in Handke's *Der kurze Brief zum lang Abschied.*" *Journal of Australian University Language and Literature Association* (November 1981), 156-166.

Pusack, James P. "An American Reading Public for Handke: Considerations on the Use of Fictional Texts in Language Teaching? " *Österreich in Amerikaner Sicht,* Vol. 2 (1981), 45-56.

Carpenter, Charles A. "The Plays of Bernhard, Bauer, and Handke: A Checklist of Major Critical Studies." *Modern Drama,* Vol. 23, no. 4 (1981), 484-491.

Schlueter, June. "Politics and Poetry: Peter Handke's *They Are Dying Out.*" *Modern Drama,* Vol. 23, no. 4 (January 1981), 339-345.

Hays, Michael. "Peter Handke and the End of the "Modern." *Modern Drama,* Vol. 23, no. 4 (January 1981), 346-366.

Critchfield, Richard. "From Abuse to Liberation: On Images of Women in Peter Handke's Writing of the Seventies." *Jahrbuch für Internationale Germanistik,* Vol. 14, no. 2 (1982), 27-36.

Herrick, Jeffrey. "Peter Handke's *Kaspar:* A Study of Linguistic Theory in Modern Drama." *Philological Quarterly,* Vol. 63, no. 2 (Spring 1984), 205-221.

Jones, Calvin N. "Learning to See, to Experience, to Write: Peter Handke's *Die Lehre der Sainte-Victoire* as Narrative." *German Review,* Vol. 59, no. 4 (Fall 1984), 149-155.

Varsava, Jerry A. "Auto-Bio-Graphy as Metafiction: Peter Handke's *A Sorrow Beyond Dreams.*" *CLIO:* A Journal of Literature, History and the Philosophy of History, Vol. 14, no. 2 (Winter 1985), 119-135.

Honegger, Gitta. "Acoustic Masks: Strategies of Language in the Theater of Canetti, Bernhard, and Handke." *Modern Austrian Literature,* Vol. 18, no. 2 (1985), 57-66.

Brown, Russell E. "Names in Handke's *Die Angst des Tormanns.*" *Literary Onomastic Studies,* Vol. 12 (1985), 63-73.

Vannatta, Dennis. "Wittgenstein, Handke's *The Goalie's Anxiety at the Penalty Kick,* and the Language of Madness." *Literary Review,* Vol. 28, no. 4 (Summer 1985), 606-616.

Zorach, Cecile Cazort. "The Artist as Joker in Peter Handke's *Langsame Heimkehr.*" *Monatshefte,* Vol. 77, no. 2 (Summer 1985), 181-194.

Kaiser, Nancy A. "Identity and Relationship in Peter Handke's Wunschloses Unglück and Kindergeschichte. *Symposium,* Vol. 4 (1986-1987), 41-58.

Demetz, Peter. "Peter Handke: A Fragile Witness." In: *After the Fires:* Recent Writings in the Germanies, Austria, and Switzerland (New York: Harcourt, Brace, Jovanovich, 1986), pp. 213-232.

Francis M. Sharp. "Peter Handke." In: *Major Figures of Contemporary Austrian Literature.* Ed., Donald G. Daviau (New York: Peter Lang, 1987), pp. 207-236.

Barry, Thomas F. "America Reflected: On the American Reception of Peter Handke's Writings/Handke's Reception of America in His Writings." *Modern Austrian Literature,* Vol. 20, nos. 3/4, 1987), 107-115.

Linstead, Michael. "Peter Handke." In: Keith Bullivant (ed.) *The Modern German* (New York: St. Martins Press, 1987), pp. 155-170.

Reviews of other Works of Peter Handke in English and German

The more than 150 reviews in newspapers and journals are too extensive to include.

Franz Innerhofer

Translations in English

Beautiful Days. Trans. Anselm Hollo (New York: Urizen Books, 1976).

Articles in English

Fetz, Gerald. "Franz Innerhofer." In: *Major Figures of Contemporary Austrian Literature.* Ed., Donald G. Daviau (New York: Peter Lang, 1987), pp. 237-263.

Reviews of English Translations

Beautiful Days (1976)

Publishers Weekly, Vol. 210 (16 August 1976), 120.
New York Times Book Review (23 January 1977), 7.
Booklist, Vol. 73 (15 March 1977), 1068.
Choice, Vol. 14 (May 1977), 381.
New Statesman, Vol. 93 (10 June 1977), 787.

Reviews of Works in German in English Periodicals

Schattseite. Times Literature Supplement (17 September 1976), 1184.

Die grossen Wörter. World Literature Today, Vol. 52, no. 3 (Summer 1978), 453.

Der Emporkömmling: Erzählung. World Literature Today, Vol. 58, no. 1 (Winter 1984), 91.

Friederike Mayröcker

Translations in English

Sinclair Sophocles, the Baby Dinosaur. Trans. Renate Moore and Linda Hayward (New York: Random House, 1974).

Pegas, the Horse. Illus. Angelika Kaumann (Neugebauer Press, 1982).

English Translations of Selected Prose and Poetry

Elizay, Michael P. *Dimension,* Vol. 4 (1971), 178-191; Vol. 6 (1973). 100-105 and 522-529; Vol. 8 (1975), 252-265.

Willson, A. Leslie. *Dimension,* Vol. 7 (1974), 214-247.

Watts, Harriett. The Malahat Review, *Vol. 37 (1976), 18-19.*

Wynand, Derk. *The Malahat Review,* Vol. 37 (1976), 17; *The Chicago Review,* Vol. 29 (1978), 132-135.

Hamburger, Michael. *German Poetry 1910-1975* (New York: Persea Books, 1977), 344-345.

Middleton, Christopher. *Modern Poetry in Translation,* Vol. 4 (1980), 5-8.

Kuhner, Herbert. *Anthology of Modern Austrian Literature.* Ed., Adolf Opel (Atlantic Highlands, New Jersey: Humanities Press, 1981), 36.

Bjorklund, Beth. *The Literary Review,* Vol. 25 (1982), 222-231.

Waldrop, Rosmarie and Harriett Watts (eds and trans.). "Friederike Mayröcker." In: *6 Major Austrian Poets: The Vienna Group* (Barrytown, NY: Station Hill Press, 1985), pp. 36-50.

Holton, Milne and Herbert Kuhner (eds and trans.). "Friederike Mayröcker." In: *Austrian Poetry Today* (New York: Schocken Books, 1985), 55-60.

Secondary Literature in English

Bjorklund, Beth. "Radical Transformation and Magical Synthesis: Interview with Friederike Mayröcker." *Literary Review,* Vol. 25, no. 2 (Winter 1982), 222-228.

———. "Friederike Mayröcker and the Austrian Avant-Garde." *Poesis,* Vol. 5, no. 3 (1984), 48-67.

———. "The Modern Muse of Friederike Mayröcker's Literary Production." In: *Major Figures of Contemporary Austrian Literature.* Ed., Donald G. Daviau (New York: Peter Lang, 1987), pp. 313-336.

Reviews of English Translations

Sinclair Sophocles, the Baby Dinosaur (1974)

Publishers Weekly, Vol. 205 (25 February 1974), 114.

Kirkus Reviews, Vol. 42 (15 April 1974), 419.

Library Journal, Vol. 99, no. 16 (15 September 1974), 2252.

Chicago University Center for Children's Books—*Bulletin,* Vol. 28 (September 1974), 13.

Pegas, the Horse (1982)

Wilson Library Bulletin, Vol. 57 (September 1982), 59.

Reviews of Friederike Mayröcker's Works in German

Fantom Fan (1972)
Times Literary Supplement (14 January 1972), 32.
Fast ein Frühling des Markus (1976)
World Literature Today, Vol. 51, no. 3 (1977), 443.
rot ist unten (1977)
World Literature Today, Vol. 52, no. 4 (Autumn 1978), 628-629.
Heiligenanstalt (1978)
World Literature Today, Vol. 53, no. 2 (Spring 1979), 291.
Ein Lesebuch (1979)
World Literature Today, Vol. 54, no. 4 (Autumn 1980), 629.
Gute Nacht, guten Morgen: Gedichte 1978-1981
World Literature Today, Vol. 57, no. 2 (Spring 1983), 280-281.
Reise durch die Nacht (1984)
World Literature Today, Vol. 60, no. 1 (Winter 1986), 106.

Gerhard Roth

Translations in English

Winterreise. Trans. Joachim Neugroschel (New York: Farrar, Straus and Giroux, 1980).

Secondary Literature in English

Steele, Wallanne Padus. "The Cityscape and Mind's Horizon in Gerhard Roth's *Der grosse Horizont.*" *Centerpoint,* Vol. 1, no. iii (1975), 15-19.

Updike, John. "Disaffection in Deutsch." In: *Hugging the Shore.* Essays in Criticism (New York: Knopf, 1983), pp. 448-452.

Bauschinger, Sigrid. "Gerhard Roth." In: *Major Figures of Contemporary Austrian Literature.* Ed., Donald G. Daviau (New York: Peter Lang, 1987), pp. 337-362.

Reviews of English Translations

Winterreise (1980)
Booklist, Vol. 71 (15 July 1975), 1167.
Booklist, Vol. 73 (15 October 1976), 310.
World Literature Today, Vol. 53 (Autumn 1979), 682.
Kirkus Reviews, Vol. 47 (1 December 1979), 1396.
Library Journal, Vol. 104 (15 December 1979), 2666.
Publishers Weekly, Vol. 216 (3 December 1979), 46.

New Statesman, Vol. 100 (19 September 1980), 23.
New Yorker, Vol. 56 (21 April 1980), 130-133.
Atlantic Monthly, Vol. 245 (March 1980), 102.
Times Literary Supplement (10 October 1980), 1145.
Choice, Vol. 17 (May 1980), 396.
Booklist, Vol. 76 (15 March 1980), 1031.

Joseph Roth

Translations in English

The Radetzky March. Trans. Eva Tucker, based on an earlier translation by Geoffrey Dunlop (Woodstock, New York: Overlook Press, 1974). Distributed by Viking Press. Paper 1984.

Flight without End. Trans. David Le Vay and Beatrice Musgrave (Woodstock, New York: Overlook Press, 1977).

The Silent Prophet. Trans. David Le Vay (Woodstock, New York: Overlook Press, 1980).

Job: The Story of a Simple Man. Trans. Dorothy Thompson (Woodstock, New York: Overlook Press, 1982). Paper 1985.

The Emperor's Tomb. Trans. John Hoare (Woodstock, New York: Overlook Press, 1984).

Confession of a Murderer: Told in One Night. Trans. Desmond I. Vesey (Woodstock, New York: Overlook Press, 1985).

Hotel Savoy. With "Fallmerayer the Stationmaster" and "The Bust of the Emperor." Trans. John Hoare (Woodstock, New York: Overlook Press, 1986).

Tarabas: A Guest on Earth. Trans. Winifred Katzin (Woodstock, New York: Overlook Press, 1987).

The Spider's Web and *Zipper and His Fathher.* Trans. John Hoare (Woodstock, New York: Overlook Press, 1989).

Reviews of English Translations

Moss, Robert. "*The Radetzky March.* By Joseph Roth." *The New Republic* (14 September 1974), 29-31.

Wiesel, Elie. "The Radetzky March. By Joseph Roth." *New York Times Book Review* (3 November 1974), sec. 7, p. 70.

Orland, Henry. "Joseph Roth's Outsider. *Flight without End,* by Joseph Roth." *St. Louis Globe Democrat* (29-30 October 1977).

Marcus, Greil. "Desolation Row, 1927." (Review of *Flight without End*). *Rolling Stone* (9 March 1978).

Gross, John. "Books of the Times: *Hotel Savoy.* With 'Fallmerayer the Stationmaster' and 'The Bust of the Emperor.' By Joseph Roth." *The New York Times* (16 December 1986).

Gold, Herbert. "Surrounded by Small Hearts. *Hotel Savoy. Fallmerayer the Stationmaster. The Bust of the Emperor.* By Joseph Roth." *New York Times Book Review* (8 February 1987), sec. 7, p. 30.

Mandel, Siegfried. "Sardonic Picaresque. *Hotel Savoy.* Joseph Roth." *American Book Review* (September/October 1987).

Lardner, Susan. "An Enemy of His Time." (*Tarabus; The Radetzky March; Flight without End; Hotel Savoy; Confession of a Murderer; The Silent Prophet; Job: The Story of a Simple Man; The Emperor's Tomb;* "The Bust of the Emperor.") *The New Yorker* (23 November 1987).

APPENDIX I

Fifty panelists, guests and students participated in the AUSTRIAN STUDIES WORKSHOP at Taos Ski Valley, July 1987. A dozen students took this workshop for university credit and had to write a report at the end. Most of them are gathered for this photograph taken on the last day.

Front row from left to right: Martin Ögg, High School Student, Theresianum, Vienna, Austria; Peter Pabisch, University Professor and Director of the Workshop, University of New Mexico; Dr. Robert James Seeley, College Teacher, Texas. Back row: Glenn S. Levine, Student, University of New Mexico and Universität Heidelberg; Michael Gienger, Artist and Language Teacher, Albuquerque, New Mexico; Richard Page, MA, Assistant Professor of Library Sciences, University of Southern California; Jean Maley, MA, College Teacher, New Mexico Military Institute, Roswell; Keith Cothrun, High School Teacher of German, Las Cruces, New Mexico; Steven Lee, Student, University of New Mexico; Donald Monheit, Student, University of New Mexico; Marlies Wierenga, Student, State University of New Mexico, Las Cruces; Tim Currie, Student, University of Colorado; Patricia Taylor, Secretary, Goethe Institute, Houston, Texas; Curt Berryman, Student, Fort Lewis College, Colorado.

Summaries of the Students' Reports
Aus den Abschlußberichten der Studenten–Zusammenfassungen

Curt Berryman points out that he learned a great deal during the Austrian Workshop because so many fields and viewpoints were represented.

Curt Berryman hebt hervor, daß er während des Österreichischen Workshops viel dazulernte, weil so viele Sachgebiete und entsprechende Gesichtspunkte repräsentiert wurden.

Richard Page, M.A., states that he also learned a great deal; however, he would have preferred fewer talks, because time was too limited to think about everything thoroughly.

Richard Page schreibt, er habe auch viel gelernt, hätte sich aber weniger Vorträge gewünscht, weil die Zeit zu kurz war, um alles gründlich verarbeiten zu können.

Dr. Robert Seeley praises the overall organization of the Workshop; he has been enlightened about the Waldheim issue by the panel discussion since most of this information he could not have acquired otherwise in the United States.

Dr. Robert Seeley lobt die Gesamtorganisation des Workshops und fand die Forumsdiskussion über das Thema Waldheim informativ. Solche Informationen hätte er sonst nicht in den USA erhalten.

The Viennese high school student Martin Ögg welcomes the historical depth of the Workshop's topic so that everyone could see that positive relations between Austria and America actually prevail over the Waldheim issue.

Der Wiener Gymnasiast Martin Ögg begrüßt die historische Breite der Workshopthematik, so daß jeder einsehen konnte, wie die positiven Beziehungen zwischen Österreich und Amerika das Waldheimthema überlagern.

Marlies Wierenga contemplates about the rise and fall of the Austro-Hungarian Monarchy. She concludes that its fall came about due to the opposing

Marlies Wierenga stellt einige Überlegungen zum Aufstieg und Fall der Österreichisch-Ungarischen Monarchie an und erklärt letzteren durch

national interests of the peoples in this now vanished empire.

die gegensätzlichen nationalen Interessen der Völker dieses verschwundenen Staates.

Donald Monheit also deals with the dual monarchy and asks how much Woodrow Wilson may have contributed to its ending. He concludes that Wilson's 14-Point-Declaration wanted to help rather than destroy. However, at the time of its announcement it was interpreted one-sidedly.

Donald Monheit beschäftigt sich ebenfalls mit der Doppelmonarchie und fragt, wie sehr Woodrow Wilson zu deren Ende gewirkt habe. Monheit kommt zu dem Schluß, daß die 14-Punkte-Erklärung Präsident Wilsons eher helfen als zerstören wollte; zur Zeit ihrer Verkündigung war sie aber durch nationale Interessen einseitig interpretiert worden.

Jean Maley is interested in Austria's neutrality. As a college professor at a Military Institute she recognizes this neutrality as a successful diplomatic status quo for a small country positioned between the two world powers.

Jean Maley interessiert sich für Österreichs Neutralität. Als Collegeprofessorin an einer Militärakademie versteht sie diese Neutralität als einen erfolgreichen diplomatischen Status für ein kleines Land zwischen den beiden Großmächten.

Keith Cothrun explains Austria's difficult economic position as she is a member of the Western economic system, but restricted through her neutrality from becoming fully integrated in the European Community.

Keith Cothrun sieht Österreichs schwierige Wirtschaftslage ein. Das Land gehöre zwar dem westlichen Wirtschaftsbereich an, könne jedoch durch seine Neutralität nicht Vollmitglied der Europäischen Gemeinschaft werden.

Glenn S. Levine understands that Waldheim's personal guilt cannot be proven but that he has become a symbol for an era that brought evil over the world. Levine cannot understand therefore how Austria could have elected him as president.

Glenn S. Levine anerkennt Waldheims persönliche Unschuld. Waldheim sei aber Symbol für eine Ära geworden, die großes Übel in die Welt brachte; daher sei nicht zu verstehen, warum ihn Österreich zum Bundespräsidenten wählen konnte.

Steven Lee begrudges Waldheim's

Steven Lee bedauert die Wahl Wald-

election to Austria's federal presidency and concludes that Austria's population has still not overcome its sympathies for the Third Reich entirely.

Jack Utley recognizes Austria as an independent and free country and interprets the United States' intervention into her internal affairs by the Meese decision as questionable. The agitation against Waldheim, also by the press, has to be called a smear campaign.

Michael Gienger views Austria as an international country with a rich world culture and the ambiente of joining nations; this example she should continue to foster.

July 1987

heims zum österreichischen Bundespräsidenten und kommt zu dem Schluß, daß Österreichs Bevölkerung ihre Sympathien für das Dritte Reich noch nicht ganz abgelegt hat.

Jack Utley anerkennt Österreich als selbständiges, freies Land und findet Amerikas Einmischung in seine internen Angelegenheiten durch die Meese-Entscheidung fragwürdig. Die auch durch die Presse aufgekommene Hetze gegen Waldheim sei einer Schmierkampagne gleichzusetzen.

Michael Gienger betrachtet Österreich als internationales Land mit völkerverbindenden Zügen und einer reichen Weltkultur. Dieses Vorbild sollte es weiterpflegen.

Juli 1987

APPENDIX II

The American String Quartet: Mitchell Stern, violin; David Geber, cello; Daniel Avshalomoff, viola; Laurie Carney, violin

Additional Programs and Events of the Taos Austrian Workshop 1987

1. Piano Concert by Robert MacDonald,
   Professor at the Taos School of Music–
   Sonata in D major, op. 28 by Beethoven
   Three pieces by Fauré:
   Impromptu in f minor, op. 31
   Nocturne in D^b major, op. 67
   Valse-Caprice in G^b major, op. 59

2. Concert by the American String Quartet, Professors at the Taos School of Music, Mitchell Stern, violin; Laurie Carney, violin; David Geber, cello; Daniel Avshalomoff, viola–
   Quartet in d minor, Koechel 421, by Mozart

3. Guided tour by Professor Robert Holzapfel to Taos, its Indian Pueblo, the Millicent Rogers Museum, etc.–see following article.

4. A Jura-Soyfer-Exhibit, produced and assembled by Professor Horst Jarka; available at the Austrian Institute New York.

5. A TV performance of Gustav Mahler–"Sterben muß ich um zu Leben," a film by Wolfgang Lesowsky, Vienna.

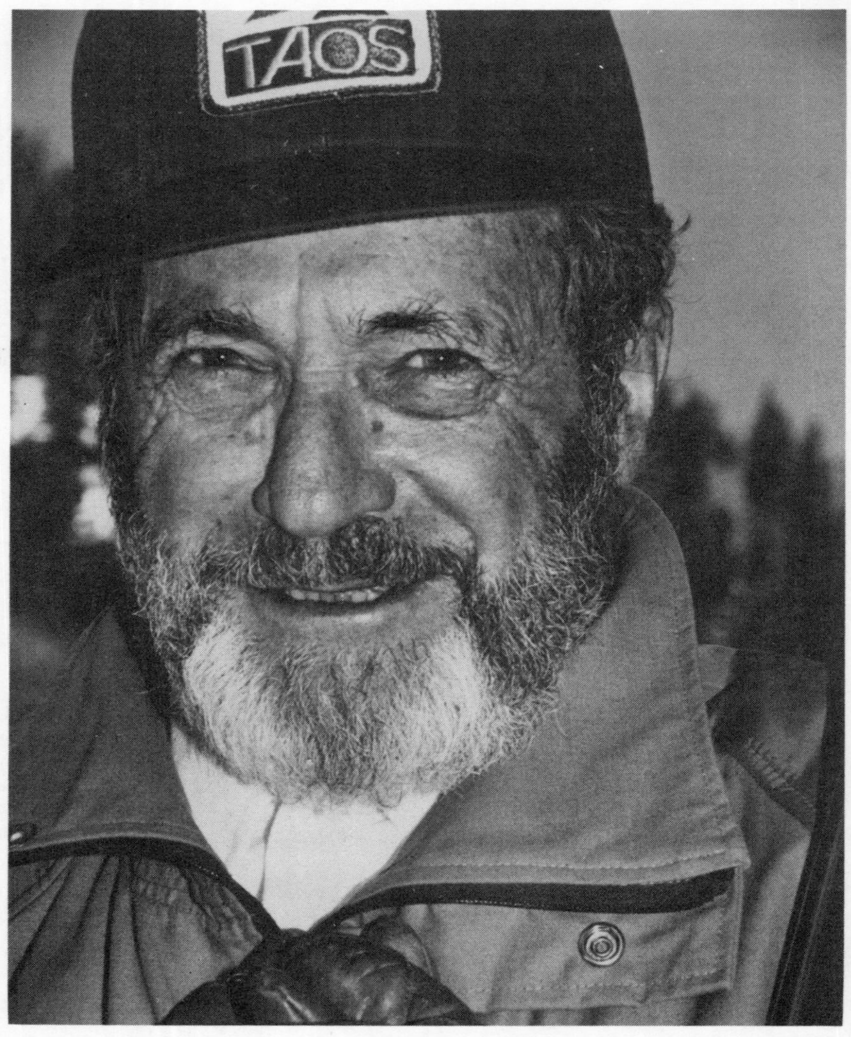

Ernest H. Blake (1913–1989), founder and director of Taos Ski Valley since 1955, was also guest professor of history at the German Summer School of New Mexico and taught seminars on "Switzerland," "The Third Reich," and "From Bismarck to Adenauer." ERNIE started skiing as a small child in St. Moritz, Switzerland, and kept at it steadily until a few weeks before he passed away. (Photo by Peter Blake, 1979)

APPENDIX III

Taos—An Ideal Location for the German Summer School of New Mexico and Its New Workshop Series

Robert Holzapfel

Als Treffpunkt der spanischen, indianischen und nordamerikanischen Kulturen hat Taos seit langem eine Tradition der internationalen Verständigung gepflegt. Das Schital von Taos, ca. 20 km außerhalb der Stadt, bietet durch seine Abgeschlossenheit und seinen alpinen Landschaftscharakter einzigartige Möglichkeiten zur Aussprache und Lehre—ein akademischer Hain im echten Sinne des Wortes.

A quote from an official tourist map summarizes with some flair the salient features of Taos:

> First established as Fernando de Taos around 1615, the town of Taos was 161 years old when the United States established her independence. The Taos Indian Pueblo was first discovered by Capt. Hernando Alvarado and his conquistadors around 1540. In 1615 it was Spain's northernmost colony, the Taos Indians being friendly and offering Spanish settlers water from their land and friendship in exchange for defense against the hostile Navajos.
>
> In the early 1800s Taos was frequented by many trappers and mountain men and became the largest fur trading center west of St. Louis. Kit Carson, famous mountain man and scout, first came to Taos at the age of sixteen after running away from an apprenticeship in Kentucky. He made his home here for some 24 years.
>
> Today Taos is a great art center with some 80 odd galleries, featuring work by many great Western artists. The quaint adobe buildings and ancient trees that shade the Plaza and line the roadways lend an Old World atmosphere, a charm of Old Mexico. The fresh water streams that flow from the mountains surrounding Taos offer excellent trout fishing. Taos Ski Valley, located 20 miles outside Taos, offers excellent skiing in the winter.
>
> (From: *Taos Map & Guide* by Ed Weiss, Taos, 1983-1984)

Taos Ski Valley lies one thousand meters (some 3000 feet) higher than Taos and looks like an Alpine village, because since 1955 European ski resort experts have tried to recreate a Swiss-Austrian ski village in the Rockies. They built a hotel Edelweiss, an Alpenhof, an Innsbruck Lodge and a St. Bernard Hotel.

Twining, the Ski Valley's actual name, was forgotten for years until the Swiss Ernest H. Blake discovered its great potential for skiing. With the help of some friends he founded the Taos Ski Valley in 1955. In the first years he was totally involved with the winter season. Once things calmed down a little, he regretted that the hotels lay idle in the summer. In 1975 he met Professors Peter Pabisch and George F. Peters, who were looking for a location for their German Summer School and in 1976, with the help of the Goethe House in New York, the Austrian Institute New York, the University of New Mexico and the University of Texas at Austin, *Die Deutsche Sommerschule von New Mexico in Taos bei Santa Fe* was founded. It has become a place of learning where GERMAN ONLY is spoken for four-and-a-half weeks and a Transatlantic

(Fig. 1) As one comes up from the Rio Grande and sees Taos Valley from the south, one is struck by the breathtaking view of the landscape that stretches from the volcanic mountains in the west over the deep gorge of the Rio Grande to the Rockies in the east.

dialogue takes place. In celebration of its tenth session in 1985 the regular summer school program was expanded by a more intensive academic program, a week long workshop concerned with German, Swiss, and Austrian Studies. The topic presented in this book, *From Wilson to Waldheim,* was the subject of the workshop in Austrian Studies in 1987.

Some photos and sketches are included to highlight the scenic and cultural uniqueness of Taos. Over the years I conducted a Workshop on Taos, and took several hundred students and professors on guided tours of the area. It was one of those rare tasks that improve with repetition.

Before reaching Taos the road passes the famous Franciscan church of Ranchos de Taos which painter Georgia O'Keeffe called the most beautiful church in the entire United States (Fig. 2)

(Fig. 2) San Francisco de Asis in Ranchos de Taos from the east. The adobe brick structure stems mostly from the early nineteenth century but is built in the style of old Catholic mission churches in New Mexico.

Driving north into the town one passes the Plaza, founded in 1617 under Habsburg rule. Here visitors admire the atmosphere which attracted, and still attracts, so many artists. The contemporary Indian artist R. C. Gorman, a great admiror of Arnold Schwarzenegger, recently invited the well-known Austrian to Taos. Millicent Rogers established her famous Indian museum in Taos which Austrian painter Georg Eisler frequented so often with his art classes from the German Summer School. D. H. Lawrence lent the town his name even though he spent but a few months north of Taos at a ranch. There a small shrine reminds one of his stay. (Fig. 3).

(Fig. 3) The D. H. Lawrence shrine where the author's ashes are buried at his former ranch some miles north of the town.

His "three women," however, lived most of their adult lives in Taos and expanded the Taos legend. Frieda von Richthofen, Mable Dodge Lujan, and Dorothy Brett were interviewed by the Austrian author Hilde Spiel in 1952 and the 94-year-old Brett again in 1977, when Spiel taught at the German Summer School. Afterwards she wrote a memorable article for the *Frankfurter Allgemeine Zeitung,* October, 1977.

Taos is well known for its Indian pueblo which is still inhabited although maintained mostly for historical purposes. In spite of the many changes surrounding them, the Indians have managed to preserve their traditions. (Photos 1 and 2).

Foto 1: Taos Pueblo around 1880 during the San Geronimo Fiesta Day.

Foto 2: Taos Pueblo in 1983, with a bread oven in the foreground and the Rockies of Taos Ski Valley in the background.

This concludes my abbreviated tour and takes us back to the Ski Valley in winter (Photo 3). Also, a sketch made in summer, when the German Summer School and the German Studies Workshop takes place. (Fig. 4).

(Photo 3) Taos Ski Valley in winter, known for its challenging and easy slopes and its ideal powder snow. Photo by Ernest H. Blake

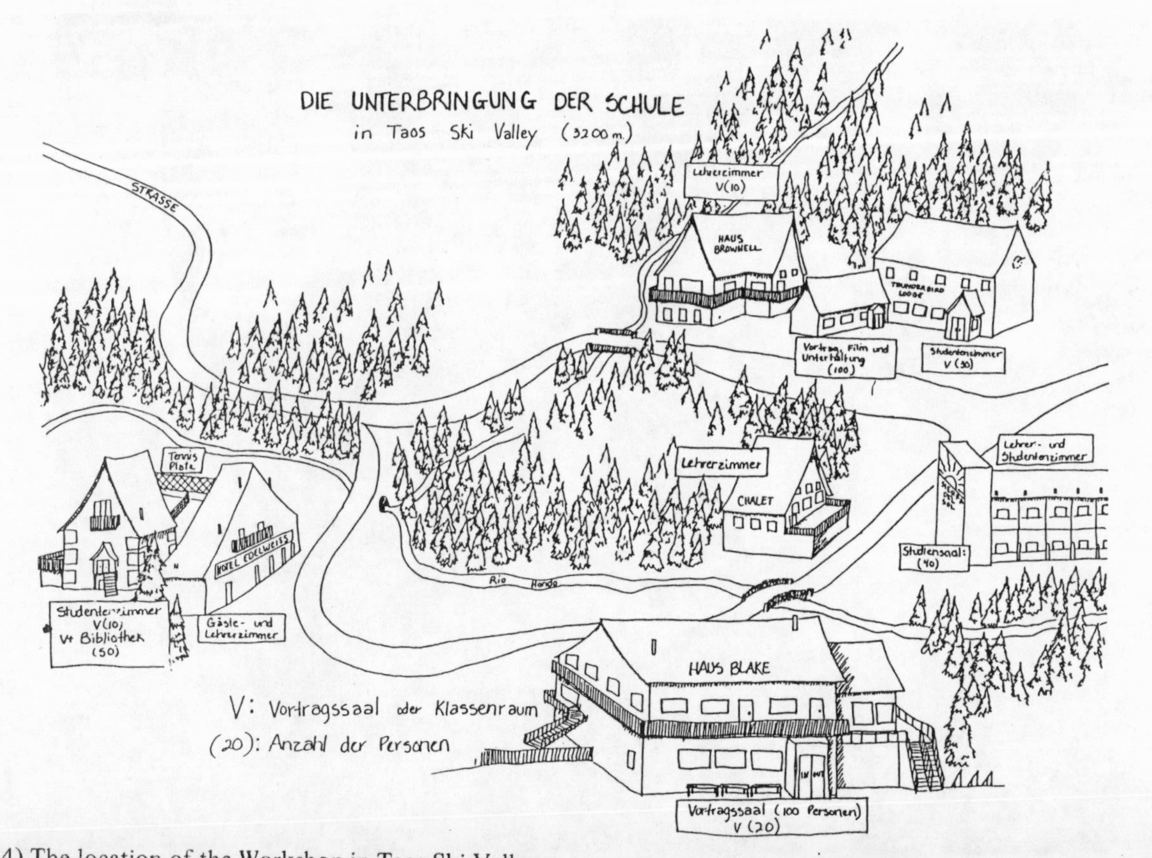

(Fig. 4) The location of the Workshop in Taos Ski Valley

Contributors

Monika Chavez is an M.A. candidate of the German Section of the University of New Mexico. She was born in Austria and lived in Melk until she married an American. Previously she studied History and German at the University of Vienna.

Donald G. Daviau is Chairman of the Department of Literatures and Languages and Professor of German at the University of California at Riverside. As the editor of the scholarly journal *Modern Austrian Literature* he has contributed greatly to research in this field. Among his many other merits for Austrian matters are his long presidency of the International Arthur Schnitzler Research Association and his presidency of the American Council for the Study of Austrian Literature.

Robert Holzapfel is Associate Professor of German at the University of New Mexico and also has a strong interest in Southwestern folklore.

Burghild Nina Holzer holds a doctorate in literary studies. She was born and raised in Austria but has lived in the United States for many years. Besides being a bilingual author she is an expert in creative writing and in translating. Her residence is in San Francisco.

McAllister Hull, former Academic Provost of the University of New Mexico for many years, has returned to teaching Physics and Astronomy. His interests are widespread and include philosophy and the humanities. Furthermore, he has been a loyal supporter of German and Austrian Studies for many years.

Horst Jarka is Chairman of his Foreign Languages Department and Professor of German at the University of Montana at Missoula. He is an Austrian married to an American. Through his university he directs a program in Austria, and he is one of the most distinguished representatives of Austrian Literature and Austrian Studies in the U.S.A. and abroad.

Jürgen Kullnigg recently returned to Austria after having been an associate to the former Austrian Trade Commissioner in Houston, Texas, Rudolf Merten (who also returned to Austria). This official Austrian agency in Houston, namely, the Austrian Trade Commission, has been an effective instrument in establishing fruitful Austro-American relations in a short period of time. This was accomplished thanks to Rudolf Merten and his helpful staff, of which Jürgen Kullnigg was an expert in economics and world trade.

Ruth Lorbe is Professor of German at the University of Illinois at Urbana-Champaign, where she has twice been named Distinguished Teacher of the Year. Among other things she teaches courses on Turn-of-the-Century Literature, Hugo von Hofmannsthal being one of her favorite authors.

Charles McClelland is Professor of History at the University of New Mexico. As an American he is fluent in German, French, and Italian. His specialty is European History and, among other research, he has written several books and articles on German and Austrian affairs.

Niclaas Moolenijzer, born and raised in Holland, is Professor of Physical Education at the University of New Mexico. He has published widely on the Natural Method, which had its origin in Austria and partly in Germany, and is now the underlying principle of teaching Physical Education in Austria and other countries. Since he is multilingual he also served as Special Director of a global P.E. program for the UNESCO in Paris.

Gerald Nash was born in Berlin, which he had to leave early on because of the holocaust. Still fluent in German he has not neglected his background about which he teaches, among other subject areas, as a Professor of History at the University of New Mexico.

Valters Nollendorfs, former Chair of the largest German department in the U.S.A. at the University of Wisconsin at Madison, is Professor of German and Co-editor of the renowned scholarly journal *Monatshefte.* Born in Latvia, he is an expert in Baltic Studies and one of the distinguished promoters of German Studies in the U.S. He recently co-edited the new "Guidelines for Curricular Organization at American Educational Instituions" in German Studies. These guidelines, by the way, also propose the special status of Austrian Studies within this larger area.

Peter Pabisch—with Professor George F. Peters, co-founder and co-director of the University of New Mexico affiliated German Summer School of New Mexico – is Professor of German with a research focus on Austrian Literature and Austrian Studies.

Ulf Pacher is Press-Attaché at the Austrian Embassy in Washington, D.C.

Ralph Parks is a medical doctor, specializing in pulmonary medicine, who has taught in a full-time and adjunct capacity at the School of Medicine at the University of New Mexico and has, thus, worked at the UNM-Hospital. He is one of the senior doctors of Pulmonary Associates in Albuquerque. His special interest lies also in the history of medicine.

Wolfgang Petritsch has a law degree and is Director of the Austrian Press and Information Service in New York. He is one of the leading contemporary experts on the status quo of Austro-American relations. In former years he was personal secretary to former Austrian Federal Chancellor Bruno Kreisky.

Walter Picard was Member of the House of Representatives (Bundestag) in Bonn, Federal Republic of Germany. For many years he was the Bundestag's special delegate for German-American cultural and educational relations who has supported – beyond the limits of his conservative (CDU) party affiliation – the expansion of these relations, as they are represented by such German agencies as the DAAD (German Academic Exchange Service) in New York, the Goethe Institutes of the U.S.A. and Canada, and the German Marshall Fund in Washington, D.C. Walter Picard has also been one of the most active promoters of the German Summer School of New Mexico.

Richard Rundell is Associate Professor of German and Director of the reputable Theatre Arts Department at New Mexico State University, Las Cruces. He is guest-editing an issue on *Liedermacher* for the University of Texas (Austin) journal *Dimension* in recognition of his universal expertise in this subject matter.

Nikolaus Scherk, Austrian Consul General in Los Angeles until 1988, lectured at the German Summer School at Taos several times. Having served also under Bruno Kreisky and, later on, at the Austrian Embassy in Washington, D.C. he is a professional expert on Austrian and Austrian-American affairs, who is also interested in furthering academic and cultural exchange on the faculty and student level between Austria and the U.S.A.

Ferdinand Trauttmansdorff has a law degree and is Special Councilor (Botschaftsrat) at the Austrian Embassy in Washington, D.C. Besides being a professional diplomat he also served as a special advisor to Kurt Waldheim during the election campaign in 1985/1986. He was delegated by Federal President Kurt Waldheim personally to be his representative during the Taos Austrian Workshop 1987.

Gerhard Weiss is Professor of German at the University of Minnesota and one of the distinguished senior academic leaders of German Studies in the U.S.A. He held several national offices in his profession, including the prestigious presidency of the American Association of Teachers of German (AATG). At the Taos Austrian Workshop 1987 he also served as the official representative of his university's Center for Austrian Studies.

Acknowledgments

Special thanks and acknowledgments go to the following persons:

Ernest H. Blake (†) for his continued support of the German Summer School of New Mexico and its enterprises.

Elisabeth and Thomas Brownell for their hospitality during the Taos Austrian Studies Workshop at the Thunderbird Lodge, Taos Ski Valley.

Monika Chavez as secretary of the workshop and her help in editing this book.

Fritz Cocron, former deputy director of the Austrian Institute in New York, for his advice and support.

Professor Donald G. Daviau for his support of Austrian matters.

Kim Frye, secretary, for helping in editing this book.

Professor Robert Herzstein for his scholarship and advice.

Dean Hobson-Wildenthal, College of Arts and Sciences, University of New Mexico, for his financial support of the Taos Austrian Workshop 1987.

Peter Marboe, former deputy director of the Austrian Institute in New York for his advice and support.

Dr. Erich H. Markel, president of the Max-Kade-Foundation in New York for his financial and personal support.

Martin Ögg for all his intelligent technical and secretarial help during the Austrian Workshop 1987.

Patricia Pabisch for advice and secretarial help.

Ulf Pacher for his friendship, his advice, humor and support as well as his communication efforts between Taos and Vienna.

Professor George F. Peters, co-director of the German Summer School, for his support and help in preparing the Taos Austrian Workshop 1987.

Dr. Wolfgang Petritsch for all his support through the Austrian Press and Information Service New York, and for his personal advice, not least of all in matters regarding this book.

Dr. Nikolaus Scherk, former Austrian Consul General in Los Angeles, for his continued support and advice.

Dr. Ferdinand Trauttmansdorff for his support, advice and collaboration in editing and publishing this book as well as his confidence in our good will concerning the Waldheim issue.

Dr. Neddy Vigil from the Language Learning Center of the University of New Mexico for his help in technical matters concerning the workshop, thereby especially enabling us to record the entire event on radio cassette.

Austrian President Kurt Waldheim and his secretary Dr. Scheide for inviting me to a private interview on 2 April 1987, concerning the Taos Austrian Workshop 1987, and for supporting this event by also delegating Dr. Trauttmansdorff as his personal representative.

Ernst Wawerka, school principal from Vienna, for recording large portions of the Taos Austrian Workshop 1987 on video cassette and for editing it to presentation standards.

Professor William E. Wright, former director of the Center for Austrian Studies at the University of Minnesota, for his financial and moral support of the Workshop.

Friederike Zeitlhofer, secretary of the Austrian Institute New York, for her tireless help by sending books and materials, but also for her public relations efforts on behalf of the Taos enterprises.

The German Studies Association of America (GSA), particularly Professors Gerald Kleinfeld, Valters Nollendorfs and Gerhard Weiss, for permitting us to advertise the Taos Institute Workshop 1987 at the National GSA Conference 1986 in Albuquerque, New Mexico.

We thank and acknowledge the following agencies and persons for their contributing of photographic material to this book issue:

The Austrian Press and Information Service New York. Wolfgang Petritsch and Sylvia Gardner-Wittgenstein. – The Center for Austrian Studies at the University of Minnesota at Minneapolis. William E. Wright. – The News and Information Center of the University of Texas at Austin. Helen Tackett. – The Santa Fe Opera Press Office. – Professor Niclaas Moolenijzer of the University of New Mexico. – The University of New Mexico Special Collections Room at Zimmerman Library. – The University of New Mexico Hospital–News Service. Arlene Vendetti. – The Taos Ski Valley, Inc. Mr. Ernest H. Blake, Director. – The Taos Chamber of Commerce, Taos, New Mexico. – Professor Horst Jarka of the University of Montana. – Professor Donald G. Daviau of the University of California at Riverside. – Dr. Robert Seeley, Texas. – Ms. Alison Freese of the University of New Mexico.

Note: The photographers' names are listed with the pictures.

Drawings and Sketches

George Eisler, artist from Vienna, Austria, drew the covers for the reproduced issues of *Modern Austrian Literature* and *Dimension* during his stay at Taos Ski Valley in 1979. One depicts the landscape near Taos Ski Valley and the other (in *Dimension*) depicts a line from a poem by Alfred Gulden inside the journal.

Ariadne von Huene, a University of New Mexico student, drew the diagram picture of Taos Ski Valley in 1980.

Peter Pabisch drew four so-called "second sketches" in 1987/1988: (1) The Santa Fe Opera, (2) The landscape around the Rio Grande Gorge near Taos, (3) detail of the San Francisco de Asis Church in Ranchos de Taos, (4) the D. H. Lawrence Shrine at the D. H. Lawrence Ranch north of Taos, New Mexico. He also drew the cover design.

Other Sources for Special Text Inclusions

1. The map of Taos with permission of the Taos Chamber of Commerce.
2. The texts from German Studies Programs, German Studies Association 1987, with permission from Professor Valters Nollendorfs, co-editor.
3. The maps of Austria and Austria-Hungary were taken from two editions of *Austria: Facts and Figures* with permission by the Austrian Press and Information Service, New York.
4. The list of titles for "Franz Joseph der Erste" was taken from *Österreich: Freies Volk, Freies Land*—Dokumente. Vienna: Bundesministerium für Unterricht, 1957. Permission for reprinting was obtained through the Austrian Press and Information Service New York.
5. Permission to reproduce E. Behrendt's cartoon from 12 February 1988, was sought from *Frankfurter Allgemeine Zeitung*.

Name Index